LSAT®

Diagnostic Exams

Version 10.7

Contents

Introduction

IN THIS BOOK

This book contains six five-section exams that you'll use as diagnostic tests. In most cases, you'll take the tests in a proctored setting at scheduled administrations. If you can't make it to a scheduled exam, see the next page for instructions on how to take the test at home and submit it for scoring.

The exams in this book are the same length as the one you will see on test day. The Law School Admission Council (LSAC) does not release its unscored "experimental" sections to the public, so we have taken sections from other Prep-Tests and inserted them to provide the most realistic testing experience possible. Because inserting extra sections into the tests can get a bit confusing, you will find a map on the score grid page that lists which sections are experimental. Please reserve these tests for use at your scheduled diagnostic tests. If you use them for other purposes, you will cheat yourself out of the opportunity to practice under simulated exam conditions.

Good luck, have fun, and if you ever have questions, please don't hesitate to ask your instructor or the office staff. We're here to help.

The Princeton Review LSAT Team

TEST-AT-HOME INSTRUCTIONS

Taking your LSAT diagnostic exams under timed, proctored conditions similar to those at the actual test is an important part of your test preparation. You should make every effort to take your diagnostic exams at the scheduled time and location. However, we realize that sometimes it's impossible to attend a scheduled exam. If you cannot take an exam with the rest of your class, you'll need to take the test on your own. The instructions below explain how to take the test at home. If you have any questions about taking the test or getting your scores, please call your local office of The Princeton Review (1-800-2Review).

Before the Test

You'll need this book, an answer sheet, pencils, and a timer. Find a place to take your test that simulates the actual testing environment. Sit at a table or desk in a quiet location. Turn off the telephone, television, and computer. Fill out the top portion of your answer sheet. In the space for Item 1 on your answer sheet, print your last name, first name, and middle initial. Fill in your birth date in Item 2 and your seven-digit phone number in Item 3. In Item 4, fill in the Test Code. Be sure to darken the corresponding ovals for Item 1 through 4. Write the Test Form in Item 7. The Test Code and Test Form numbers are listed on the title page of each test. Write the information requested in Item 9.

Test	Test Form	Test Code
PrepTest 69	4LSN106	9698
PrepTest 70	3LSN105	9708
PrepTest 71	3LSN104	9718
PrepTest 72	5LSN113	9728
PrepTest 73	4LSN110	9738
PrepTest 74	4LSN111	9748

During the Test

Make your testing experience as much like the real LSAT as possible. Take the entire test in one sitting. At the LSAT, you get just one break. It comes after the third section and lasts 10–15 minutes. Follow the same plan when you take a test on your own. Use a timer to monitor your time in each section. Give yourself 35 minutes for each section. If you finish a section early, you may review your work in that section only. Do not go back to a previous section and do not go on to the next section. When you're ready to begin, open to the appropriate page, start the timer, and begin.

After the Test

To find out your score right away, you can calculate your score using the information in your exam book, or you can enter your responses in the Score My Tests section of the Online Content. Log on and choose the Score My Tests link; then select the appropriate diagnostic exam listed under Core Tests. Follow the online instructions for entering your responses. You'll get a score and a full score report immediately.

To score the test yourself using the exams book, turn to the answer key and scoring information, which can be found at the end of the each test. Use the answer key to check your answers in each section. Count the number of correct responses in each section, and enter them into the Scoring Worksheet. Add up the number correct in each section to get your Raw Score. The Raw Score includes the four scored sections and excludes the experimental section. Check the Conversion Chart to find the Scaled Score (120–180) that corresponds to your Raw Score.

If you don't score your test online, take your answer sheet to your local office of The Princeton Review or give it to your teacher, and we'll score your test for you.

TEST ANALYSIS

Getting the most from your diagnostic exams involves more than just taking tests. Improving your score is a three-part process.

- **Assess.** You'll take diagnostic exams to assess your progress throughout the course.
- **Analyze.** You'll receive a detailed score report each time you take a test. After you receive your score report from an exam, complete the post-test analysis. This will help you identify strengths and weaknesses and adjust your pacing plan. It will also help you identify any patterns that may be limiting your score improvement. This analysis is one of the most important elements in your preparation.
- **Act.** Decide how to adjust your approach and set goals for the next test.

Overall Performance

Return to the goals/analysis chart. Look at your scratch work to determine the number of questions attempted, and use your score report to fill in the number of questions correct in each section.

Games

Use the Games chart to analyze your work in this section. Indicate whether you attempted each game, specify in what order you worked the games, describe the diagram and elements, and make notes about the games. If you missed one or two questions on a game, rework those questions. If you missed three or four questions on a game, reread the game and check your setup. You might have incorrectly symbolized a clue or missed a piece of information. Then, work the entire game again. If you didn't attempt a game, do the game from scratch. If you get stumped by a game, use the online explanations to see the full setup and deductions.

Reading Comprehension

Use the Reading Comprehension chart to analyze your work in this section. Indicate whether you attempted each passage, describe the topic, and make notes about the passage and questions. Review each question you missed to determine why you chose the wrong answer and why the credited response is correct. If you missed one or two questions with a passage, rework those questions. If you missed three or four questions on a passage, reread the passage. You might have missed the important ideas. Then, work all the questions again. If you didn't attempt a passage, do it from scratch. Use the print explanations online to help you understand each passage.

Arguments

Use the Arguments chart to analyze your work in these sections. Review each question you missed to determine why you chose the wrong answer and why the credited response is correct. Explanations that break down each argument and answer choice can be found in your online resources.

The Official LSAT PrepTest™ 69
Test code 9698
Form 4LSN106

SECTION I

Time—35 minutes

25 Questions

Directions: The questions in this section are based on the reasoning contained in brief statements or passages. For some questions, more than one of the choices could conceivably answer the question. However, you are to choose the best answer; that is, the response that most accurately and completely answers the question. You should not make assumptions that are by commonsense standards implausible, superfluous, or incompatible with the passage. After you have chosen the best answer, blacken the corresponding space on your answer sheet.

1. Police chief: This department's officers are, of course, prohibited from drinking on the job. However, there is one exception: it is extremely valuable for officers to work undercover to investigate nightclubs that have chronic crime problems, and officers may drink in moderation during such work.

Which one of the following, if true, most helps to justify the exception to the police department's rule stated above?

(A) Only very experienced police officers are allowed to work undercover investigating nightclubs.
(B) Many nightclub patrons would suspect that people in a nightclub who refrained from drinking were police officers.
(C) Over the last several years, the police department has significantly increased its undercover operations in nightclubs.
(D) Most police officers believe that allowing officers to drink during undercover work in nightclubs does not cause significant problems.
(E) For the most part, the public is aware that police officers are allowed to drink during undercover operations in nightclubs.

2. Jake: Companies have recently introduced antibacterial household cleaning products that kill common bacteria on surfaces like countertops and floors. It's clear that people who want to minimize the amount of bacteria in their homes should use cleaning products that contain antibacterial agents.

Karolinka: But studies also suggest that the use of these antibacterial cleaning products can be harmful, since common bacteria that survive the use of these products will eventually produce strains of bacteria that are resistant to antibiotics. That's why antibacterial agents should not be used in household cleaning products.

The discussion above indicates that Jake and Karolinka agree with each other that which one of the following is true?

(A) Household cleaning products with antibacterial agents kill some common bacteria.
(B) Household cleaning products with antibacterial agents remove dirt better than do products lacking those agents.
(C) The use of antibacterial agents in household cleaning products can produce antibiotic resistant strains of bacteria.
(D) Common household bacteria are a serious health concern.
(E) People should use household cleaning products with antibacterial agents to clean their homes.

GO ON TO THE NEXT PAGE.

3. A study of the dietary habits of a group of people who had recently developed cancer and a group without cancer found that during the previous five years the diets of the two groups' members closely matched each other in the amount of yogurt they contained. Yogurt contains galactose, which is processed in the body by an enzyme. In the people with cancer the levels of this enzyme were too low to process the galactose in the yogurt they were consuming. It can be concluded that galactose in amounts exceeding the body's ability to process it is carcinogenic.

Of the following, which one constitutes the strongest objection to the reasoning in the argument?

(A) The argument fails to consider whether the dietary habits of everyone in the two groups were the same in all other respects.
(B) The argument neglects to recommend that people with low levels of the enzyme avoid eating yogurt.
(C) The argument focuses on only one substance that can increase the risk of cancer, when it is well known that there are many such substances.
(D) The argument overlooks the possibility that cancer causes low levels of the enzyme.
(E) The argument does not specify whether any member of either group lacked the enzyme entirely.

4. Chemical-company employee: A conservation group's study of the pollutants released into the environment by 30 small chemical companies reveals that our company and four other companies together account for 60 percent of the total. Clearly, our company releases more pollutants than most chemical companies similar to us in size.

Which one of the following is an assumption required by the employee's argument?

(A) The conservation group that produced the study is not hostile to the chemical industry.
(B) The employee's company does not produce chemicals whose processing naturally produces more pollutants than the chemicals produced by other small chemical companies.
(C) The total pollution produced by all small chemical companies combined is not greatly outweighed by that produced by large chemical companies.
(D) The four other companies mentioned by the employee do not together account for very close to 60 percent of the total pollution by the 30 companies.
(E) There is no significant variation in the quantities of pollutants released by the other 25 small chemical companies.

5. Journalist: A recent study showed that people who drink three cups of decaffeinated coffee per day are twice as likely to develop arthritis—inflammation of joints resulting from damage to connective tissue— as those who drink three cups of regular coffee per day. Clearly, decaffeinated coffee must contain something that damages connective tissue and that is not present in regular coffee.

Which one of the following would be most useful to know in order to evaluate the journalist's argument?

(A) whether people who exercise regularly are more likely to drink decaffeinated beverages than those who do not
(B) whether people who drink decaffeinated coffee tend to drink coffee less often than those who drink regular coffee
(C) whether the degeneration of connective tissue is slowed by consumption of caffeine and other stimulants
(D) whether most coffee drinkers drink more than three cups of coffee per day
(E) whether people who have arthritis are less likely than the general population to drink coffee of any kind

6. A company that imports and sells collectibles sought to have some of its collectible figurines classified as toys, which are subject to lower import tariffs than collectibles. The company argued that the figurines amuse customers, just as toys do. However, the government agency responsible for tariffs rejected the company's request on the grounds that the figurines are marketed as collector's items rather than toys.

Which one of the following principles, if valid, most helps to justify the government agency's decision?

(A) The tariff classification of an item should depend primarily on how the item is marketed.
(B) When importing products, a company should seek the tariff classification that results in the lowest tariffs.
(C) An object should not be classified as a collectible if it is typically used as a toy.
(D) Objects that are developed primarily to provide amusement should be subject to lower tariffs than other objects.
(E) A company should market its products as collectibles rather than toys if doing so enables it to sell them for higher prices.

GO ON TO THE NEXT PAGE.

7. The photographs that the store developed were quite unsatisfactory. The customer claims to have handled the film correctly. Neither the film nor the camera was defective. If a store does not process pictures properly, the customer is owed a refund, so if the customer's claim is correct, the store owes her a refund.

The argument relies on assuming which one of the following?

(A) If the store owes the customer a refund, then neither the camera nor the film was defective.

(B) If neither the film nor the camera was defective, and the customer handled the film correctly, then the store processed it improperly.

(C) If pictures are taken with a defective camera, then it is not possible for the store to develop those pictures improperly.

(D) If the customer handled the film incorrectly, that is what caused the photographs that the store developed to be unsatisfactory.

(E) If the customer's claim was not correct, then the store does not owe her a refund.

8. When weeding a vegetable garden, one should not try to remove all the weeds. It is true that the more weeds, the less productive the garden. Nevertheless, avoiding the painstaking effort of finding and pulling every single weed more than compensates for the slight productivity loss resulting from leaving a few.

The principle underlying which one of the following arguments is most similar to the principle underlying the argument above?

(A) It is a mistake to try to remove every imperfection from one's personality. Personality imperfections make life difficult sometimes, but people cannot be truly happy if their personalities lack defects.

(B) One should not try to change every aspect of one's personality. Such a radical change is more likely to make one worse off than better off.

(C) If one is trying to improve one's personality by removing imperfections, one should not try to remove them all. For while each imperfection makes one's personality worse, it is no longer worth one's time to remove imperfections if there are only a few left.

(D) One who is trying to improve one's personality by removing imperfections should not try to remove them all. Granted, the fewer imperfections one's personality has, the happier one will be. However, it is never possible to remove all of the imperfections from one's personality.

(E) When one is trying to improve one's personality, one should not try to remove imperfections that do not cause one serious difficulties. Often, removing such an imperfection will only lead to greater imperfections.

GO ON TO THE NEXT PAGE.

9. Doctor: It would benefit public health if junk food were taxed. Not only in this country but in many other countries as well, the excessive proportion of junk food in people's diets contributes to many common and serious health problems. If junk food were much more expensive than healthful food, people would be encouraged to make dietary changes that would reduce these problems.

Which one of the following most accurately expresses the conclusion drawn in the doctor's argument?

(A) Taxing junk food would benefit public health.
(B) In many countries, the excessive proportion of junk food in people's diets contributes to many common and serious health problems.
(C) If junk food were much more expensive than healthful food, people would be encouraged to make dietary changes that would reduce many common and serious health problems.
(D) Taxing junk food would encourage people to reduce the proportion of junk food in their diets.
(E) Junk food should be taxed if doing so would benefit public health.

10. Large deposits of the rare mineral nahcolite formed in salty lakes 50 million to 52 million years ago during the Eocene epoch. Laboratory tests found that, in salty water, nahcolite can form only when the atmosphere contains at least 1,125 parts per million of carbon dioxide.

The statements above, if true, most strongly support which one of the following?

(A) For most of the time since the Eocene epoch, the level of carbon dioxide in the atmosphere has been lower than it was during most of the Eocene epoch.
(B) Levels of carbon dioxide in the atmosphere fluctuated greatly during the Eocene epoch.
(C) Lakes were more likely to be salty during periods when the level of carbon dioxide in the atmosphere was at least 1,125 parts per million.
(D) The atmosphere contained at least 1,125 parts per million of carbon dioxide during at least some part of the Eocene epoch.
(E) No significant deposits of nahcolite have formed at any time since the Eocene epoch.

11. Editor: When asked to name a poet contemporaneous with Shakespeare, 60 percent of high school students picked a twentieth-century poet. Admittedly, it is hard to interpret this result accurately. Does it show that most high school students do not know any poets of Shakespeare's era, or do they just not know what "contemporaneous" means? However, either way, there is clearly something deeply wrong with the educational system.

The statement that the majority of students picked a twentieth-century poet functions primarily in the argument

(A) as evidence that the educational system is producing students who are ignorant of the history of poetry
(B) as evidence of the ambiguity of some questions
(C) to illustrate that research results are difficult to interpret
(D) as evidence that the ambiguity of data should not prevent us from drawing conclusions from them
(E) as evidence that something is deeply wrong with the educational system

12. One should apologize only to a person one has wronged, and only for having wronged that person. To apologize sincerely is to acknowledge that one has acted wrongfully. One cannot apologize sincerely unless one intends not to repeat that wrongful act. To accept an apology sincerely is to acknowledge a wrong, but also to vow not to hold a grudge against the wrongdoer.

The statements above, if true, most strongly support which one of the following?

(A) If one apologizes and subsequently repeats the wrongful act for which one has apologized, then one has not apologized sincerely.
(B) One cannot sincerely accept an apology that was not sincerely offered.
(C) If one commits a wrongful act, then one should sincerely apologize for that act.
(D) An apology that cannot be sincerely accepted cannot be sincerely offered.
(E) An apology cannot be both sincerely offered and sincerely accepted unless each person acknowledges that a wrongful act has occurred.

GO ON TO THE NEXT PAGE.

13. A small collection of copper-alloy kitchen implements was found in an abandoned Roman-era well. Beneath them was a cache of coins, some of which dated to 375 A.D. The implements, therefore, were dropped into the well no earlier than 375 A.D.

Which one of the following, if true, most strengthens the argument?

(A) The coins used in the Roman Empire often remained in circulation for many decades.
(B) The coins were found in a dense cluster that could not have been formed by coins slipping through an accumulation of larger objects.
(C) The coins had far more value than the kitchen implements did.
(D) The items in the well were probably thrown there when people evacuated the area and would have been retrieved if the people had returned.
(E) Items of jewelry found beneath the coins were probably made around 300 A.D.

14. Investigators have not proved that the forest fire was started by campers. Nor have they proved that lightning triggered the fire. So the investigators have not proved that the blaze was caused by campers or lightning.

The flawed pattern of reasoning in which one of the following arguments most closely resembles the flawed pattern of reasoning in the argument above?

(A) Kim has no reason to believe that Sada will win the election. Kim also has no reason to believe that Brown will win the election. So Kim has no reason to believe that either Sada or Brown will win the election.
(B) We have no proof either for the theory that the thief escaped through the vent in the ceiling or for the theory that the thief escaped through the window. Therefore, one theory is as plausible as the other.
(C) Most of the students in my dormitory are engineering majors, and most of the students in my dormitory are from out of town. So most of the engineering majors in my dormitory are from out of town.
(D) In some parts of the forest camping is permitted. Also, hunting is permitted in some parts of the forest. So there are some parts of the forest in which both hunting and camping are permitted.
(E) The evidence shows that the car could have been driven by Jones at the time of the accident; however, it also shows that it could have been driven by Katsarakis at the time of the accident. Therefore, the evidence shows that the car could have been driven by both Jones and Katsarakis at the time of the accident.

15. To reduce the mosquito population in a resort area, hundreds of trees were planted that bear fruit attractive to birds. Over the years, as the trees matured, they attracted a variety of bird species and greatly increased the summer bird population in the area. As expected, the birds ate many mosquitoes. However, the planting of the fruit trees had the very opposite of its intended effect.

Which one of the following, if true, most helps to explain the apparently paradoxical result?

(A) Most of the species of birds that were attracted by the trees that were planted did not eat mosquitoes.
(B) The species of birds that were attracted in the greatest number by the fruit of the trees that were planted did not eat mosquitoes.
(C) The birds attracted to the area by the trees ate many more insects that prey on mosquitoes than they did mosquitoes.
(D) Since the trees were planted, the annual precipitation has been below average, and drier weather tends to keep mosquito populations down.
(E) Increases and decreases in mosquito populations tend to follow a cyclical pattern.

16. Roxanne promised Luke that she would finish their report while he was on vacation; however, the deadline for that report was postponed. Clearly, if you promised a friend that you would meet them for lunch but just before lunch you felt ill, it would not be wrong for you to miss the lunch; your friend would not expect you to be there if you felt ill. Similarly, _____.

Which one of the following most logically completes the argument?

(A) if Roxanne believes that Luke would not expect her to finish the report under the circumstances, then it would be wrong for Roxanne to finish it
(B) it would not be wrong for Roxanne to finish the report if Luke did not expect the deadline to be postponed
(C) if Luke would expect Roxanne to finish the report even after the deadline has been postponed, then it would be wrong for Roxanne not to finish it
(D) if Luke would not expect Roxanne to finish the report under the circumstances, then it would not be wrong for Roxanne to fail to finish it
(E) Luke would not expect Roxanne to finish the report and it would be wrong if she did finish it

GO ON TO THE NEXT PAGE.

17. Politician: A major social problem is children hurting other children. The results of a recent experiment by psychologists establish that watching violent films is at least partly responsible for this aggressive behavior. The psychologists conducted an experiment in which one group of children watched a film of people punching Bobo the Clown dolls. A second group of children was not shown the film. Afterward, both groups of children played together in a room containing a Bobo doll. Most of the children who had seen the film punched the Bobo doll, while most of the other children did not.

Which one of the following, if true, most weakens the politician's argument?

(A) Some of the children who did not punch the Bobo doll, including some who had been shown the film, chastised those who did punch the doll.

(B) The child who punched the Bobo doll the hardest and the most frequently had not been shown the film.

(C) The children who had been shown the film were found to be no more likely than the children who had not been shown the film to punch other children.

(D) Some children who had not been shown the film imitated the behavior of those who had been shown the film and who punched the doll.

(E) Many of the children who participated in the experiment had never seen a Bobo doll before the experiment.

18. Editorial: In order to encourage personal responsibility in adults, society should not restrict the performance of any of the actions of adults or interfere with the likely results except to prevent negative effects on others.

Which one of the following expresses a view that is inconsistent with the principle stated in the editorial?

(A) We should not prevent the students from wasting the classroom time set aside for homework. But this does not mean that they may spend the time any way they wish. Activities disruptive to others should not be tolerated.

(B) The scientist who invented this technology is not the only one who should be allowed to profit from it. After all, there is no evidence that allowing others to profit from this technology will reduce the scientist's own profits.

(C) Even though public smoking may lead to indirect harm to others, it should not be banned. There are several other ways to eliminate this harm that do not restrict the conduct of smokers and hence are preferable to a complete ban on public smoking.

(D) Highway speed limits are a justified restriction of freedom. For drivers who speed do not risk only their own lives; such drivers often injure or kill other people. Moreover, speed limits have been shown to significantly reduce highway accident and fatality rates.

(E) It is not enough that consumable products containing harmful substances have warning labels. Many adults simply ignore such warnings and continue to consume these substances in spite of the harm it may cause them. This is why consuming such substances should be illegal.

GO ON TO THE NEXT PAGE.

19. The goblin fern, which requires a thick layer of leaf litter on the forest floor, is disappearing from North American forests. In spots where it has recently vanished, the leaf litter is unusually thin and, unlike those places where this fern still thrives, is teeming with the European earthworm *Lumbricus rubellus*, which eats leaf litter. *L. rubellus* is thus probably responsible for the fern's disappearance.

Which one of the following is an assumption on which the argument depends?

(A) Wherever there is a thick layer of leaf litter in North American forests, goblin ferns can be found.
(B) None of the earthworms that are native to North America eat leaf litter.
(C) Dead leaves from goblin ferns make up the greater part of the layer of leaf litter on the forest floors where the goblin fern has recently vanished.
(D) There are no spots in the forests of North America where both goblin ferns and earthworms of the species *L. rubellus* can be found.
(E) *L. rubellus* does not favor habitats where the leaf litter layer is considerably thinner than what is required by goblin ferns.

20. Medical reporter: Studies have consistently found that taking an aspirin a day thins the blood slightly, thereby helping to prevent or reduce the severity of heart disease. Since heart disease is one of the most common types of ill health in industrialized nations, most people in such nations would therefore be in better health if they took an aspirin a day.

The reasoning in the doctor's argument is most vulnerable to criticism on which one of the following grounds?

(A) It takes for granted that if medication can reduce the severity of heart disease, it can also prevent some cases of heart disease.
(B) It overlooks the possibility that even if a disease is one of the most common in a nation, most people in that nation are not in significant danger of developing that disease.
(C) It overlooks the possibility that preventing or reducing the severity of heart disease has little or no effect on any of the other most common diseases in industrialized nations.
(D) It fails to address the possibility that taking an aspirin a day is not the single most effective measure for preventing heart disease.
(E) It fails to address the possibility that the studies on the beneficial effects of aspirin were conducted only in industrialized nations.

21. Essayist: Winners of a Nobel prize for science, who are typically professional scientists, have all made significant contributions to science. But amateur scientists have also provided many significant contributions. And unlike professional scientists, who are often motivated by economic necessity or a desire for fame, amateur scientists are motivated by the love of discovery alone.

If the essayist's statements are true, then which one of the following must also be true?

(A) Some amateur scientists who did not win a Nobel prize for science nevertheless made significant contributions to science.
(B) Typically, winners of a Nobel prize for science are not motivated at all by the love of discovery.
(C) The love of discovery is the motive behind many significant contributions to science.
(D) Professional scientists have made a greater overall contribution to science than have amateur scientists.
(E) A professional scientist is more likely to make a significant contribution to science if he or she is motivated by the love of discovery.

22. Company president: Most of our best sales representatives came to the job with a degree in engineering but little or no sales experience. Thus, when we hire sales representatives, we should favor applicants who have engineering degrees but little or no sales experience over applicants with extensive sales experience but no engineering degrees.

Which one of the following, if true, most seriously weakens the company president's argument?

(A) Some of the company's sales representatives completed a degree in engineering while working for the company.
(B) Most of the people hired by the company as sales representatives have had a degree in engineering but no sales experience.
(C) Most of the customers that the company's sales representatives work with have a degree in engineering.
(D) Most of the people who apply for a sales representative position with the company do not have a degree in engineering.
(E) Some of the people whom the company has hired as sales representatives and who were subsequently not very good at the job did not have extensive previous sales experience.

GO ON TO THE NEXT PAGE.

23. Anthropologist: Every human culture has taboos against eating certain animals. Some researchers have argued that such taboos originated solely for practical reasons, pointing out, for example, that in many cultures it is taboo to eat domestic animals that provide labor and that are therefore worth more alive than dead. But that conclusion is unwarranted; taboos against eating certain animals might instead have arisen for symbolic, ritualistic reasons, and the presence of the taboos might then have led people to find other uses for those animals.

In the argument, the anthropologist

(A) calls an explanation of a phenomenon into question by pointing out that observations cited as evidence supporting it are also compatible with an alternative explanation of the phenomenon

(B) establishes that an explanation of a phenomenon is false by demonstrating that the evidence that had been cited in support of that explanation was inadequate

(C) rejects the reasoning used to justify a hypothesis about the origins of a phenomenon, on the grounds that there exists another, more plausible hypothesis about the origins of that phenomenon

(D) argues in support of one explanation of a phenomenon by citing evidence incompatible with a rival explanation

(E) describes a hypothesis about the sequence of events involved in the origins of a phenomenon, and then argues that those events occurred in a different sequence

24. In an effort to reduce underage drinking, the Department of Health has been encouraging adolescents to take a pledge not to drink alcohol until they reach the legal age. This seems to be successful. A survey of seventeen-year-olds has found that many who do not drink report having taken a pledge to refrain from drinking, whereas almost all who drink report having never taken such a pledge.

The reasoning in the argument is most vulnerable to criticism because the argument

(A) bases a conclusion about the efficacy of a method to reduce underage drinking merely on a normative judgment about the morality of underage drinking

(B) fails to consider that an alternative method of reducing underage drinking might be more effective

(C) infers from an association between pledging not to drink and refraining from drinking that the pledging was the cause of refraining from drinking

(D) treats a condition that is sufficient to produce an outcome as though it were necessary for the outcome to occur

(E) confuses the claim that many adolescents who do not drink report having taken the pledge with the claim that many who report having taken the pledge do not drink

25. Literary critic: A folktale is a traditional story told in an entertaining way, which may lead some to think that folktales lack deeper meaning. But this is not the case. A folktale is passed along by a culture for generations, and each storyteller adds something of his or her own to the story, and in this way folktales provide great insight into the wisdom of the culture.

The main conclusion of the literary critic's argument can be properly inferred if which one of the following is assumed?

(A) Any tale that is passed along by a culture for generations can provide great insight into the wisdom of that culture.

(B) Any tale that provides insight into the wisdom of a culture is deeply meaningful in some respect.

(C) Not every tale that lacks deep meaning or beauty is told solely for entertainment.

(D) Any tale with deep meaning provides great insight into the wisdom of the culture by which it has been passed on.

(E) A story that is told primarily for entertainment does not necessarily lack deeper meaning.

STOP
IF YOU FINISH BEFORE TIME IS CALLED, YOU MAY CHECK YOUR WORK ON THIS SECTION ONLY. DO NOT
WORK ON ANY OTHER SECTION IN THE TEST.

SECTION II

Time—35 minutes

23 Questions

<u>Directions</u>: Each group of questions in this section is based on a set of conditions. In answering some of the questions, it may be useful to draw a rough diagram. Choose the response that most accurately and completely answers each question and blacken the corresponding space on your answer sheet.

<u>Questions 1–5</u>

A researcher is studying seven manuscripts—F, G, H, L, M, P, and S—to determine their relative ages. It is known that no two manuscripts were written at the same time. The researcher has also determined the following:

  H was written earlier than S but later than F.
  P was the next manuscript written after G.
  At least four of the manuscripts were written earlier
    than L.
  At least four of the manuscripts were written later
    than M.
  H was not written fifth.

1. Which one of the following could be the order in which the manuscripts were written, from first to last?

  (A) F, M, G, H, P, L, S
  (B) G, P, M, F, H, S, L
  (C) H, F, M, G, P, L, S
  (D) L, F, M, G, P, H, S
  (E) M, F, H, S, L, G, P

GO ON TO THE NEXT PAGE.

2. Which one of the following manuscripts CANNOT have been written third?

   (A) S
   (B) P
   (C) M
   (D) H
   (E) G

3. If H was the next manuscript written after M, which one of the following could be true?

   (A) F was written second.
   (B) G was written third.
   (C) H was written fourth.
   (D) P was written third.
   (E) S was written fourth.

4. Which one of the following manuscripts CANNOT have been written fourth?

   (A) F
   (B) G
   (C) H
   (D) P
   (E) S

5. If P was written earlier than H, then any of the following could be true EXCEPT:

   (A) F was written first.
   (B) G was written third.
   (C) H was written sixth.
   (D) L was written seventh.
   (E) M was written second.

GO ON TO THE NEXT PAGE.

Questions 6–11

Exactly six petri dishes—labeled dish 1 through dish 6—are to be stored in an otherwise empty refrigerator. There are three available shelves—the bottom shelf, the middle shelf, and the top shelf. The placement of the dishes must be consistent with the following conditions:

    No more than three dishes are stored on any shelf.

    Dish 2 is stored at least one shelf above dish 6.

    Dish 6 is stored either one shelf above or one shelf below dish 5.

    Dish 1 is not stored on the same shelf as dish 4.

6. Which one of the following is an acceptable placement of dishes on the bottom, middle, and top shelves?

(A)   bottom: dish 1
       middle: dish 6
       top: dishes 2, 3, 4, 5

(B)   bottom: dishes 1, 3
       middle: dish 6
       top: dishes 2, 4, 5

(C)   bottom: dish 2
       middle: dishes 4, 6
       top: dishes 1, 3, 5

(D)   bottom: dishes 3, 5
       middle: dish 6
       top: dishes 1, 2, 4

(E)   bottom: dishes 4, 6
       middle: dishes 1, 3
       top: dishes 2, 5

GO ON TO THE NEXT PAGE.

7. If dish 6 is the only dish stored on the bottom shelf, which one of the following could be the list of dishes that are stored together on the middle shelf?

    (A) dish 1, dish 3
    (B) dish 2, dish 4
    (C) dish 2, dish 3
    (D) dish 3, dish 5
    (E) dish 4, dish 5

8. If dish 1, dish 2, and dish 3 are stored on the same shelf as each other, which one of the following could be true?

    (A) Exactly one of the dishes is stored on the top shelf.
    (B) Exactly two of the dishes are stored on the top shelf.
    (C) Exactly two of the dishes are stored on the middle shelf.
    (D) Exactly three of the dishes are stored on the middle shelf.
    (E) Exactly three of the dishes are stored on the bottom shelf.

9. If exactly one of the shelves has no dish stored on it, which one of the following must be true?

    (A) Exactly three of the dishes are stored on the bottom shelf.
    (B) Exactly three of the dishes are stored on the middle shelf.
    (C) Dish 1 is stored on the same shelf as dish 5.
    (D) Dish 2 is stored on the same shelf as dish 3.
    (E) Dish 4 is stored on the same shelf as dish 5.

10. If dish 5 is the only dish stored on the bottom shelf and if exactly two of the dishes are stored on the middle shelf, then which one of the following is a pair of dishes that must be among the dishes stored on the top shelf?

    (A) dish 1 and dish 2
    (B) dish 1 and dish 6
    (C) dish 2 and dish 3
    (D) dish 2 and dish 4
    (E) dish 3 and dish 4

11. If exactly one of the dishes is stored on the middle shelf, which one of the following could be the list of dishes stored on the top shelf?

    (A) dish 1, dish 2
    (B) dish 1, dish 5
    (C) dish 2, dish 3
    (D) dish 3, dish 4
    (E) dish 3, dish 5

GO ON TO THE NEXT PAGE.

<u>Questions 12–17</u>

A company operates vending machines in four schools: Ferndale, Gladstone, Hafford, and Isley. The company delivers juices in one of its two trucks and snacks in the other truck. Each week, exactly one delivery of juices and exactly one delivery of snacks is made to each school, subject to the following conditions:

    Snacks must be delivered to Ferndale at some time before they are delivered to Hafford.

    Gladstone cannot be the fourth school to which juices are delivered.

    Gladstone must be the third school to which snacks are delivered.

    The first school to which juices are delivered must be the fourth one to which snacks are delivered.

12. Which one of the following could be the schedule of deliveries to the schools, from the first to the fourth?

(A)   Juices: Hafford, Ferndale, Gladstone, Isley
       Snacks: Ferndale, Isley, Gladstone, Hafford

(B)   Juices: Hafford, Isley, Ferndale, Gladstone
       Snacks: Isley, Ferndale, Gladstone, Hafford

(C)   Juices: Isley, Ferndale, Gladstone, Hafford
       Snacks: Hafford, Ferndale, Gladstone, Isley

(D)   Juices: Isley, Gladstone, Ferndale, Hafford
       Snacks: Ferndale, Gladstone, Hafford, Isley

(E)   Juices: Isley, Hafford, Gladstone, Ferndale
       Snacks: Ferndale, Isley, Gladstone, Hafford

GO ON TO THE NEXT PAGE.

13. If Hafford is the fourth school to which juices are delivered, which one of the following must be true?

(A) Ferndale is the second school to which juices are delivered.
(B) Gladstone is the third school to which juices are delivered.
(C) Ferndale is the second school to which snacks are delivered.
(D) Hafford is the second school to which snacks are delivered.
(E) Isley is the first school to which snacks are delivered.

14. If Isley is the third school to which juices are delivered, which one of the following could be true?

(A) Juices are delivered to Gladstone at some time before they are delivered to Hafford.
(B) Juices are delivered to Isley at some time before they are delivered to Hafford.
(C) Snacks are delivered to Ferndale at some time before they are delivered to Isley.
(D) Snacks are delivered to Gladstone at some time before they are delivered to Isley.
(E) Snacks are delivered to Hafford at some time before they are delivered to Gladstone.

15. If Isley is the first school to which snacks are delivered, which one of the following could be true?

(A) Ferndale is the second school to which juices are delivered.
(B) Hafford is the second school to which juices are delivered.
(C) Hafford is the third school to which juices are delivered.
(D) Isley is the first school to which juices are delivered.
(E) Hafford is the second school to which snacks are delivered.

16. Which one of the following could be true?

(A) Both juices and snacks are delivered to Gladstone at some time before they are delivered to Ferndale.
(B) Both juices and snacks are delivered to Gladstone at some time before they are delivered to Isley.
(C) Both juices and snacks are delivered to Hafford at some time before they are delivered to Isley.
(D) Both juices and snacks are delivered to Isley at some time before they are delivered to Ferndale.
(E) Both juices and snacks are delivered to Isley at some time before they are delivered to Hafford.

17. Which one of the following, if substituted for the condition that Gladstone cannot be the fourth school to which juices are delivered, would have the same effect in determining the delivery schedule?

(A) Ferndale must be either the second school or the fourth school to which juices are delivered.
(B) Gladstone must be either the second school or the third school to which juices are delivered.
(C) Hafford must be either the first school or the fourth school to which juices are delivered.
(D) The first school to which juices are delivered must be either Ferndale or Isley.
(E) The fourth school to which juices are delivered must be either Hafford or Isley.

GO ON TO THE NEXT PAGE.

Questions 18–23

Each of five paralegals—Frank, Gina, Hiro, Kevin, and Laurie—is being assigned to exactly one of three cases—the Raimes, Sicoli, or Thompson case. At least one paralegal will be assigned to each case. The following conditions must apply:

   Either Frank is assigned to Raimes and Kevin is assigned to Thompson, or Frank is not assigned to Raimes and Kevin is not assigned to Thompson.

   Either Frank is the sole paralegal assigned to his case or Gina is the sole paralegal assigned to her case, but not both.

   Hiro is assigned to Sicoli.

18. Which one of the following could be the assignment of paralegals to cases?

   (A) Raimes: Frank
        Sicoli: Gina, Hiro, Kevin
        Thompson: Laurie
   (B) Raimes: Kevin
        Sicoli: Gina
        Thompson: Frank, Hiro, Laurie
   (C) Raimes: Gina, Kevin
        Sicoli: Frank, Hiro
        Thompson: Laurie
   (D) Raimes: Kevin, Laurie
        Sicoli: Gina, Hiro
        Thompson: Frank
   (E) Raimes: Frank, Kevin, Laurie
        Sicoli: Hiro
        Thompson: Gina

GO ON TO THE NEXT PAGE.

19. Which one of the following CANNOT be the complete assignment of paralegals to the Sicoli case?

(A) Frank, Hiro, Kevin
(B) Frank, Hiro, Laurie
(C) Gina, Hiro, Kevin
(D) Gina, Hiro, Laurie
(E) Hiro, Kevin, Laurie

20. If exactly two of the paralegals are assigned to the Thompson case, then which one of the following could be the complete assignment of paralegals to the Raimes case?

(A) Gina
(B) Kevin
(C) Laurie
(D) Gina, Kevin
(E) Kevin, Laurie

21. If one of the cases has Gina and Laurie as the only paralegals assigned to it, then each of the following must be false EXCEPT:

(A) Frank is assigned to the Raimes case.
(B) Frank is assigned to the Sicoli case.
(C) Gina is assigned to the Raimes case.
(D) Kevin is assigned to the Raimes case.
(E) Laurie is assigned to the Thompson case.

22. Which one of the following CANNOT be the complete assignment of paralegals to the Thompson case?

(A) Gina
(B) Laurie
(C) Gina, Kevin
(D) Gina, Laurie
(E) Kevin, Laurie

23. If Kevin is the sole paralegal assigned to one of the cases, then which one of the following lists all of the paralegals any one of whom could be assigned to the Raimes case?

(A) Frank, Kevin, Laurie
(B) Frank, Kevin
(C) Frank
(D) Gina
(E) Kevin

STOP
IF YOU FINISH BEFORE TIME IS CALLED, YOU MAY CHECK YOUR WORK ON THIS SECTION ONLY. DO NOT WORK ON ANY OTHER SECTION IN THE TEST.

SECTION III

Time—35 minutes

27 Questions

<u>Directions</u>: Each set of questions in this section is based on a single passage or a pair of passages. The questions are to be answered on the basis of what is <u>stated</u> or <u>implied</u> in the passage or pair of passages. For some of the questions, more than one of the choices could conceivably answer the question. However, you are to choose the <u>best</u> answer; that is, the response that most accurately and completely answers the question, and blacken the corresponding space on your answer sheet.

The prevailing trend in agriculture toward massive and highly mechanized production, with its heavy dependence on debt and credit as a means of raising capital, has been linked to the growing problem
(5) of bankruptcy among small farms. African American horticulturalist Booker T. Whatley has proposed a comprehensive approach to small farming that runs counter to this trend. Whatley maintains that small farms can operate profitably despite these economic
(10) obstacles, and he provides guidelines that he believes will bring about such profitability when combined with smart management and hard work.

Whatley emphasizes that small farms must generate year-round cash flow. To this end, he
(15) recommends growing at least ten different crops, which would alleviate financial problems should one crop fail completely. To minimize the need to seek hard-to-obtain loans, the market for the farm products should be developed via a "clientele membership club"
(20) (CMC), whereby clients pay in advance for the right to go to the farm and harvest what they require. To help guarantee small farmers a market for all of their crops, Whatley encourages them to grow only crops that clients ask for, and to comply with client requests
(25) regarding the use of chemicals.

Whatley stresses that this "pick-your-own" farming is crucial for profitability because 50 percent of a farmer's production cost is tied up with harvesting, and using clients as harvesters allows the farmer to
(30) charge 60 percent of what supermarkets charge and still operate the farm at a profit. Whatley's plan also affords farmers the advantage of selling directly to consumers, thus eliminating distribution costs. To realize profits on a 25-acre farm, for example,
(35) Whatley suggests that a CMC of about 1,000 people is needed. The CMC would consist primarily of people from metropolitan areas who value fresh produce.

The success of this plan, Whatley cautions, depends in large part on a farm's location: the farm
(40) should be situated on a hard-surfaced road within 40 miles of a population center of at least 50,000 people, as studies suggest that people are less inclined to travel any greater distances for food. In this way, Whatley reverses the traditional view of hard-surfaced
(45) roads as farm-to-market roads, calling them instead "city-to-farm" roads. The farm should also have well-drained soil and a ready water source for irrigation, since inevitably certain preferred crops will not be drought resistant. Lastly, Whatley recommends
(50) carrying liability insurance upwards of $1 million to

cover anyone injured on the farm. Adhering to this plan, Whatley contends, will allow small farms to exist as a viable alternative to sprawling corporate farms while providing top-quality agricultural goods
(55) to consumers in most urban areas.

1. Which one of the following most accurately states the main point of the passage?

(A) In reaction to dominant trends in agriculture, Booker T. Whatley has advanced a set of recommendations he claims will enable small farms to thrive.

(B) Booker T. Whatley's approach to farming is sensitive to the demands of the consumer, unlike the dominant approach to farming that focuses on massive and efficient production and depends on debt and credit.

(C) As part of a general critique of the trend in agriculture toward massive production, Booker T. Whatley assesses the ability of small farms to compete against large corporate farms.

(D) While CMCs are not the only key to successful small farming, Booker T. Whatley shows that without them small farms risk failure even with a diversity of crops and a good location.

(E) The adoption of Booker T. Whatley's methods of small farming will eventually threaten the dominance of large-scale production and reliance on debt and credit that mark corporate farming.

GO ON TO THE NEXT PAGE.

2. Based on the information in the passage, which one of the following would Whatley be most likely to view as facilitating adherence to an aspect of his plan for operating a small farm?

   (A) a farmer's planting a relatively unknown crop to test the market for that crop
   (B) a farmer's leaving large lanes between plots of each crop to allow people easy access at harvest time
   (C) a farmer's traveling into the city two afternoons a week to sell fresh produce at a farmer's market
   (D) a farmer's using an honor system whereby produce is displayed on tables in view of the road and passersby can buy produce and leave their money in a box
   (E) a farmer's deciding that for environmental reasons chemicals will no longer be used on the farm to increase yields

3. According to the passage, "pick-your-own" farming is seen by Whatley as necessary to the operation of small farms for which one of the following reasons?

   (A) Customers are given the chance to experience firsthand where their produce comes from.
   (B) It guarantees a substantial year-round cash flow for the farm.
   (C) It allows farmers to maintain profits while charging less for produce than what supermarkets charge.
   (D) Only those varieties of crops that have been specifically selected by clients within the CMC will be grown by the farmer.
   (E) Consumers who are willing to drive to farms to harvest their own food comprise a strong potential market for farmers.

4. The author of the passage is primarily concerned with

   (A) summarizing the main points of an innovative solution to a serious problem
   (B) examining contemporary trends and isolating their strengths and weaknesses
   (C) criticizing widely accepted practices within a key sector of the economy
   (D) demonstrating the advantages and disadvantages of a new strategy within an industry
   (E) analyzing the impact of a new idea on a tradition-driven industry

5. The passage provides the most support for inferring which one of the following statements?

   (A) A corporate farm is more likely to need a loan than a small farm is.
   (B) If small farms charged what supermarkets charge for produce that is fresher than that sold by supermarkets, then small farms would see higher profits in the long term.
   (C) Consumers who live in rural areas are generally less inclined than those who live in metropolitan areas to join a CMC.
   (D) If a CMC requests fewer than ten different crops to be grown, then at least one of Whatley's recommendations will not be followed.
   (E) Distribution costs are accounted for in the budget of a small farm with a CMC and are paid directly by customers.

6. According to the passage, Whatley advocates which one of the following actions because it would help to guarantee that small farms have buyers for all of their produce?

   (A) growing at least ten different crops
   (B) charging 60 percent of what supermarkets charge for the same produce
   (C) recruiting only clients who value fresh produce
   (D) honoring the crop requests and chemical-use preferences of clients
   (E) irrigating crops that are susceptible to drought

7. Which one of the following inferences is most supported by the information in the passage?

   (A) The advance payment to the farmer by CMC members guarantees that members will get the produce they want.
   (B) Hard-surfaced roads are traditionally the means by which some farmers transport their produce to their customers in cities.
   (C) A typical population center of 50,000 should be able to support CMCs on at least fifty 25-acre farms.
   (D) Consumers prefer hard-surfaced roads to other roads because the former cause less wear and tear on their vehicles.
   (E) Most roads with hard surfaces were originally given these surfaces primarily for the sake of farmers.

GO ON TO THE NEXT PAGE.

When Jayne Hinds Bidaut saw her first tintype, she was so struck by its rich creamy tones that she could hardly believe this photographic process had been abandoned. She set out to revive it. Bidaut had
(5) been searching for a way to photograph insects from her entomological collection, but paper prints simply seemed too flat to her. The tintype, an image captured on a thin, coated piece of iron (there is no tin in it), provided the detail and dimensionality she wanted.
(10) The image-containing emulsion can often create a raised surface on the plate.

For the photographer Dan Estabrook, old albumen prints and tintypes inspired a fantasy. He imagines planting the ones he makes in flea markets and antique
(15) shops, to be discovered as "originals" from a bygone time that never existed.

On the verge of a filmless, digital revolution, photography is moving forward into its past. In addition to reviving the tintype process, photographers
(20) are polishing daguerreotype plates, coating paper with egg whites, making pinhole cameras, and mixing emulsions from nineteenth-century recipes in order to coax new expressive effects from old photographic techniques. So diverse are the artists returning to
(25) photography's roots that the movement is more like a groundswell.

The old techniques are heavily hands-on and idiosyncratic. That is the source of their appeal. It is also the prime reason for their eclipse. Most became
(30) obsolete in a few decades, replaced by others that were simpler, cheaper, faster, and more consistent in their results. Only the tintype lasted as a curiosity into the twentieth century. Today's artists quickly discover that to exploit the past is to court the very uncertainty that
(35) early innovators sought to banish. Such unpredictability attracted Estabrook to old processes. His work embraces accident and idiosyncrasy in order to foster the illusion of antiquity. In his view, time leaches meaning from every photograph and renders it a lost object, enabling
(40) us to project onto it our sentiments and associations. So while the stains and imperfections of prints made from gum bichromate or albumen coatings would probably have been cropped out by a nineteenth-century photographer, Estabrook retains them to
(45) heighten the sense of nostalgia.

This preoccupation with contingency offers a clue to the deeper motivations of many of the antiquarian avant-gardists. The widely variable outcome of old techniques virtually guarantees that
(50) each production is one of a kind and bears, on some level, the indelible mark of the artist's encounter with a particular set of circumstances. At the same time, old methods offer the possibility of recovering an intimacy with photographic communication that
(55) mass media have all but overwhelmed.

8. In the context of the third paragraph, the function of the phrase "on the verge of a filmless, digital revolution" (line 17) is to

(A) highlight the circumstances that make the renewed interest in early photographic processes ironic
(B) indicate that most photographers are wary of advanced photographic techniques
(C) reveal the author's skeptical views regarding the trend toward the use of old photographic techniques
(D) suggest that most photographers who are artists see little merit in the newest digital technology
(E) imply that the groundswell of interest by photographers in old processes will probably turn out to be a passing fad

9. Based on the passage, which one of the following most accurately describes an attitude displayed by the author toward artists' uses of old photographic techniques?

(A) doubtful hesitation about the artistic value of using old techniques
(B) appreciative understanding of the artists' aesthetic goals
(C) ironic amusement at the continued use of techniques that are obsolete
(D) enthusiastic endorsement of their implicit critique of modern photographic technology
(E) whimsical curiosity about the ways in which the processes work

10. Information in the passage most helps to answer which one of the following questions?

(A) What are some nineteenth-century photographic techniques that have not been revived?
(B) What is the chemical makeup of the emulsion applied to the iron plate in the tintype process?
(C) What are the names of some contemporary photographers who are using pinhole cameras?
(D) What effect is produced when photographic paper is coated with egg whites?
(E) What were the perceived advantages of the innovations that led to the obsolescence of many early photographic techniques and processes?

GO ON TO THE NEXT PAGE.

11. Which one of the following most accurately describes the primary purpose of the passage?

(A) to make a case for the aesthetic value of certain old photographic processes
(B) to provide details of how certain old methods of photographic processing are used in producing artistic photographs
(C) to give an account of a surprising recent development in the photographic arts
(D) to explain the acclaim that photographers using old photographic techniques have received
(E) to contrast the approaches used by two contemporary photographers

12. Which one of the following is most analogous to the use of old photographic techniques for artistic purposes by late-twentieth-century artists, as described in the passage?

(A) A biomedical researcher in a pharmaceutical firm researches the potential of certain traditional herbal remedies for curing various skin conditions.
(B) An architect investigates ancient accounts of classical building styles in order to get inspiration for designing a high-rise office building.
(C) An engineer uses an early-twentieth-century design for a highly efficient turbocharger in preference to a new computer-aided design.
(D) A clothing designer uses fabrics woven on old-fashioned looms in order to produce the irregular texture of handwoven garments.
(E) An artist uses a computer graphics program to reproduce stylized figures from ancient paintings and insert them into a depiction of a modern city landscape.

13. Based on the information in the passage, it can be inferred that Estabrook believes that

(A) photography in the nineteenth century tended to focus on subjects that are especially striking and aesthetically interesting
(B) artists can relinquish control over significant aspects of the process of creating their work and still produce the aesthetic effects they desire
(C) photographs produced in the nineteenth and early twentieth centuries were generally intended to exploit artistically the unpredictability of photographic processing
(D) it is ethically questionable to produce works of art intended to deceive the viewer into believing that the works are older than they really are
(E) the aesthetic significance of a photograph depends primarily on factors that can be manipulated after the photograph has been taken

14. The reasoning by which, according to the passage, Estabrook justifies his choice of certain strategies in photographic processing would be most strengthened if which one of the following were true?

(A) When advanced modern photographic techniques are used to intentionally produce prints with imperfections resembling those in nineteenth-century prints, the resulting prints invariably betray the artifice involved.
(B) The various feelings evoked by a work of art are independent of the techniques used to produce the work and irrelevant to its artistic value.
(C) Most people who use photographs as a way of remembering or learning about the past value them almost exclusively for their ability to record their subjects accurately.
(D) People who are interested in artistic photography seldom see much artistic value in photographs that appear antique but are not really so.
(E) The latest photographic techniques can produce photographs that are almost completely free of blemishes and highly resistant to deterioration over time.

GO ON TO THE NEXT PAGE.

Passage A is from a 2007 article on the United States patent system; passage B is from a corporate statement.

Passage A

Theoretically, the patent office is only supposed to award patents for "nonobvious" inventions, and the concept of translating between an Internet address and a telephone number certainly seems obvious. Still,
(5) a court recently held that a technology company had infringed on patents covering computer servers that perform these translations.

In an ideal world, patents would be narrow enough that companies could "invent around" others'
(10) patents if licensing agreements cannot be reached. Unfortunately, the patent system has departed from this ideal. In recent decades, the courts have dramatically lowered the bar for obviousness. As a result, some patents being granted are so broad that
(15) inventing around them is practically impossible.

Large technology companies have responded to this proliferation of bad patents with the patent equivalent of nuclear stockpiling. By obtaining hundreds or even thousands of patents, a company
(20) can develop a credible deterrent against patent lawsuits: if someone sues it for patent infringement, it can find a patent the other company has infringed and countersue. Often, however, a fundamental mistake is made: not joining this arms race. As a result, a
(25) company can find itself defenseless against lawsuits.

Software patents are particularly ripe for abuse because software is assembled from modular components. If the patent system allows those components to be patented, it becomes almost
(30) impossible to develop a software product without infringing numerous patents. Moreover, because of the complexity of software, it is often prohibitively expensive to even find all the patents a given software product might in principle be infringing. So even a
(35) software maker that wanted to find and license all of the patents relevant to its products is unlikely to be able to do so.

Passage B

Software makers like ours have consistently taken the position that patents generally impede innovation
(40) in software development and are inconsistent with open-source/free software. We will continue to work to promote this position and are pleased to join our colleagues in the open-source/free software community, as well as those proprietary vendors who have publicly
(45) stated their opposition to software patents.

At the same time, we are forced to live in the world as it is, and that world currently permits software patents. A small number of very large companies have amassed large numbers of software
(50) patents. We believe such massive software patent portfolios are ripe for misuse because of the questionable nature of many software patents generally and because of the high cost of patent litigation.

One defense against such misuse is to develop a
(55) corresponding portfolio of software patents for

defensive purposes. Many software makers, both open-source and proprietary, pursue this strategy. In the interests of our company and in an attempt to protect and promote the open-source community,
(60) we have elected to adopt this same stance. We do so reluctantly because of the perceived inconsistency with our stance against software patents; however, prudence dictates this position.

15. Which one of the following pairs would be most appropriate as titles for passage A and passage B, respectively?

(A) "The Use and Abuse of Patents"
    "The Necessary Elimination of Software Patents"
(B) "Reforming Patent Laws"
    "In Defense of Software Patents"
(C) "Patenting the Obvious"
    "Patents: A Defensive Policy"
(D) "A Misunderstanding of Patent Policies"
    "Keeping Software Free but Safe"
(E) "Developing a Credible Deterrent Against Patent Lawsuits"
    "An Apology to Our Customers"

16. Which one of the following is mentioned in passage A but not in passage B?

(A) the amassing of patents by software companies
(B) the cost of finding all the patents a product may infringe
(C) the negative effect of patents on software development
(D) the high cost of patent litigation in general
(E) the dubious nature of many software patents

17. Which one of the following comes closest to capturing the meaning of the phrase "invent around" (line 9)?

(A) invent a product whose use is so obvious that no one can have a patent on it
(B) conceal the fact that a product infringes a patent
(C) implement a previously patented idea in a way other than that intended by the patent holder
(D) develop new products based on principles that are entirely different from those for products affected by competitors' patents
(E) devise something that serves the same function as the patented invention without violating the patent

GO ON TO THE NEXT PAGE.

18. Which one of the following most accurately describes the relationship between the two passages?

(A) Passage A objectively reports a set of events; passage B subjectively takes issue with aspects of the reported events.

(B) Passage A discusses a problem in an industry; passage B states the position of a party dealing with that problem.

(C) Passage A is highly critical of a defensive strategy used by an industry; passage B is a clarification of that strategy.

(D) Passage A describes an impasse within an industry; passage B suggests a way out of this impasse.

(E) Passage A lays out both sides of a dispute; passage B focuses on one of those sides.

19. The authors of the passages would be most likely to agree that software companies would be well advised to

(A) amass their own portfolios of software patents

(B) attempt to license software patented by other companies

(C) exploit patents already owned by competitors

(D) refrain from infringing on any patents held by other companies

(E) research the patents relevant to their products more thoroughly

20. In terms of what it alludes to, "this same stance" (line 60) is most closely related to which one of the following phrases in passage A?

(A) nonobvious (line 2)
(B) invent around (line 9)
(C) lowered the bar (line 13)
(D) credible deterrent (line 20)
(E) modular components (lines 27–28)

21. Which one of the following, if true, would cast doubt on the position concerning innovation in software development taken in the first paragraph of passage B?

(A) Most patents for software innovations have a duration of only 20 years or less.

(B) Software companies that do not patent software generally offer products that are more reliable than those that do.

(C) Some proprietary vendors oppose software patents for self-interested reasons.

(D) Software innovation would be less profitable if software could not be patented.

(E) The main beneficiaries of software innovations are large corporations rather than individual innovators.

GO ON TO THE NEXT PAGE.

Calvaria major is a rare but once-abundant tree found on the island of Mauritius, which was also home to the dodo, a large flightless bird that became extinct about three centuries ago. In 1977 Stanley Temple,
(5) an ecologist whose investigation of *Calvaria major* was a sidelight to his research on endangered birds of Mauritius, proposed that the population decline of *Calvaria major* was linked to the demise of the dodo, a hypothesis that subsequently gained considerable
(10) currency. Temple had found only thirteen *Calvaria major* trees on Mauritius, all overmature and dying, and all estimated by foresters at over 300 years old. These trees produced fruits that appeared fertile but that Temple assumed could no longer germinate,
(15) given his failure to find younger trees.

The temporal coincidence between the extinction of the dodo and what Temple considered the last evidence of natural germination of *Calvaria major* seeds led him to posit a causal connection. Specifically,
(20) he hypothesized that the fruit of *Calvaria major* had developed its extremely thick-walled pit as an evolutionary response to the dodo's habitual consumption of those fruits, a trait enabling the pits to withstand the abrasive forces exerted on them in
(25) the birds' digestive tracts. This defensive thickness, though, ultimately prevented the seeds within the pits from germinating without the thinning caused by abrasion in the dodo's gizzard. What had once been adaptive, Temple maintained, became a lethal
(30) imprisonment for the seeds after the dodo vanished.

Although direct proof was unattainable, Temple did offer some additional findings in support of his hypothesis, which lent his argument a semblance of rigor. From studies of other birds, he estimated the
(35) abrasive force generated within a dodo's gizzard. Based on this estimate and on test results determining the crush-resistant strength of *Calvaria major* pits, he concluded that the pits could probably have withstood a cycle through a dodo's gizzard. He also fed *Calvaria*
(40) *major* pits to turkeys, and though many of the pits were destroyed, ten emerged, abraded yet intact. Three of these sprouted when planted, which he saw as vindicating his hypothesis.

Though many scientists found this dramatic and
(45) intriguing hypothesis plausible, Temple's proposals have been strongly challenged by leading specialists in the field. Where Temple had found only thirteen specimens of *Calvaria major*, Wendy Strahm, the foremost expert on the plant ecology of Mauritius,
(50) has identified hundreds, many far younger than three centuries. So *Calvaria major* seeds have in fact germinated, and the tree's reproductive cycle has thus continued, since the dodo's disappearance. Additional counterevidence comes from horticultural
(55) research by Anthony Speke, which shows that while only a minority of unabraded *Calvaria major* seeds germinate, the number is still probably sufficient to keep this species from becoming extinct. The population decline, while clearly acute, could easily
(60) be due to other factors, including disease and damage done by certain nonindigenous animals introduced onto Mauritius in the past few centuries.

22. Which one of the following most accurately expresses the main point of the passage?

(A) *Calvaria major* germination, though rare, is probably adequate to avoid extinction of the species.
(B) The appeal of Temple's hypothesis notwithstanding, the scarcity of *Calvaria major* is probably not due to the extinction of the dodo.
(C) Temple's experimentation with *Calvaria major* pits, though methodologically unsound, nevertheless led to a probable solution to the mystery of the tree's decline.
(D) Temple's dramatic but speculative hypothesis, though presented without sufficient supporting research, may nevertheless be correct.
(E) *Calvaria major* would probably still be scarce today even if the dodo had not become extinct.

23. The author indicates that Temple's research on birds of the island of Mauritius

(A) was largely concerned with species facing the threat of extinction
(B) furnished him with the basis for his highly accurate estimates of the crush-resistant strength of *Calvaria major* pits
(C) provided experimental evidence that some modern birds' gizzards exert roughly the same amount of abrasive force on their contents as did dodo gizzards
(D) was comprehensive in scope and conducted with methodological precision
(E) was originally inspired by his observation that apparently fertile *Calvaria major* pits were nevertheless no longer able to germinate

GO ON TO THE NEXT PAGE.

24. In saying that Temple's supporting evidence lent his argument a "semblance of rigor" (lines 33–34), the author most likely intends to indicate that

    (A) despite his attempts to use strict scientific methodology, Temple's experimental findings regarding *Calvaria major* pits were not carefully derived and thus merely appeared to support his hypothesis
    (B) direct proof of a hypothesis of the sort Temple was investigating is virtually impossible to obtain, even with the most exact measurements and observations
    (C) in contrast to Temple's secondhand information concerning the age of the thirteen overmature *Calvaria major* trees he found, his experiments with turkeys and other birds represented careful and accurate firsthand research
    (D) in his experimentation on *Calvaria major* pits, Temple produced quantitative experimental results that superficially appeared to bolster the scientific credibility of his hypothesis
    (E) although the consensus among experts is that Temple's overall conclusion is mistaken, the scientific precision and the creativity of Temple's experimentation remain admirable

25. The passage indicates which one of the following about the abrasion of *Calvaria major* pit walls?

    (A) Thinning through abrasion is not necessary for germination of *Calvaria major* seeds.
    (B) In Temple's experiment, the abrasion caused by the digestive tracts of turkeys always released *Calvaria major* seeds, undamaged, from their hard coverings.
    (C) Temple was mistaken in believing that the abrasion caused by dodos would have been sufficient to thin the pit walls to any significant degree.
    (D) Abrasion of *Calvaria major* pit walls by the digestive tracts of animals occurred commonly in past centuries but rarely occurs in nature today.
    (E) Temple overlooked the fact that other natural environmental forces have been abrading *Calvaria major* pit walls since the dodo ceased to fulfill this role.

26. It can be most logically inferred from the passage that the author regards Temple's hypothesis that the extinction of the dodo was the cause of *Calvaria major's* seeming loss of the ability to reproduce as which one of the following?

    (A) essentially correct, but containing some inaccurate details
    (B) initially implausible, but vindicated by his empirical findings
    (C) an example of a valuable scientific achievement outside a researcher's primary area of expertise
    (D) laudable for its precise formulation and its attention to historical detail
    (E) an attempt to explain a state of affairs that did not in fact exist

27. Based on the passage, it can be inferred that the author would be likely to agree with each of the following statements about *Calvaria major* EXCEPT:

    (A) The causes of the evolution of the tree's particularly durable pit wall have not been definitively identified by Temple's critics.
    (B) The notion that the thickness of the pit wall in the tree's fruit has been a factor contributing to the decline of the tree has not been definitively discredited.
    (C) In light of the current rate of germination of seeds of the species, it is surprising that the tree has not been abundant since the dodo's disappearance.
    (D) There is good reason to believe that the tree is not threatened with imminent extinction.
    (E) *Calvaria major* seeds can germinate even if they do not first pass through a bird's digestive system.

STOP
IF YOU FINISH BEFORE TIME IS CALLED, YOU MAY CHECK YOUR WORK ON THIS SECTION ONLY. DO NOT WORK ON ANY OTHER SECTION IN THE TEST.

SECTION IV

Time—35 minutes

23 Questions

<u>Directions</u>: Each group of questions in this section is based on a set of conditions. In answering some of the questions, it may be useful to draw a rough diagram. Choose the response that most accurately and completely answers each question and blacken the corresponding space on your answer sheet.

<u>Questions 1–5</u>

On a particular Saturday, a student will perform six activities—grocery shopping, hedge trimming, jogging, kitchen cleaning, laundry, and motorbike servicing. Each activity will be performed once, one at a time. The order in which the activities are performed is subject to the following conditions:

    Grocery shopping has to be immediately after hedge trimming.

    Kitchen cleaning has to be earlier than grocery shopping.

    Motorbike servicing has to be earlier than laundry.

    Motorbike servicing has to be either immediately before or immediately after jogging.

1. Which one of the following could be the order, from first to last, of the student's activities?

  (A) jogging, kitchen cleaning, hedge trimming, grocery shopping, motorbike servicing, laundry

  (B) jogging, motorbike servicing, laundry, hedge trimming, grocery shopping, kitchen cleaning

  (C) kitchen cleaning, hedge trimming, grocery shopping, laundry, motorbike servicing, jogging

  (D) kitchen cleaning, jogging, motorbike servicing, laundry, hedge trimming, grocery shopping

  (E) motorbike servicing, jogging, laundry, hedge trimming, kitchen cleaning, grocery shopping

GO ON TO THE NEXT PAGE.

2. Which one of the following activities CANNOT be third?

    (A) grocery shopping
    (B) hedge trimming
    (C) jogging
    (D) kitchen cleaning
    (E) motorbike servicing

3. Which one of the following CANNOT be true?

    (A) Hedge trimming is fourth.
    (B) Jogging is fourth.
    (C) Kitchen cleaning is second.
    (D) Laundry is third.
    (E) Motorbike servicing is second.

4. Which one of the following activities CANNOT be fifth?

    (A) grocery shopping
    (B) hedge trimming
    (C) jogging
    (D) laundry
    (E) motorbike servicing

5. Which one of the following, if substituted for the condition that motorbike servicing has to be earlier than laundry, would have the same effect in determining the order of the student's activities?

    (A) Laundry has to be one of the last three activities.
    (B) Laundry has to be either immediately before or immediately after jogging.
    (C) Jogging has to be earlier than laundry.
    (D) Laundry has to be earlier than hedge trimming.
    (E) Laundry has to be earlier than jogging.

GO ON TO THE NEXT PAGE.

<u>Questions 6–11</u>

Each of exactly three actors—Gombrich, Otto, and Raines—auditions for parts on exactly two of the following days of a particular week: Wednesday, Thursday, Friday, and Saturday. On each of these days at least one of the actors auditions for parts. The order of that week's auditions must meet the following conditions:

> The first day on which Otto auditions is some day before the first day on which Raines auditions.
>
> There is at least one day on which both Gombrich and Raines audition.
>
> At least one of the actors auditions on both Thursday and Saturday.

6. Which one of the following could be an accurate matching of the actors to the days on which they audition?

(A) Gombrich: Thursday, Friday
   Otto: Wednesday, Saturday
   Raines: Friday, Saturday

(B) Gombrich: Thursday, Saturday
   Otto: Wednesday, Friday
   Raines: Friday, Saturday

(C) Gombrich: Friday, Saturday
   Otto: Thursday, Saturday
   Raines: Wednesday, Friday

(D) Gombrich: Wednesday, Thursday
   Otto: Wednesday, Saturday
   Raines: Thursday, Saturday

(E) Gombrich: Wednesday, Friday
   Otto: Wednesday, Thursday
   Raines: Thursday, Saturday

GO ON TO THE NEXT PAGE.

7. If Otto auditions on both Thursday and Saturday, then Gombrich could audition on both

    (A) Wednesday and Thursday
    (B) Wednesday and Friday
    (C) Thursday and Friday
    (D) Thursday and Saturday
    (E) Friday and Saturday

8. Which one of the following CANNOT be true of the week's auditions?

    (A) Gombrich's last audition is on Thursday.
    (B) Gombrich's last audition is on Friday.
    (C) Otto's last audition is on Saturday.
    (D) Raines's last audition is on Friday.
    (E) Raines's last audition is on Thursday.

9. Which one of the following pairs of days CANNOT be the two days on which Otto auditions?

    (A) Wednesday and Thursday
    (B) Wednesday and Friday
    (C) Wednesday and Saturday
    (D) Thursday and Friday
    (E) Thursday and Saturday

10. Which one of the following could be true?

    (A) All three actors audition on Wednesday.
    (B) All three actors audition on Friday.
    (C) All three actors audition on Saturday.
    (D) Otto auditions on Friday and on Saturday.
    (E) Raines auditions on Wednesday and on Friday.

11. If Gombrich auditions on both Wednesday and Saturday, then which one of the following could be true?

    (A) Otto auditions on both Wednesday and Thursday.
    (B) Otto auditions on both Wednesday and Friday.
    (C) Otto auditions on both Wednesday and Saturday.
    (D) Raines auditions on both Wednesday and Saturday.
    (E) Raines auditions on both Thursday and Friday.

GO ON TO THE NEXT PAGE.

Questions 12–17

Each of seven toy dinosaurs—an iguanadon, a lambeosaur, a plateosaur, a stegosaur, a tyrannosaur, an ultrasaur, and a velociraptor—is completely colored either green, mauve, red, or yellow. A display is to consist entirely of exactly five of these toys. The display must meet the following specifications:

Exactly two mauve toys are included.

The stegosaur is red and is included.

The iguanadon is included only if it is green.

The plateosaur is included only if it is yellow.

The velociraptor is included only if the ultrasaur is not.

If both the lambeosaur and the ultrasaur are included, at least one of them is not mauve.

12. Which one of the following could be the toys included in the display?

(A) the lambeosaur, the plateosaur, the stegosaur, the ultrasaur, the velociraptor

(B) the lambeosaur, the plateosaur, the stegosaur, the tyrannosaur, the ultrasaur

(C) the iguanadon, the lambeosaur, the plateosaur, the stegosaur, the ultrasaur

(D) the iguanadon, the lambeosaur, the plateosaur, the tyrannosaur, the velociraptor

(E) the iguanadon, the lambeosaur, the stegosaur, the ultrasaur, the velociraptor

GO ON TO THE NEXT PAGE.

13. If the tyrannosaur is not included in the display, then the display must contain each of the following EXCEPT:

    (A) a green iguanadon
    (B) a mauve velociraptor
    (C) a mauve lambeosaur
    (D) a mauve ultrasaur
    (E) a yellow plateosaur

14. Which one of the following is a pair of toys that could be included in the display together?

    (A) a green lambeosaur and a mauve velociraptor
    (B) a green lambeosaur and a yellow tyrannosaur
    (C) a green lambeosaur and a yellow ultrasaur
    (D) a yellow tyrannosaur and a green ultrasaur
    (E) a yellow tyrannosaur and a red velociraptor

15. If the display includes a yellow tyrannosaur, then which one of the following must be true?

    (A) The iguanadon is included in the display.
    (B) The plateosaur is not included in the display.
    (C) The display includes two yellow toy dinosaurs.
    (D) The display contains a green lambeosaur.
    (E) The display contains a mauve velociraptor.

16. If both the iguanadon and the ultrasaur are included in the display, then the display must contain which one of the following?

    (A) a mauve tyrannosaur
    (B) a mauve ultrasaur
    (C) a yellow lambeosaur
    (D) a yellow plateosaur
    (E) a yellow ultrasaur

17. If the display includes two green toys, then which one of the following could be true?

    (A) There is exactly one yellow toy included in the display.
    (B) The tyrannosaur is included in the display and it is green.
    (C) Neither the lambeosaur nor the velociraptor is included in the display.
    (D) Neither the tyrannosaur nor the velociraptor is included in the display.
    (E) Neither the ultrasaur nor the velociraptor is included in the display.

GO ON TO THE NEXT PAGE.

Questions 18–23

A charitable foundation awards grants in exactly four areas—medical services, theater arts, wildlife preservation, and youth services—each grant being in one of these areas. One or more grants are awarded in each of the four quarters of a calendar year. Additionally, over the course of a calendar year, the following must obtain:

    Grants are awarded in all four areas.
    No more than six grants are awarded.
    No grants in the same area are awarded in the same quarter or in consecutive quarters.
    Exactly two medical services grants are awarded.
    A wildlife preservation grant is awarded in the second quarter.

18.   Which one of the following is a possible allocation of grants in a particular calendar year?

    (A)   first quarter: theater arts
            second quarter: wildlife preservation
            third quarter: medical services, youth services
            fourth quarter: theater arts

    (B)   first quarter: wildlife preservation
            second quarter: medical services
            third quarter: theater arts
            fourth quarter: medical services, youth services

    (C)   first quarter: youth services
            second quarter: wildlife preservation, medical services
            third quarter: theater arts
            fourth quarter: medical services, youth services

    (D)   first quarter: medical services, theater arts
            second quarter: theater arts, wildlife preservation
            third quarter: youth services
            fourth quarter: medical services

    (E)   first quarter: medical services, theater arts
            second quarter: wildlife preservation, youth services
            third quarter: theater arts
            fourth quarter: medical services, youth services

GO ON TO THE NEXT PAGE.

4 4 4 4 4 4

19. Which one of the following CANNOT be true in a particular calendar year?

(A) In each of the two quarters in which a medical services grant is awarded, no other grant is awarded.
(B) Exactly two theater arts grants are awarded, one in the second quarter and one in the fourth quarter.
(C) Exactly two youth services grants are awarded, one in the first quarter and one in the third quarter.
(D) Two wildlife preservation grants and two youth services grants are awarded.
(E) Three grants are awarded in the fourth quarter.

20. If a wildlife preservation grant and a youth services grant are awarded in the same quarter of a particular calendar year, then any of the following could be true that year EXCEPT:

(A) A medical services grant is awarded in the second quarter.
(B) A theater arts grant is awarded in the first quarter.
(C) A theater arts grant is awarded in the second quarter.
(D) A wildlife preservation grant is awarded in the fourth quarter.
(E) A youth services grant is awarded in the third quarter.

21. If exactly two grants are awarded in just one of the four quarters of a particular calendar year, then which one of the following could be true that year?

(A) Two youth services grants are awarded.
(B) Neither a medical services grant nor a youth services grant is awarded in the first quarter.
(C) A wildlife preservation grant is awarded in the fourth quarter.
(D) Both a youth services grant and a theater arts grant are awarded in the first quarter.
(E) A youth services grant is awarded in the first quarter and a theater arts grant is awarded in the second quarter.

22. Which one of the following CANNOT be true in a particular calendar year?

(A) Three grants are awarded in a quarter, none of which is a medical services grant.
(B) Exactly two grants are awarded in the first quarter and exactly two in the third quarter.
(C) Exactly two grants are awarded in the first quarter and exactly two in the fourth quarter.
(D) Theater arts grants are awarded in the first and fourth quarters, and no other grants are awarded in those two quarters.
(E) Wildlife preservation grants are awarded in the second and fourth quarters, and no other grants are awarded in those two quarters.

23. It is fully determined which grants are awarded for each quarter of a particular calendar year if which one of the following is true that year?

(A) Two theater arts grants are awarded.
(B) Two youth services grants are awarded.
(C) Three grants are awarded in the first quarter.
(D) Three grants are awarded in the second quarter.
(E) Three grants are awarded in the third quarter.

STOP
IF YOU FINISH BEFORE TIME IS CALLED, YOU MAY CHECK YOUR WORK ON THIS SECTION ONLY. DO NOT WORK ON ANY OTHER SECTION IN THE TEST.

SECTION V

Time—35 minutes

25 Questions

Directions: The questions in this section are based on the reasoning contained in brief statements or passages. For some questions, more than one of the choices could conceivably answer the question. However, you are to choose the best answer; that is, the response that most accurately and completely answers the question. You should not make assumptions that are by commonsense standards implausible, superfluous, or incompatible with the passage. After you have chosen the best answer, blacken the corresponding space on your answer sheet.

1. Scientists generally believe that no deep-sea creature can detect red light, but they need to reassess that view. Researchers recently discovered a foot-long deep-sea creature of the genus *Erenna* with bioluminescent red lights on some of its tentacles. These red lights, which are shaped like a common food source for small, deep-sea fish, probably function as lures to attract prey.

    Which one of the following most accurately expresses the overall conclusion drawn in the argument?

    (A) Red lights on the tentacles of a newly discovered deep-sea creature probably function as lures.
    (B) Red lights on the tentacles of a newly discovered deep-sea creature are shaped like a common food source for small, deep-sea fish.
    (C) A foot-long deep-sea creature of the genus *Erenna* has been discovered recently.
    (D) Scientists generally believe that deep-sea creatures cannot detect red light.
    (E) Scientists need to reconsider the belief that deep-sea creatures cannot detect red light.

2. For house painting, acrylic paints are an excellent choice. They provide everything that a good paint should provide: smooth and even coverage, quick drying time, durability, and easy cleanup. Even acrylics, however, cannot correct such surface defects as badly cracked paint. Such conditions indicate some underlying problem, such as water damage, that needs repair.

    Which one of the following is most strongly supported by the statements above?

    (A) Badly cracked paint is not a result of harsh weather conditions.
    (B) Acrylics are the only paints that provide everything that most homeowners need from a paint.
    (C) Acrylics should not be used to paint over other types of house paint.
    (D) It is not a requirement of house paints that they correct surface defects such as badly cracked paint.
    (E) Acrylic paints come in as wide a range of colors as do any other paints.

3. Letter to the editor: You have asserted that philanthropists want to make the nonprofit sector as efficient as private business in this country. Philanthropists want no such thing, of course. Why would anyone want to make nonprofits as inefficient as Byworks Corporation, which has posted huge losses for years?

    The reasoning of the argument in the letter is most vulnerable to criticism on the grounds that the argument

    (A) draws a conclusion about what ought to be the case from premises that are entirely about what is the case
    (B) takes the condition of one member of a category to be representative of the category in general
    (C) rejects a claim by attacking the proponent of the claim rather than addressing the claim itself
    (D) concludes that a claim must be false because of the mere absence of evidence in its favor
    (E) concludes that a phenomenon will have a certain property merely because the phenomenon's cause has that property

GO ON TO THE NEXT PAGE.

4. Statistical records of crime rates probably often reflect as much about the motives and methods of those who compile or cite them as they do about the actual incidence of crime. The police may underreport crime in order to convey the impression of their own success or overreport crime to make the case for a budget increase. Politicians may magnify crime rates to get elected or minimize them to remain in office. Newspapers, of course, often sensationalize crime statistics to increase readership.

The argument proceeds by doing which one of the following?

(A) evaluating evidence for and against its conclusion
(B) citing examples in support of its conclusion
(C) deriving implications of a generalization that it assumes to be true
(D) enumerating problems for which it proposes a general solution
(E) showing how evidence that apparently contradicts its conclusion actually supports that conclusion

5. Physiologist: The likelihood of developing osteoporosis is greatly increased by a deficiency of calcium in the diet. Dairy products usually contain more calcium per serving than do fruits and vegetables. Yet in countries where dairy products are rare, and fruits and vegetables are the main source of calcium, the incidence of osteoporosis is much lower than in countries where people consume a great deal of calcium from dairy products.

Which one of the following, if true, would most help to resolve the apparent discrepancy described by the physiologist?

(A) A healthy human body eventually loses the excess calcium that it takes in.
(B) Many people who eat large quantities of fruits and vegetables also consume dairy products.
(C) There are more people who have a calcium deficiency than there are who have developed osteoporosis.
(D) People who have calcium deficiencies are also likely to have deficiencies in other minerals.
(E) The fats in dairy products tend to inhibit the body's calcium absorption.

6. A first-term board member should not be on the finance committee unless he or she is an accountant or his or her membership on the committee is supported by all the members of the board.

Which one of the following arguments most closely conforms to the principle stated above?

(A) Simkins is a first-term board member and not an accountant; thus, Simkins should not be on the finance committee.
(B) Timmons is a third-term board member but not an accountant; thus, if all other board members think that Timmons should be on the finance committee, then Timmons should be on that committee.
(C) Ruiz is on the finance committee but is not an accountant; thus, Ruiz's membership must have been supported by all the members of the board.
(D) Klein is a first-term board member who is not an accountant; thus, Klein should not be allowed on the finance committee if any board member opposes Klein's appointment to that committee.
(E) Mabry is a board member who is not an accountant; thus, because Mabry's membership on the finance committee is opposed by most board members, Mabry should not be allowed on that committee.

7. Most respondents to a magazine survey who had recently listened to a taped reading of a certain best-selling novel said that they had enjoyed the novel, while most respondents who had recently read the novel themselves said they had not enjoyed it. These survey results support the contention that a person who listens to a taped reading of a novel is more likely to enjoy the novel than a person who reads it is.

Which one of the following, if true, would most weaken the argument?

(A) Most of the respondents who had listened to a taped reading of the novel had never read it, and most of the respondents who had read the novel had never listened to a taped reading of it.
(B) Most people can read a novel in considerably less time than it would take them to listen to a taped reading of it.
(C) When people are asked their opinion of a bestselling novel that they have read or listened to on tape, they are more likely to say that they enjoyed the novel than that they did not enjoy it.
(D) Many novels that are available in text versions are not available in audio versions.
(E) The novel in question, unlike most novels, included dialogue in many different dialects that are more understandable when heard than when read.

GO ON TO THE NEXT PAGE.

8. To qualify as a medical specialist, one must usually graduate from a university, then complete approximately four years of medical school, followed by a residency of two to six years in one's specialty. Finally, a physician who desires to become a recognized specialist must complete an evaluation program directed by a medical specialty board. Therefore, anyone who has qualified as a recognized medical specialist is competent to practice in his or her specialty.

Which one of the following is an assumption on which the argument depends?

(A) People who are not highly motivated will not complete the demanding course of study and examination required to become qualified as a recognized medical specialist.

(B) Only the most talented people will successfully complete the rigorous course of study necessary for qualification as a recognized medical specialist.

(C) No one incompetent to practice a particular specialty completes the evaluation program for that specialty.

(D) Usually, six to ten years of medical training beyond a university degree is sufficient to render someone competent to practice in his or her medical specialty.

(E) Usually, six to ten years of medical training beyond a university degree is necessary to render someone competent to practice in his or her medical specialty.

9. Archaeologists are currently analyzing plant remains found at a site that was last occupied more than 10,000 years ago. If the plants were cultivated, then the people who occupied the site discovered agriculture thousands of years before any other people are known to have done so. On the other hand, if the plants were wild—that is, uncultivated—then the people who occupied the site ate a wider variety of wild plants than did any other people at the time.

The statements above, if true, most strongly support which one of the following?

(A) The archaeologists analyzing the plant remains at the site will be able to determine whether the plants were cultivated or were wild.

(B) The people who occupied the site used some plants in ways that no other people did at that time.

(C) If the people who occupied the site had reached a more advanced stage in the use of wild plants than any other people at the time, then the plants found at the site were uncultivated.

(D) If the people who occupied the site discovered agriculture thousands of years before people anywhere else are known to have done so, then there are remains of cultivated plants at the site.

(E) It is more likely that the people who occupied the site discovered agriculture thousands of years before people anywhere else did than it is that they ate a wider variety of wild plants than any other people at the time.

GO ON TO THE NEXT PAGE.

10. In a test of fuel efficiency, car X and car Y yielded the same average fuel mileage, even though car X was driven in a less fuel-efficient manner than car Y was. Thus, car X is more fuel efficient than car Y.

Which one of the following arguments is most similar in its reasoning to the argument above?

(A) In an experiment, subject X consistently gave lower pain ratings in response to pinpricks than subject Y did. Therefore, it is reasonable to conclude that subjects X and Y experience pain differently.

(B) Our hamster gained the same amount of weight as our neighbors' hamster, even though our hamster ate more than theirs. So it must be that our hamster burned more calories than theirs did.

(C) When on his bicycle, Roland makes better time coasting down a hill than pedaling on a horizontal path. So he would make even better time on the hills if he were to pedal rather than coast.

(D) When asked to judge the value of various pieces of antique furniture, I gave lower estimates on average than you did. So in those cases where we both gave the same estimate, I must have overestimated the piece's value.

(E) Jean demonstrates a high level of visual acuity when she wears prescription glasses. Thus, it must be that without those prescription glasses, she would demonstrate a lower level of visual acuity.

11. Plumb-Ace advertises that its plumbers are more qualified than plumbers at any other major plumbing firm in the region because Plumb-Ace plumbers must complete a very difficult certification process. Plumb-Ace plumbers may or may not be more qualified, but clearly the certification process is not very difficult, because nearly everyone who takes the written portion of the certification exam passes it very easily.

The reasoning in the argument is flawed in that it

(A) treats something that is necessary to make a certification process very difficult as if it were sufficient by itself to make the process very difficult

(B) takes for granted that plumbers are not qualified unless they complete some certification process

(C) overlooks the possibility that plumbers at other firms in the region complete certification processes that are even easier than that completed by Plumb-Ace's plumbers

(D) infers that a claim is false on the grounds that an inadequate argument has been given for that claim

(E) presumes that since one part of a whole lacks a certain characteristic, the whole must lack that characteristic as well

12. Historian: The early Egyptian pharaohs spent as much wealth on largely ceremonial and hugely impressive architecture as they did on roads and irrigation systems. This was not mere frivolousness, however, for if people under a pharaoh's rule could be made to realize the extent of their ruler's mastery of the physical world, their loyalty could be maintained without military coercion.

The claim that early Egyptian expenditure on largely ceremonial architecture was not frivolous plays which one of the following roles in the historian's argument?

(A) It is a conclusion purportedly justified by the argument's appeal to the psychological effects of these structures on the Egyptian population.

(B) It is offered in support of the claim that Egyptian pharaohs spent as much on ceremonial architecture as they did on roads and irrigation systems.

(C) It is a premise given in support of the claim that the loyalty of people under a pharaoh's rule was maintained over time without reliance on military force.

(D) It is offered as an illustration of the principle that social and political stability do not depend ultimately on force.

(E) It is a premise used to justify the pharaohs' policy of spending scarce resources on structures that have only military utility.

13. The proposed change to the patent system is bound to have a chilling effect on scientific research. Under current rules, researchers have one full year after the initial publication of a new discovery to patent the discovery. This allows research results to be shared widely prior to the patent application. The proposed change would have the application precede initial publication, which would delay the communication of discoveries.

The conclusion drawn above follows logically if which one of the following is assumed?

(A) The proposed change will encourage more patent applications to be filed.

(B) Dramatic advances in scientific research have occurred while the current patent system has been in place.

(C) Delays in the communication of discoveries will have a chilling effect on scientific research.

(D) Most researchers oppose the proposed change to the patent system.

(E) The current rules for patent applications facilitate progress in scientific research by rewarding the communication of discoveries.

GO ON TO THE NEXT PAGE.

14. Every time people get what they want they feel pleasure. Pleasure is a natural result of getting what one wants. We can conclude that no one fundamentally desires anything except pleasure.

Which one of the following uses questionable reasoning most similar to that used in the argument above?

(A) I sure am enjoying the party even though I was sure I would not, so I guess I wanted to come after all.

(B) I have never been skiing, but just thinking about it terrifies me, so I guess I must not want to learn how.

(C) Every time I eat pizza I get a stomachache, so I suppose the reason I eat pizza in the first place is so that I can have a stomachache.

(D) Every time I have gone to a party with Julio I have enjoyed myself, so I expect I will enjoy myself if Julio and I go to a party tonight.

(E) I never enjoy a soccer game without eating hot dogs, so I guess I would not enjoy going to a basketball game if I could not eat hot dogs at the game.

15. Linguist: You philosophers say that we linguists do not have a deep understanding of language, but you have provided no evidence.

Philosopher: Well, you have said that you believe that "Joan and Ivan are siblings" is identical in meaning to "Ivan and Joan are siblings." But this cannot be the case, for the sentences are physically different; yet for two things to be identical, they must have all the same attributes.

Of the following, which one is the strongest logical counter that the linguist can make to the philosopher?

(A) Two things can have a few minor differences and still be identical.

(B) Two sentences can be identical physically, and yet, depending on the context in which they are uttered, not be identical in meaning.

(C) It is necessarily true that Joan is Ivan's sibling if Ivan is Joan's sibling.

(D) The issue is not whether the two sentences are completely identical, but whether they mean the same thing.

(E) A linguist has more experience with language than a philosopher, and so is in a better position to answer such questions.

16. Salespeople always steer customers toward products from which they make their highest commissions, and all salespeople in major health stores work on commission. Hence, when you buy vitamin supplements in a major health store, you can be sure that the claims the salespeople make about the quality of the products are inaccurate.

The reasoning in the argument is flawed in that the argument

(A) offers as a premise a claim that merely paraphrases the conclusion and for which no support is provided

(B) infers that some claims are inaccurate solely on the basis of the source of those claims

(C) infers that just because a group of people has a certain property, each member of the group has that property

(D) takes a condition that is sufficient for the conclusion to be true as one that is necessary for the conclusion to be true

(E) relies on the claims of an authority on a topic outside that authority's area of expertise

GO ON TO THE NEXT PAGE.

17. Because no other theory has been able to predict it so simply and accurately, the advance of the perihelion of Mercury is sometimes cited as evidence in support of Einstein's theory of general relativity. However, this phenomenon was already well known when Einstein developed his theory, and he quite probably adjusted his equations to generate the correct numbers for the perihelion advance. Therefore, accounting for this advance should not be counted as evidence in support of Einstein's theory.

Which one of the following principles, if valid, most helps to justify the argument above?

(A) Unless a phenomenon predicted by a scientific theory is unknown at the time the theory is developed, the theory should not be credited with the discovery of that phenomenon.

(B) A phenomenon that is predicted by a scientific theory should not count as evidence in favor of that theory unless the theory was developed with that phenomenon in mind.

(C) Unless a theory can accurately account for all relevant phenomena that are already well known at the time of its development, it cannot be regarded as well supported.

(D) If a theory is adjusted specifically to account for some particular phenomenon, a match between that theory and that phenomenon should not count as evidence in favor of the theory.

(E) If a theory is adjusted to generate the correct predictions for some phenomenon that is already known to the scientist developing the theory, the theory should not be counted as predicting that phenomenon.

18. Computer store manager: Last year we made an average of 13 percent profit on the high-end computer models—those priced over $1,000—that we sold, while low-end models—those priced below $1,000—typically returned at least 25 percent profit. Since there is a limit to how many models we can display and sell, we should sell only low-end models. This would maximize our profits, since we would probably sell as many low-end models if that is all we sold as we would sell both kinds combined if we continued to sell both.

The reasoning in the manager's argument is vulnerable to criticism on which one of the following grounds?

(A) The argument fails to consider the possibility that the money earned on each high-end computer is significantly higher than the money earned on each low-end computer.

(B) The argument fails to address the possibility that, despite the price differential, the store sold as many high-end models as low-end models last year.

(C) The argument ignores the possibility that some customers who come into a computer store expecting to purchase a low-end model end up purchasing a high-end model.

(D) The argument presumes, without providing justification, that the sole objective in managing the computer store should be maximizing profits.

(E) The argument fails to recognize that future sales of low-end computers may not be the same as past sales.

GO ON TO THE NEXT PAGE.

19. Professor: Economists argue that buying lottery tickets is an unwise use of resources, because the average payoff for the tickets sold in a lottery is much lower than the cost of a ticket. But this reasoning is faulty. The average amount paid out on individual insurance policies is much lower than the average cost of a policy, yet nobody would argue that purchasing insurance is an unwise use of resources.

Which one of the following, if true, most weakens the professor's argument?

(A) Individuals spend, on average, much more on insurance than on lottery tickets.

(B) Insurance companies generally retain a higher proportion of total revenue than do organizations that sponsor lotteries.

(C) Taking small financial risks can often greatly increase one's chances of obtaining much larger benefits.

(D) In general, the odds of winning the grand prize in a lottery are significantly lower than the odds of collecting a settlement from a typical insurance policy.

(E) The protection against loss that insurance provides is more important to one's well-being than is the possibility of a windfall gain.

20. Unusually large and intense forest fires swept the tropics in 1997. The tropics were quite susceptible to fire at that time because of the widespread drought caused by an unusually strong El Niño, an occasional global weather phenomenon. Many scientists believe the strength of the El Niño was enhanced by the global warming caused by air pollution.

Which one of the following can be properly inferred from the information above?

(A) Air pollution was largely responsible for the size and intensity of the forest fires that swept the tropics in 1997.

(B) If the El Niño in 1997 had not been unusually strong, few if any large and intense forest fires would have swept the tropics in that year.

(C) Forest fires in the tropics are generally larger and more intense than usual during a strong El Niño.

(D) At least some scientists believe that air pollution was responsible for the size and intensity of the forest fires that swept the tropics in 1997.

(E) If air pollution enhanced the strength of the El Niño in 1997, then it also contributed to the widespread drought in that year.

21. If Skiff's book is published this year, Professor Nguyen vows she will urge the dean to promote Skiff. Thus, if Skiff's book is as important and as well written as Skiff claims, he will be promoted, for Nguyen will certainly keep her promise, and the dean will surely promote Skiff if Nguyen recommends it.

The argument's conclusion can be properly inferred if which one of the following is assumed?

(A) Skiff's book will be published this year if it is as important as he claims it is.

(B) Skiff needs to publish a book before he can be promoted.

(C) Professor Nguyen believes that Skiff's book is well written.

(D) Skiff's book will not be published unless it is as important and as well written as he claims it is.

(E) Skiff will not be promoted unless Professor Nguyen urges the dean to do so.

22. If the magazine's circulation continues to rise as it has over the last ten years, in another ten years it will be the largest-selling martial arts magazine in the world. Unfortunately, it has now become clear that the magazine's publisher will not allow the managing editor to make the changes she has proposed, and without these changes, the magazine's circulation will not rise as quickly over the next ten years as it has over the last ten. So the magazine will not be the largest-selling martial arts magazine ten years from now.

The argument's reasoning is flawed because the argument

(A) identifies some changes required for the magazine's circulation to continue its rapid increase and concludes from this that no other changes are needed

(B) equates a reduction in the rate at which the magazine's circulation is increasing with a decline in the magazine's circulation

(C) draws a conclusion that simply restates a claim that is presented in support of that conclusion

(D) takes a single fact that is incompatible with a general claim as enough to show that claim to be false

(E) treats an occurrence that will ensure a certain outcome as something that is required for that outcome

GO ON TO THE NEXT PAGE.

23. Botanist: In an experiment, scientists raised domesticated radishes in a field with wild radishes, which are considered weeds. Within several generations, the wild radishes began to show the same flower color as the domesticated ones. This suggests that resistance to pesticides, which is often a genetically engineered trait, would also be passed from domesticated crop plants to their relatives that are considered weeds.

Which one of the following, if true, most strengthens the botanist's argument?

(A) It is much easier in principle for genetic traits to be passed from wild plants to their domesticated relatives than it is for such traits to be passed from the domesticated plant to the wild relative.

(B) When the ratio of domesticated radishes to wild radishes in the field increased, the speed with which the flower color passed to the wild radishes also increased.

(C) Radishes are not representative of crop plants in general with respect to the ease with which various traits are passed among members of closely related species.

(D) The flower color of the domesticated radishes had not been introduced into them via genetic engineering.

(E) It is more difficult for flower color to be transferred between domesticated and wild radishes than it is for almost any other trait to be passed between any two similarly related plant species.

24. Parents who consistently laud their children for every attempt to accomplish something, whether successful or not, actually erode the youngsters' sense of self-esteem. Children require commendation for their achievements, but if uniformly praised for both what they have accomplished and what they have merely attempted, they will eventually discount all words of commendation. In effect, such children never hear any praise at all.

Which one of the following most accurately expresses the overall conclusion of the argument?

(A) Parents should praise their children for their achievements.

(B) Children whose actions are praised undeservedly eventually learn to discount all words of praise.

(C) Parents need to distinguish between their own expectations for their children and what their children are actually capable of accomplishing.

(D) Children's self-esteem will suffer if their parents uniformly praise their attempts to accomplish things regardless of their success or failure.

(E) Children will develop low self-esteem if their parents do not praise them when they succeed.

25. Pauline: Some environmentalists claim that for the salmon to be saved, the hydroelectric dams on the river must be breached. But if the dams are breached, given the region's growing population and booming industry, electrical costs will skyrocket.

Roger: The dams are already producing electricity at optimal capacity. So regardless of whether they are breached, we will have to find additional energy sources for the region.

The dialogue provides the most support for the claim that Pauline and Roger agree that

(A) production from other energy sources cannot be increased in the near future to compensate for electricity production lost by breaching the dams

(B) there will be no significant decrease in demand for electricity in the region in the near future

(C) if the dams remain in service but do not operate at optimal capacity, electrical costs in the region will rise

(D) some environmentalists who advocate saving the salmon believe that that goal overrides concerns about electrical costs

(E) finding additional energy sources will not decrease the electrical costs in the region

STOP

IF YOU FINISH BEFORE TIME IS CALLED, YOU MAY CHECK YOUR WORK ON THIS SECTION ONLY. DO NOT WORK ON ANY OTHER SECTION IN THE TEST.

LSAT WRITING SAMPLE TOPIC

WildCare, a donor-supported organization that rescues and rehabilitates injured or sick wild animals, currently rents a portion of the facility that houses the local animal shelter. WildCare is deciding whether to stay where it is or relocate to a new facility. Using the facts below, write an essay in which you argue for one option over the other based on the following two criteria:

• WildCare's mission is to provide the highest quality care to the greatest number of animals.

• WildCare wants to maintain a strong donor base.

The building that houses both the animal shelter and WildCare is located in town, where it is easily accessible to both the local community and the surrounding region. WildCare is often able to borrow supplies such as cages, heating pads, and towels from the animal shelter. Most of WildCare's donors and volunteers learn of WildCare through interactions with the animal shelter. There is friction between WildCare and the building management over WildCare's need for upgraded electrical and water services and its desire to house more animals on the grounds. WildCare has foundation grants for supplies and staff support that are contingent on its remaining in the town.

At the new location WildCare would be the only occupant of a freestanding building adjacent to a nature preserve. An environmental education organization hosts a variety of wildlife-oriented activities for the public at the preserve. The director of the nature preserve would like WildCare to relocate there and has offered assistance with the move. Several of WildCare's larger donors are supportive of the move. The location is some distance from the town and is difficult to reach. There would be room to house more animals.

Directions:

1. Use the Answer Key on the next page to check your answers.

2. Use the Scoring Worksheet below to compute your raw score.

3. Use the Score Conversion Chart to convert your raw score into the 120–180 scale.

Scoring Worksheet

1. Enter the number of questions you answered correctly in each section.

	Number Correct
SECTION I..	_____
SECTION II	_____
SECTION III	_____
SECTION V	_____

2. Enter the sum here:_____
   This is your Raw Score.

Section Map

SECTION I: PrepTest 69, Section 1
SECTION II: PrepTest 69, Section 2
SECTION III: PrepTest 69, Section 3
SECTION IV: Experimental (PrepTest 57, Section 1)
SECTION V: PrepTest 69, Section 4

Conversion Chart
For Converting Raw Score to the 120–180 LSAT
Scaled Score
LSAT Form 4LSN106

Reported Score	Lowest	Highest
180	98	100
179	*	*
178	97	97
177	96	96
176	95	95
175	94	94
174	93	93
173	92	92
172	91	91
171	90	90
170	89	89
169	87	88
168	86	86
167	84	85
166	83	83
165	81	82
164	80	80
163	78	79
162	76	77
161	74	75
160	73	73
159	71	72
158	69	70
157	67	68
156	65	66
155	63	64
154	62	62
153	60	61
152	58	59
151	56	57
150	54	55
149	52	53
148	51	51
147	49	50
146	47	48
145	45	46
144	44	44
143	42	43
142	40	41
141	39	39
140	37	38
139	36	36
138	34	35
137	33	33
136	31	32
135	30	30
134	29	29
133	28	28
132	26	27
131	25	25
130	24	24
129	23	23
128	22	22
127	21	21
126	20	20
125	19	19
124	*	*
123	18	18
122	16	17
121	*	*
120	0	15

*There is no raw score that will produce this scaled score for this form.

SECTION I

1. B	8. C	15. C	22. B
2. A	9. A	16. D	23. A
3. D	10. D	17. C	24. C
4. D	11. E	18. E	25. B
5. C	12. E	19. E	
6. A	13. B	20. B	
7. B	14. A	21. C	

SECTION II

1. E	8. C	15. A	22. D
2. A	9. B	16. D	23. B
3. E	10. C	17. B	
4. C	11. A	18. D	
5. D	12. A	19. E	
6. B	13. D	20. A	
7. E	14. C	21. C	

SECTION III

1. A	8. A	15. C	22. B
2. B	9. B	16. B	23. A
3. C	10. E	17. E	24. D
4. A	11. C	18. B	25. A
5. D	12. D	19. A	26. E
6. D	13. B	20. D	27. C
7. B	14. A	21. D	

SECTION IV

1. D	8. E	15. E	22. D
2. B	9. D	16. A	23. E
3. C	10. C	17. B	
4. D	11. B	18. C	
5. C	12. B	19. D	
6. B	13. D	20. E	
7. B	14. A	21. B	

SECTION V

1. E	8. C	15. D	22. E
2. D	9. B	16. B	23. E
3. B	10. B	17. D	24. D
4. B	11. E	18. A	25. B
5. E	12. A	19. E	
6. D	13. C	20. E	
7. E	14. C	21. A	

TEST ANALYSIS

Section	Overall Performance Score: _____ Percentile: _____		
	Number attempted	Number of guesses	Number correct
Games			
Reading Comprehension			
Arguments 1			
Arguments 2			
TOTAL			

Games			
	Attempted? What order?	Diagram and Elements	Notes
Game 1			
Game 2			
Game 3			
Game 4			

Reading Comprehension

	Attempted? What order?	Passage Notes	Question Notes
Passage 1			
Passage 2			
Passage 3			
Passage 4			

Arguments

Page	Question Number	Question Task	Notes

Arguments

Page	Question Number	Question Task	Notes

The Official LSAT
PrepTest™ 70
Test code 9708
Form 3LSN105

SECTION I

Time—35 minutes

25 Questions

Directions: The questions in this section are based on the reasoning contained in brief statements or passages. For some questions, more than one of the choices could conceivably answer the question. However, you are to choose the best answer; that is, the response that most accurately and completely answers the question. You should not make assumptions that are by commonsense standards implausible, superfluous, or incompatible with the passage. After you have chosen the best answer, blacken the corresponding space on your answer sheet.

1. The television star Markus Hermann refuses to grant interviews with newspapers unless he is given the right to approve the article before publication. *The Greyburg Messenger* newspaper refuses to do anything that its editors believe will compromise their editorial integrity. So the *Messenger* will not interview Hermann, since _____.

   The conclusion of the argument is properly drawn if which one of the following completes the passage?

   (A) the editors of the *Messenger* believe that giving an interviewee the right to approve an article before publication would compromise their editorial integrity
   (B) the *Messenger* has never before given an interviewee the right to approve an article before publication
   (C) most television stars are willing to grant interviews with the *Messenger* even if they are not given the right to approve the articles before publication
   (D) Hermann usually requests substantial changes to interview articles before approving them
   (E) Hermann believes that the *Messenger* frequently edits interviews in ways that result in unflattering portrayals of the interviewees

2. Columnist: An information design expert has argued that using the popular presentation-graphics software GIAPS, with its autopresentation wizard and simplistic premade templates, leads people to develop ineffective presentations. But that is absurd. GIAPS is just a tool, so it cannot be responsible for bad presentations. The responsibility must lie with those who use the tool poorly.

   The columnist's argument is most vulnerable to criticism on the grounds that it

   (A) bases its conclusion on claims that are inconsistent with each other
   (B) takes for granted that any presentation that is not ineffective is a good presentation
   (C) bases an endorsement of a product entirely on that product's popularity
   (D) fails to consider that a tool might not effectively perform its intended function
   (E) rejects a claim because of its source rather than its content

3. Editorial: The legislature is considering allowing oil drilling in the Cape Simmons Nature Preserve. Supporters claim that, because modern drilling methods will be used, there will be no damage to the environment. However, that claim is easily disproven by looking at nearby Alphin Bay, where oil drilling began five years ago. The land there is marred by industrial sprawl, drilling platforms, and thousands of miles of roads and pipelines.

   Which one of the following, if true, most strengthens the argument in the editorial?

   (A) The Cape Simmons Nature Preserve is one of the few areas of pristine wilderness in the region.
   (B) The companies drilling for oil at Alphin Bay never claimed that drilling there would not cause any environmental damage.
   (C) The editorialist believes that oil drilling should not be allowed in a nature preserve unless it would cause no environmental damage.
   (D) There have been no significant changes in oil drilling methods in the last five years.
   (E) Oil drilling is only one of several industrial activities that takes place at Alphin Bay.

GO ON TO THE NEXT PAGE.

4. James: Community colleges, by their very nature, work to meet the educational needs of the communities they are in. The same is not true of universities, whose primary goals differ from those of community colleges.

   Margaret: A primary goal of any university is to serve the needs of the community where it is located. The main reason people have for attending a university is the same as that for attending a community college: preparing oneself for a career.

   James's and Margaret's statements provide the most support for the claim that they disagree over the truth of which one of the following?

   (A) A primary goal of any university is to serve the educational needs of its community.
   (B) Most universities adequately serve the educational needs of the communities in which they are located.
   (C) The main reason people have for attending a university is to prepare themselves for a career.
   (D) In a typical community, the primary educational need is to prepare community residents for careers.
   (E) The main reason people have for attending a university is the same as the main reason people have for attending a community college.

5. Most people who have taken a seminar for building organizational skills in the workplace have indeed become more organized as a result; however, despite having become more organized, few have become any more efficient.

   Which one of the following, if true, would most help to resolve the apparent discrepancy described above?

   (A) Some of the people who are most efficient in the workplace are not among the most organized.
   (B) Most people whose organizational skills in the workplace are below average do not take seminars for building organizational skills in the workplace.
   (C) Most seminars for building organizational skills in the workplace are designed for people who have been selected for management training.
   (D) Most people who have taken a seminar for building organizational skills in the workplace have below-average organizational skills before they enroll in the seminar.
   (E) Most people who have taken a seminar for building organizational skills in the workplace consequently expend a great amount of time organizing their activities.

6. Problem: The Thimble Corporation recently distributed rebate coupons for one of its products. Some of the coupons bore an expiration date that was too early. This created an unfair situation in which some customers believed, incorrectly, that the rebate offer had already expired.

   Principle: Anyone who creates an unfair situation has an obligation to rectify any unfair result of that situation.

   The principle, if valid, most helps to justify which one of the following judgments concerning the problem?

   (A) If a customer believed that the expiration date had passed but applied for the rebate anyway, the Thimble Corporation is not obligated to give a rebate to that customer.
   (B) Because some customers who knew that they were eligible for the rebate chose not to apply for it, the Thimble Corporation is not solely responsible for creating the unfair situation.
   (C) If there is a chance that any customers did not apply for the rebate because of an incorrect expiration date on their rebate coupon, the Thimble Corporation is obligated to try to identify them and offer them the rebate.
   (D) Because it cannot identify all of the customers who were adversely affected by the incorrect expiration date, the Thimble Corporation should deny the rebate to all of the customers who applied for it.
   (E) If a customer did not rely on an incorrect expiration date when applying for the rebate but was denied the rebate for any other reason, the Thimble Corporation is not obligated to offer that customer the rebate.

7. Critic: The recent biography of Shakespeare does not explain what is of most interest about him. It is by an expert on the history of Elizabethan England, and so does a good job of showing what life would have been like for Shakespeare as a man of that time. But it does not explain what made Shakespeare different from his contemporaries.

   The conclusion of the argument can be properly drawn if which one of the following is assumed?

   (A) There is no way to know what made Shakespeare different from his contemporaries.
   (B) The life of the average man in Elizabethan England is uninteresting.
   (C) Shakespeare was very different from the other men of his time.
   (D) A biography should always focus on what makes its subject distinctive.
   (E) What is most interesting about Shakespeare is what made him different from his contemporaries.

GO ON TO THE NEXT PAGE.

8. The result of attempting to whip cream in a blender is a thick, velvety substance rather than fluffy whipped cream. This is because a blender's container does not let in enough air to whip cream effectively. Although using a special whipping-cream attachment in a blender can help somewhat, it cannot fully compensate for the container's poor air intake.

If all of the statements above are true, which one of the following must be true?

(A) Cream that has been whipped ineffectively generally becomes a thick, velvety substance rather than fluffy whipped cream.
(B) The use of a special whipping-cream attachment in a blender does not suffice to whip cream completely effectively.
(C) When attempting to whip cream in a blender, using a special whipping-cream attachment always produces a fluffier result than could be obtained without using such an attachment.
(D) The use of a special whipping-cream attachment in a blender can reduce the total amount of air required to whip cream effectively in that blender.
(E) The use of a blender, with or without any special attachments, is not the most common way to attempt to produce whipped cream.

9. Astronomer: Proponents of the hypothesis that life evolved extraterrestrially and drifted here in spores point out that, 3.8 billion years ago, Earth was bombarded by meteorites that would have destroyed any life already here. Yet 3.5 billion years ago, Earth had life forms complex enough to leave fossil remains. Such life could not have evolved here in the 0.3 billion years following the meteorite bombardments, they claim. There is good reason to regard their hypothesis as false, however, for they merely offer empirical arguments against the view that life evolved on Earth; neither they nor anyone else has provided positive support for the extraterrestrial-spore theory of the origin of terrestrial life.

The reasoning in the astronomer's argument is flawed because the argument

(A) concludes, simply because there is no evidence in favor of a hypothesis, that there is evidence against that hypothesis
(B) fails to justify its claim that the view being criticized is inherently implausible
(C) reasons that a hypothesis is false simply because there is another hypothesis that is equally likely to be true
(D) attempts to derive a conclusion from premises that contradict it
(E) grants the truth of claims that are made by the advocates of the hypothesis but that do nothing to strengthen the astronomer's own argument

10. Advertisement: VIVVY, a video-based foreign language course for children, was introduced seventeen years ago. Amy, Matt, and Evelyn were among the first children to use VIVVY. Now they are successful university students. So if your child uses VIVVY, you can expect him or her to become a successful university student.

Which one of the following demonstrates most effectively by parallel reasoning that the argument in the advertisement is flawed?

(A) Similarly, you could conclude that you can expect to win the lottery if you carry a good-luck charm. After all, Annie, Francisco, and Sean carry good-luck charms, and these three people are lottery winners.
(B) Similarly, you could conclude that Jesse should not expect to get food poisoning. After all, Jesse, Doris, and Christine all attended the company picnic, and only Christine has gotten food poisoning as a result.
(C) Similarly, you could conclude that Eric, Diane, and Martin are the only employees who will be laid off. After all, any employee hired within the last year can expect to be laid off, and these three employees are the only ones who were hired within the last year.
(D) Similarly, you could conclude that Ken, Norma, and Mary routinely drive faster than the speed limit. After all, if you routinely exceed the speed limit, you can expect to get a speeding ticket eventually, and these three people have gotten speeding tickets.
(E) Similarly, you could conclude that Jack, Stephen, and Tina can expect to get jobs after they complete their university education. After all, these three people attend Perry University, and most people who graduated from Perry last year found jobs.

GO ON TO THE NEXT PAGE.

11. Activist: Accidents at the Three Mile Island and Chernobyl nuclear plants have shown the dangers of nuclear power. It was earlier argued that nuclear power was necessary because fossil fuels will eventually run out. Recently, however, a technology has been developed for deriving from sewage sludge an oil that can be used to generate power. This new technology, therefore, together with the possibility of using alternative sources of energy like solar, wind, and hydroelectric power, raises the hope that we can dispense altogether with nuclear power and that we can meet our energy needs in a way that better protects the environment from harm than we do at present.

Which one of the following considerations is LEAST relevant in evaluating the degree of practicability of the hope expressed by the activist above?

(A) whether the current methods of disposing of sewage sludge by dumping do environmental damage

(B) whether the processes that are used to turn sewage into clean water and sewage sludge have been improved in recent decades

(C) whether the cost of producing and using oil from sewage sludge would be economically sustainable

(D) whether the burning of oil from sewage sludge would, in contrast to nuclear power production, produce gases that would have a harmful warming effect on climate worldwide

(E) whether waste products that would be produced in deriving oil from sewage sludge and burning it would be as dangerous as those produced by the mining and use of nuclear fuel

12. In a study of tropical forests it was found that while the species of trees that is most common in a particular forest also reproduces the most, trees of the species that is rarest there tend to survive longer. This pattern holds regardless of which species of trees is the most common and which is the rarest.

Which one of the following, if true, most helps to explain why trees of the rarest species tend to survive longer than trees of the most common species?

(A) The species of trees that is most common in a forest thrives there because it is best suited to the local climate.

(B) Older trees tend to reproduce the least.

(C) The study tracked preexisting tree species but did not introduce any new species to the tropical forests.

(D) The survival of the trees of the rarer species enables tropical forests to recover more easily from moderate destruction.

(E) The trees of the common species have more competition for the resources they need than do the trees of the rare species.

13. The television network's advertisement for its new medical drama grossly misrepresents what that program is like. Thus, it will not as effectively attract the sort of viewers likely to continue watching the program as would the advertisement that the program's producers favored; people who tune in to the first episode based on false expectations will be unlikely to watch subsequent episodes.

The argument relies on which one of the following assumptions?

(A) Most viewers who tune in to the first episode of the program will do so because of the network's advertisement for the program.

(B) The advertisement that the program's producers favored would not have grossly misrepresented what the program would be like.

(C) Most people who tune in to the first episode of the program and become loyal viewers will not have tuned in to the first episode as a result of the network's advertisement for the program.

(D) If the advertisement that the program's producers favored were used instead of the network's advertisement, almost all of the viewers who tuned in to the first episode would tune in to subsequent episodes as well.

(E) Most people who become loyal viewers of a program do not miss the program's first episode.

14. Sharon heard her favorite novelist speak out against a political candidate that Sharon has supported for years. As a result, Sharon's estimation of the novelist declined but her estimation of the candidate did not change.

The situation described above conforms most closely to which one of the following principles?

(A) Artists who speak out on political matters will have influence only among their most dedicated fans.

(B) A political statement from an artist should be considered only if the artist has established a reputation for being an honest and knowledgeable observer of politics.

(C) Artists should limit their public political statements to issues that are somehow related to the arts.

(D) Someone who hears testimony that contradicts a long-standing opinion will generally entertain doubts about the source of the testimony rather than the correctness of the opinion.

(E) People are far less likely to renounce an allegiance that they have had for many years than to renounce an allegiance that is new to them.

GO ON TO THE NEXT PAGE.

15. Advertisement: In a carefully controlled study, blindfolded volunteers were divided evenly into five groups. Each volunteer tasted Sparkle Cola and one of five competing colas, each group tasting a different cola. Most of the volunteers said they preferred Sparkle Cola to the competing cola tasted. This shows that Sparkle Cola elicits a more favorable response from consumers than any of the competing colas tested.

The reasoning in the advertisement is most vulnerable to criticism on which one of the following grounds?

(A) It overlooks the possibility that a generalization true of the entire group of volunteers was not true of each of the five smaller groups.
(B) It takes for granted that most of the volunteers would buy Sparkle Cola rather than one of the other colas tasted, at least in situations where Sparkle Cola is not much more expensive.
(C) It overlooks the possibility that some cola not tested in the study would have elicited a more favorable response than Sparkle Cola.
(D) It overlooks the possibility that many people may prefer Sparkle Cola to competing colas for reasons such as the packaging or price of Sparkle Cola, rather than its taste.
(E) It is based on a study that does not elicit consumers' responses to any beverages other than colas.

16. Evidently, watching too much television can lead people to overestimate the risks that the world poses to them. A recent study found that people are more likely to think that they will be victims of a natural disaster if they watch an above-average amount of television than if they do not.

Which one of the following, if true, most weakens the reasoning above?

(A) Many people overestimate the dangers that the world poses to them, regardless of the amount of television they watch.
(B) A person is less likely to live in an area that is prone to natural disasters if that person watches an above-average amount of television than if that person watches a below-average amount of television.
(C) People who watch a below-average amount of television tend to have a fairly accurate idea of the likelihood that they will be victims of a natural disaster.
(D) People who are well informed about the risks posed by natural disasters tend to have become well informed in some way other than by watching television.
(E) A person is more likely to watch an above-average amount of television if that person lives in an area that is prone to natural disasters than if that person lives in an area that is not.

17. Meteorologist: Heavy downpours are likely to become more frequent if Earth's atmosphere becomes significantly warmer. A warm atmosphere heats the oceans, leading to faster evaporation, and the resulting water vapor forms rain clouds more quickly. A warmer atmosphere also holds more moisture, resulting in larger clouds. In general, as water vapor in larger clouds condenses, heavier downpours are more likely to result.

Which one of the following most accurately describes the role played in the meteorologist's argument by the claim that, in general, as water vapor in larger clouds condenses, heavier downpours are more likely to result?

(A) It is the only conclusion in the argument.
(B) It is the conclusion of the argument as a whole but is not the only explicitly stated conclusion in the argument.
(C) It is a statement that the argument is intended to support but is not the conclusion of the argument as a whole.
(D) It is used to support the only conclusion in the argument.
(E) It provides a causal explanation of the phenomenon described by the conclusion of the argument as a whole, but it is not intended to provide support for that conclusion.

18. Field studies, which have long been a staple of anthropological research, involve the researcher living within the community being studied. However, the usefulness of field studies tends to be overrated by anthropologists. Although most anthropologists do realize that living within the community one is studying affects that community, they generally underestimate the extent of such effects.

Which one of the following most accurately expresses the conclusion drawn in the argument?

(A) Anthropologists tend to overestimate the value of field studies.
(B) In a field study, the researcher lives within the community being studied.
(C) Field studies have been a central feature of anthropological research for a long time.
(D) Most anthropologists know that when they live within a community being studied, the community is affected at least somewhat.
(E) Most anthropologists underestimate how much of an effect the researcher's presence has on a community being studied.

GO ON TO THE NEXT PAGE.

19. Juarez thinks that the sales proposal will be rejected by the committee if it is not rewritten before they see it. Juarez's opinion is very reliable on such matters. Thus, since the proposal will not be rewritten, it will probably be rejected by the committee.

The reasoning in which one of the following arguments is most similar to the reasoning in the argument above?

(A) A leading science journal has concluded that data provided by the manufacturer of a certain controversial new medication are accurate. The journal is generally reliable on such matters. Thus, the medication is probably safe, for if the company's data are accurate, the medication must be safe.

(B) The data from the manufacturer of a controversial new medication prove that the medication is safe, because a leading science journal has concluded that the medication is safe, and it would not have done so had the manufacturer's data not proven that the medication is safe.

(C) A leading science journal states that a certain controversial new medication is safe if the data provided by the company that developed the drug are accurate. Thus, the medication is probably safe, for the science journal is rarely wrong about such matters, and the company's data are accurate.

(D) A leading science journal states that the data provided by the manufacturer of a controversial new medication are probably accurate and that if they are accurate, the medication is safe. Thus, the manufacturer's data are probably accurate, for the science journal is fairly reliable on such matters.

(E) The data from the manufacturer of a controversial new medication are probably accurate, because a leading science journal has published the data and has concluded that the data are probably accurate. Moreover, the journal is fairly reliable on such matters.

20. Advertisement: In a recent survey, a sample representative of all new Popelka Auto Insurance policyholders reported savings of $250 a year, on average, as a result of switching their auto insurance coverage to Popelka. Thus, most people who hold auto insurance policies with other companies could save hundreds of dollars by switching to Popelka.

The argument in the advertisement is most vulnerable to criticism on which one of the following grounds?

(A) It overlooks the possibility that at least some of the new Popelka Auto Insurance policyholders surveyed reported that they saved little or no money when they switched their auto insurance coverage to Popelka.

(B) It takes for granted that the new Popelka Auto Insurance policyholders pay no less for their auto insurance, on average, than do people who have held Popelka Auto Insurance policies for a longer period of time.

(C) It fails to address adequately the possibility that switching to another insurance company would enable many auto insurance policyholders to save even more money than they would save by switching to Popelka.

(D) It takes for granted that few if any of the Popelka Auto Insurance policyholders surveyed underestimated how much they saved when they switched their auto insurance coverage to Popelka.

(E) It fails to address adequately the possibility that people capable of saving hundreds of dollars by switching their auto insurance coverage to Popelka are disproportionately represented among the new Popelka auto insurance policyholders.

GO ON TO THE NEXT PAGE.

21. Consumer magazine: Because front-loading washers use less water than top-loading washers, ordinary powder detergent does not dissolve readily in front-loading washers. So, to get clothes really clean in a front-loading machine you need to use a detergent formulated especially for front-loading washers, instead of ordinary powder detergent.

Which one of the following is an assumption required by the argument in the consumer magazine?

(A) All top-loading washing machines use the same amount of water.
(B) A laundry detergent formulated especially for front-loading washers dissolves more readily in them than it does in top-loading washers.
(C) A washing machine gets clothes really clean only with a laundry detergent specially formulated for that machine.
(D) A laundry detergent does not get clothes really clean in a washer unless it dissolves readily in it.
(E) Washers that use more water get clothes cleaner than those that use less.

22. In marketing their products, drug companies often send gifts to physicians. According to a recent survey, most physicians believe that their own choices when prescribing drugs are not influenced by drug companies' gifts. The same survey indicates that the majority of physicians believe that most other physicians' prescription choices are influenced by such gifts.

If the survey results are accurate, which one of the following must be true?

(A) Physicians who do not accept gifts from drug companies are less likely to prescribe unnecessary drugs than those who do accept such gifts.
(B) Most physicians believe that drug companies should adopt new guidelines that regulate their practices in sending gifts to physicians.
(C) Some physicians are mistaken either about the degree to which they are influenced by gifts from drug companies or about the degree to which such gifts influence other physicians.
(D) Some physicians who admit that their own choices when prescribing drugs are influenced by drug companies' gifts believe that other physicians' prescription choices are influenced to a greater degree by such gifts.
(E) All physicians who admit that their own choices when prescribing drugs are influenced by drug companies' gifts believe that most other physicians' prescription choices are also influenced by such gifts.

23. Columnist: Although most people favor the bill and the bill does not violate anyone's basic human rights, it will not be passed for many years, if at all; nor will any similar bill. Those people who would be adversely affected were it to become law are very influential. This shows that, if this country is a democracy at all, it is not a well-functioning one.

Which one of the following principles, if valid, most helps to justify the columnist's reasoning?

(A) In a well-functioning democracy, any bill that would benefit most people will be passed into law within a few years if it does not violate anyone's basic human rights.
(B) If a democracy is well functioning, then any bill that is opposed by influential people but favored by most other people will eventually pass into law.
(C) In a well-functioning democracy, a bill that is favored by most people will become law within a few years only if those who oppose it are not very influential.
(D) Any bill passed into law in a well-functioning democracy will be favored by most people and be consistent with individuals' basic human rights.
(E) A bill that most people favor will be passed promptly into law in a well-functioning democracy if the bill does not violate anyone's basic human rights.

GO ON TO THE NEXT PAGE.

24. Many homeowners regularly add commercial fertilizers to their lawns and gardens to maintain a healthy balance of nutrients in soil. The widely available commercial fertilizers contain only macronutrients—namely, nitrogen, phosphorus, and potassium. To remain healthy in the long term, soil for lawns requires the presence of these macronutrients and also trace amounts of micronutrients such as zinc, iron, and copper, which are depleted when grass clippings are raked up rather than allowed to decay and return to the soil.

Which one of the following can be properly inferred from the statements above?

(A) There is no single fertilizer that provides both the macronutrients and micronutrients necessary for maintaining soil's long-term health.

(B) The macronutrients nitrogen, phosphorus, and potassium are available to homeowners only in commercial fertilizers.

(C) Widely available commercial fertilizers are not alone sufficient to maintain a healthy balance of nutrients in soil for lawns where grass clippings are not allowed to decay and return to the soil.

(D) For soil to remain healthy in the long term, it requires the regular addition of both commercial fertilizers and a source of micronutrients such as grass clippings that are allowed to decay and return to the soil.

(E) Homeowners who rake up their grass clippings are unable to maintain the long-term health of the soil in their lawns and gardens.

25. In most industrial waste products that contain the toxic chemical XTX, the concentration of this chemical is approximately 1,000 parts per million. A federal law intended to reduce the harm that can result from the introduction of XTX into the environment permits a company to dispose of these waste products in a dump for hazardous waste, but only if the concentration of XTX is below 500 parts per million. Waste products with concentrations above that level must be destroyed by incineration. The law further specifies that manufacturers may not dilute XTX-containing waste products to bring their concentration of XTX down to a permissible level for dumping.

Which one of the following, if true, argues most strongly for the inclusion of the antidilution provision of the law?

(A) If improperly incinerated, waste products containing undiluted concentrations of XTX can release into the environment a gaseous form of the chemical that is more than twice as toxic as XTX is in its usual liquid state.

(B) If present in the environment in sufficient quantities, the diluted XTX is as harmful as the more concentrated XTX.

(C) When XTX is exposed to sunlight and oxygen, it eventually breaks down into a number of components that individually and collectively carry no risk of environmental harm.

(D) Most owners of dumps for hazardous waste are willing to accept XTX for disposal in their facilities only in concentrations below 800 parts per million.

(E) To manufacturers, the cost of diluting and disposing of waste products containing XTX is approximately the same as the cost of destroying these products by incineration.

STOP
IF YOU FINISH BEFORE TIME IS CALLED, YOU MAY CHECK YOUR WORK ON THIS SECTION ONLY. DO NOT WORK ON ANY OTHER SECTION IN THE TEST.

SECTION II

Time—35 minutes

26 Questions

Directions: The questions in this section are based on the reasoning contained in brief statements or passages. For some questions, more than one of the choices could conceivably answer the question. However, you are to choose the best answer; that is, the response that most accurately and completely answers the question. You should not make assumptions that are by commonsense standards implausible, superfluous, or incompatible with the passage. After you have chosen the best answer, blacken the corresponding space on your answer sheet.

1. Many doctors cater to patients' demands that they be prescribed antibiotics for their colds. However, colds are caused by viruses, and antibiotics have no effect on viruses, and so antibiotics have no effect on colds. Such treatments are also problematic because antibiotics can have dangerous side effects. So doctors should never prescribe antibiotics to treat colds.

The reasoning above most closely conforms to which one of the following principles?

(A) A doctor should not prescribe a drug for a condition if it cannot improve that condition and if the drug potentially has adverse side effects.

(B) A doctor should not prescribe any drug that might have harmful effects on the patient even if the drug might have a positive effect on the patient.

(C) A doctor should attempt to prescribe every drug that is likely to affect the patient's health positively.

(D) A doctor should withhold treatment from a patient if the doctor is uncertain whether the treatment will benefit the patient.

(E) A doctor should never base the decision to prescribe a certain medication for a patient on the patient's claims about the effectiveness of that medication.

2. Long-distance runners use two different kinds of cognitive strategies: "associative" and "dissociative." Associative strategies involve attending closely to physical sensations, while dissociative strategies involve mostly ignoring physical sensations. Associative strategies, unlike dissociative ones, require so much concentration that they result in mental exhaustion lasting more than a day. Since it is important for long-distance runners to enter a race mentally refreshed, _____.

Which one of the following most logically completes the argument?

(A) long-distance runners should not rely heavily on associative strategies during training the day before they run in a race

(B) unless they regularly train using associative strategies, long-distance runners should use dissociative strategies during races

(C) maximizing the benefits of training for long-distance running involves frequently alternating associative and dissociative strategies

(D) long-distance runners are about evenly divided between those who use dissociative strategies during races and those who use associative strategies during races

(E) in long-distance running, dissociative strategies are generally more effective for a day's training run than are associative strategies

GO ON TO THE NEXT PAGE.

3. MetroBank made loans to ten small companies, in amounts ranging from $1,000 to $100,000. These ten loans all had graduated payment plans, i.e., the scheduled monthly loan payment increased slightly each month over the five-year term of the loan. Nonetheless, the average payment received by MetroBank for these ten loans had decreased by the end of the five-year term.

Which one of the following, if true, most helps to resolve the apparent discrepancy in the statements above?

(A) The number of small companies receiving new loans from MetroBank increased over the five-year term.
(B) Several of the ten small companies also borrowed money from other banks.
(C) Most banks offer a greater number of loans for under $100,000 than for over $100,000.
(D) Of the ten small companies, the three that had borrowed the largest amounts paid off their loans within three years.
(E) For some loans made by MetroBank, the monthly payment decreases slightly over the term of the loan.

4. Professor: A guest speaker recently delivered a talk entitled "The Functions of Democratic Governments" to a Political Ideologies class at this university. The talk was carefully researched and theoretical in nature. But two students who disagreed with the theory hurled vicious taunts at the speaker. Several others applauded their attempt to humiliate the speaker. This incident shows that universities these days do not foster fair-minded and tolerant intellectual debate.

The professor's reasoning is flawed in that it

(A) draws a conclusion based on the professor's own opinion rather than on that of the majority of the students present at the talk
(B) is inconsistent in advocating tolerance while showing intolerance of the dissenting students' views
(C) relies primarily on an emotional appeal
(D) draws a general conclusion based on too small a sample
(E) incorrectly focuses on the behavior of the dissenting students rather than relating the reasons for that behavior

5. Studies reveal that most people select the foods they eat primarily on the basis of flavor, and that nutrition is usually a secondary concern at best. This suggests that health experts would have more success in encouraging people to eat wholesome foods if they emphasized how flavorful those foods truly are rather than how nutritious they are.

Which one of the following, if true, most strengthens the argument above?

(A) Most people currently believe that wholesome foods are more flavorful, on average, than unwholesome foods are.
(B) Few people, when given a choice between foods that are flavorful but not nutritious and foods that are nutritious but not flavorful, will choose the foods that are nutritious but not flavorful.
(C) Health experts' attempts to encourage people to eat wholesome foods by emphasizing how nutritious those foods are have been moderately successful.
(D) The studies that revealed that people choose the foods they eat primarily on the basis of flavor also revealed that people rated as most flavorful those foods that were least nutritious.
(E) In a study, subjects who were told that a given food was very flavorful were more willing to try the food and more likely to enjoy it than were subjects who were told that the food was nutritious.

6. Studies show that individuals with a high propensity for taking risks tend to have fewer ethical principles to which they consciously adhere in their business interactions than do most people. On the other hand, individuals with a strong desire to be accepted socially tend to have more such principles than do most people. And, in general, the more ethical principles to which someone consciously adheres, the more ethical is that person's behavior. Therefore, business schools can promote more ethical behavior among future businesspeople by promoting among their students the desire to be accepted socially and discouraging the propensity for taking risks.

The reasoning in the argument is flawed because the argument

(A) infers from the fact that something is usually true that it is always true
(B) takes for granted that promoting ethical behavior is more important than any other goal
(C) concludes merely from the fact that two things are correlated that one causes the other
(D) takes for granted that certain actions are morally wrong simply because most people believe that they are morally wrong
(E) draws a conclusion that simply restates a claim presented in support of that conclusion

GO ON TO THE NEXT PAGE.

7. Essayist: Lessing contended that an art form's medium dictates the kind of representation the art form must employ in order to be legitimate; painting, for example, must represent simultaneous arrays of colored shapes, while literature, consisting of words read in succession, must represent events or actions occurring in sequence. The claim about literature must be rejected, however, if one regards as legitimate the imagists' poems, which consist solely of amalgams of disparate images.

Which one of the following, if assumed, enables the essayist's conclusion to be properly drawn?

(A) An amalgam of disparate images cannot represent a sequence of events or actions.
(B) Poems whose subject matter is not appropriate to their medium are illegitimate.
(C) Lessing was not aware that the imagists' poetry consists of an amalgam of disparate images.
(D) All art, even the imagists' poetry, depicts or represents some subject matter.
(E) All art represents something either as simultaneous or as successive.

8. A psychiatrist argued that there is no such thing as a multiple personality disorder on the grounds that in all her years of clinical practice, she had never encountered one case of this type.

Which one of the following most closely parallels the questionable reasoning cited above?

(A) Anton concluded that colds are seldom fatal on the grounds that in all his years of clinical practice, he never had a patient who died of a cold.
(B) Lyla said that no one in the area has seen a groundhog and so there are probably no groundhogs in the area.
(C) Sauda argued that because therapy rarely had an effect on her patient's type of disorder, therapy was not warranted.
(D) Thomas argued that because Natasha has driven her car to work every day since she bought it, she would probably continue to drive her car to work.
(E) Jerod had never spotted a deer in his area and concluded from this that there are no deer in the area.

9. Even if many more people in the world excluded meat from their diet, world hunger would not thereby be significantly reduced.

Which one of the following, if true, most calls into question the claim above?

(A) Hunger often results from natural disasters like typhoons or hurricanes, which sweep away everything in their path.
(B) Both herds and crops are susceptible to devastating viral and other diseases.
(C) The amount of land needed to produce enough meat to feed one person for a week can grow enough grain to feed more than ten people for a week.
(D) Often people go hungry because they live in remote barren areas where there is no efficient distribution for emergency food relief.
(E) Most historical cases of famine have been due to bad social and economic policies or catastrophes such as massive crop failure.

10. Dairy farmer: On our farm, we have great concern for our cows' environmental conditions. We have recently made improvements that increase their comfort, such as providing them with special sleeping mattresses. These changes are intended to increase blood flow to the udder. This increased blood flow would boost milk output and thus increase profits.

Of the following propositions, which one is best illustrated by the dairy farmer's statements?

(A) Dairy cows cannot have comfortable living conditions unless farmers have some knowledge about the physiology of milk production.
(B) Farming practices introduced for the sake of maximizing profits can improve the living conditions of farm animals.
(C) More than other farm animals, dairy cows respond favorably to improvements in their living environments.
(D) The productivity of dairy farms should be increased only if the quality of the product is not compromised.
(E) The key to maximizing profits on a dairy farm is having a concern for dairy cows' environment.

GO ON TO THE NEXT PAGE.

11. Pat: E-mail fosters anonymity, which removes barriers to self-revelation. This promotes a degree of intimacy with strangers that would otherwise take years of direct personal contact to attain.

Amar: Frankness is not intimacy. Intimacy requires a real social bond, and social bonds cannot be formed without direct personal contact.

The dialogue most strongly supports the claim that Pat and Amar disagree with each other about whether

(A) barriers to self-revelation hinder the initial growth of intimacy
(B) E-mail can increase intimacy between friends
(C) intimacy between those who communicate with each other solely by e-mail is possible
(D) real social bonds always lead to intimacy
(E) the use of e-mail removes barriers to self-revelation

12. Criminologist: The main purpose of most criminal organizations is to generate profits. The ongoing revolutions in biotechnology and information technology promise to generate enormous profits. Therefore, criminal organizations will undoubtedly try to become increasingly involved in these areas.

The conclusion of the criminologist's argument is properly inferred if which one of the following is assumed?

(A) If an organization tries to become increasingly involved in areas that promise to generate enormous profits, then the main purpose of that organization is to generate profits.
(B) At least some criminal organizations are or will at some point become aware that the ongoing revolutions in biotechnology and information technology promise to generate enormous profits.
(C) Criminal organizations are already heavily involved in every activity that promises to generate enormous profits.
(D) Any organization whose main purpose is to generate profits will try to become increasingly involved in any technological revolution that promises to generate enormous profits.
(E) Most criminal organizations are willing to become involved in legal activities if those activities are sufficiently profitable.

13. Administrators of educational institutions are enthusiastic about the educational use of computers because they believe that it will enable schools to teach far more courses with far fewer teachers than traditional methods allow. Many teachers fear computers for the same reason. But this reason is mistaken. Computerized instruction requires more, not less, time of instructors, which indicates that any reduction in the number of teachers would require an accompanying reduction in courses offered.

The statement that the educational use of computers enables schools to teach far more courses with far fewer teachers figures in the argument in which one of the following ways?

(A) It is presented as a possible explanation for an observation that follows it.
(B) It is a statement of the problem the argument sets out to solve.
(C) It is a statement that the argument is designed to refute.
(D) It is a statement offered in support of the argument's main conclusion.
(E) It is the argument's main conclusion.

14. Scientists have shown that older bees, which usually forage outside the hive for food, tend to have larger brains than do younger bees, which usually do not forage but instead remain in the hive to tend to newly hatched bees. Since foraging requires greater cognitive ability than does tending to newly hatched bees, it appears that foraging leads to the increased brain size of older bees.

Which one of the following, if true, most seriously weakens the argument above?

(A) Bees that have foraged for a long time do not have significantly larger brains than do bees that have foraged for a shorter time.
(B) The brains of older bees that stop foraging to take on other responsibilities do not become smaller after they stop foraging.
(C) Those bees that travel a long distance to find food do not have significantly larger brains than do bees that locate food nearer the hive.
(D) In some species of bees, the brains of older bees are only marginally larger than those of younger bees.
(E) The brains of older bees that never learn to forage are the same size as those of their foraging counterparts of the same age.

GO ON TO THE NEXT PAGE.

15. Carla: Professors at public universities should receive paid leaves of absence to allow them to engage in research. Research not only advances human knowledge, but also improves professors' teaching by keeping them abreast of the latest information in their fields.

David: But even if you are right about the beneficial effects of research, why should our limited resources be devoted to supporting professors taking time off from teaching?

David's response to Carla is most vulnerable to criticism on the grounds that it

(A) ignores the part of Carla's remarks that could provide an answer to David's question
(B) takes for granted that the only function of a university professor is teaching
(C) incorrectly takes Carla's remarks as claiming that all funding for professors comes from tax money
(D) takes for granted that providing the opportunity for research is the only function of paid leaves of absence
(E) presumes, without providing justification, that professors do not need vacations

16. Software reviewer: Dictation software allows a computer to produce a written version of sentences that are spoken to it. Although dictation software has been promoted as a labor-saving invention, it fails to live up to its billing. The laborious part of writing is in the thinking and the editing, not in the typing. And proofreading the software's error-filled output generally squanders any time saved in typing.

Which one of the following most accurately describes the role played in the software reviewer's argument by the claim that dictation software fails to live up to its billing?

(A) It is the argument's main conclusion but not its only conclusion.
(B) It is the argument's only conclusion.
(C) It is an intermediate conclusion that is offered as direct support for the argument's main conclusion.
(D) It is a premise offered in support of the argument's conclusion.
(E) It is a premise offered as direct support for an intermediate conclusion of the argument.

17. Poetry journal patron: Everybody who publishes in *The Brick Wall Review* has to agree in advance that if a poem is printed in one of its regular issues, the magazine also has the right to reprint it, without monetary compensation, in its annual anthology. *The Brick Wall Review* makes enough money from sales of its anthologies to cover most operating expenses. So, if your magazine also published an anthology of poems first printed in your magazine, you could depend less on donations. After all, most poems published in your magazine are very similar to those published in *The Brick Wall Review*.

Which one of the following, if true, most weakens the patron's argument?

(A) Neither *The Brick Wall Review* nor the other magazine under discussion depends on donations to cover most operating expenses.
(B) Many of the poets whose work appears in *The Brick Wall Review* have had several poems rejected for publication by the other magazine under discussion.
(C) The only compensation poets receive for publishing in the regular issues of the magazines under discussion are free copies of the issues in which their poems appear.
(D) *The Brick Wall Review* depends on donations to cover most operating expenses not covered by income from anthology sales.
(E) *The Brick Wall Review*'s annual poetry anthology always contains a number of poems by famous poets not published in the regular issues of the magazine.

18. No one with a serious medical problem would rely on the average person to prescribe treatment. Similarly, since a good public servant has the interest of the public at heart, _____.

Which one of the following statements would most reasonably complete the argument?

(A) public servants should not be concerned about the outcomes of public opinion surveys
(B) the average public servant knows more about what is best for society than the average person does
(C) public servants should be more knowledgeable about the public good than they are
(D) public servants should base decisions on something other than the average person's recommendations
(E) one is a good public servant if one is more knowledgeable about the public good than is the average person

GO ON TO THE NEXT PAGE.

19. Team captain: Winning requires the willingness to cooperate, which in turn requires motivation. So you will not win if you are not motivated.

The pattern of reasoning in which one of the following is most similar to that in the argument above?

(A) Being healthy requires exercise. But exercising involves risk of injury. So, paradoxically, anyone who wants to be healthy will not exercise.

(B) Learning requires making some mistakes. And you must learn if you are to improve. So you will not make mistakes without there being a noticeable improvement.

(C) Our political party will retain its status only if it raises more money. But raising more money requires increased campaigning. So our party will not retain its status unless it increases its campaigning.

(D) You can repair your own bicycle only if you are enthusiastic. And if you are enthusiastic, you will also have mechanical aptitude. So if you are not able to repair your own bicycle, you lack mechanical aptitude.

(E) Getting a ticket requires waiting in line. Waiting in line requires patience. So if you do not wait in line, you lack patience.

20. In the past, when there was no highway speed limit, the highway accident rate increased yearly, peaking a decade ago. At that time, the speed limit on highways was set at 90 kilometers per hour (kph) (55 miles per hour). Every year since the introduction of the highway speed limit, the highway accident rate has been at least 15 percent lower than that of its peak rate. Thus, setting the highway speed limit at 90 kph (55 mph) has reduced the highway accident rate by at least 15 percent.

Which one of the following, if true, most seriously weakens the argument?

(A) In the years prior to the introduction of the highway speed limit, many cars could go faster than 90 kph (55 mph).

(B) Ten years ago, at least 95 percent of all automobile accidents in the area occurred on roads with a speed limit of under 80 kph (50 mph).

(C) Although the speed limit on many highways is officially set at 90 kph (55 mph), most people typically drive faster than the speed limit.

(D) Thanks to changes in automobile design in the past ten years, drivers are better able to maintain control of their cars in dangerous situations.

(E) It was not until shortly after the introduction of the highway speed limit that most cars were equipped with features such as seat belts and airbags designed to prevent harm to passengers.

21. Editorial: It is a travesty of justice, social critics say, that we can launch rockets into outer space but cannot solve social problems that have plagued humanity. The assumption underlying this assertion is that there are greater difficulties involved in a space launch than are involved in ending long-standing social problems, which in turn suggests that a government's failure to achieve the latter is simply a case of misplaced priorities. The criticism is misplaced, however, for rocket technology is much simpler than the human psyche, and until we adequately understand the human psyche we cannot solve the great social problems.

The statement that rocket technology is much simpler than the human psyche plays which one of the following roles in the editorial's argument?

(A) It is cited as a possible objection to the argument's conclusion.

(B) According to the argument, it is a fact that has misled some social critics.

(C) It is the argument's conclusion.

(D) It is claimed to be a false assumption on which the reasoning that the argument seeks to undermine rests.

(E) It is used by the argument to attempt to undermine the reasoning behind a viewpoint.

GO ON TO THE NEXT PAGE.

22. Archaeologist: After the last ice age, groups of paleohumans left Siberia and crossed the Bering land bridge, which no longer exists, into North America. Archaeologists have discovered in Siberia a cache of Clovis points—the distinctive stone spear points made by paleohumans. This shows that, contrary to previous belief, the Clovis point was not invented in North America.

Which one of the following, if true, would most strengthen the archaeologist's argument?

(A) The Clovis points found in Siberia are older than any of those that have been found in North America.

(B) The Bering land bridge disappeared before any of the Clovis points found to date were made.

(C) Clovis points were more effective hunting weapons than earlier spear points had been.

(D) Archaeologists have discovered in Siberia artifacts that date from after the time paleohumans left Siberia.

(E) Some paleohuman groups that migrated from Siberia to North America via the Bering land bridge eventually returned to Siberia.

23. Taxi drivers, whose income is based on the fares they receive, usually decide when to finish work each day by setting a daily income target; they stop when they reach that target. This means that they typically work fewer hours on a busy day than on a slow day.

The facts described above provide the strongest evidence against which one of the following?

(A) The number of hours per day that a person is willing to work depends on that person's financial needs.

(B) People work longer when their effective hourly wage is high than when it is low.

(C) Workers will accept a lower hourly wage in exchange for the freedom to set their own schedules.

(D) People are willing to work many hours a day in order to avoid a reduction in their standard of living.

(E) People who are paid based on their production work more efficiently than those who are paid a fixed hourly wage.

24. Sometimes one reads a poem and believes that the poem expresses contradictory ideas, even if it is a great poem. So it is wrong to think that the meaning of a poem is whatever the author intends to communicate to the reader by means of the poem. No one who is writing a great poem intends it to communicate contradictory ideas.

Which one of the following is an assumption on which the argument depends?

(A) Different readers will usually disagree about what the author of a particular poem intends to communicate by means of that poem.

(B) If someone writes a great poem, he or she intends the poem to express one primary idea.

(C) Readers will not agree about the meaning of a poem if they do not agree about what the author of the poem intended the poem to mean.

(D) Anyone reading a great poem can discern every idea that the author intended to express in the poem.

(E) If a reader believes that a poem expresses a particular idea, then that idea is part of the meaning of the poem.

GO ON TO THE NEXT PAGE.

25. The law of the city of Weston regarding contributions to mayoral campaigns is as follows: all contributions to these campaigns in excess of $100 made by nonresidents of Weston who are not former residents of Weston must be registered with the city council. Brimley's mayoral campaign clearly complied with this law since it accepted contributions only from residents and former residents of Weston.

If all the statements above are true, which one of the following statements must be true?

(A) No nonresident of Weston contributed in excess of $100 to Brimley's campaign.
(B) Some contributions to Brimley's campaign in excess of $100 were registered with the city council.
(C) No contributions to Brimley's campaign needed to be registered with the city council.
(D) All contributions to Brimley's campaign that were registered with the city council were in excess of $100.
(E) Brimley's campaign did not register any contributions with the city council.

26. Historian: Flavius, an ancient Roman governor who believed deeply in the virtues of manual labor and moral temperance, actively sought to discourage the arts by removing state financial support for them. Also, Flavius was widely unpopular among his subjects, as we can conclude from the large number of satirical plays that were written about him during his administration.

The historian's argumentation is most vulnerable to criticism on the grounds that it

(A) fails to consider the percentage of plays written during Flavius's administration that were not explicitly about Flavius
(B) treats the satirical plays as a reliable indicator of Flavius's popularity despite potential bias on the part of the playwrights
(C) presumes, without providing evidence, that Flavius was unfavorably disposed toward the arts
(D) takes for granted that Flavius's attempt to discourage the arts was successful
(E) fails to consider whether manual labor and moral temperance were widely regarded as virtues in ancient Rome

STOP
IF YOU FINISH BEFORE TIME IS CALLED, YOU MAY CHECK YOUR WORK ON THIS SECTION ONLY. DO NOT WORK ON ANY OTHER SECTION IN THE TEST.

SECTION III

Time—35 minutes

27 Questions

Directions: Each set of questions in this section is based on a single passage or a pair of passages. The questions are to be answered on the basis of what is stated or implied in the passage or pair of passages. For some of the questions, more than one of the choices could conceivably answer the question. However, you are to choose the best answer; that is, the response that most accurately and completely answers the question, and blacken the corresponding space on your answer sheet.

An organism is considered to have an infection when a disease-causing agent, called a pathogen, establishes a viable presence in the organism. This can occur only if the pathogenic agent is able to reproduce
(5) itself in the host organism. The only agents believed until recently to be responsible for infections—viruses, bacteria, fungi, and parasites—reproduce and regulate their other life processes by means of genetic material, composed of nucleic acid (DNA or RNA). It was thus
(10) widely assumed that all pathogens contain such genetic material in their cellular structure.

This assumption has been challenged, however, by scientists seeking to identify the pathogen that causes Creutzfeldt-Jakob disease (CJD), a degenerative
(15) form of dementia in humans. CJD causes the brain to become riddled with tiny holes, like a sponge (evidence of extensive nerve cell death). Its symptoms include impaired muscle control, loss of mental acuity, memory loss, and chronic insomnia. Extensive experiments
(20) aimed at identifying the pathogen responsible for CJD have led surprisingly to the isolation of a disease agent lacking nucleic acid and consisting mainly, if not exclusively, of protein. Researchers coined the term "prion" for this new type of protein pathogen.

(25) Upon further study, scientists discovered that prions normally exist as harmless cellular proteins in many of the body's tissues, including white blood cells and nerve cells in the brain; however, they possess the capability of converting their structures into a
(30) dangerous abnormal shape. Prions exhibiting this abnormal conformation were found to have infectious properties and the ability to reproduce themselves in an unexpected way, by initiating a chain reaction that induces normally shaped prions to transform
(35) themselves on contact, one after another, into the abnormal, pathogenic conformation. This cascade of transformations produces a plaque, consisting of thread-like structures, that collects in the brain and ultimately destroys nerve cells. Because prions, unlike
(40) other pathogens, occur naturally in the body as proteins, the body does not produce an immune response when they are present. And in the absence of any effective therapy for preventing the cascade process by which affected prions reproduce
(45) themselves, CJD is inevitably fatal, though there are wide variations in pre-symptomatic incubation times and in how aggressively the disease progresses.

Although the discovery of the link between prions and CJD was initially received with great skepticism
(50) in the scientific community, subsequent research has supported the conclusion that prions are an entirely new class of infectious pathogens. Furthermore, it is now believed that a similar process of protein malformation may be involved in other, more
(55) common degenerative neurological conditions such as Alzheimer's disease and Parkinson's disease. This possibility has yet to be fully explored, however, and the exact mechanisms by which prions reproduce themselves and cause cellular destruction have yet to
(60) be completely understood.

1. Which one of the following most accurately expresses the main point of the passage?

(A) Although most organisms are known to produce several kinds of proteins, the mechanism by which isolated protein molecules such as prions reproduce themselves is not yet known in detail.

(B) Research into the cause of CJD has uncovered a deadly class of protein pathogens uniquely capable of reproducing themselves without genetic material.

(C) Recent research suggests that prions may be responsible not only for CJD, but for most other degenerative neurological conditions as well.

(D) The assertion that prions cause CJD has been received with great skepticism in the scientific community because it undermines a firmly entrenched view about the nature of pathogens.

(E) Even though prions contain no genetic material, it has become clear that they are somehow capable of reproducing themselves.

GO ON TO THE NEXT PAGE.

2. Which one of the following is most strongly supported by the passage?

   (A) Understanding the cause of CJD has required scientists to reconsider their traditional beliefs about the causes of infection.
   (B) CJD is contagious, though not highly so.
   (C) The prevention of CJD would be most efficiently achieved by the prevention of certain genetic abnormalities.
   (D) Although patients with CJD exhibit different incubation times, the disease progresses at about the same rate in all patients once symptoms are manifested.
   (E) The prion theory of infection has weak support within the scientific community.

3. If the hypothesis that CJD is caused by prions is correct, finding the answer to which one of the following questions would tend most to help a physician in deciding whether a patient has CJD?

   (A) Has the patient suffered a severe blow to the skull recently?
   (B) Does the patient experience occasional bouts of insomnia?
   (C) Has the patient been exposed to any forms of radiation that have a known tendency to cause certain kinds of genetic damage?
   (D) Has any member of the patient's immediate family ever had a brain disease?
   (E) Does the patient's brain tissue exhibit the presence of any abnormal thread-like structures?

4. Which one of the following is most strongly supported by the passage?

   (A) The only way in which CJD can be transmitted is through the injection of abnormally shaped prions from an infected individual into an uninfected individual.
   (B) Most infectious diseases previously thought to be caused by other pathogens are now thought to be caused by prions.
   (C) If they were unable to reproduce themselves, abnormally shaped prions would not cause CJD.
   (D) Alzheimer's disease and Parkinson's disease are caused by different conformations of the same prion pathogen that causes CJD.
   (E) Prion diseases generally progress more aggressively than diseases caused by other known pathogens.

5. It can be inferred from the passage that the author would be LEAST likely to agree with which one of the following?

   (A) The presence of certain abnormally shaped prions in brain tissue is a sign of neurological disease.
   (B) Some patients currently infected with CJD will recover from the disease.
   (C) Prions do not require nucleic acid for their reproduction.
   (D) The body has no natural defense against CJD.
   (E) Scientists have only a partial understanding of the mechanism by which prions reproduce.

6. Given the manner in which the term "pathogen" is used in the passage, and assuming that the prion theory of infection is correct, which one of the following statements must be false?

   (A) Nothing that lacks nucleic acid is a pathogen.
   (B) Prions are a relatively newly discovered type of pathogen.
   (C) All pathogens can cause infection.
   (D) Pathogens contribute in some manner to the occurrence of CJD.
   (E) There are other pathogens besides viruses, bacteria, fungi, and parasites.

7. Which one of the following, if true, would most undermine the claim that prions cause CJD?

   (A) Several symptoms closely resembling those of CJD have been experienced by patients known to have a specific viral infection.
   (B) None of the therapies currently available for treating neurological diseases is designed to block the chain reaction by which abnormal prions are believed to reproduce.
   (C) Research undertaken subsequent to the studies on CJD has linked prions to degenerative conditions not affecting the brain or the central nervous system.
   (D) Epidemiological studies carried out on a large population have failed to show any hereditary predisposition to CJD.
   (E) A newly developed antibacterial drug currently undergoing clinical trials is proving to be effective in reversing the onset of CJD.

GO ON TO THE NEXT PAGE.

One of the more striking developments in modern North American dance was African American choreographer Katherine Dunham's introduction of a technique known as dance-isolation, in which one part
(5) of the body moves in one rhythm while other parts are kept stationary or are moved in different rhythms. The incorporation of this technique into North American and European choreography is relatively recent, although various forms of the technique have long
(10) been essential to traditional dances of certain African, Caribbean, and Pacific-island cultures. Dunham's success in bringing dance-isolation and other traditional techniques from those cultures into the mainstream of modern North American dance is due
(15) in no small part to her training in both anthropological research and choreography.

As an anthropologist in the 1930s, Dunham was one of the pioneers in the field of dance ethnology. Previously, dance had been neglected as an area of
(20) social research, primarily because most social scientists gravitated toward areas likely to be recognized by their peers as befitting scientifically rigorous, and therefore legitimate, modes of inquiry. Moreover, no other social scientist at that time was sufficiently
(25) trained in dance to be able to understand dance techniques, while experts in dance were not trained in the methods of social research.

Starting in 1935, Dunham conducted a series of research projects into traditional Caribbean dance
(30) forms, with special interest in their origins in African culture. Especially critical to her success was her approach to research, which diverged radically from the methodology that prevailed at the time. Colleagues in anthropology advised her not to become too closely
(35) involved in the dances she was observing, both because of the extreme physical demands of the dances, and because they subscribed to the long-standing view, now fortunately recognized as unrealistic, that effective data gathering can and must be conducted
(40) from a position of complete detachment. But because of her interest and her skill as a performer, she generally eschewed such caution and participated in the dances herself. Through prolonged immersion of this kind, Dunham was able not only to comprehend
(45) various dances as complex cultural practices, but also to learn the techniques well enough to teach them to others and incorporate them into new forms of ballet.

Between 1937 and 1945, Dunham developed a research-to-performance method that she used to adapt
(50) Caribbean dance forms for use in theatrical performance, combining them with modern dance styles she learned in Chicago. The ballets she created in this fashion were among the first North American dances to rectify the exclusion of African American themes from the
(55) medium of modern dance. Her work was thus crucial in establishing African American dance as an art form in its own right, making possible future companies such as Arthur Mitchell's Dance Theater of Harlem.

8. Which one of the following most accurately expresses the main point of the passage?

(A) Katherine Dunham transformed the field of anthropology by developing innovative research methodologies for studying Caribbean and other traditional dance styles and connecting them with African American dance.
(B) Katherine Dunham's ballets were distinct from others produced in North America in that they incorporated authentic dance techniques from traditional cultures.
(C) Katherine Dunham's expertise as an anthropologist allowed her to use Caribbean and African dance traditions to express the aesthetic and political concerns of African American dancers and choreographers.
(D) The innovative research methods of Katherine Dunham made possible her discovery that the dance traditions of the Caribbean were derived from earlier African dance traditions.
(E) Katherine Dunham's anthropological and choreographic expertise enabled her to make contributions that altered the landscape of modern dance in North America.

9. According to the passage, Dunham's work in anthropology differed from that of most other anthropologists in the 1930s in that Dunham

(A) performed fieldwork for a very extended time period
(B) related the traditions she studied to those of her own culture
(C) employed a participative approach in performing research
(D) attached a high degree of political significance to her research
(E) had prior familiarity with the cultural practices of the peoples she set out to study

GO ON TO THE NEXT PAGE.

10. The passage suggests that the "peers" mentioned in line 22 would have been most likely to agree with which one of the following statements about the study of dance?

    (A) Most social scientists who have attempted to study dance as a cultural phenomenon have misinterpreted it.
    (B) Social scientists need not be well versed in dance traditions in order to obtain reliable data about them.
    (C) Research into dance as a cultural form cannot be conducted with a high degree of scientific precision.
    (D) Most experts in the field of dance are too preoccupied to conduct studies in the field of dance ethnology.
    (E) Dance forms are too variable across cultures to permit rigorous means of data collection.

11. In the last sentence of the second paragraph, the author mentions "experts in dance" primarily in order to

    (A) suggest why a group of social scientists did not embrace the study of a particular cultural form
    (B) suggest that a certain group was more qualified to study a particular cultural form than was another group
    (C) identify an additional factor that motivated a particular social scientist to pursue a specific new line of research
    (D) contribute to an explanation of why a particular field of research was not previously pursued
    (E) indicate an additional possible reason for the tension between the members of two distinct fields of research

12. According to the passage, which one of the following was true of the dance forms that Dunham began studying in 1935?

    (A) They were more similar to dance forms used in Pacific-island cultures than to any other known dance forms.
    (B) They represented the first use of the technique of dance-isolation within a culture outside of Africa.
    (C) They shared certain rhythmic characteristics with the dance forms employed in North American ballets.
    (D) They had already influenced certain popular dances in North America.
    (E) They were influenced by the traditions of non-Caribbean cultures.

13. Which one of the following is most analogous to Dunham's work in anthropology and choreography as that work is described in the passage?

    (A) A French archaeologist with training in musicology researches instruments used in seventeenth century France, and her findings become the basis for a Korean engineer's designs for devices to simulate the sounds those instruments most likely made.
    (B) An Australian medical researcher with training in botany analyzes the chemical composition of plants that other researchers have collected in the Philippines, and then an Australian pharmaceutical company uses her findings to develop successful new medicines.
    (C) A Canadian surgeon uses her skill in drawing to collaborate with a Vietnamese surgeon to develop a manual containing detailed illustrations of the proper techniques for certain types of reconstructive surgery performed in both countries.
    (D) A Brazilian teacher with training in social psychology conducts a detailed study of teaching procedures while working with teachers in several Asian countries, then introduces the most effective of those procedures to teachers in his own country.
    (E) An Italian fashion designer researches the social significance of clothing design in several cultures and then presents his research in a highly acclaimed book directed toward his colleagues in fashion design.

14. The passage suggests that the author would be most likely to agree with which one of the following statements about the colleagues mentioned in line 33?

    (A) They were partly correct in recommending that Dunham change her methods of data collection, since injury sustained during fieldwork might have compromised her research.
    (B) They were partly correct in advising Dunham to exercise initial caution in participating in the Caribbean dances, since her skill in performing them improved with experience.
    (C) They were incorrect in advising Dunham to increase the degree of her detachment, since extensive personal investment in fieldwork generally enhances scientific rigor.
    (D) They were incorrect in assuming that researchers in the social sciences are able to gather data in an entirely objective manner.
    (E) They were incorrect in assuming that dance could be studied with the same degree of scientific rigor possible in other areas of ethnology.

GO ON TO THE NEXT PAGE.

Passage A

Research concerning happiness and wealth reveals a paradox: at any one time richer people report higher levels of happiness than poorer people in the same society report, and yet over time advanced societies
(5) have not grown happier as they have grown richer. Apparently, people are comparing their income with some norm, and that norm must be rising along with actual income. Two phenomena—habituation and rivalry—push up the norm.
(10) When our living standards increase, we love it initially but then we adjust and it makes little difference. For example, if we ask people with different incomes what income they consider sufficient, the "required income" correlates strongly with their actual income:
(15) a rise in actual income causes a roughly equivalent rise in required income. We can also look at reported happiness over time. Job satisfaction depends little on the absolute level of wages but rises if wages rapidly increase.
(20) We do not have the same experience with other aspects of our lives. We do not foresee how we adjust to material possessions, so we overinvest in acquiring them, at the expense of leisure.

Now consider the phenomenon of rivalry. In a
(25) study conducted by Solnick and Hemenway, people were asked to choose between two options, with all prices held constant:

A. You earn $50,000 a year while everyone else earns $25,000;
(30) B. You earn $100,000 a year while others make $200,000.

The majority chose the first. They were happy to be poorer, provided their relative position improved.

And indeed, how people compare to their "reference
(35) group"—those most like them—is crucial for happiness. In East Germany, for example, living standards have soared since 1990, but the level of happiness has plummeted because people now compare themselves with West Germans, rather than with people in other
(40) Soviet bloc countries.

Passage B

Does the Solnick and Hemenway study mean that we care most about one-upmanship? Perhaps out of our primeval past comes the urge to demonstrate our superiority in order to help ensure mating prospects,
(45) keeping our genetic lines going. Still programmed like this, we get unexplainable pleasure from having a bigger house than our neighbors.

This theory may sound good and is commonly heard, but it is not the explanation best supported by
(50) the evidence. Rather, the data show that earning more makes people happier because relative prosperity makes them feel that they are successful, that they have created value.

If two people feel equally successful, they will be
(55) equally happy even if their incomes differ greatly. Of course, people who earn more generally view themselves as successful. But it is the success—not the money per se—that provides the happiness. We use material wealth to show not just that we are
(60) prosperous, but that we are prosperous because we create value.

What scholars often portray as an ignoble tendency—wanting to have more than others— is really evidence of a desire to create value. Wanting
(65) to create value benefits society. It is a bonus that it also brings happiness.

15. Both passages are primarily concerned with explaining which one of the following?

(A) the human desire to create value
(B) the relationship between income and happiness
(C) the biological basis of people's attitudes toward wealth
(D) the human propensity to become habituated to wealth
(E) the concept of "required income"

16. The author of passage B would be most likely to agree with which one of the following statements?

(A) The desire to demonstrate that one is wealthier than others is a remnant of human beings' primeval past.
(B) Very few people would be willing to accept a lower standard of living in return for greater relative wealth.
(C) Being wealthier than other people would not make one happier if one believed that one's wealth was due merely to luck.
(D) Gradual increases in employees' wages do not increase their job satisfaction.
(E) The overall level of happiness in a society usually increases as the society becomes wealthier.

17. The author of passage B would be most likely to regard the conclusion that the Solnick and Hemenway study points to the existence of a "phenomenon of rivalry" (line 24) as

(A) ungenerous in its view of human nature and mistaken in its interpretation of the evidence
(B) flattering in its implications about human nature but only weakly supported by the available evidence
(C) plausible in its account of human nature but based largely upon ambiguous evidence
(D) unflattering in its implications about human nature but more or less valid in the conclusions drawn from the evidence
(E) accurate concerning human nature and strongly supported by the evidence

GO ON TO THE NEXT PAGE.

18. Which one of the following pairs most accurately describes why the authors of passage A and passage B, respectively, mention the study by Solnick and Hemenway?

    (A) to present a view that will be argued against
        to present a view for which additional evidence will be provided
    (B) to present a view that will be argued against
        to provide evidence for one explanation of a phenomenon
    (C) to provide evidence for one explanation of a phenomenon
        to present a view for which additional evidence will be provided
    (D) to provide evidence for one explanation of a phenomenon
        to introduce the main topic to be discussed
    (E) to introduce the main topic to be discussed
        to present a view that will be argued against

19. Which one of the following pairs of terms would most likely be used by the authors of passage A and passage B, respectively, to describe a person who wants to make more money than his or her neighbors?

    (A) insular, cosmopolitan
    (B) altruistic, egocentric
    (C) happy, miserable
    (D) misguided, admirable
    (E) lucky, primitive

20. In arguing for their respective positions, the author of passage A and the author of passage B both do which one of the following?

    (A) explain a phenomenon by pointing to its biological origins
    (B) endorse a claim simply because it is widely believed
    (C) accept a claim for the sake of argument
    (D) attempt to resolve an apparent paradox
    (E) assert that their positions are supported by data

GO ON TO THE NEXT PAGE.

It is generally believed that while in some cases government should intervene to protect people from risk—by imposing air safety standards, for example—in other cases, such as mountain climbing, the onus
(5) should be on the individual to protect himself or herself. In the eyes of the public at large, the demarcation between the two kinds of cases has mainly to do with whether the risk in question is incurred voluntarily. This distinction between voluntary and involuntary
(10) risk may in fact be the chief difference between lay and expert judgments about risk. Policy experts tend to focus on aggregate lives at stake; laypeople care a great deal whether a risk is undertaken voluntarily. However, judgments about whether a risk is
(15) "involuntary" often stem from confusion and selective attention, and the real reason for such judgments frequently lies in an antecedent judgment of some other kind. They are thus of little utility in guiding policy decisions.
(20) First, it is not easy to determine when a risk is voluntarily incurred. Although voluntariness may be entirely absent in the case of an unforeseeable collision with an asteroid, with most environmental, occupational, and other social risks, it is not an all-or-
(25) nothing matter, but rather one of degree. Risks incurred by airline passengers are typically thought to be involuntary, since passengers have no control over whether a plane is going to crash. But they can choose airlines on the basis of safety records or choose not to
(30) fly. In characterizing the risks as involuntary, people focus on a small part of a complex interaction, not the decision to fly, but the accident when it occurs.
Second, people often characterize risks as "voluntary" when they do not approve of the purpose
(35) for which people run the risks. It is unlikely that people would want to pour enormous taxpayer resources into lowering the risks associated with skydiving, even if the ratio of dollars spent to lives saved were quite good. By contrast, people would
(40) probably not object to spending enormous resources on improving the safety of firefighters, even though the decision to become a firefighter is voluntary. In short, there is no special magic in notions like "voluntary" and "involuntary." Therefore, regulatory
(45) policy should be guided by a better understanding of the factors that underlie judgments about voluntariness.
In general, the government should attempt to save as many lives as it can, subject to the limited public and private resources devoted to risk reduction.
(50) Departures from this principle should be justified not by invoking the allegedly voluntary or involuntary nature of a particular risk, but rather by identifying the more specific considerations for which notions of voluntariness serve as proxies.

21. Which one of the following most accurately expresses the main point of the passage?

(A) In general, whether people characterize a risk as voluntary or involuntary depends on whether they approve of the purpose for which the risk is taken.

(B) Decisions about government intervention to protect people from risks should be based primarily on how many lives can be saved rather than on whether the risks are considered voluntary.

(C) Though laypeople may object, experts should be the ones to determine whether the risk incurred in a particular action is voluntary or involuntary.

(D) Public-policy decisions related to the protection of society against risk are difficult to make because of the difficulty of distinguishing risks incurred voluntarily from those incurred involuntarily.

(E) People who make judgments about the voluntary or involuntary character of a risk are usually unaware of the complicated motivations that lead people to take risks.

22. The passage indicates that which one of the following is usually a significant factor in laypeople's willingness to support public funding for specific risk-reduction measures?

(A) an expectation about the ratio of dollars spent to lives saved

(B) deference to expert judgments concerning whether the government should intervene

(C) a belief as to whether the risk is incurred voluntarily or involuntarily

(D) a judgment as to whether the risk puts a great number of lives at stake

(E) a consideration of the total resources available for risk reduction

23. According to the passage, which one of the following do laypeople generally consider to involve risk that is not freely assumed?

(A) traveling in outer space
(B) participating in skydiving
(C) serving as a firefighter
(D) traveling in airplanes
(E) climbing mountains

GO ON TO THE NEXT PAGE.

24. It can be inferred from the passage that the author would be most likely to agree with which one of the following statements?

    (A) People should generally not be protected against the risks incurred through activities, such as skydiving, that are dangerous and serve no socially useful purpose.
    (B) The fact that plane crash victims chose to fly would usually be deemed by policy experts to be largely irrelevant to decisions about the government's role in regulating air safety.
    (C) Both the probability of occurrence and the probability of resulting death or injury are higher for plane crashes than for any other kind of risk incurred by airline passengers.
    (D) For public-policy purposes, a risk should be deemed voluntarily incurred if people are not subject to that risk unless they make a particular choice.
    (E) The main category of risk that is usually incurred completely involuntarily is the risk of natural disaster.

25. The author's use of the phrase "no special magic" (line 43) is most likely meant primarily to convey that notions like "voluntary" and "involuntary"

    (A) do not exhaustively characterize the risks that people commonly face
    (B) have been used to intentionally conceal the factors motivating government efforts to protect people from risks
    (C) have no meaning beyond their literal, dictionary definitions
    (D) are mistakenly believed to be characteristics that inform people's understanding of the consequences of risk
    (E) provide a flawed mechanism for making public policy decisions relating to risk reduction

26. The passage most strongly supports the inference that the author believes which one of the following?

    (A) Whenever an activity involves the risk of loss of human life, the government should intervene to reduce the degree of risk incurred.
    (B) Some environmental risks are voluntary to a greater degree than others are.
    (C) Policy experts are more likely than laypeople to form an accurate judgment about the voluntariness or involuntariness of an activity.
    (D) The government should increase the quantity of resources devoted to protecting people from risk.
    (E) Government policies intended to reduce risk are not justified unless they comport with most people's beliefs.

27. Which one of the following most accurately describes the author's attitude in the passage?

    (A) chagrin at the rampant misunderstanding of the relative risks associated with various activities
    (B) concern that policy guided mainly by laypeople's emphasis on the voluntariness of risk would lead to excessive government regulation
    (C) skepticism about the reliability of laypeople's intuitions as a general guide to deciding government risk-management policy
    (D) conviction that the sole criterion that can justify government intervention to reduce risk is the saving of human lives
    (E) eagerness to persuade the reader that policy experts' analysis of risk is distorted by subtle biases

STOP

IF YOU FINISH BEFORE TIME IS CALLED, YOU MAY CHECK YOUR WORK ON THIS SECTION ONLY. DO NOT WORK ON ANY OTHER SECTION IN THE TEST.

SECTION IV

Time—35 minutes

23 Questions

Directions: Each group of questions in this section is based on a set of conditions. In answering some of the questions, it may be useful to draw a rough diagram. Choose the response that most accurately and completely answers each question and blacken the corresponding space on your answer sheet.

Questions 1–7

A concert promoter is filling the six slots at a benefit concert. The slots, from earliest to latest, are numbered slot one through slot six. The slots will be filled by six bands— Uneasy, Vegemite, Wellspring, Xpert, Yardsign, and Zircon. Each band will perform in just one slot. The order must meet the following constraints:

Vegemite performs in an earlier slot than Zircon.
Wellspring and Zircon each perform in an earlier slot than Xpert.
Uneasy performs in one of the last three slots.
Yardsign performs in one of the first three slots.

1. Which one of the following CANNOT be the band that performs in slot five?

(A) Uneasy
(B) Vegemite
(C) Wellspring
(D) Xpert
(E) Zircon

GO ON TO THE NEXT PAGE.

2. If Zircon performs in an earlier slot than Yardsign, which one of the following is the earliest slot in which Wellspring could perform?

   (A) two
   (B) three
   (C) four
   (D) five
   (E) six

3. If Vegemite performs in slot three, which one of the following must be true?

   (A) Uneasy performs in an earlier slot than Xpert.
   (B) Wellspring performs in an earlier slot than Zircon.
   (C) Xpert performs in an earlier slot than Uneasy.
   (D) Yardsign performs in an earlier slot than Wellspring.
   (E) Zircon performs in an earlier slot than Uneasy.

4. If Zircon performs immediately before Wellspring, which one of the following must be true?

   (A) Uneasy performs in slot five.
   (B) Vegemite performs in slot one.
   (C) Xpert performs in slot five.
   (D) Yardsign performs in slot two.
   (E) Zircon performs in slot three.

5. Which one of the following is a complete and accurate list of bands any one of which could be the band that performs in slot one?

   (A) Yardsign
   (B) Vegemite, Wellspring
   (C) Vegemite, Yardsign
   (D) Vegemite, Wellspring, Yardsign
   (E) Vegemite, Wellspring, Yardsign, Zircon

6. If Wellspring performs immediately before Xpert, which one of the following could be true?

   (A) Uneasy performs in slot five.
   (B) Vegemite performs in slot three.
   (C) Wellspring performs in slot three.
   (D) Zircon performs in slot two.
   (E) Zircon performs in slot four.

7. Which one of the following, if substituted for the constraint that Wellspring and Zircon each perform in an earlier slot than Xpert, would have the same effect in determining the order in which the bands perform?

   (A) Only Uneasy can perform in a later slot than Xpert.
   (B) Vegemite performs in an earlier slot than Wellspring, which performs in an earlier slot than Zircon.
   (C) Vegemite and Wellspring each perform in an earlier slot than Xpert.
   (D) Xpert performs either immediately before or immediately after Uneasy.
   (E) Xpert performs in either slot five or slot six.

GO ON TO THE NEXT PAGE.

Questions 8–12

A corporate manager is selecting employees for a research team. The team will include at least four employees, all from among the following eight: Myers, Ortega, Paine, Schmidt, Thomson, Wong, Yoder, and Zayre. The selection is constrained by the following conditions:

If Myers is on the team, neither Ortega nor Paine can be.

If Schmidt is on the team, both Paine and Thomson must also be.

If Wong is on the team, both Myers and Yoder must also be.

8. Which one of the following is a possible selection of employees for the team?

(A) Myers, Paine, Schmidt, and Thomson
(B) Ortega, Paine, Thomson, and Zayre
(C) Paine, Schmidt, Yoder, and Zayre
(D) Schmidt, Thomson, Yoder, and Zayre
(E) Thomson, Wong, Yoder, and Zayre

GO ON TO THE NEXT PAGE.

9. Which one of the following is a pair of employees who CANNOT be on the team together?

    (A) Myers and Thomson
    (B) Ortega and Yoder
    (C) Paine and Zayre
    (D) Schmidt and Wong
    (E) Wong and Yoder

10. If Yoder is not on the team, then any of the following could be on the team EXCEPT:

    (A) Zayre
    (B) Thomson
    (C) Paine
    (D) Ortega
    (E) Myers

11. If Paine is not on the team, which one of the following could be true?

    (A) Neither Myers nor Ortega is on the team.
    (B) Neither Myers nor Thomson is on the team.
    (C) Neither Myers nor Zayre is on the team.
    (D) Neither Ortega nor Thomson is on the team.
    (E) Neither Ortega nor Yoder is on the team.

12. Which one of the following is a pair of employees at least one of whom must be on the team?

    (A) Ortega and Schmidt
    (B) Ortega and Wong
    (C) Paine and Schmidt
    (D) Thomson and Yoder
    (E) Yoder and Zayre

GO ON TO THE NEXT PAGE.

Questions 13–18

Exactly five movies are showing at the repertory theater this evening: a horror film, a mystery, a romance, a sci-fi film, and a western. Each movie is shown exactly once, on one of the theater's three screens: screens 1, 2, and 3. Screens 1 and 2 show two movies each, one beginning at 7 P.M. and the other at 9 P.M.; screen 3 shows exactly one movie, at 8 P.M. The following conditions apply to this evening's schedule:

    The western begins at some time before the horror film does.

    The sci-fi film is not shown on screen 3.

    The romance is not shown on screen 2.

    The horror film and the mystery are shown on different screens.

13. Which one of the following is an acceptable schedule of the movies for this evening?

(A)   screen 1: romance at 7 P.M., horror film at 9 P.M.
    screen 2: western at 7 P.M., sci-fi film at 9 P.M.
    screen 3: mystery at 8 P.M.

(B)   screen 1: mystery at 7 P.M., romance at 9 P.M.
    screen 2: horror film at 7 P.M., sci-fi film at 9 P.M.
    screen 3: western at 8 P.M.

(C)   screen 1: western at 7 P.M., sci-fi film at 9 P.M.
    screen 2: mystery at 7 P.M., horror film at 9 P.M.
    screen 3: romance at 8 P.M.

(D)   screen 1: romance at 7 P.M., mystery at 9 P.M.
    screen 2: western at 7 P.M., horror film at 9 P.M.
    screen 3: sci-fi film at 8 P.M.

(E)   screen 1: western at 7 P.M., mystery at 9 P.M.
    screen 2: sci-fi film at 7 P.M., romance at 9 P.M.
    screen 3: horror film at 8 P.M.

GO ON TO THE NEXT PAGE.

14. Which one of the following CANNOT be an accurate list of the movies scheduled to be shown on screen 2 this evening, listing the 7 P.M. movie first?

(A) the sci-fi film, the horror film
(B) the sci-fi film, the mystery
(C) the sci-fi film, the western
(D) the western, the horror film
(E) the western, the mystery

15. If the western and the sci-fi film are scheduled to be shown on the same screen, then which one of the following could be true of this evening's schedule?

(A) The horror film is shown on screen 2.
(B) The mystery begins at 9 P.M.
(C) The romance is shown on screen 3.
(D) The sci-fi film begins at 7 P.M.
(E) The western begins at 8 P.M.

16. If the romance is scheduled to begin before the western does, then which one of the following must be true of this evening's schedule?

(A) The horror film is shown on screen 1.
(B) The mystery begins at 7 P.M.
(C) The mystery is shown on screen 2.
(D) The sci-fi film begins at 9 P.M.
(E) The sci-fi film is shown on screen 2.

17. Which one of the following CANNOT be an accurate list of the movies scheduled to be shown on screen 1 this evening, listing the 7 P.M. movie first?

(A) the sci-fi film, the horror film
(B) the sci-fi film, the mystery
(C) the western, the horror film
(D) the western, the mystery
(E) the western, the sci-fi film

18. If the sci-fi film and the romance are to be shown on the same screen, then which one of the following must be true of this evening's schedule?

(A) The western begins at 7 P.M.
(B) The sci-fi film begins at 9 P.M.
(C) The mystery begins at 8 P.M.
(D) The romance begins at 9 P.M.
(E) The horror film begins at 8 P.M.

GO ON TO THE NEXT PAGE.

<u>Questions 19–23</u>

A naturalist will give five lectures, each on a different type of bird: oystercatchers, petrels, rails, sandpipers, or terns. The lectures must be given in either Gladwyn Hall or Howard Auditorium, in an order that meets the following conditions:

    The first lecture is in Gladwyn Hall.

    The fourth lecture is in Howard Auditorium.

    Exactly three of the lectures are in Gladwyn Hall.

    The lecture on sandpipers is in Howard Auditorium and is given earlier than the lecture on oystercatchers.

    The lecture on terns is given earlier than the lecture on petrels, which is in Gladwyn Hall.

19. Which one of the following is an acceptable order for the lectures, from first to fifth?

(A) oystercatchers, petrels, rails, sandpipers, terns
(B) petrels, sandpipers, oystercatchers, terns, rails
(C) rails, sandpipers, terns, petrels, oystercatchers
(D) sandpipers, terns, oystercatchers, rails, petrels
(E) terns, petrels, sandpipers, oystercatchers, rails

GO ON TO THE NEXT PAGE.

20. Which one of the following must be false?

    (A) The first and second lectures are both in Gladwyn Hall.
    (B) The second and third lectures are both in Howard Auditorium.
    (C) The second and fifth lectures are both in Gladwyn Hall.
    (D) The third and fourth lectures are both in Howard Auditorium.
    (E) The third and fifth lectures are both in Gladwyn Hall.

21. If the lecture on terns is given in Howard Auditorium, which one of the following could be true of the third lecture?

    (A) It is on oystercatchers and is in Gladwyn Hall.
    (B) It is on rails and is in Howard Auditorium.
    (C) It is on rails and is in Gladwyn Hall.
    (D) It is on sandpipers and is in Howard Auditorium.
    (E) It is on terns and is in Howard Auditorium.

22. Which one of the following could be true of the fifth lecture?

    (A) It is on oystercatchers and is in Gladwyn Hall.
    (B) It is on petrels and is in Howard Auditorium.
    (C) It is on rails and is in Howard Auditorium.
    (D) It is on sandpipers and is in Howard Auditorium.
    (E) It is on terns and is in Gladwyn Hall.

23. If the third lecture is on sandpipers, which one of the following could be true?

    (A) The second lecture is on oystercatchers and is in Gladwyn Hall.
    (B) The fifth lecture is on oystercatchers and is in Howard Auditorium.
    (C) The second lecture is on rails and is in Howard Auditorium.
    (D) The second lecture is on terns and is in Gladwyn Hall.
    (E) The fourth lecture is on terns and is in Howard Auditorium.

STOP
IF YOU FINISH BEFORE TIME IS CALLED, YOU MAY CHECK YOUR WORK ON THIS SECTION ONLY. DO NOT WORK ON ANY OTHER SECTION IN THE TEST.

SECTION V

Time—35 minutes

25 Questions

<u>Directions:</u> The questions in this section are based on the reasoning contained in brief statements or passages. For some questions, more than one of the choices could conceivably answer the question. However, you are to choose the best answer; that is, the response that most accurately and completely answers the question. You should not make assumptions that are by commonsense standards implausible, superfluous, or incompatible with the passage. After you have chosen the best answer, blacken the corresponding space on your answer sheet.

1. The quantity and type of pollution that entered the river last Thursday night suggest that the local auto repair shop is responsible. But the penalty for this type of pollution is so severe that, unless stronger evidence is discovered or the perpetrator admits responsibility, we cannot be sufficiently certain of the identity of the polluter to justify imposing the penalty.

   Which one of the following principles, if valid, most helps to justify the reasoning in the argument?

   (A) The more severe the penalty for an infraction is, the more certain one must be of the guilt of a party before being justified in imposing the penalty on that party.

   (B) Penalties for crimes should be severe enough to deter people from committing them, but not so severe as to undermine one's willingness to impose them.

   (C) The severity of the penalty imposed for an infraction should be proportional to the harm caused by that infraction.

   (D) The more severe the penalty for an offense is, the less likely it is that someone will come forward and admit responsibility for the offense.

   (E) The severity of the penalty for an offense should not be so great that one can never be sufficiently certain of guilt to justify punishment for that offense.

2. Depression is a serious problem for residents of nursing homes. However, a recent study has found that residents who developed personal bonds with pets had significantly lower rates of depression than did residents who did not develop personal bonds with pets.

   Which one of the following statements is most strongly supported by the information above?

   (A) Nursing-home residents are more subject to depression than any other individuals.

   (B) The best method for helping a nursing-home resident to overcome depression is to provide access to a pet.

   (C) High rates of depression among nursing-home residents may result at least in part from a lack of companionship.

   (D) Animal companionship is essential for psychological well-being.

   (E) Allowing free access to pets in nursing homes would eliminate problems relating to depression.

3. Humorous television advertisements are the only effective ones. For if something is humorous it will not only attract people's attention, it will hold their attention long enough for a message to be conveyed. And, obviously, for an advertisement to be effective it must convey its message.

   Which one of the following most accurately describes a flaw in the argument?

   (A) It takes for granted that nothing but humor can attract a person's attention and hold it long enough for a message to be conveyed.

   (B) It confuses attracting a person's attention with holding a person's attention long enough for a message to be conveyed.

   (C) It treats a necessary condition for an advertisement's being effective as if it were a sufficient condition.

   (D) It uses two senses of the term "effective" without differentiating them.

   (E) It takes for granted that an advertisement's only purpose is to convey its message.

GO ON TO THE NEXT PAGE.

4. Physician: Stories of people developing serious health problems shortly after receiving vaccinations have given rise to the question of whether vaccination is safe. But even if these stories are true, they need not be cause for concern. With millions of people being vaccinated every year, it is to be expected that some will develop health problems purely by coincidence shortly after receiving vaccinations.

Which one of the following, if true, would most strengthen the physician's argument?

(A) For the most part, stories of people developing serious health problems shortly after receiving vaccinations involve vaccines that were recently introduced.

(B) Some of the illnesses that vaccines are designed to prevent have become so rare that even if people are not vaccinated, they are unlikely to contract those illnesses.

(C) People are no more likely, on average, to develop serious health problems shortly after receiving vaccinations than shortly before receiving vaccinations.

(D) The health problems that some people have developed shortly after receiving vaccinations have been more serious than the health problems that the vaccines were intended to prevent.

(E) In a few cases in which people developed serious health problems shortly after taking other medications, these problems were initially attributed to coincidence but were later determined to be due to the medications.

5. Sharita: Anyone who owns a cat should have it spayed or neutered unless they are willing to take care of the cat's offspring. It is because people fail to do this that there are so many stray cats around.

Chad: Stray cats are not only a nuisance, they spread diseases and cause injuries to other cats and to humans. People feed these animals out of kindness, but doing so only exacerbates the problem unless the cats are then captured and adopted.

Sharita's and Chad's statements provide the most support for the claim that they agree about which one of the following?

(A) It is usually wrong to feed stray cats.
(B) There are more stray cats than there should be.
(C) Stray cats are a problem because of the risk they pose to humans.
(D) Stray cats spread diseases to other cats.
(E) It is mainly out of kindness that people feed stray cats.

6. Detective: People who repeatedly commit crimes like embezzlement or bribery without being caught tend to become more confident. With each success, they believe that getting caught is less likely. However, the more crimes a person commits, the greater the chance that one of those crimes will be solved. It is therefore likely that most people who commit embezzlement or bribery will eventually be caught.

Which one of the following is an assumption required by the detective's argument?

(A) The majority of people who commit embezzlement or bribery do so repeatedly.
(B) People who commit embezzlement or bribery tend to be people who feel confident.
(C) Embezzlement and bribery are more likely to be solved than are many other types of crimes.
(D) People who repeatedly commit embezzlement or bribery become more and more careless the longer they avoid detection.
(E) No one who commits embezzlement or bribery is ever caught the first time.

7. If grain prices double then the average price of a loaf of bread will rise between 10 and 15 percent, whereas the price of grain-fed beef will come close to doubling.

Which one of the following would, if true, most contribute to an explanation of the phenomenon described above?

(A) Farmers engaged in very large-scale cattle production generally try to reduce the labor costs involved in the production and sale of beef.
(B) The wholesale price per pound of beef is approximately ten times the wholesale price per pound of bread.
(C) The labor and marketing costs in producing and selling bread represent most of its cost, but the cost of feeding cattle represents most of the cost of producing beef.
(D) Only an insignificantly small proportion of the beef sold in retail markets is produced from cattle fed on grass rather than grain.
(E) The vast majority of retail grocery outlets purchase the bread they sell from small independent bakers but purchase the meat they sell from large wholesale processing operations.

GO ON TO THE NEXT PAGE.

8. Mark: The decongestant drug Zokaz was discontinued by its manufacturer because long-term studies revealed that it increased the risk of heart attack. Qualzan, another decongestant, works by essentially the same physiological mechanism as Zokaz. So Qualzan probably also increases the risk of heart attack.

Kathy: The decongestive effects of the two drugs do stem from the same physiological mechanism. But since they are different chemically, the two drugs probably have different side effects.

Which one of the following is a technique of reasoning used in Kathy's response to Mark?

(A) using a product's overall record of safety as evidence that the product is not linked to a particular health problem
(B) attempting to discredit an argument by comparing it to another obviously flawed argument that is logically parallel
(C) arguing against a conclusion by raising questions about the validity of scientific studies cited in support of that conclusion
(D) attempting to undermine an argument by showing that it is incompatible with a fundamental principle of medicine
(E) challenging an argument from analogy by focusing on a dissimilarity between the things being compared

9. CEO: We have been falsely criticized for not being an environmentally responsible corporation. Environmentally responsible corporations are corporations that do all they can to pollute less. Our current production methods pollute significantly less than our old methods did, and there currently are no methods that do not produce any pollution.

The reasoning in the CEO's argument is flawed in that it

(A) takes for granted that production methods that do not produce pollution cannot be developed
(B) fails to take into account the possibility that different causes can have similar effects
(C) generalizes too hastily from the inapplicability of a specific criticism to the inapplicability of a class of criticisms
(D) takes for granted that because the company has attempted to reduce the amount of pollution produced, they must have succeeded
(E) ignores the possibility that there are currently production methods that would allow the corporation to produce less pollution than it does now

10. A recent study showed that people who address problems quickly and directly are significantly less likely to have gum disease than are people who react to problems by refusing to think about them. Since stress can have a negative effect on the immune system, the study's results clearly indicate that some forms of gum disease are caused or aggravated by suppression of the immune system.

The argument requires the assumption that

(A) painful conditions will interfere with a person's ability to address problems quickly and directly
(B) refusing to think about something troubling contributes to a person's level of stress
(C) people who have highly stressful lives tend to address problems quickly and directly
(D) people who tend to address problems quickly and directly will invariably seek dental care at the first sign of problems
(E) the reason some people refuse to think about problems is that they find addressing problems to be stressful

11. A science class stored one selection of various fruits at 30 degrees Celsius, a similar selection in similar conditions at 20 degrees, and another similar selection in similar conditions at 10 degrees. Because the fruits stored at 20 degrees stayed fresh longer than those stored at 30 degrees, and those stored at 10 degrees stayed fresh longest, the class concluded that the cooler the temperature at which these varieties of fruits are stored, the longer they will stay fresh.

The class's reasoning is flawed in that the class

(A) generalized too readily from the fruits it tested to fruits it did not test
(B) ignored the effects of other factors such as humidity and sunlight on the rate of spoilage
(C) too readily extrapolated from a narrow range of temperatures to the entire range of temperatures
(D) assumed without proof that its thermometer was reliable
(E) neglected to offer any explanation for the results it discovered

GO ON TO THE NEXT PAGE.

12. Though Earth's human population is increasing, it currently uses only a relatively small fraction of the supply of fresh water. Thus, claims that water shortages will plague humankind in the near future unless population growth trends change are simply mistaken.

Which one of the following, if true, most seriously weakens the argument above?

(A) Population growth trends are notoriously hard to predict with reasonable accuracy.
(B) The amount of fresh water available to meet the needs of Earth's population varies significantly from region to region.
(C) Not all of Earth's population will adopt water conservation methods in the near future.
(D) If Earth's population continues to increase, it will eventually outstrip all available resources.
(E) The percentage of fresh water used for agriculture is likely to grow more quickly than is the percentage used for industry.

13. Consultant: The dramatic improvements in productivity achieved during the Industrial Revolution resulted in large part from standardization of processes and procedures coupled with centralization of planning and decision making. Yet, in recent years, many already productive companies have further improved their productivity by giving individual employees greater influence in decision making and in how they do their work.

Which one of the following, if true, most helps to resolve the apparent paradox in the consultant's statements?

(A) Most companies still try to improve productivity mainly through greater standardization and centralization of decision making.
(B) Increased productivity is not the only benefit of giving individual employees greater control over their work; job satisfaction increases as well.
(C) Most of the increases in industrial productivity that have occurred in recent years have been due to the introduction of advanced technology like industrial robots.
(D) The innovations of the Industrial Revolution are only now being applied in those companies in which individual employees have traditionally been entirely in control of how they do their work.
(E) Increases in productivity in highly productive companies depend on management's broad application of innovative ideas solicited from individual employees about their work.

14. Professor: The most important function of epic poetry is to transmit the values by which a group of people is to live. This transmission is accomplished not by an explicit discussion of those values, but rather by their embodiment in heroic figures, who are presented as role models. Imitating those role models gives meaning and direction to the lives of those who hear the poems.

If the professor's statements are true, which one of the following must also be true?

(A) An important function of poetry is to give meaning and direction to the lives of those who hear or read it.
(B) Epic poems accomplish their most important function by presenting heroic figures as role models.
(C) When values are represented in poetry, they are rarely if ever set forth explicitly.
(D) For many groups of people, heroic figures serve as role models embodying the values by which those people are to live.
(E) Only epic poetry presents heroic figures as role models that, if imitated, give meaning and direction to the lives of those who hear it.

15. Letter to the editor: You say that if the government were to confiscate a portion of the wages of convicted burglars when they reenter the workforce, it would be a form of stealing, hence an abuse of power. Yet under the proposal now being considered, the government would confiscate such wages in order to fund an account to compensate burglary victims. So even if confiscating a portion of burglars' wages were a form of stealing, it would still be justified.

Which one of the following principles, if valid, most helps to support the argument in the letter to the editor?

(A) Money stolen from a burglar should be given to that burglar's victims.
(B) Burglars are obligated to provide compensation to the same individuals they victimized.
(C) The motive prompting an action determines whether or not that action is justified.
(D) A crime is justified only if it is a means of compensating people who deserve compensation.
(E) Stealing is never justified even if it benefits someone who has been a burglary victim.

GO ON TO THE NEXT PAGE.

16. Some heartburn-medication advertisements imply that unrelieved heartburn is likely to cause esophageal cancer. This is simply false. The fact is that only about 5 percent of people with severe heartburn have a condition called Barrett's esophagus, in which cells similar to those in the stomach's lining develop in the lower esophagus. Only these people have an increased risk of developing cancer because of heartburn.

Which one of the following most accurately expresses the overall conclusion drawn in the argument?

(A) Only those people with Barrett's esophagus can suffer an increased risk of developing cancer from heartburn.

(B) An increase in the risk of esophageal cancer arises from cells similar to those in the stomach's lining developing in the lower esophagus.

(C) Unrelieved heartburn is not likely to cause esophageal cancer.

(D) Some heartburn-medication advertisements imply that unrelieved heartburn is likely to cause esophageal cancer.

(E) The dangers touted by heartburn-medication advertisements will affect relatively few of the people who see those advertisements.

17. We can be sure that at least some halogen lamps are well crafted, because halogen lamps from most major manufacturers are on display at Furniture Labyrinth. Any item on display at Furniture Labyrinth is well crafted.

Which one of the following arguments is most similar in its reasoning to the argument above?

(A) We can be confident that the temperature will drop abruptly on at least one day this week, for there is a chance of storms most days this week; whenever there are storms, the temperature drops suddenly.

(B) We can be positive that there are at least a few disturbing sonnets, given that Melinda has written several different kinds of sonnets; everything Melinda writes is disturbing.

(C) We can be sure that Gianna will get at least some good mechanical work done to her car, because she can have her car worked on at any of several shops in the city, and every shop is capable of doing good mechanical work.

(D) We can be positive that at least some minnows are healthy, because many different species of minnow can be found in lakes nearby, and every lake nearby is teeming with healthy fish.

(E) We can be confident that the cornmeal used at Matteo's Trattoria is healthful and organic, since cornmeal is among the ingredients used in preparing meals there; whenever a meal is prepared at Matteo's Trattoria, only healthful, organic ingredients are used.

18. Psychologists have found that the implementation of policies allowing work schedules to be tailored to individuals' needs does not typically increase managers' job satisfaction or their efficiency—although this may be because most managers already have the autonomy to adjust their own schedules. But these flexible-schedule policies do increase job satisfaction, productivity, and attendance among nonmanagerial employees. The benefits dissipate somewhat over time, however, and they are reduced even further if schedules are too elastic.

Which one of the following statements is most supported by the information above?

(A) Implementing flexible schedules would be an effective means of increasing the job satisfaction and efficiency of managers who do not already have scheduling autonomy.

(B) Flexible-schedule policies should be expected to improve the morale of some individual employees but not the overall morale of a company's workforce.

(C) Flexible schedules should be expected to substantially improve a company's productivity and employee satisfaction in the long run.

(D) There is little correlation between managers' job satisfaction and their ability to set their own work schedules.

(E) The typical benefits of flexible-schedule policies cannot be reliably inferred from observations of the effects of such policies on managers.

GO ON TO THE NEXT PAGE.

19. Viewers surveyed immediately after the televised political debate last year between Lopez and Tanner tended to think that Lopez had made the better arguments, but the survey respondents who reported that Lopez's arguments were better may have been biased in favor of Lopez. After all, Lopez eventually did win the election.

Which one of the following, if true, most seriously undermines the argument?

(A) Most people who voted in the election that Lopez won did not watch the debate.
(B) Most people in the live audience watching the debate who were surveyed immediately afterward said that they thought that Tanner was more persuasive in the debate than was Lopez.
(C) The people who watched the televised debate were more likely to vote for Tanner than were the people who did not watch the debate.
(D) Most of the viewers surveyed immediately prior to the debate said that they would probably vote for Tanner.
(E) Lopez won the election over Tanner by a very narrow margin.

20. Recent medical and anthropological data show that prohibitions on the use of certain foods served important social, economic, and medical functions in ancient cultures. But these data cannot explain the origin of the prohibitions involved, since those who originally adopted and enforced them did not have access to the same data as modern researchers.

Which one of the following is an assumption required by the argument?

(A) The origin of a food prohibition must be explained with reference to the understanding that the people who adopted and enforced the prohibition had.
(B) The social, economic, and medical problems of a society may lead to the adoption of contradictory food prohibitions.
(C) The social importance of the origin of a food prohibition is independent of the nutritional value of the food prohibited.
(D) The original purpose of a food prohibition is often forgotten a few generations after the prohibition is introduced.
(E) The people who originally adopted and enforced food prohibitions in ancient cultures generally had a nontechnical understanding of the medical functions of those prohibitions.

21. Editor: Most of the books of fiction we have published were submitted by literary agents for writers they represented; the rest were received directly from fiction writers from whom we requested submissions. No nonfiction manuscript has been given serious attention, let alone been published, unless it was from a renowned figure or we had requested the manuscript after careful review of the writer's book proposal.

Which one of the following can be properly inferred from the editor's statements?

(A) Most unrequested manuscripts that the publishing house receives are not given serious attention.
(B) Most of the books that the publishing house publishes that are not by renowned authors are books of fiction.
(C) If a manuscript has received careful attention at the publishing house, then it is either a work of fiction or the work of a renowned figure.
(D) The publishing house is less likely to give careful consideration to a manuscript that was submitted directly by a writer than one that was submitted by a writer's literary agent.
(E) Any unrequested manuscripts not submitted by literary agents that the publishing house has published were written by renowned figures.

GO ON TO THE NEXT PAGE.

22. If the budget does not allow for more dairy inspectors to be hired, most of the large dairies in the central valley will not meet federal standards governing the disposal of natural wastes, which can seep into streams and groundwater. The new district budget, however, does not allow for the hiring of more dairy inspectors. Consequently, most of the district's drinking water is likely to become polluted.

The conclusion above follows logically if which one of the following is assumed?

(A) If most of the dairies in the central valley meet federal standards for the disposal of natural wastes, it is unlikely that most of the district's drinking water will become polluted.
(B) To keep all the drinking water in the district clean requires more dairy inspectors to monitor the dairies' disposal of natural wastes.
(C) All of the district's drinking water is likely to become polluted only if all of the large dairies in the central valley do not meet federal standards for the disposal of natural wastes.
(D) Most of the district's drinking water is likely to become polluted if most of the large dairies in the central valley do not meet federal standards for the disposal of natural wastes.
(E) If none of the large dairies in the central valley meets federal standards for the disposal of natural wastes, most of the district's drinking water is likely to become polluted.

23. Company president: Almost every really successful product introduced in the last ten years has been launched by a massive television advertising campaign. We are using a massive television advertising campaign to introduce the Vegetaste Burger. So the Vegetaste Burger will probably be very successful.

The flawed nature of the company president's argument can most effectively be demonstrated by noting that, by parallel reasoning, we could conclude that

(A) the president of Corbin Corporation has an office that is not in Corbin's headquarters building, since almost all of the offices in Corbin's headquarters building are small, whereas Corbin's president has a large office
(B) Donna has at least ten years of experience as a computer programmer, since almost every programmer who works for Coderight Software has at least ten years experience, and Donna will probably be hired as a programmer by Coderight
(C) almost all of Acme's employees oppose the pending merger with Barrington Corporation, since almost all of Acme's employees are factory workers, and almost all of the factory workers at Acme oppose the merger
(D) Robinson will probably be appointed as president of Sifton University, since almost every one of Sifton's previous presidents had a Ph.D., and Robinson has a Ph.D.
(E) the novel Safekeeping will probably earn a profit for its publisher, Peninsula Press, since almost every novel published by Peninsula over the last ten years has been profitable

GO ON TO THE NEXT PAGE.

24. Biologist: Scientists have discovered fossilized bacteria in rocks 3.5 billion years old. The fossils indicate that these bacteria were quite complex and so must have already had a long evolutionary history when fossilized 3.5 billion years ago. However, Earth is only 4.6 billion years old, so the first life on Earth must have appeared soon after the planet's formation, when conditions were extremely harsh. This suggests that life may be able to arise under many difficult conditions throughout the universe.

Which one of the following most accurately describes the role played in the biologist's argument by the claim that the fossilized bacteria discovered in rocks 3.5 billion years old must have had a long evolutionary history?

(A) It is a claim for which no support is provided in the argument, and that is used to illustrate the conclusion of the argument as a whole.
(B) It is a claim for which no support is provided in the argument, and that is used to support a claim that in turn lends support to the conclusion of the argument as a whole.
(C) It is a claim for which some support is provided in the argument, and that itself is used to support another claim that in turn lends support to the conclusion of the argument as a whole.
(D) It is a claim for which some support is provided in the argument, and that itself is not used to support any other claim in the argument.
(E) It is a claim for which some support is provided in the argument, and that itself is used to support two distinct conclusions, neither of which is intended to provide support for the other.

25. At one time, many astronomers assumed that Earth remains motionless while the stars revolve around it. They concluded from this that the stars were not more than a few million miles from Earth. They reasoned that if the stars were farther away, they would have to move at tremendously great speeds in order to circle Earth during the day and reappear in roughly the same positions each night.

Which one of the following is an assumption required by the reasoning described above?

(A) If the stars do not revolve around Earth, it is possible for at least some stars to be more than a few million miles from Earth.
(B) All stars move at exactly the same speed when they are revolving around Earth.
(C) Earth does not remain motionless while the stars revolve around it.
(D) Stars do not move at tremendously great speeds.
(E) A star that is more than a million miles from Earth could reappear in roughly the same position each night.

26. People may praise the talent of a painter capable of realistically portraying a scene and dismiss as artistically worthless the efforts of abstract expressionists, but obviously an exact replica of the scene depicted is not the only thing people appreciate in a painting, for otherwise photography would have entirely displaced painting as an art form.

The argument proceeds by

(A) using a claim about what most people appreciate to support an aesthetic principle
(B) appealing to an aesthetic principle to defend the tastes that people have
(C) explaining a historical fact in terms of the artistic preferences of people
(D) appealing to a historical fact to support a claim about people's artistic preferences
(E) considering historical context to defend the artistic preferences of people

STOP
IF YOU FINISH BEFORE TIME IS CALLED, YOU MAY CHECK YOUR WORK ON THIS SECTION ONLY. DO NOT WORK ON ANY OTHER SECTION IN THE TEST.

LSAT WRITING SAMPLE TOPIC

Karen Dalton, the CEO and founder of a successful company, is deciding whether to remain CEO of the company or to step down to run for political office. Using the facts below write an essay in which you argue for one option over the other based on the following criteria:

• Dalton wants the company to continue to be successful.

• Dalton wants to advance political ideas that are important to her.

Dalton was instrumental in developing all of the product lines her company produces. The work needed to maintain and grow existing product lines is handled by Dalton's employees and has generally been successful. Dalton has some ideas that she thinks might be developed into new product lines. She has been frustrated by some limitations to her company's expansion due to regulations of her industry that she considers burdensome. She currently contributes heavily to politicians whose policies she supports. She is influential enough to get meetings with politicians across the political spectrum.

If Dalton runs for office, she has been promised the support of the leaders of her political party, which has been out of power but has seen its political representation steadily grow. The party has an antibusiness reputation. It would benefit from being represented by a successful businesswoman. Dalton agrees with the majority of its platform. She thinks that advancing the party's platform would be good for the success of her company. Even if she is elected to office, her party might not achieve majority status. If her party does achieve majority status, it is likely to focus on regulatory reform that affects her industry.

Directions:

1. Use the Answer Key on the next page to check your answers.

2. Use the Scoring Worksheet below to compute your raw score.

3. Use the Score Conversion Chart to convert your raw score into the 120–180 scale.

Scoring Worksheet

1. Enter the number of questions you answered correctly in each section.

	Number Correct
SECTION I...	_____
SECTION III	_____
SECTION IV	_____
SECTION V	_____

2. Enter the sum here:_____

   This is your Raw Score.

Section Map

SECTION I: PrepTest 70, Section 1
SECTION II: Experimental (PrepTest 57, Section 2)
SECTION III: PrepTest 70, Section 2
SECTION IV: PrepTest 70, Section 3
SECTION V: PrepTest 70, Section 4

Conversion Chart
For Converting Raw Score to the 120–180 LSAT Scaled Score
LSAT Form 3LSN105

Reported Score	Lowest	Highest
180	99	101
179	98	98
178	*	*
177	97	97
176	96	96
175	95	95
174	94	94
173	93	93
172	92	92
171	91	91
170	89	90
169	88	88
168	87	87
167	85	86
166	84	84
165	82	83
164	80	81
163	79	79
162	77	78
161	75	76
160	73	74
159	72	72
158	70	71
157	68	69
156	66	67
155	64	65
154	63	63
153	61	62
152	59	60
151	57	58
150	55	56
149	54	54
148	52	53
147	50	51
146	49	49
145	47	48
144	46	46
143	44	45
142	43	43
141	41	42
140	40	40
139	38	39
138	37	37
137	35	36
136	34	34
135	33	33
134	32	32
133	30	31
132	29	29
131	28	28
130	27	27
129	26	26
128	25	25
127	23	24
126	22	22
125	21	21
124	20	20
123	19	19
122	18	18
121	17	17
120	0	16

*There is no raw score that will produce this scaled score for this form.

SECTION I

1. A	8. B	15. A	22. C
2. D	9. A	16. E	23. E
3. D	10. A	17. D	24. C
4. A	11. B	18. A	25. B
5. E	12. E	19. C	
6. C	13. B	20. E	
7. E	14. D	21. D	

SECTION II

1. A	8. E	15. A	22. A
2. A	9. C	16. B	23. B
3. D	10. B	17. E	24. E
4. D	11. C	18. D	25. C
5. E	12. D	19. C	26. B
6. C	13. C	20. D	
7. A	14. E	21. E	

SECTION III

1. B	8. E	15. B	22. C
2. A	9. C	16. C	23. D
3. E	10. C	17. A	24. B
4. C	11. D	18. D	25. E
5. B	12. E	19. D	26. B
6. A	13. D	20. E	27. C
7. E	14. D	21. B	

SECTION IV

1. B	8. B	15. B	22. A
2. C	9. D	16. E	23. D
3. B	10. E	17. E	
4. E	11. D	18. A	
5. D	12. D	19. E	
6. D	13. A	20. B	
7. A	14. C	21. A	

SECTION V

1. A	8. E	15. C	22. D
2. C	9. E	16. C	23. D
3. A	10. B	17. B	24. C
4. C	11. C	18. E	25. D
5. B	12. B	19. D	26. D
6. A	13. E	20. A	
7. C	14. B	21. E	

TEST ANALYSIS

Section	Overall Performance Score: _____ Percentile: _____		
	Number attempted	Number of guesses	Number correct
Games			
Reading Comprehension			
Arguments 1			
Arguments 2			
TOTAL			

Games			
	Attempted? What order?	Diagram and Elements	Notes
Game 1			
Game 2			
Game 3			
Game 4			

Reading Comprehension

	Attempted? What order?	Passage Notes	Question Notes
Passage 1			
Passage 2			
Passage 3			
Passage 4			

Arguments

Page	Question Number	Question Task	Notes

Arguments

Page	Question Number	Question Task	Notes

The Official LSAT PrepTest™ 71
Test code 9718
Form 3LSN104

SECTION I

Time—35 minutes

25 Questions

<u>Directions</u>: The questions in this section are based on the reasoning contained in brief statements or passages. For some questions, more than one of the choices could conceivably answer the question. However, you are to choose the <u>best</u> answer; that is, the response that most accurately and completely answers the question. You should not make assumptions that are by commonsense standards implausible, superfluous, or incompatible with the passage. After you have chosen the best answer, blacken the corresponding space on your answer sheet.

1. Several years ago, most of one country's large banks ailed and were taken over by a government agency. The agency is now selling these banks, aiming to strengthen the banking system in the process. But the banking system will not be strengthened if the former owners of these banks buy them back. So the agency is unlikely to achieve its goal, since _____.

The conclusion of the argument is properly drawn if which one of the following completes the passage?

(A) the agency may be unable to sell some of the banks

(B) a single company could buy more than one of the banks

(C) the country's overall economy is not much stronger than it was when the large banks failed

(D) the banks sold by the agency will be financially weaker than the country's other banks for some time

(E) all of the bidders for the banks are their former owners

2. Accountant: The newspaper industry habitually cites the rising cost of newsprint to explain falling profits. But when corrected for inflation, the cost of newsprint is no more than it was ten years ago. Far from being victims of high costs, newspapers have been benefiting from cheap newsprint for decades. The real threats to their profitability are falling circulation and falling advertising.

The accountant's argument proceeds by

(A) reinterpreting a popular analogy in order to use that analogy to support an alternative conclusion

(B) using economic data to raise doubts about the current effectiveness of a historically accepted approach

(C) criticizing a newly developed method by demonstrating that a conventional method shows better results

(D) challenging an explanation that has been given for a phenomenon in order to introduce a different explanation

(E) calling into question a justification for a practice by showing how the same justification can be used to support a clearly undesirable practice

3. Peter: Recent evidence suggests that moderate alcohol consumption has certain beneficial effects on health. In particular, alcohol creates an inhospitable environment in the human body for certain bacteria that can cause illness. Thus, alcohol consumption is, on balance, beneficial.

Which one of the following most accurately expresses a flaw in the reasoning in Peter's argument?

(A) It takes for granted that people choose to consume alcohol because they believe it is beneficial to their health.

(B) It draws a comparison based on popular belief rather than on scientific opinion.

(C) It fails to consider methods of achieving the same beneficial effects that do not involve alcohol.

(D) It draws a conclusion about alcohol consumption in general from a premise about moderate alcohol consumption.

(E) It fails to consider that alcohol may have no effect on many bacteria that cause illness in human beings.

GO ON TO THE NEXT PAGE.

4. Consultant: Children taught using innovative new educational methods learn to think more creatively than children taught using rote methods such as drills, but they are less adept at memorizing large amounts of information. Most jobs at Grodex Corporation require the ability to think creatively but do not require a strong ability to memorize. So Grodex should probably conduct its employee-training seminars using the innovative methods, because _____.

Which one of the following most logically completes the consultant's argument?

(A) most of the employees at Grodex began in high school to learn the creative thinking skills that they later used on the job

(B) corporations that conduct training seminars for employees using innovative educational methods are generally more successful than are corporations that do not conduct training seminars

(C) less than half of the employees at Grodex regularly attend the company's training seminars

(D) the effects of teaching methods in the education of adults are generally very similar to the effects of those methods in the education of children

(E) knowing how to think creatively helps people to compensate for deficiencies in memorization skills

5. Essayist: If Earth's population continues to grow geometrically, then in a few centuries there will be ten people for every square meter (approximately one person per square foot) of Earth's surface. Some people have claimed that this will probably not be a problem, since humans will have learned by then how to colonize other planets. This would, however, be a temporary solution at best: if the population continues to double every 30 years, and if in the year 2500 half of Earth's population emigrated to Mars, then by the year 2530 Earth would be just as crowded as it had been before the emigration.

Which one of the following most accurately expresses the conclusion drawn in the essayist's argument?

(A) If Earth's population continues to grow geometrically, then in a few centuries the population density of Earth's surface will be ten people per square meter.

(B) Due to the continuing geometric growth of Earth's population, the problem of overpopulation of Earth will probably persist.

(C) If Earth's population continues to double every 30 years, and if at some point half of the population of Earth emigrated elsewhere, then after 30 years Earth would be just as crowded as it had been before the emigration.

(D) The population of Earth's surface will probably continue to grow geometrically even if temporary solutions to population growth, such as colonizing other planets, are adopted.

(E) Learning how to colonize other planets would, at best, be a temporary solution to the overcrowding of Earth.

6. A recent taste test reveals that most people like low-fat chocolate ice cream as much as its full-fat counterpart. Previous tests with vanilla ice cream found that people tended to dislike low-fat versions, complaining of a harsher taste. Chemists point out that chocolate is a very complex flavor, requiring around 500 distinct chemical compounds to produce it. Hence, this complexity probably masks any difference in taste due to the lack of fat.

Which one of the following, if true, most strengthens the argument?

(A) Most people prefer full-fat chocolate ice cream to full-fat vanilla ice cream.

(B) The subjects of the previous tests were not informed of the difference in fat content.

(C) The more distinct compounds required to produce a flavor, the better people like it.

(D) Vanilla is known to be a significantly less complex flavor than chocolate.

(E) Most people are aware of the chemical complexities of different flavors.

GO ON TO THE NEXT PAGE.

7. Ethicist: Robert Gillette has argued that because a thorough knowledge of genetics would enable us to cure the over 3,000 inherited disorders that affect humanity, deciphering the human genetic code will certainly benefit humanity despite its enormous cost. Gillette's argument is not persuasive, however, because he fails to consider that such knowledge might ultimately harm human beings more than it would benefit them.

Which one of the following most accurately expresses the conclusion of the ethicist's argument?

(A) Gillette's argument wrongly assumes that deciphering the genetic code will lead to cures for genetic disorders.
(B) Deciphering the genetic code might ultimately harm human beings more than benefit them.
(C) Because of its possible negative consequences, genetic research should not be conducted.
(D) Gillette's claim that a thorough knowledge of genetics would enable us to cure over 3,000 disorders is overstated.
(E) Gillette's argument is unconvincing because it ignores certain possible consequences of genetic research.

8. Many uses have been claimed for hypnosis, from combating drug addiction to overcoming common phobias. A recent experimental study helps illuminate the supposed connection between hypnosis and increased power of recall. A number of subjects listened to a long, unfamiliar piece of instrumental music. Under subsequent hypnosis, half the subjects were asked to recall salient passages from the musical piece and half were asked to describe scenes from "the film they had just viewed," despite their not having just seen a film. The study found that the subjects in the second group were equally confident and detailed in their movie recollections as the subjects in the first group were in their music recollections.

Which one of the following statements is most supported by the information above?

(A) Many of the claims made on behalf of hypnosis are overstated.
(B) Hypnosis cannot significantly increase a person's power of recall.
(C) Recalling events under hypnosis inevitably results in false memories.
(D) What people recall under hypnosis depends to at least some extent on suggestion.
(E) Visual memory is enhanced more by hypnosis than is auditory memory.

9. Records from 1850 to 1900 show that in a certain region, babies' birth weights each year varied with the success of the previous year's crops: the more successful the crops, the higher the birth weights. This indicates that the health of a newborn depends to a large extent on the amount of food available to the mother during her pregnancy.

The argument proceeds by

(A) inferring from a claimed correlation between two phenomena that two other phenomena are causally connected to one another
(B) inferring from the claim that two phenomena have fluctuated together that one of those phenomena must be the sole cause of the other
(C) inferring from records concerning a past correlation between two phenomena that that correlation still exists
(D) inferring from records concerning two phenomena the existence of a common cause of the phenomena and then presenting a hypothesis about that common cause
(E) inferring the existence of one causal connection from that of another and then providing an explanation for the existence of the two causal connections

10. Vincent: No scientific discipline can study something that cannot be measured, and since happiness is an entirely subjective experience, it cannot be measured.

Yolanda: Just as optometry relies on patients' reports of what they see, happiness research relies on subjects' reports of how they feel. Surely optometry is a scientific discipline.

Vincent's and Yolanda's statements provide the most support for concluding that they disagree over which one of the following?

(A) Happiness is an entirely subjective experience.
(B) Optometry is a scientific discipline.
(C) A scientific discipline can rely on subjective reports.
(D) Happiness research is as much a scientific discipline as optometry is.
(E) Experiences that cannot be measured are entirely subjective experiences.

GO ON TO THE NEXT PAGE.

11. Although large cities are generally more polluted than the countryside, increasing urbanization may actually reduce the total amount of pollution generated nationwide. Residents of large cities usually rely more on mass transportation and live in smaller, more energy-efficient dwellings than do people in rural areas. Thus, a given number of people will produce less pollution if concentrated in a large city than if dispersed among many small towns.

Which one of the following most accurately describes the role played in the argument by the claim that increasing urbanization may actually reduce the total amount of pollution generated nationwide?

(A) It is used to support the conclusion that people should live in large cities.
(B) It is a statement offered to call into question the claim that large cities are generally more polluted than the countryside.
(C) It is a statement serving merely to introduce the topic to be addressed in the argument and plays no logical role.
(D) It is a premise offered in support of the conclusion that large cities are generally more polluted than the countryside.
(E) It is a claim that the rest of the argument is designed to establish.

12. Climatologist: Over the coming century, winter temperatures are likely to increase in the Rocky Mountains due to global warming. This will cause a greater proportion of precipitation to fall as rain instead of snow. Therefore, the mountain snowpack will probably melt more rapidly and earlier in the season, leading to greater spring flooding and less storable water to meet summer demands.

Which one of the following, if true, most strengthens the climatologist's argument?

(A) Global warming will probably cause a substantial increase in the average amount of annual precipitation in the Rocky Mountains over the coming century.
(B) In other mountainous regions after relatively mild winters, the melting of snowpacks has led to greater spring flooding and less storable water, on average, than in those mountainous regions after colder winters.
(C) On average, in areas of the Rocky Mountains in which winters are relatively mild, there is less storable water to meet summer demands than there is in areas of the Rocky Mountains that experience colder winters.
(D) On average, in the regions of the world with the mildest winters, there is more spring flooding and less storable water than in regions of the world with much colder winters.
(E) The larger a mountain snowpack is, the greater the amount of spring flooding it is likely to be responsible for producing.

13. Animal feed should not include genetically modified plants. A study found that laboratory rats fed genetically modified potatoes for 30 days tended to develop intestinal deformities and a weakened immune system, whereas rats fed a normal diet of foods that were not genetically modified did not develop these problems.

Which one of the following, if true, most weakens the argument?

(A) Potatoes are not normally a part of the diet of laboratory rats.
(B) The rats tended to eat more of the genetically modified potatoes at the beginning of the 30 days than they did toward the end of the 30 days.
(C) Intestinal deformities at birth are not uncommon among rats bred in laboratory conditions.
(D) Genetically modified potatoes have the same nutritional value to rats as do potatoes that are not genetically modified.
(E) The researchers conducting the study were unable to explain how the genetic modifications of the potatoes would have caused the intestinal deformities or a weakened immune system in the rats.

GO ON TO THE NEXT PAGE.

14. Some philosophers explain visual perception by suggesting that when we visually perceive an object, a mental image of that object forms in our mind. However, this hypothesis cannot be correct, since it would require an inner self visually perceiving the newly formed mental image; this would in turn require that the inner self have a mental image of that mental image, and so on. But such an infinite regress is absurd.

Which one of the following arguments is most similar in its pattern of reasoning to the argument above?

(A) According to some linguists, many of the world's languages can be traced back to a common source known as Indo-European. However, Indo-European cannot be the earliest language, for if it were, then there would be no language from which it was derived. But this is highly unlikely, given the overwhelming evidence that humans spoke long before the advent of Indo-European.

(B) The claim that any scientific theory is adequate as long as it agrees with all the empirical data cannot be correct. For there are an infinite number of theories all of which account equally well for the empirical data, and they cannot all be true at the same time.

(C) Some historians claim that no theory is ever genuinely new; no matter how clever a theory is, there is always a precedent theory that contains its gist. But if this were true, then every theory would have a precedent theory containing its gist, and this precedent theory would also have a precedent theory, and so on, without end. Since this is clearly impossible, the historians' claim must be false.

(D) Some engineers define a structure's foundation as that part of the structure that supports the rest of the structure. This definition is unfortunate, however, because it evokes the suggestion that the foundation itself does not have any support, which, of course, is absurd.

(E) Some people claim that the first library was the library of Alexandria, which for many centuries contained the largest collection of books in the world. However, Alexandria's collection was itself put together from smaller collections, small libraries in themselves. It follows that the library of Alexandria was not the first in the world.

15. Greatly exceeding the recommended daily intake of vitamins A and D is dangerous, for they can be toxic at high levels. For some vitamin-fortified foods, each serving, as defined by the manufacturer, has 100 percent of the recommended daily intake of these vitamins. But many people overestimate what counts as a standard serving of vitamin-fortified foods such as cereal, consuming two to three times what the manufacturers define as standard servings.

Which one of the following is most strongly supported by the information above?

(A) Few people who consume vitamin-fortified foods are aware of the recommended daily intake of vitamins A and D.

(B) Some people who consume vitamin-fortified foods exceed the recommended daily intake of vitamins A and D.

(C) Some people mistakenly believe it is healthy to consume more than the recommended daily intake of vitamins A and D.

(D) Most people who eat vitamin-fortified foods should not take any vitamin supplements.

(E) Manufacturers are unaware that many people consume vitamin-fortified foods in amounts greater than the standard serving sizes.

GO ON TO THE NEXT PAGE.

16. At the end of 1997 several nations stated that their oil reserves had not changed since the end of 1996. But oil reserves gradually drop as old oil fields are drained and rise suddenly as new oil fields are discovered. Therefore, oil reserves are unlikely to remain unchanged from one year to the next. So most of the nations stating that their oil reserves were unchanged are probably incorrect.

Which one of the following is an assumption the argument requires?

(A) For any nation with oil reserves, it is more likely that the nation was mistaken in its statements about changes in its oil reserves than that the nation's oil reserves remained unchanged.

(B) It is likely that in 1997, in most of the nations that stated that their oil reserves were unchanged, old oil fields were drained or new oil fields were discovered, or both.

(C) During the course of 1997, the oil reserves of at least one nation not only gradually dropped but also rose suddenly.

(D) If a nation incorrectly stated at the end of 1997 that its oil reserves had not changed since the end of 1996, then during 1997 that nation drained its old oil fields and discovered new ones.

(E) If a nation's oil reserves change from one year to the next, then that nation is obligated to report the change correctly.

17. If a motor is sound-insulated, then it is quiet enough to use in home appliances. If a motor is quiet enough to use in home appliances, then it can be used in institutional settings. None of the motors manufactured by EM Industries are quiet enough to use in home appliances.

If the statements above are true, which one of the following must be true?

(A) If a motor can be used in institutional settings, then it is sound-insulated.

(B) None of the motors manufactured by EM Industries are sound-insulated.

(C) At least some of the motors manufactured by EM Industries can be used in institutional settings.

(D) If a motor is quiet enough to use in home appliances, then it is sound-insulated.

(E) None of the motors manufactured by EM Industries can be used in institutional settings.

18. Mayor: A huge protest against plans to build a chemical plant in this town was held yesterday. The protesters claim that the factory could cause health problems. But this worry can be dismissed. Most of the protesters were there only because they were paid to show up by property developers who are concerned that the factory would lower the value of nearby land that they own.

Which one of the following most accurately expresses a flaw in reasoning in the mayor's argument?

(A) The argument mischaracterizes an opposing view and then attacks this mischaracterized view.

(B) The argument attempts to persuade by inducing fear of the consequences of rejecting its conclusion.

(C) The argument rejects a claim simply because of the motivation that some people have for making it.

(D) The argument generalizes on the basis of a few unrepresentative cases.

(E) The argument mistakes a claim that a result is possible for a claim that the result is inevitable.

19. One should not intentionally misrepresent another person's beliefs unless one's purpose in doing so is to act in the interest of that other person.

Which one of the following actions most clearly violates the principle stated?

(A) Ann told someone that Bruce thought the Apollo missions to the moon were elaborate hoaxes, even though she knew he did not think this; she did so merely to make him look ridiculous.

(B) Claude told someone that Thelma believed in extraterrestrial beings, even though he knew she believed no such thing; he did so solely to keep this other person from bothering her.

(C) In Maria's absence John had told people that Maria believed that university education should be free of charge. He knew that Maria would not want him telling people this, but he wanted these people to think highly of Maria.

(D) Harvey told Josephine that he thought Josephine would someday be famous. Harvey did not really think that Josephine would ever be famous, but he said she would because he thought she would like him as a result.

(E) Wanda told people that George thought Egypt is in Asia. Wanda herself knew that Egypt is in Africa, but she told people that George thought it was in Asia because she wanted people to know that George knew little about geography.

GO ON TO THE NEXT PAGE.

20. Adjusted for inflation, the income earned from wool sales by a certain family of Australian sheep farmers grew substantially during the period from 1840 to 1860. This is because the price for wool sold on the international market was higher than the price paid on domestic markets and the percentage and amount of its wool that this family sold internationally increased dramatically during that period. But even though the family generated more income from selling their wool, they failed to enjoy a commensurate increase in prosperity.

Which one of the following would, if true, help most to resolve the apparent paradox described above?

(A) At the end of the 1800s, prices in general in Australia rose more rapidly than did the wholesale price of wool sold domestically.

(B) The prices of wool sold to domestic markets by Australian sheep farmers decreased dramatically during the period in question.

(C) The international and domestic prices for mutton, sheepskins, and certain other products produced by all Australian sheep farmers fell sharply during the period in question.

(D) Competition in wool sales increased during the period in question, leaving Australian wool producers in a less favorable position than previously.

(E) Among Australian sheep farmers, the percentage who made their living exclusively from international wool sales increased significantly during the period in question.

21. Lawyer: If you take something that you have good reason to think is someone else's property, that is stealing, and stealing is wrong. However, Meyers had no good reason to think that the compost in the public garden was anyone else's property, so it was not wrong for Meyers to take it.

The reasoning in the lawyer's argument is flawed in that the argument

(A) confuses a factual claim with a moral judgment

(B) takes for granted that Meyers would not have taken the compost if he had good reason to believe that it was someone else's property

(C) takes a condition that by itself is enough to make an action wrong to also be necessary in order for the action to be wrong

(D) fails to consider the possibility that the compost was Meyers' property

(E) concludes that something is certainly someone else's property when there is merely good, but not conclusive, reason to think that it is someone else's property

22. From time to time there is a public outcry against predatory pricing—where a company deliberately sells its products at prices low enough to drive its competitors out of business. But this practice clearly should be acceptable, because even after its competitors go out of business, the mere threat of renewed competition will prevent the company from raising its prices to unreasonable levels.

Which one of the following is an assumption on which the argument depends?

(A) Any company that is successful will inevitably induce competitors to enter the market.

(B) It is unlikely that several competing companies will engage in predatory pricing simultaneously.

(C) Only the largest and wealthiest companies can engage in predatory pricing for a sustained period of time.

(D) It is only competition or the threat of competition that keeps companies from raising prices.

(E) Any pricing practice that does not result in unreasonable prices should be acceptable.

23. If the prosecutor wanted to charge Frank with embezzlement, then Frank would already have been indicted. But Frank has not been indicted. So clearly Frank is not an embezzler.

The flawed pattern of reasoning exhibited by which one of the following is most similar to that exhibited by the argument above?

(A) If Rosita knew that her 9:00 appointment would cancel, she would not come in to work until 10:00. She did not come in until 10:00. So she must have known her 9:00 appointment would cancel.

(B) If Barry had won the lottery, he would stay home to celebrate. But Barry did not win the lottery, so he will be in to work today.

(C) If Makoto believed that he left the oven on, he would rush home. But Makoto is still at work. So obviously he did not leave the oven on.

(D) If Tamara believed she was getting a promotion, she would come in to work early. She did come in early. So apparently she is getting a promotion.

(E) If Lucy believed she was going to be fired, she would not come in to work today. She is going to be fired, so clearly she will not be coming in today.

GO ON TO THE NEXT PAGE.

24. Pediatrician: Swollen tonsils give rise to breathing problems during sleep, and the surgical removal of children's swollen tonsils has been shown to alleviate sleep disturbances. So removing children's tonsils before swelling even occurs will ensure that the children do not experience any breathing problems during sleep.

The pediatrician's argument is most vulnerable to the criticism that it

(A) relies on an inappropriate appeal to authority
(B) relies on an assumption that is tantamount to assuming that the conclusion is true
(C) infers from the fact that an action has a certain effect that the action is intended to produce that effect
(D) fails to consider the possibility that there may be other medical reasons for surgically removing a child's tonsils
(E) fails to consider the possibility that some breathing problems during sleep may be caused by something other than swollen tonsils

25. It is unethical for government officials to use their knowledge of impending policies to financially benefit themselves if that knowledge is not available to the general public.

Which one of the following actions would be unethical according to the principle stated above?

(A) A company whose former manager is now an official with the Department of Natural Resources was one of several bidders for an extremely lucrative contract with the department; the names of the bidders were not disclosed to the public.
(B) A retired high-ranking military officer now owns a company that contracts with the Department of Defense. He uses his contacts with department officials to help his company obtain contracts.
(C) After a tax reform law was enacted, an official with the government's revenue agency obtained a 20 percent reduction in personal income tax by setting up tax shelters that were allowed by the new law.
(D) A Finance Department official, one of the few people who knew of a plan to tax luxury cars, bought a luxury car just before the plan was announced to the public in order to avoid paying the tax.
(E) An official with a government agency that regulates securities sold her stock in Acme just after she announced to the public that her agency was investigating Acme for improper accounting.

STOP
IF YOU FINISH BEFORE TIME IS CALLED, YOU MAY CHECK YOUR WORK ON THIS SECTION ONLY. DO NOT WORK ON ANY OTHER SECTION IN THE TEST.

SECTION II

Time—35 minutes

23 Questions

Directions: Each group of questions in this section is based on a set of conditions. In answering some of the questions, it may be useful to draw a rough diagram. Choose the response that most accurately and completely answers each question and blacken the corresponding space on your answer sheet.

Questions 1–5

A movie studio is scheduling the release of six films—*Fiesta, Glaciers, Hurricanes, Jets, Kangaroos,* and *Lovebird.* No two of these films can be released on the same date. The release schedule is governed by the following conditions:

Fiesta must be released earlier than both *Jets* and *Lovebird.*

Kangaroos must be released earlier than *Jets,* and *Jets* must be released earlier than *Hurricanes.*

Lovebird must be released earlier than *Glaciers.*

1. Which one of the following CANNOT be true?

   (A) *Fiesta* is released second.
   (B) *Glaciers* is released third.
   (C) *Hurricanes* is released fourth.
   (D) *Kangaroos* is released fourth.
   (E) *Kangaroos* is released fifth.

GO ON TO THE NEXT PAGE.

2. Which one of the following must be true?

(A) *Fiesta* is released earlier than *Hurricanes*.
(B) *Jets* is released earlier than *Glaciers*.
(C) *Kangaroos* is released earlier than *Glaciers*.
(D) *Lovebird* is released earlier than *Hurricanes*.
(E) *Lovebird* is released earlier than *Jets*.

3. If *Glaciers* is released earlier than *Hurricanes*, then each of the following could be true EXCEPT:

(A) *Glaciers* is released fourth.
(B) *Jets* is released third.
(C) *Kangaroos* is released second.
(D) *Lovebird* is released third.
(E) *Lovebird* is released fifth.

4. If *Lovebird* is released earlier than *Kangaroos*, which one of the following could be true?

(A) *Lovebird* is released third.
(B) *Lovebird* is released fourth.
(C) *Hurricanes* is released earlier than *Lovebird*.
(D) *Jets* is released earlier than *Glaciers*.
(E) *Jets* is released earlier than *Lovebird*.

5. Which one of the following, if substituted for the condition that *Fiesta* must be released earlier than both *Jets* and *Lovebird*, would have the same effect on the order in which the films are released?

(A) Only *Kangaroos* can be released earlier than *Fiesta*.
(B) *Kangaroos* must be released earlier than *Lovebird*.
(C) *Fiesta* must be released either first or second.
(D) *Fiesta* must be released earlier than both *Kangaroos* and *Lovebird*.
(E) Either *Fiesta* or *Kangaroos* must be released first.

GO ON TO THE NEXT PAGE.

Questions 6–11

The applications of seven job candidates—Farrell, Grant, Hong, Inman, Kent, Lopez, and Madsen—will be evaluated by four human resource officers—Rao, Smith, Tipton, and Ullman. Each application will be evaluated by exactly one officer, and each officer will evaluate at least one application, subject to the following constraints:

> Grant's application must be evaluated by Ullman.
> Farrell's application must be evaluated by the same officer who evaluates Lopez's application.
> Neither Hong's application nor Madsen's application can be evaluated by the same officer who evaluates Inman's application.
> The officer who evaluates Kent's application cannot evaluate any other applications.
> Smith must evaluate more of the applications than Tipton does.

6. Which one of the following could be the assignment of applications to officers?

(A) Rao: Hong
Smith: Farrell, Lopez, Madsen
Tipton: Kent
Ullman: Grant, Inman

(B) Rao: Inman
Smith: Hong, Lopez, Madsen
Tipton: Kent
Ullman: Farrell, Grant

(C) Rao: Madsen
Smith: Farrell, Lopez
Tipton: Kent
Ullman: Grant, Hong, Inman

(D) Rao: Farrell, Lopez
Smith: Hong, Kent, Madsen
Tipton: Inman
Ullman: Grant

(E) Rao: Farrell, Grant, Lopez
Smith: Hong, Madsen
Tipton: Kent
Ullman: Inman

GO ON TO THE NEXT PAGE.

7. If Hong's application is evaluated by Rao, which one of the following could be true?

    (A) Farrell's application is evaluated by Rao.
    (B) Inman's application is evaluated by Smith.
    (C) Kent's application is evaluated by Rao.
    (D) Lopez's application is evaluated by Ullman.
    (E) Madsen's application is evaluated by Tipton.

8. If exactly two of the applications are evaluated by Tipton, then each of the following must be true EXCEPT:

    (A) Exactly one of the applications is evaluated by Rao.
    (B) Exactly one of the applications is evaluated by Ullman.
    (C) Farrell's application is evaluated by Tipton.
    (D) Inman's application is evaluated by Smith.
    (E) Lopez's application is evaluated by Smith.

9. If the officer who evaluates Madsen's application does not evaluate any other application, which one of the following must be true?

    (A) Madsen's application is evaluated by Tipton.
    (B) Lopez's application is evaluated by Smith.
    (C) Kent's application is evaluated by Tipton.
    (D) Inman's application is evaluated by Smith.
    (E) Hong's application is evaluated by Smith.

10. If Farrell's application is evaluated by the same officer who evaluates Inman's application, then any of the following could be true EXCEPT:

    (A) Hong's application is evaluated by Ullman.
    (B) Kent's application is evaluated by Tipton.
    (C) Lopez's application is evaluated by Ullman.
    (D) Madsen's application is evaluated by Smith.
    (E) Madsen's application is evaluated by Ullman.

11. If Farrell's application is evaluated by Rao, then for how many of the other applications is the identity of the officer who evaluates it fully determined?

    (A) one
    (B) two
    (C) three
    (D) four
    (E) five

GO ON TO THE NEXT PAGE.

Questions 12–16

A six-week literature course is being planned in which six books—F, K, N, O, R, and T—will be discussed. The books will be discussed one at a time, one book per week. In addition, written summaries will be required for one or more of the books. The order in which the books are discussed and the selection of books to be summarized is subject to the following conditions:

No two books that are summarized are discussed in consecutive weeks.

If N is not summarized, then both R and T are summarized.

N is discussed earlier than T, and T is discussed earlier than O.

F is discussed earlier than O, and O is discussed earlier than both K and R.

12. Which one of the following could be the plan for the course, showing the order, from first to last, in which the books are discussed and the choice of books to be summarized?

(A) F, N, T, O, R, K; with only T and R summarized

(B) F, T, N, O, K, R; with only N and K summarized

(C) N, F, T, O, K, R; with only T, O, and R summarized

(D) N, T, F, O, K, R; with only T and O summarized

(E) N, T, O, F, K, R; with only T and R summarized

GO ON TO THE NEXT PAGE.

13. If N is the second book discussed and it is not summarized, which one of the following could be true?

   (A) F is summarized.
   (B) K is summarized.
   (C) O is summarized.
   (D) T is discussed earlier than F.
   (E) The third book discussed is not summarized.

14. If O is summarized, which one of the following CANNOT be true?

   (A) F is the first book discussed.
   (B) K is the sixth book discussed.
   (C) F is summarized.
   (D) K is not summarized.
   (E) N is not summarized.

15. If neither of the last two books discussed is summarized, which one of the following could be true?

   (A) K is summarized.
   (B) O is summarized.
   (C) R is summarized.
   (D) F and T are summarized.
   (E) N is not summarized.

16. Which one of the following, if substituted for the condition that F is discussed earlier than O, and O is discussed earlier than both K and R, would have the same effect in determining the plan for the literature course?

   (A) T is discussed third, and the last two books discussed are K and R, not necessarily in that order.
   (B) T is discussed earlier than F, and the last two books discussed are K and R, not necessarily in that order.
   (C) K and R are among the last three books discussed, and F is among the first three books discussed.
   (D) K and R are discussed in consecutive weeks, not necessarily in that order, and O is discussed fourth.
   (E) K and R are discussed in consecutive weeks, not necessarily in that order, and F is discussed third.

GO ON TO THE NEXT PAGE.

Questions 17–23

A museum curator is arranging seven paintings—a Morisot, a Pissarro, a Renoir, a Sisley, a Turner, a Vuillard, and a Whistler. The paintings will be arranged in a horizontal row of seven positions, with the first position being closest to the entrance and the seventh being furthest from the entrance. The arrangement is subject to the following constraints:

The Turner must be closer to the entrance than the Whistler is.

The Renoir must be closer to the entrance than the Morisot is, with exactly one other painting between them.

The Pissarro and the Sisley must be next to each other.

If the Vuillard is not in the third position, it must be in the fourth position.

17. Which one of the following could be the arrangement of the paintings, listed in order from the first position to the seventh?

(A) Morisot, Turner, Renoir, Vuillard, Whistler, Sisley, Pissarro

(B) Pissarro, Sisley, Renoir, Vuillard, Morisot, Whistler, Turner

(C) Renoir, Turner, Morisot, Vuillard, Whistler, Sisley, Pissarro

(D) Sisley, Turner, Pissarro, Vuillard, Renoir, Whistler, Morisot

(E) Turner, Vuillard, Pissarro, Sisley, Renoir, Whistler, Morisot

GO ON TO THE NEXT PAGE.

18. If the Sisley is in the seventh position, which one of the following could be the position that the Turner is in?

    (A) second
    (B) third
    (C) fourth
    (D) fifth
    (E) sixth

19. If the Pissarro is in the fifth position, which one of the following must be true?

    (A) The Morisot is in the fourth position.
    (B) The Renoir is in the second position.
    (C) The Sisley is in the sixth position.
    (D) The Turner is in the first position.
    (E) The Vuillard is in the third position.

20. Any one of the following could be in the third position EXCEPT:

    (A) the Morisot
    (B) the Renoir
    (C) the Sisley
    (D) the Turner
    (E) the Whistler

21. If the Renoir and the Morisot are both between the Turner and the Whistler, which one of the following could be true?

    (A) The Pissarro is in the fifth position.
    (B) The Sisley is in the second position.
    (C) The Turner is in the third position.
    (D) The Vuillard is in the fourth position.
    (E) The Whistler is in the sixth position.

22. If there is exactly one painting between the Turner and the Whistler, which one of the following must be true?

    (A) The Morisot is in the seventh position.
    (B) The Pissarro is in the first position.
    (C) The Renoir is in the fourth position.
    (D) The Turner is in the second position.
    (E) The Vuillard is in the third position.

23. If the Turner is next to the Vuillard, which one of the following is a pair of paintings in which the one mentioned first must be closer to the entrance than the one mentioned second?

    (A) the Pissarro and the Sisley
    (B) the Renoir and the Whistler
    (C) the Turner and the Vuillard
    (D) the Vuillard and the Turner
    (E) the Whistler and the Renoir

STOP
IF YOU FINISH BEFORE TIME IS CALLED, YOU MAY CHECK YOUR WORK ON THIS SECTION ONLY. DO NOT
WORK ON ANY OTHER SECTION IN THE TEST.

SECTION III

Time—35 minutes

25 Questions

<u>Directions</u>: The questions in this section are based on the reasoning contained in brief statements or passages. For some questions, more than one of the choices could conceivably answer the question. However, you are to choose the <u>best</u> answer; that is, the response that most accurately and completely answers the question. You should not make assumptions that are by commonsense standards implausible, superfluous, or incompatible with the passage. After you have chosen the best answer, blacken the corresponding space on your answer sheet.

1. Educators studied the performance of 200 students in a university's history classes. They found that those students who performed the best had either part-time jobs or full-time jobs, had their history classes early in the morning, and had a very limited social life, whereas those students who performed the worst had no jobs, had their history classes early in the morning, and had a very active social life.

    Which one of the following, if true, most helps to explain the educators' findings?

    (A) The students compensated for any study time lost due to their jobs but they did not compensate for any study time lost due to their social lives.
    (B) The students who had full-time jobs typically worked late-night hours at those jobs.
    (C) Better students tend to choose classes that are scheduled to meet early in the morning.
    (D) A larger percentage of those students interested in majoring in history had part-time jobs than had full-time jobs.
    (E) Although having a job tends to provide a release from stress, thus increasing academic performance, having a full-time job, like having an active social life, can distract a student from studying.

2. Politician: Most of those at the meeting were not persuaded by Kuyler's argument, nor should they have been, for Kuyler's argument implied that it would be improper to enter into a contract with the government; and yet—as many people know—Kuyler's company has had numerous lucrative contracts with the government.

    Which one of the following describes a flaw in the politician's argument?

    (A) It concludes that an argument is defective merely on the grounds that the argument has failed to persuade anyone of the truth of its conclusion.
    (B) It relies on testimony that is likely to be biased.
    (C) It rejects an argument merely on the grounds that the arguer has not behaved in a way that is consistent with the argument.
    (D) It rejects a position merely on the grounds that an inadequate argument has been given for it.
    (E) It rejects an argument on the basis of an appeal to popular opinion.

GO ON TO THE NEXT PAGE.

3. Although free international trade allows countries to specialize, which in turn increases productivity, such specialization carries risks. After all, small countries often rely on one or two products for the bulk of their exports. If those products are raw materials, the supply is finite and can be used up. If they are foodstuffs, a natural disaster can wipe out a season's production overnight.

Which one of the following most accurately expresses the conclusion of the argument as a whole?

(A) Specialization within international trade comes with risks.
(B) A natural disaster can destroy a whole season's production overnight, devastating a small country's economy.
(C) A small country's supply of raw materials can be used up in a short period.
(D) Some countries rely on a small number of products for the export-based sectors of their economies.
(E) When international trade is free, countries can specialize in what they export.

4. Two randomly selected groups of 30 adults each were asked to write short stories on a particular topic. One group was told that the best stories would be awarded cash prizes, while the other group was not told of any prizes. Each story was evaluated by a team of judges who were given no indication of the group from which the story came. The stories submitted by those who thought they were competing for prizes were ranked on average significantly lower than the stories from the other group.

Which one of the following, if true, most helps to explain the difference in average ranking between the two groups' stories?

(A) The cash prizes were too small to motivate an average adult to make a significant effort to produce stories of high quality.
(B) People writing to win prizes show a greater than usual tendency to produce stereotypical stories that show little creativity.
(C) Most adults show little originality in writing stories on a topic suggested by someone else.
(D) The team of judges was biased in favor of stories that they judged to be more realistic.
(E) No one explained clearly to either group what standards would be used in judging their stories.

5. Hernandez: I recommend that staff cars be replaced every four years instead of every three years. Three-year-old cars are still in good condition and this would result in big savings.

Green: I disagree. Some of our salespeople with big territories wear out their cars in three years.

Hernandez: I meant three-year-old cars subjected to normal use.

In the conversation, Hernandez responds to Green's objection in which one of the following ways?

(A) by explicitly qualifying a premise used earlier
(B) by criticizing salespeople who wear out their cars in three years
(C) by disputing the accuracy of Green's evidence
(D) by changing the subject to the size of sales territories
(E) by indicating that Green used a phrase ambiguously

6. Economist: As should be obvious, raising the minimum wage significantly would make it more expensive for businesses to pay workers for minimum-wage jobs. Therefore, businesses could not afford to continue to employ as many workers for such jobs. So raising the minimum wage significantly will cause an increase in unemployment.

Which one of the following, if true, most weakens the economist's argument?

(A) Businesses typically pass the cost of increased wages on to consumers without adversely affecting profits.
(B) When the difference between minimum wage and a skilled worker's wage is small, a greater percentage of a business's employees will be skilled workers.
(C) A modest increase in unemployment is acceptable because the current minimum wage is not a livable wage.
(D) Most workers are earning more than the current minimum wage.
(E) The unemployment rate has been declining steadily in recent years.

GO ON TO THE NEXT PAGE.

7. Scientists removed all viruses from a seawater sample and then measured the growth rate of the plankton population in the water. They expected the rate to increase dramatically, but the population actually got smaller.

Which one of the following, if true, most helps to explain the unexpected result described above?

(A) Viruses in seawater help to keep the plankton population below the maximum level that the resources in the water will support.

(B) Plankton and viruses in seawater compete for some of the same nutrients.

(C) Plankton utilize the nutrients released by the death of organisms killed by viruses.

(D) The absence of viruses can facilitate the flourishing of bacteria that sometimes damage other organisms.

(E) At any given time, a considerable portion of the plankton in seawater are already infected by viruses.

8. City council member: The Senior Guild has asked for a temporary exception to the ordinance prohibiting automobiles in municipal parks. Their case does appear to deserve the exception. However, if we grant this exception, we will find ourselves granting many other exceptions to this ordinance, some of which will be undeserved. Before long, we will be granting exceptions to all manner of other city ordinances. If we are to prevent anarchy in our city, we must deny the Senior Guild's request.

The city council member's argument is most vulnerable to criticism on the grounds that it

(A) distorts an argument and then attacks this distorted argument

(B) dismisses a claim because of its source rather than because of its content

(C) presumes, without sufficient warrant, that one event will lead to a particular causal sequence of events

(D) contains premises that contradict one another

(E) fails to make a needed distinction between deserved exceptions and undeserved ones

9. Physician: In comparing our country with two other countries of roughly the same population size, I found that even though we face the same dietary, bacterial, and stress-related causes of ulcers as they do, prescriptions for ulcer medicines in all socioeconomic strata are much rarer here than in those two countries. It's clear that we suffer significantly fewer ulcers, per capita, than they do.

Which one of the following, if true, most strengthens the physician's argument?

(A) The two countries that were compared with the physician's country had approximately the same ulcer rates as each other.

(B) The people of the physician's country have a cultural tradition of stoicism that encourages them to ignore physical ailments rather than to seek remedies for them.

(C) Several other countries not covered in the physician's comparisons have more prescriptions for ulcer medication than does the physician's country.

(D) A person in the physician's country who is suffering from ulcers is just as likely to obtain a prescription for the ailment as is a person suffering from ulcers in one of the other two countries.

(E) The physician's country has a much better system for reporting the number of prescriptions of a given type that are obtained each year than is present in either of the other two countries.

10. Columnist: The failure of bicyclists to obey traffic regulations is a causal factor in more than one quarter of the traffic accidents involving bicycles. Since inadequate bicycle safety equipment is also a factor in more than a quarter of such accidents, bicyclists are at least partially responsible for more than half of the traffic accidents involving bicycles.

The columnist's reasoning is flawed in that it

(A) presumes, without providing justification, that motorists are a factor in less than half of the traffic accidents involving bicycles

(B) improperly infers the presence of a causal connection on the basis of a correlation

(C) fails to consider the possibility that more than one factor may contribute to a given accident

(D) fails to provide the source of the figures it cites

(E) fails to consider that the severity of injuries to bicyclists from traffic accidents can vary widely

GO ON TO THE NEXT PAGE.

11. Many vaccines create immunity to viral diseases by introducing a certain portion of the disease-causing virus's outer coating into the body. Exposure to that part of a virus is as effective as exposure to the whole virus in stimulating production of antibodies that will subsequently recognize and kill the whole virus. To create a successful vaccine of this type, doctors must first isolate in the disease-causing virus a portion that stimulates antibody production. Now that a suitable portion of the virus that causes hepatitis E has been isolated, doctors claim they can produce a vaccine that will produce permanent immunity to that disease.

Which one of the following, if true, most strongly counters the doctors' claim?

(A) Most of the people who contract hepatitis E are young adults who were probably exposed to the virus in childhood also.

(B) Some laboratory animals exposed to one strain of the hepatitis virus developed immunity to all strains of the virus.

(C) Researchers developed a successful vaccine for another strain of hepatitis, hepatitis B, after first isolating the virus that causes it.

(D) The virus that causes hepatitis E is very common in some areas, so the number of people exposed to that virus is likely to be quite high in those areas.

(E) Many children who are exposed to viruses that cause childhood diseases such as chicken pox never develop those diseases.

12. Editorial: To qualify as an effective law, as opposed to merely an impressive declaration, a command must be backed up by an effective enforcement mechanism. That is why societies have police. The power of the police to enforce a society's laws makes those laws effective. But there is currently no international police force. Hence, what is called "international law" is not effective law.

Which one of the following is an assumption required by the editorial's argument?

(A) No one obeys a command unless mechanisms exist to compel obedience.

(B) If an international police force were established, then so-called international law would become effective law.

(C) The only difference between international law and the law of an individual society is the former's lack of an effective enforcement mechanism.

(D) The primary purpose of a police force is to enforce the laws of the society.

(E) Only an international police force could effectively enforce international law.

13. Art historian: More than any other genre of representational painting, still-life painting lends itself naturally to art whose goal is the artist's self-expression, rather than merely the reflection of a preexisting external reality. This is because in still-life painting, the artist invariably chooses, modifies, and arranges the objects to be painted. Thus, the artist has considerably more control over the composition and subject of a still-life painting than over those of a landscape painting or portrait, for example.

Which one of the following is most strongly supported by the art historian's statements?

(A) Landscape painting and portraiture are the artistic genres that lend themselves most naturally to the mere reflection of a preexisting external reality.

(B) The only way in which artists control the composition and subject of a painting is by choosing, modifying, and arranging the objects to be represented in that painting.

(C) Nonrepresentational painting does not lend itself as naturally as still-life painting does to the goal of the artist's self-expression.

(D) In genres of representational painting other than still-life painting, the artist does not always choose, modify, and arrange the objects to be painted.

(E) When painting a portrait, artists rarely attempt to express themselves through the choice, modification, or arrangement of the background elements against which the subject of the portrait is painted.

14. Food labeling regulation: Food of a type that does not ordinarily contain fat cannot be labeled "nonfat" unless most people mistakenly believe the food ordinarily contains fat. If most people mistakenly believe that a food ordinarily contains fat, the food may be labeled "nonfat" if the label also states that the food ordinarily contains no fat.

Which one of the following situations violates the food labeling regulation?

(A) Although most people know that bran flakes do not normally contain fat, Lester's Bran Flakes are not labeled "nonfat."

(B) Although most people are aware that lasagna ordinarily contains fat, Lester's Lasagna, which contains no fat, is not labeled "nonfat."

(C) Although most garlic baguettes contain fat, Lester's Garlic Baguettes are labeled "nonfat."

(D) Although most people are aware that applesauce does not ordinarily contain fat, Lester's Applesauce is labeled "nonfat."

(E) Although most people mistakenly believe that salsa ordinarily contains fat, the label on Lester's Zesty Salsa says "This product, like all salsas, is nonfat."

GO ON TO THE NEXT PAGE.

15. Medical ethicist: Assuming there is a reasonable chance for a cure, it is acceptable to offer experimental treatments for a disease to patients who suffer from extreme symptoms of that disease. Such patients are best able to weigh a treatment's risks against the benefits of a cure. Therefore, it is never acceptable to offer experimental treatments to patients who experience no extreme symptoms of the relevant disease.

The flawed reasoning in which one of the following is most similar to the flawed reasoning in the medical ethicist's argument?

(A) Even a geological engineer with a background in economics can lose money investing in mineral extraction. So, those who are less knowledgeable about geology or economics should not expect to make money in every investment in mineral extraction.

(B) One is always in a better position to judge whether an automobile would be worth its cost if one has test-driven that automobile. Therefore, if an automobile proves to be not worth its cost, it is likely that it was not test-driven.

(C) Someone born and raised in a country, who has lived abroad and then returned, is exceptionally qualified to judge the merits of living in that country. That is why someone who has not lived in that country should not form judgments about the merits of living there.

(D) One can never eliminate all of the risks of daily life, and even trying to avoid every risk in life is costly. Therefore, anyone who is reasonable will accept some of the risks of daily life.

(E) Almost any industrial development will have unwelcome environmental side effects. Therefore, it is not worthwhile to weigh the costs of potential environmental side effects since such side effects are unavoidable.

16. Critic: As modern methods of communication and transportation have continued to improve, the pace of life today has become faster than ever before. This speed has created feelings of impermanence and instability, making us feel as if we never have enough time to achieve what we want—or at least what we think we want.

The critic's statements most closely conform to which one of the following assessments?

(A) The fast pace of modern life has made it difficult for people to achieve their goals.

(B) The disadvantages of technological progress often outweigh the advantages.

(C) Changes in people's feelings about life can result from technological changes.

(D) The perception of impermanence in contemporary life makes it more difficult for people to know what they want.

(E) Changes in people's feelings fuel the need for technological advancement.

17. Consumer: If you buy a watch at a department store and use it only in the way it was intended to be used, but the watch stops working the next day, then the department store will refund your money. So by this very reasonable standard, Bingham's Jewelry Store should give me a refund even though they themselves are not a department store, since the watch I bought from them stopped working the very next day.

The consumer's argument relies on the assumption that

(A) one should not sell something unless one expects that it will function in the way it was originally designed to function

(B) a watch bought at a department store and a watch bought at Bingham's Jewelry Store can both be expected to keep working for about the same length of time if each is used only as it was intended to be used

(C) a seller should refund the money that was paid for a product if the product does not perform as the purchaser expected it to perform

(D) the consumer did not use the watch in a way contrary to the way it was intended to be used

(E) the watch that was purchased from Bingham's Jewelry Store was not a new watch

GO ON TO THE NEXT PAGE.

18. A study found that patients referred by their doctors to psychotherapists practicing a new experimental form of therapy made more progress with respect to their problems than those referred to psychotherapists practicing traditional forms of therapy. Therapists practicing the new form of therapy, therefore, are more effective than therapists practicing traditional forms.

Which one of the following most accurately describes a flaw in the argument?

(A) It ignores the possibility that therapists trained in traditional forms of therapy use the same techniques in treating their patients as therapists trained in the new form of therapy do.

(B) It ignores the possibility that the patients referred to therapists practicing the new form of therapy had problems more amenable to treatment than did those referred to therapists practicing traditional forms.

(C) It presumes, without providing justification, that any psychotherapist trained in traditional forms of therapy is untrained in the new form of therapy.

(D) It ignores the possibility that therapists practicing the new form of therapy systematically differ from therapists practicing traditional forms of therapy with regard to some personality attribute relevant to effective treatment.

(E) It presumes, without providing justification, that the personal rapport between therapist and patient has no influence on the effectiveness of the treatment the patient receives.

19. Essayist: One of the drawbacks of extreme personal and political freedom is that free choices are often made for the worst. To expect people to thrive when they are given the freedom to make unwise decisions is frequently unrealistic. Once people see the destructive consequences of extreme freedom, they may prefer to establish totalitarian political regimes that allow virtually no freedom. Thus, one should not support political systems that allow extreme freedom.

Which one of the following principles, if valid, most helps to justify the essayist's reasoning?

(A) One should not support any political system that will inevitably lead to the establishment of a totalitarian political regime.

(B) One should not expect everyone to thrive even in a political system that maximizes people's freedom in the long run.

(C) One should support only those political systems that give people the freedom to make wise choices.

(D) One should not support any political system whose destructive consequences could lead people to prefer totalitarian political regimes.

(E) One should not support any political system that is based on unrealistic expectations about people's behavior under that system.

GO ON TO THE NEXT PAGE.

20. Ethicist: Every moral action is the keeping of an agreement, and keeping an agreement is nothing more than an act of securing mutual benefit. Clearly, however, not all instances of agreement-keeping are moral actions. Therefore, some acts of securing mutual benefit are not moral actions.

The pattern of reasoning in which one of the following arguments is most similar to that in the ethicist's argument?

(A) All calculators are kinds of computers, and all computers are devices for automated reasoning. However, not all devices for automated reasoning are calculators. Therefore, some devices for automated reasoning are not computers.

(B) All exercise is beneficial, and all things that are beneficial promote health. However, not all things that are beneficial are forms of exercise. Therefore, some exercise does not promote health.

(C) All metaphors are comparisons, and not all comparisons are surprising. However, all metaphors are surprising. Therefore, some comparisons are not metaphors.

(D) All architecture is design and all design is art. However, not all design is architecture. Therefore, some art is not design.

(E) All books are texts, and all texts are documents. However, not all texts are books. Therefore, some documents are not books.

21. Sociologist: The more technologically advanced a society is, the more marked its members' resistance to technological innovations. This is not surprising, because the more technologically advanced a society is, the more aware its members are of technology's drawbacks. Specifically, people realize that sophisticated technologies deeply affect the quality of human relations.

The claim that the more technologically advanced a society is, the more aware its members are of technology's drawbacks plays which one of the following roles in the sociologist's argument?

(A) It is a conclusion supported by the claim that people realize that sophisticated technologies deeply affect the quality of human relations.

(B) It is offered as an explanation of why people's resistance to technological innovations is more marked the more technologically advanced the society in which they live is.

(C) It is a premise in support of the claim that the quality of human relations in technologically advanced societies is extremely poor.

(D) It is a generalization based on the claim that the more people resist technological innovations, the more difficult it is for them to adjust to those innovations.

(E) It is an example presented to illustrate the claim that resistance to technological innovations deeply affects the quality of human relations.

22. To win democratic elections that are not fully subsidized by the government, nonwealthy candidates must be supported by wealthy patrons. This makes plausible the belief that these candidates will compromise their views to win that support. But since the wealthy are dispersed among the various political parties in roughly equal proportion to their percentage in the overall population, this belief is false.

The argument is vulnerable to criticism on the grounds that it fails to consider that

(A) the primary function of political parties in democracies whose governments do not subsidize elections might not be to provide a means of negating the influence of wealth on elections

(B) in democracies in which elections are not fully subsidized by the government, positions endorsed by political parties might be much less varied than the positions taken by candidates

(C) in democracies, government-subsidized elections ensure that the views expressed by the people who run for office might not be overly influenced by the opinions of the wealthiest people in those countries

(D) in democracies in which elections are not fully subsidized by the government, it might be no easier for a wealthy person to win an election than it is for a nonwealthy person to win an election

(E) a democracy in which candidates do not compromise their views in order to be elected to office might have other flaws

23. In modern "brushless" car washes, cloth strips called mitters have replaced brushes. Mitters are easier on most cars' finishes than brushes are. This is especially important with the new clear-coat finishes found on many cars today, which are more easily scratched than older finishes are.

Which one of the following is most strongly supported by the statements above, if those statements are true?

(A) When car washes all used brushes rather than mitters, there were more cars on the road with scratched finishes than there are today.

(B) Modern "brushless" car washes were introduced as a direct response to the use of clear-coat finishes on cars.

(C) Modern "brushless" car washes usually do not produce visible scratches on cars with older finishes.

(D) Brushes are more effective than mitters and are preferred for cleaning cars with older finishes.

(E) More cars in use today have clear-coat finishes rather than older finishes.

GO ON TO THE NEXT PAGE.

24. It is widely believed that lancelets—small, primitive sea animals—do not have hearts. Each lancelet has a contracting vessel, but this vessel is considered an artery rather than a heart. However, this vessel is indeed a heart. After all, it strongly resembles the structure of the heart of certain other sea animals. Moreover, the muscular contractions in the lancelet's vessel closely resemble the muscular contractions of other animals' hearts.

The argument's conclusion follows logically if which one of the following is assumed?

(A) Only animals that have contracting vessels have hearts.
(B) Some primitive animals other than lancelets have what is widely held to be a heart.
(C) A vessel whose structure and actions closely resemble those of other animal hearts is a heart.
(D) For a vessel in an animal to be properly considered a heart, that vessel must undergo muscular contractions.
(E) No animal that has a heart lacks an artery.

25. Manager: I recommend that our company reconsider the decision to completely abandon our allegedly difficult-to-use computer software and replace it companywide with a new software package advertised as more flexible and easier to use. Several other companies in our region officially replaced the software we currently use with the new package, and while their employees can all use the new software, unofficially many continue to use their former software as much as possible.

Which one of the following is most strongly supported by the manager's statements?

(A) The current company software is as flexible as the proposed new software package.
(B) The familiarity that employees have with a computer software package is a more important consideration in selecting software than flexibility or initial ease of use.
(C) The employees of the manager's company would find that the new software package lacks some of the capabilities of the present software.
(D) Adopting the new software package would create two classes of employees, those who can use it and those who cannot.
(E) Many of the employees in the manager's company would not prefer the new software package to the software currently in use.

STOP
IF YOU FINISH BEFORE TIME IS CALLED, YOU MAY CHECK YOUR WORK ON THIS SECTION ONLY. DO NOT WORK ON ANY OTHER SECTION IN THE TEST.

SECTION IV

Time—35 minutes

26 Questions

Directions: The questions in this section are based on the reasoning contained in brief statements or passages. For some questions, more than one of the choices could conceivably answer the question. However, you are to choose the best answer; that is, the response that most accurately and completely answers the question. You should not make assumptions that are by commonsense standards implausible, superfluous, or incompatible with the passage. After you have chosen the best answer, blacken the corresponding space on your answer sheet.

1. Advertisement: GreenBank gives all of its customers unlimited free automatic teller machine (ATM) use. TekBank charges 25 cents for each ATM transaction. So, clearly, it costs more to bank at TekBank than at GreenBank.

The reasoning in the advertisement's argument is misleading in that the argument

(A) bases a recommendation solely on economic factors without considering whether other factors are more important

(B) presents claims that are irrelevant to the issue under discussion in order to divert attention away from that issue

(C) draws a conclusion about the overall cost of a service solely on the basis of a claim about the cost of one component of that service

(D) concludes that a component of a service must have a property that the service as a whole possesses

(E) concludes that a claim must be false because of the mere absence of evidence in its favor

2. Klein: The fact that the amount of matter that we have found in our galaxy is only one-tenth of what Einstein's theory predicts gives us good reason for abandoning his view.

Brown: Given the great successes of Einstein's theory, it would be better to conclude that most of the matter in our galaxy has not yet been found.

On the basis of their statements, Klein and Brown are committed to disagreeing over the truth of which one of the following statements?

(A) Scientists have found only one-tenth of the matter that Einstein's theory predicts.

(B) Einstein's theory has achieved many successes.

(C) It is possible to determine the amount of matter in our galaxy without relying on Einstein's theory.

(D) The failure to find all of the matter predicted by Einstein's theory should lead us to abandon it.

(E) Scientists are able to accurately judge the amount of matter that has been found in our galaxy.

3. When chimpanzees become angry at other chimpanzees, they often engage in what primatologists call "threat gestures": grunting, spitting, or making abrupt, upsweeping arm movements. Chimpanzees also sometimes attack other chimpanzees out of anger. However, when they do attack, they almost never take time to make threat gestures first. And, conversely, threat gestures are rarely followed by physical attacks.

Which one of the following, if true, most helps to explain the information about how often threat gestures are accompanied by physical attacks?

(A) Chimpanzees engage in threat gestures when they are angry in order to preserve or enhance social status.

(B) Making threat gestures helps chimpanzees vent aggressive feelings and thereby avoid physical aggression.

(C) Threat gestures and physical attacks are not the only means by which chimpanzees display aggression.

(D) Chimpanzees often respond to other chimpanzees' threat gestures with threat gestures of their own.

(E) The chimpanzees that most often make threat gestures are the ones that least often initiate physical attacks.

GO ON TO THE NEXT PAGE.

4. The Magno-Blanket is probably able to relieve arthritic pain in older dogs. A hospital study of people suffering from severe joint pain found that 76 percent of those who were treated with magnets reported reduced pain after just 3 weeks. Dogs and humans have similar physiologies and the Magno-Blanket brings magnets into the same proximity to the dog's joints as they were to patients' joints in the hospital study.

Which one of the following, if true, most strengthens the argument?

(A) The Magno-Blanket is likely to be effective on cats and other pets as well if it is effective at reducing joint pain in arthritic dogs.
(B) Magnets have been shown to be capable of intensifying the transmission of messages from people's nerve cells to their brains.
(C) There are currently fewer means of safely alleviating arthritic pain in dogs than in humans.
(D) The patients in the hospital study suffering from severe joint pain who, after being treated with magnets, did not report reduced pain tended not to be those suffering from the most severe pain.
(E) Most of the patients in the hospital study suffering from severe joint pain who received a placebo rather than treatment with magnets did not report reduced pain.

5. Some people believe that advertising is socially pernicious—it changes consumers' preferences, thereby manipulating people into wanting things they would not otherwise want. However, classes in music and art appreciation change people's preferences for various forms of art and music, and there is nothing wrong with these classes. Therefore, _____.

Which one of the following most logically completes the argument?

(A) consumers would still want most of the things they want even if they were not advertised
(B) the social perniciousness of advertising is not limited to its effect on people's preferences
(C) the fact that advertising changes consumers' preferences does not establish that it is bad
(D) if advertising changes consumers' preferences, it generally does so in a positive way
(E) it is not completely accurate to say that advertising changes people's preferences

6. Many high school students interested in journalism think of journalism careers as involving glamorous international news gathering. But most journalists cover primarily local news, and the overwhelming majority of reporters work for local newspapers. Thus, high school career counselors should tell students who are interested in journalism what life is like for a typical reporter, that is, a reporter for a local newspaper.

Which one of the following principles would, if valid, most help to justify the reasoning above?

(A) High school students who have misconceptions about a career should not be encouraged to pursue that career.
(B) One should not encourage people to seek unattainable goals if one wishes to maximize those people's chances to lead happy lives.
(C) Students who are choosing a career should be encouraged to try to reach the top levels of that career.
(D) A career counselor should try to disabuse students of any unrealistic conceptions they may have about the likely consequences of choosing a particular career.
(E) Career counselors are not doing their job properly if they encourage people to make career choices that are initially appealing but that those people will later regret.

7. More pedestrian injuries occur at crosswalks marked by both striping on the roadway and flashing lights than occur at crosswalks not so marked. Obviously these so-called safety features are a waste of taxpayer money.

The reasoning in the argument is most vulnerable to criticism because the argument

(A) fails to consider that crosswalks marked by both striping and flashing lights are marked in this way precisely because they are the most dangerous ones
(B) takes for granted that safety features that fail to reduce the number of injuries are a waste of taxpayer money
(C) presumes that there are less expensive features that will reduce the number of pedestrian injuries just as effectively as striping and flashing lights
(D) takes for granted that crosswalks with both striping and flashing lights have no other safety features
(E) fails to consider that, in accidents involving pedestrians and cars, the injuries to pedestrians are nearly always more serious than the injuries to occupants of cars

GO ON TO THE NEXT PAGE.

8. John of Worcester, an English monk, recorded the sighting, on December 8, 1128, of two unusually large sunspots. Five days later a brilliant aurora borealis (northern lights) was observed in southern Korea. Sunspot activity is typically followed by the appearance of an aurora borealis, after a span of time that averages five days. Thus, the Korean sighting helps to confirm John of Worcester's sighting.

Which one of the following, if true, most strengthens the argument?

(A) An aurora borealis can sometimes occur even when there has been no significant sunspot activity in the previous week.

(B) Chinese sources recorded the sighting of sunspots more than 1000 years before John of Worcester did.

(C) Only heavy sunspot activity could have resulted in an aurora borealis viewable at a latitude as low as that of Korea.

(D) Because it is impossible to view sunspots with the naked eye under typical daylight conditions, the sighting recorded by John of Worcester would have taken place under unusual weather conditions such as fog or thin clouds.

(E) John of Worcester's account included a drawing of the sunspots, which could be the earliest illustration of sunspot activity.

9. Anyone believing that no individual can have an effect on society's future will as a result feel too helpless to act to change society for the better. Thus, anyone who wants to improve society should reject the belief that its future will be determined entirely by vast historical forces that individuals are powerless to change.

Which one of the following principles, if valid, most helps to justify the argument?

(A) Anyone who believes that individuals can have an effect on society's future should act to change society for the better.

(B) No one who rejects the belief that society's future will be determined by vast historical forces should believe that individuals cannot have an effect on it.

(C) Anyone who feels too helpless to act to change society for the better should reject the belief that its future will be determined by vast historical forces that individuals are powerless to change.

(D) No one who wants to improve society should accept any belief that makes him or her feel too helpless to act to change society for the better.

(E) Each individual should act to improve society if individuals in general feel powerless in the face of vast historical forces.

10. Company president: Whenever you subcontract the manufacturing of a product, you lose some control over the quality of that product. We do subcontract some manufacturing, but only with companies that maintain complete control over the quality of the products they supply.

Which one of the following can be properly inferred from the company president's statements?

(A) When the president's company subcontracts manufacturing of a product, it does not allow the subcontractor to further subcontract manufacturing of that product.

(B) Companies that subcontract the manufacturing of products are often disappointed in the quality of those products.

(C) The company president insists on having as much control as possible over the quality of the company's products.

(D) When consumers know that a product has been manufactured by a subcontractor, they are generally dubious about the product's quality.

(E) When a company manufactures some products in-house and subcontracts the manufacturing of others, the products made in-house will be of uniformly better quality.

11. Secondary school students achieve broad mastery of the curriculum if they are taught with methods appropriate to their learning styles and they devote significant effort to their studies. Thus, if such broad mastery is not achieved by the students in a particular secondary school, those students are not being taught with methods appropriate to their learning styles.

The conclusion can be properly drawn if which one of the following is assumed?

(A) As long as secondary school students are taught with methods appropriate to their learning styles, they will devote significant effort to their studies.

(B) Even if secondary school students are taught with methods appropriate to their learning styles, they will not achieve broad mastery of the curriculum if they do not devote significant effort to their studies.

(C) Secondary school students do not achieve broad mastery of the curriculum if they are not taught with methods appropriate to their learning styles.

(D) Teaching secondary school students with methods appropriate to their learning styles does not always result in broad mastery of the curriculum by those students.

(E) Secondary school students who devote significant effort to their studies do not always achieve broad mastery of the curriculum.

GO ON TO THE NEXT PAGE.

12. Consumer advocate: Even if one can of fruit or vegetables weighs more than another, the heavier can does not necessarily contain more food. Canned fruits and vegetables are typically packed in water, which can make up more than half the total weight of the can's contents. And nothing stops unscrupulous canning companies from including more water per can than others include.

Which one of the following most accurately expresses the conclusion drawn in the consumer advocate's argument?

(A) The heavier of two cans of fruit or vegetables does not necessarily contain more food than the lighter of the two cans contains.

(B) The weight of the water in a can of fruit or vegetables can be more than half the total weight of the can's contents.

(C) Nothing stops unscrupulous canning companies from including more water per can than others include.

(D) Some canning companies include less food in cans of a given weight than others include.

(E) The heavier of two cans of fruits or vegetables may include more water than the lighter of the two cans contains.

13. Several three-year-olds who had learned to count to ten were trying to learn their telephone numbers. Although each child was familiar with the names of all the digits, no child could remember his or her phone number. Their teacher then taught each child a song whose lyrics contained his or her phone number. By the end of the day the children could remember their telephone numbers.

The situation described above best illustrates which one of the following propositions?

(A) There are some things that children cannot learn without the aid of songs.

(B) Familiarity with a concept is not always sufficient for knowing the words used to express it.

(C) Mnemonic devices such as songs are better than any other method for memorizing numbers.

(D) Children can learn to count without understanding the meaning of numbers.

(E) Songs are useful in helping children remember the order in which familiar words occur.

14. Some theorists argue that literary critics should strive to be value-neutral in their literary criticism. These theorists maintain that by exposing the meaning of literary works without evaluating them, critics will enable readers to make their own judgments about the works' merits. But literary criticism cannot be completely value-neutral. Thus, some theorists are mistaken about what is an appropriate goal for literary criticism.

The argument's conclusion follows logically if which one of the following is assumed?

(A) Any critic who is able to help readers make their own judgments about literary works' merits should strive to produce value-neutral criticism.

(B) If it is impossible to produce completely value-neutral literary criticism, then critics should not even try to be value-neutral.

(C) Critics are more likely to provide criticisms of the works they like than to provide criticisms of the works they dislike.

(D) The less readers understand the meaning of a literary work, the less capable they will be of evaluating that work's merits.

(E) Critics who try to avoid rendering value judgments about the works they consider tend to influence readers' judgments less than other critics do.

GO ON TO THE NEXT PAGE.

15. Amoebas, like human beings, generally withdraw from stimuli that cause them physical damage. Humans do this because such stimuli cause them pain. Thus all microscopic organisms must also be capable of feeling pain.

Which one of the following exhibits flawed reasoning most similar to that exhibited by the argument above?

(A) Poets, like people under hypnosis, frequently use language in odd, incomprehensible ways. People under hypnosis do this because their inhibitions are lower than those of most people. Thus all artists must have lower inhibitions than most people have.

(B) Like nonprofit organizations, corporations usually provide some free public services. Nonprofit organizations do this solely because of their members' desire to make the world a better place. Thus this is probably also the main motive of most corporations.

(C) Most professional athletes practice regularly for the same reason. Professional boxers spend several hours a day practicing in order to excel in competition. Thus professional skaters probably also practice in order to excel in competition.

(D) Predatory birds, like many predatory animals, are generally solitary hunters. Some predatory mammals hunt alone because there is not enough food to support a pack of them in one area. Thus hawks, which are predatory birds, probably hunt alone.

(E) Hiking trails in British Columbia, like those in New Mexico, are concentrated in mountainous regions. In New Mexico this is partly because low-lying areas are too hot and arid for comfortable hiking. Thus hikers must also feel less comfortable hiking in low-lying areas of British Columbia.

16. Zoologist: In the Lake Champlain area, as the North American snowshoe hare population grows, so do the populations of its predators. As predator numbers increase, the hares seek food in more heavily forested areas, which contain less food, and so the hare population declines. Predator populations thus decline, the hare population starts to increase, and the cycle begins again. Yet these facts alone cannot explain why populations of snowshoe hares everywhere behave simultaneously in this cyclical way. Since the hare population cycle is well correlated with the regular cycle of sunspot activity, that activity is probably a causal factor as well.

Each of the following, if true, supports the zoologist's reasoning EXCEPT:

(A) Reproduction in predator populations increases when sunspot activity indirectly affects hormonal processes associated with reproduction.

(B) Local weather patterns that can affect species' population changes can occur both in the presence of sunspot activity and in its absence.

(C) Brighter light during sunspot activity subtly but significantly improves the ability of predators to detect and capture hares.

(D) The variation from cycle to cycle in the magnitude of the highs and lows in snowshoe hare populations is highly correlated with variations from cycle to cycle in the intensity of highs and lows in sunspot activity.

(E) Sunspot activity is correlated with increases and decreases in the nutritional value of vegetation eaten by the hares.

GO ON TO THE NEXT PAGE.

17. Science teacher: In any nation, a flourishing national scientific community is essential to a successful economy. For such a community to flourish requires that many young people become excited enough about science that they resolve to become professional scientists. Good communication between scientists and the public is necessary to spark that excitement.

The science teacher's statements provide the most support for which one of the following?

(A) If scientists communicate with the public, many young people will become excited enough about science to resolve to become professional scientists.

(B) The extent to which a national scientific community flourishes depends principally on the number of young people who become excited enough about science to resolve to become professional scientists.

(C) No nation can have a successful economy unless at some point scientists have communicated well with the public.

(D) It is essential to any nation's economy that most of the young people in that nation who are excited about science become professional scientists.

(E) An essential component of success in any scientific endeavor is good communication between the scientists involved in that endeavor and the public.

18. A recent magazine article argued that most companies that do not already own videoconferencing equipment would be wasting their money if they purchased it. However, this is clearly not true. In a recent survey of businesses that have purchased such equipment, most of the respondents stated that the videoconferencing equipment was well worth its cost.

The reasoning in the argument is flawed in that the argument

(A) concludes that something is worth its cost merely on the grounds that many businesses have purchased it

(B) takes a condition sufficient to justify purchasing costly equipment to be necessary in order for the cost of the purchase to be justified

(C) rejects a position merely on the grounds that an inadequate argument has been given for it

(D) relies on a sample that it is reasonable to suppose is unrepresentative of the group about which it draws its conclusion

(E) confuses the cost of an item with its value to the purchaser

19. Auditor: XYZ, a construction company, purchased 20 new trucks 3 years ago, and there is no record of any of those trucks being sold last year. Records indicate, however, that XYZ sold off all of its diesel-powered trucks last year. We can thus conclude that none of the 20 trucks purchased 3 years ago were diesel powered.

Which one of the following is an assumption required by the auditor's reasoning?

(A) All of the trucks that XYZ sold last year were diesel powered.

(B) XYZ did not purchase any used trucks 3 years ago.

(C) XYZ did not purchase any new trucks since it purchased the 20 trucks 3 years ago.

(D) None of the 20 trucks was sold before last year.

(E) XYZ no longer owns any trucks that it purchased more than 3 years ago.

20. Taylor: From observing close friends and relatives, it is clear to me that telepathy is indeed possible between people with close psychic ties. The amazing frequency with which a good friend or family member knows what one is thinking or feeling cannot be dismissed as mere coincidence.

Taylor's reasoning is most vulnerable to criticism on the grounds that it

(A) is based on too small a sample to yield a reliable conclusion

(B) fails to address a highly plausible alternative explanation for all instances of the observed phenomenon

(C) relies crucially on an illegitimate appeal to emotion

(D) presumes, without providing justification, that one can never know what a stranger is thinking or feeling

(E) appeals to a premise one would accept only if one already accepted the truth of the conclusion

GO ON TO THE NEXT PAGE.

21. Prolonged exposure to sulfur fumes permanently damages one's sense of smell. In one important study, 100 workers from sulfur-emitting factories and a control group of 100 workers from other occupations were asked to identify a variety of chemically reproduced scents, including those of foods, spices, and flowers. On average, the factory workers successfully identified 10 percent of the scents compared to 50 percent for the control group.

Each of the following, if true, weakens the argument EXCEPT:

(A) The chemicals used in the study closely but not perfectly reproduced the corresponding natural scents.

(B) The subjects in the study were tested in the environments where they usually work.

(C) Most members of the control group had participated in several earlier studies that involved the identification of scents.

(D) Every sulfur-emitting factory with workers participating in the study also emits other noxious fumes.

(E) Because of the factories' locations, the factory workers were less likely than those in the control group to have been exposed to many of the scents used in the study.

22. Principle: Anyone who has more than one overdue book out on loan from the library at the same time must be fined if some of the overdue books are not children's books and that person has previously been fined for overdue books.

Application: Since three of the books that Kessler currently has out on loan from the library are overdue, Kessler must be fined.

Which one of the following, if true, justifies the above application of the principle?

(A) Some of the books that Kessler currently has out on loan from the library are not children's books, and Kessler was fined last year for returning a children's book late.

(B) One of the overdue books that Kessler currently has out on loan from the library is a novel for adults, and Kessler was fined last year for returning this book late.

(C) None of the books that Kessler currently has out on loan from the library is a children's book and in previous years Kessler has returned various books late.

(D) Kessler was fined by the library several times in the past for overdue books, but none of the overdue books for which Kessler was fined were children's books.

(E) Kessler has never before been fined for overdue books, but the three overdue books that Kessler currently has out on loan from the library are months overdue.

23. Medical school professor: Most malpractice suits arise out of patients' perceptions that their doctors are acting negligently or carelessly. Many doctors now regard medicine as a science rather than an art, and are less compassionate as a result. Harried doctors sometimes treat patients rudely, discourage them from asking questions, or patronize them. Lawsuits could be avoided if doctors learned to listen better to patients. Unfortunately, certain economic incentives encourage doctors to treat patients rudely.

The medical school professor's statements, if true, most strongly support which one of the following?

(A) Economic incentives to treat patients rudely are the main cause of doctors being sued for malpractice.

(B) The economic incentives in the health care system encourage doctors to regard medicine as a science rather than as an art.

(C) Malpractice suits brought against doctors are, for the most part, unjustified.

(D) The scientific outlook in medicine should be replaced by an entirely different approach to medicine.

(E) Doctors foster, by their actions, the perception that they do not really care about their patients.

GO ON TO THE NEXT PAGE.

24. If the concrete is poured while the ground is wet, it will not form a solid foundation. If the concrete does not form a solid foundation, it will either settle unevenly or crack. So if the concrete settles evenly, either it was poured while the ground was dry or it will crack.

Which one of the following arguments is most closely parallel in its reasoning to the reasoning in the argument above?

(A) The film will not be properly exposed if the camera is not working properly. If the film is not properly exposed, then the photograph will be either blurred or dark. So if the photograph is not blurred, either the camera is working properly or the photograph will be dark.

(B) If the camera is working properly, the photograph will not be blurred. The photograph will be blurred if the film is either not properly exposed or not properly developed. So if the camera is working properly, the film will be both properly exposed and properly developed.

(C) The photograph will either be blurred or dark if the camera is not working properly. This photograph is not blurred, so if the photograph is not dark, the camera is working properly.

(D) If the camera is working properly, the film will be properly exposed. If either the film is properly exposed or corrections are made during the developing process, the photograph will not be dark. So if the camera is working properly, the photograph will not be dark.

(E) The camera will work properly only if the film is properly exposed. But the film cannot be properly exposed if there is either not enough or too much light. So the camera will not work properly if there is either too much or not enough light.

25. New evidence indicates that recent property development bordering a national park has not adversely affected the park's wildlife. On the contrary, a comparison of the most recent survey of the park's wildlife with one conducted just prior to the development shows that the amount of wildlife has in fact increased over the intervening decade. Moreover, the park's resources can support its current wildlife populations without strain.

Which one of the following, if true, most strengthens the argument?

(A) While both surveys found the same species of animals in the park, the more recent survey found greater numbers of animals belonging to each species.

(B) The more recent survey was taken in the summer, when the diversity of wildlife in the park is at its greatest.

(C) Migration of wildlife into the park from the adjacent developing areas has increased animal populations to levels beyond those that the resources of the park could have supported a decade ago.

(D) The most recent techniques for surveying wildlife are better at locating difficult-to-find animals than were older techniques.

(E) The more recent survey not only involved counting the animals found in the park but, unlike the earlier survey, also provided an inventory of the plant life found within the park.

26. As advances in medical research and technology have improved the ability of the medical profession to diagnose and treat a wide variety of illnesses and injuries, life spans have increased and overall health has improved. Yet, over the past few decades there has been a steady and significant increase in the rate of serious infections.

Which one of the following, if true, most helps to resolve the apparent discrepancy in the information above?

(A) It remains true that doctors sometimes prescribe ineffective medications due to misdiagnosis.

(B) Life spans have increased precisely because overall health has improved.

(C) The vast majority of serious infections are now curable, although many require hospitalization.

(D) As a population increases in size, there is a directly proportional increase in the number of serious infections.

(E) Modern treatments for many otherwise fatal illnesses increase the patient's susceptibility to infection.

STOP

IF YOU FINISH BEFORE TIME IS CALLED, YOU MAY CHECK YOUR WORK ON THIS SECTION ONLY. DO NOT WORK ON ANY OTHER SECTION IN THE TEST.

SECTION V

Time—35 minutes

27 Questions

Directions: Each set of questions in this section is based on a single passage or a pair of passages. The questions are to be answered on the basis of what is <u>stated</u> or <u>implied</u> in the passage or pair of passages. For some of the questions, more than one of the choices could conceivably answer the question. However, you are to choose the <u>best</u> answer; that is, the response that most accurately and completely answers the question, and blacken the corresponding space on your answer sheet.

African American painter Sam Gilliam (b. 1933) is internationally recognized as one of the foremost painters associated with the Washington Color School, a group of Color Field style painters practicing in
(5) Washington, D.C. during the 1950s and 1960s. The Color Field style was an important development in abstract art that emerged after the rise of abstract expressionism. It evolved from complex and minimally representational abstractions in the 1950s to totally
(10) nonrepresentational, simplified works of bright colors in the 1960s.

Gilliam's participation in the Color Field movement was motivated in part by his reaction to the art of his African American contemporaries, much of which was
(15) strictly representational and was intended to convey explicit political statements. Gilliam found their approach to be aesthetically conservative: the message was unmistakable, he felt, and there was little room for the expression of subtlety or ambiguity or, more
(20) importantly, the exploration of new artistic territory through experimentation and innovation. For example, one of his contemporaries worked with collage, assembling disparate bits of images from popular magazines into loosely structured compositions that
(25) depicted the period's political issues—themes such as urban life, the rural South, and African American music. Though such art was quite popular with the general public, Gilliam was impatient with its straightforward, literal approach to representation.
(30) In its place he sought an artistic form that was more expressive than a painted figure or a political slogan, more evocative of the complexity of human experience in general, and of the African American experience in particular. In this he represented a view that was then
(35) rare among African American artists.

Gilliam's highly experimental paintings epitomized his refusal to conform to the public's expectation that African American artists produce explicitly political art. His early experiments included
(40) pouring paint onto stained canvases and folding canvases over onto themselves. Then around 1965 Gilliam became the first painter to introduce the idea of the unsupported canvas. Partially inspired by the sight of neighbors hanging laundry on clotheslines,
(45) Gilliam began to drape huge pieces of loose canvas along floors and fold them up and down walls, even suspending them from ceilings, giving them a third dimension and therefore a sculptural quality. These efforts demonstrate a sensitivity to the texture of daily
(50) experience, as well as the ability to generate tension by juxtaposing conceptual opposites—such as surface and depth or chaos and control—to form a cohesive whole. In this way, Gilliam helped advance the notion that the deepest, hardest-to-capture emotions
(55) and tensions of being African American could not be represented directly, but were expressed more effectively through the creation of moods that would allow these emotions and tensions to be felt by all audiences.

1. In the passage, the author is primarily concerned with

(A) describing the motivation behind and nature of an artist's work
(B) describing the political themes that permeate an artist's work
(C) describing the evolution of an artist's style over a period of time
(D) demonstrating that a certain artist's views were rare among African American artists
(E) demonstrating that a certain artist was able to transcend his technical limitations

2. Which one of the following would come closest to exemplifying the characteristics of Gilliam's work as described in the passage?

(A) a brightly colored painting carefully portraying a man dressed in work clothes and holding a shovel in his hands
(B) a large, wrinkled canvas painted with soft, blended colors and overlaid with glued-on newspaper photographs depicting war scenes
(C) a painted abstract caricature of a group of jazz musicians waiting to perform
(D) a long unframed canvas painted with images of the sea and clouds and hung from a balcony to simulate the unfurling of sails
(E) a folded and crumpled canvas with many layers of colorful dripped and splashed paint interwoven with one another

GO ON TO THE NEXT PAGE.

3. The author mentions a collage artist in the second paragraph primarily to

(A) exemplify the style of art of the Washington Color School
(B) point out the cause of the animosity between representational artists and abstract artists
(C) establish that representational art was more popular with the general public than abstract art was
(D) illustrate the kind of art that Gilliam was reacting against
(E) show why Gilliam's art was primarily concerned with political issues

4. The passage most strongly suggests that Gilliam's attitude toward the strictly representational art of his contemporaries is which one of the following?

(A) derisive condescension
(B) open dissatisfaction
(C) whimsical dismissal
(D) careful neutrality
(E) mild approval

5. The passage says all of the following EXCEPT:

(A) Draping and folding canvases gives them a sculptural quality.
(B) Gilliam refused to satisfy the public's expectations concerning what African American art ought to address.
(C) Gilliam's views on explicitly political art were rare among African American artists.
(D) The Color Field style involved experimentation more than Gilliam believed the art of his African American contemporaries did.
(E) Everyday images such as laundry hanging out to dry are most likely to give artists great inspiration.

6. The passage suggests that Gilliam would be most likely to agree with which one of the following statements?

(A) Artists need not be concerned with aesthetic restrictions of any sort.
(B) The images portrayed in paintings, whether representational or not, should be inspired by real-life images.
(C) Artists ought to produce art that addresses the political issues of the period.
(D) The Color Field style offers artists effective ways to express the complexity of human experience.
(E) The public's expectations concerning what kind of art a certain group of artists produces should be a factor in that artist's work.

GO ON TO THE NEXT PAGE.

Passage A is from a source published in 2004 and passage B is from a source published in 2007.

Passage A

Millions of people worldwide play multiplayer online games. They each pick, say, a medieval character to play, such as a warrior. Then they might band together in quests to slay magical beasts; their
(5) avatars appear as tiny characters striding across a Tolkienesque land.

The economist Edward Castronova noticed something curious about the game he played: it had its own economy, a bustling trade in virtual goods.
(10) Players generate goods as they play, often by killing creatures for their treasure and trading it. The longer they play, the wealthier they get.

Things got even more interesting when Castronova learned about the "player auctions." Players would
(15) sometimes tire of the game and decide to sell off their virtual possessions at online auction sites.

As Castronova stared at the auction listings, he recognized with a shock what he was looking at. It was a form of currency trading! Each item had a value
(20) in the virtual currency traded in the game; when it was sold on the auction site, someone was paying cold hard cash for it. That meant that the virtual currency was worth something in real currency. Moreover, since players were killing monsters or skinning animals to
(25) sell their pelts, they were, in effect, creating wealth.

Passage B

Most multiplayer online games prohibit real-world trade in virtual items, but some actually encourage it, for example, by granting participants intellectual property rights in their creations.
(30) Although it seems intuitively the case that someone who accepts real money for the transfer of a virtual item should be taxed, what about the player who only accumulates items or virtual currency within a virtual world? Is "loot" acquired in a game taxable,
(35) as a prize or award is? And is the profit in a purely in-game trade or sale for virtual currency taxable? These are important questions, given the tax revenues at stake, and there is pressure on governments to answer them, given that the economies of some virtual
(40) worlds are comparable to those of small countries.

Most people's intuition probably would be that accumulation of assets within a game should not be taxed even though income tax applies even to noncash accessions to wealth. This article will argue that
(45) income tax law and policy support that result. Loot acquisitions in game worlds should not be treated as taxable prizes and awards, but rather should be treated like other property that requires effort to obtain, such as fish pulled from the ocean, which is taxed only
(50) upon sale. Moreover, in-game trades of virtual items should not be treated as taxable barter.

By contrast, tax doctrine and policy counsel taxation of the sale of virtual items for real currency,
and, in games that are intentionally commodified,
(55) even of in-world sales for virtual currency, regardless of whether the participant cashes out. This approach would leave entertainment value untaxed without creating a tax shelter for virtual commerce.

7. Which one of the following pairs of titles would be most appropriate for passage A and passage B, respectively?

(A) "The Economic Theories of Edward Castronova"
    "Intellectual Property Rights in Virtual Worlds"
(B) "An Economist Discovers New Economic Territory"
    "Taxing Virtual Property"
(C) "The Surprising Growth of Multiplayer Online Games"
    "Virtual Reality and the Law"
(D) "How to Make Money Playing Games"
    "Closing Virtual Tax Shelters"
(E) "A New Economic Paradigm"
    "An Untapped Source of Revenue"

8. Which one of the following most accurately expresses how the use of the phrase "skinning animals" in passage A (line 24) relates to the use of the phrase "fish pulled from the ocean" in passage B (line 49)?

(A) The former refers to an activity that generates wealth, whereas the latter refers to an activity that does not generate wealth.
(B) The former refers to an activity in an online game, whereas the latter refers to an analogous activity in the real world.
(C) The former, unlike the latter, refers to the production of a commodity that the author of passage B thinks should be taxed.
(D) The latter, unlike the former, refers to the production of a commodity that the author of passage B thinks should be taxed.
(E) Both are used as examples of activities by which game players generate wealth.

9. With regard to their respective attitudes toward commerce in virtual items, passage A differs from passage B in that passage A is more

(A) critical and apprehensive
(B) academic and dismissive
(C) intrigued and excited
(D) undecided but curious
(E) enthusiastic but skeptical

GO ON TO THE NEXT PAGE.

10. Based on what can be inferred from their titles, the relationship between which one of the following pairs of documents is most analogous to the relationship between passage A and passage B?

   (A) "Advances in Artificial Intelligence"
   "Human Psychology Applied to Robots"
   (B) "Internet Retailers Post Good Year"
   "Lawmakers Move to Tax Internet Commerce"
   (C) "New Planet Discovered in Solar System"
   "Planet or Asteroid: Scientists Debate"
   (D) "Biologists Create New Species in Lab"
   "Artificially Created Life: How Patent Law Applies"
   (E) "A Renegade Economist's Views on Taxation"
   "Candidate Runs on Unorthodox Tax Plan"

11. The passages were most likely taken from which one of the following pairs of sources?

   (A) passage A: a magazine article addressed to a general audience
   passage B: a law journal article
   (B) passage A: a technical journal for economists
   passage B: a magazine article addressed to a general audience
   (C) passage A: a science-fiction novel
   passage B: a technical journal for economists
   (D) passage A: a law journal article
   passage B: a speech delivered before a legislative body
   (E) passage A: a speech delivered before a legislative body
   passage B: a science-fiction novel

12. Which one of the following most accurately describes the relationship between the two passages?

   (A) Passage A summarizes a scholar's unanticipated discovery, while passage B proposes solutions to a problem raised by the phenomenon discovered.
   (B) Passage A explains an economic theory, while passage B identifies a practical problem resulting from that theory.
   (C) Passage A reports on a subculture, while passage B discusses the difficulty of policing that subculture.
   (D) Passage A challenges the common interpretation of a phenomenon, while passage B reaffirms that interpretation.
   (E) Passage A states a set of facts, while passage B draws theoretical consequences from those facts.

13. Based on passage B, which one of the following is a characteristic of some "games that are intentionally commodified" (line 54)?

   (A) The game allows selling real items for virtual currency.
   (B) The game allows players to trade avatars with other players.
   (C) Players of the game grow wealthier the longer they play.
   (D) Players of the game own intellectual property rights in their creations.
   (E) Players of the game can exchange one virtual currency for another virtual currency.

GO ON TO THE NEXT PAGE.

In certain fields of human endeavor, such as music, chess, and some athletic activities, the performance of the best practitioners is so outstanding, so superior even to the performance of other highly
(5) experienced individuals in the field, that some people believe some notion of innate talent must be invoked to account for this highest level of performance. Certain psychologists have supported this view with data concerning the performance of prodigies and the
(10) apparent heritability of relevant traits. They have noted, for example, that most outstanding musicians are discovered by the age of six, and they have found evidence that some of the qualities necessary for exceptional athletic performance, including superior
(15) motor coordination, speed of reflexes, and hand-eye coordination, can be inborn.

Until recently, however, little systematic research was done on the topic of superior performance, and previous estimates of the heritability of traits relevant
(20) to performance were based almost exclusively on random samples of the general population rather than on studies of highly trained superior performers as compared with the general population. Recent research in different domains of excellence suggests that
(25) exceptional performance arises predominantly from acquired complex skills and physiological adaptations, rather than from innate abilities. For example, it has been found that the most accomplished athletes show a systematic advantage in reaction time or perceptual
(30) discrimination only in their particular fields of performance, not in more general laboratory tests for these factors. Similarly, superior chess players have exceptional memory for configurations of chess pieces, but only if those configurations are typical of
(35) chess games.

The vast majority of exceptional adult performers were not exceptional as children, but started instruction early and improved their performance through sustained high-level training. Only extremely rarely is
(40) outstanding performance achieved without at least ten years of intensive, deliberate practice. With such intensive training, chess players who may not have superior innate capacities can acquire skills that circumvent basic limits on such factors as memory
(45) and the ability to process information. Recent research shows that, with the clear exception of some traits such as height, a surprisingly large number of anatomical characteristics, including aerobic capacity and the percentage of muscle fibers, show specific
(50) changes that develop from extended intense training.

The evidence does not, therefore, support the claim that a notion of innate talent must be invoked in order to account for the difference between good and outstanding performance, since it suggests instead that
(55) extended intense training, together with that level of talent common to all reasonably competent performers, may suffice to account for this difference. Since sustained intense training usually depends on an appropriate level of interest and desire, and since those

(60) who eventually become superior performers more often show early signs of exceptional interest than early evidence of unusual ability, motivational factors are more likely to be effective predictors of superior performance than is innate talent.

14. Which one of the following most accurately states the main point of the passage?

(A) Researchers have recently found that many inborn traits, including a surprising number of physical characteristics and motivational factors, can be altered through training and practice.

(B) Recent research into the origins of superior performance gives evidence that in sports, music, and some other fields of activity, anyone can achieve exceptional levels of performance with sustained intense practice and training.

(C) Contrary to previously accepted theories of the development of expertise, researchers have now shown that innate characteristics are irrelevant to the differences in performance among individual practitioners in various fields of activity.

(D) Recent research involving superior performers in various fields indicates that outstanding performance may result from adaptations due to training rather than from innate factors.

(E) Psychologists who previously attributed early childhood proficiency in such activities as music and chess to innate talent have revised their theories in light of new evidence of the effectiveness of training and practice.

15. Which one of the following most accurately represents the primary function of the final paragraph?

(A) It makes proposals for educational reform based on the evidence cited by the author.

(B) It demonstrates that two consequences of the findings regarding superior performance are at odds with one another.

(C) It recapitulates the evidence against the supposed heritability of outstanding talent and advocates a particular direction to be taken in future research on the topic.

(D) It raises and answers a possible objection to the author's view of the importance of intense training.

(E) It draws two inferences regarding the explanatory and predictive roles of possible factors in the development of superior performance.

GO ON TO THE NEXT PAGE.

16. Which one of the following can most reasonably be inferred from the passage?

   (A) In at least some fields of human endeavor, it would be difficult, or perhaps even impossible, to ascertain whether or not a superior performer with extensive training has exceptional innate talent.

   (B) Performance at the very highest level generally requires both the highest level of innate talent and many years of intensive, deliberate practice.

   (C) Exceptional innate talent is a prerequisite to exceptional performance in some fields of human endeavor but not others.

   (D) Exceptional innate talent is probably an obstacle to the development of superior performance, since such talent results in complacency.

   (E) The importance of motivation and interest in the development of superior performance shows that in some fields the production of exceptional skill does not depend in any way on innate talents of individuals.

17. Which one of the following does the passage say is usually necessary in order for one to keep up intense practice?

   (A) desire and interest
   (B) emotional support from other people
   (C) appropriate instruction at the right age
   (D) sufficient leisure time to devote to practice
   (E) self-discipline and control

18. Which one of the following most accurately describes the author's main purpose in the passage?

   (A) to illustrate the ways in which a revised theoretical model can be applied to problematic cases for which previous versions of the theory offered no plausible explanation

   (B) to argue that the evidence that was previously taken to support a particular theory in fact supports an opposing theory

   (C) to show how a body of recent research provides evidence that certain views based on earlier research are not applicable to a particular class of cases

   (D) to defend the author's new interpretation of data against probable objections that might be raised against it

   (E) to explain how a set of newly formulated abstract theoretical postulations relates to a long-standing body of experimental data in a different, but related, field of inquiry

19. The passage says that superior chess players do not have exceptional memory for which one of the following?

   (A) some sequences of moves that are typical of games other than chess

   (B) some types of complex sequences without spatial components

   (C) some chess games that have not been especially challenging

   (D) some kinds of arrangements of chess pieces

   (E) some types of factors requiring logical analysis in the absence of competition

GO ON TO THE NEXT PAGE.

Physicists are often asked why the image of an object, such as a chair, appears reversed left-to-right rather than, say, top-to-bottom when viewed in a mirror. Their answer is simply that an image viewed in
(5) a mirror appears reversed about the axis around which the viewer rotates his or her field of sight in turning from the object to its reflected image. That is, the reversal in question is relative to the position and orientation of the observer when the object is viewed
(10) directly. Since we ordinarily rotate our field of sight about a vertical axis, mirror images usually appear reversed left-to-right. This is the field-of-sight explanation.

However, some physicists offer a completely
(15) different explanation of what mirrors "do," suggesting that mirrors actually reverse things front-to-back. If we place a chair in front of a mirror we can envision how its reflected image will appear by imagining another chair in the space "inside" the mirror. The
(20) resulting reflection is identical to, and directly facing, the original chair. The most notable thing about this explanation is that it is clearly based on a false premise: the chair "inside" the mirror is not real, yet the explanation treats it as though it were as real and
(25) three dimensional as the original chair.

This explanation appeals strongly to many people, however, because it is quite successful at explaining what a mirror does—to a point. It seems natural because we are accustomed to dealing with our mental
(30) constructs of objects rather than with the primary sense perceptions on which those constructs are based. In general, we can safely presume a fairly reliable equation between our perceptions and their associated mental constructs, but mirrors are an exception. They
(35) present us with sense perceptions that we naturally construe in a way that is contrary to fact. Indeed, mirrors are "designed" to make a two-dimensional surface appear to have depth. Note, for example, that mirrors are among the few objects on which we
(40) almost never focus our eyes; rather, we look into them, with our focal lengths adjusted into the imagined space.

In addition to its intuitive appeal, the front-to-back explanation is motivated in part by the traditional desire in science to separate the observer
(45) from the phenomenon. Scientists like to think that what mirrors do should be explainable without reference to what the observer does (e.g., rotating a field of sight). However, questions about the appearances of images can be properly answered only
(50) if we consider both what mirrors do and what happens when we look into mirrors. If we remove the observer from consideration, we are no longer addressing images and appearances, because an image entails an observer and a point of view.

20. The main point of the passage is that an adequate explanation of mirror images

(A) must include two particular elements
(B) has yet to be determined
(C) must be determined by physicists
(D) is still subject to debate
(E) is extremely complicated

21. According to the passage, the left-to-right reversal of objects reflected in mirrors is

(A) a result of the front-to-back reversal of objects reflected in mirrors
(B) a result of the fact that we ordinarily rotate our field of sight about a vertical axis
(C) explained by the size and position of the object reflected in the mirror
(D) explained by the difference between two-dimensional and three-dimensional objects
(E) explained by the mental constructs of those who observe objects reflected in mirrors

22. According to the passage, the fact that we are accustomed to dealing with our mental constructs rather than the primary sense perceptions on which those constructs are based facilitates our ability to

(A) accept the top-to-bottom explanation of what mirrors do
(B) understand the front-to-back explanation of what mirrors do
(C) challenge complex explanations of common perceptual observations
(D) reject customarily reliable equations between perceptions and their associated mental constructs
(E) overemphasize the fact that mirrors simulate sense impressions of objects

23. It can be inferred that the author of the passage believes that the front-to-back explanation of what mirrors do is

(A) successful because it is based on incongruous facts that can be reconciled
(B) successful because it rejects any consideration of mental constructs
(C) successful because it involves the rotation of a field of sight about an axis
(D) successful only to a point because it is consistent with the traditional explanations that physicists have offered
(E) successful only to a point because it does not include what happens when we look into a mirror

GO ON TO THE NEXT PAGE.

24. In the passage the author is primarily concerned with doing which one of the following?

    (A) evaluating the experimental evidence for and against two diametrically opposed explanations of a given phenomenon

    (B) demonstrating that different explanations of the same phenomenon are based on different empirical observations

    (C) describing the difficulties that must be overcome if a satisfactory explanation of a phenomenon is to be found

    (D) showing why one explanation of a phenomenon falls short in explaining the phenomenon

    (E) relating the theoretical support for an explanation of a phenomenon to the acceptance of that explanation

25. With which one of the following statements would the author of the passage be most likely to agree?

    (A) The failure of one recent explanation of what mirrors do illustrates the need for better optical equipment in future experiments with mirrors.

    (B) Explanations of what mirrors do generally fail because physicists overlook the differences between objects and reflections of objects.

    (C) One explanation of what mirrors do reveals the traditional tendency of physicists to separate a phenomenon to be explained from the observer of the phenomenon.

    (D) The degree to which human beings tend to deal directly with mental constructs rather than with primary sense perceptions depends on their training in the sciences.

    (E) Considering objects reflected in mirrors to be mental constructs interferes with an accurate understanding of how primary perceptions function.

26. The author would be most likely to agree with which one of the following statements about the field-of-sight explanation of what mirrors do?

    (A) This explanation is based on the traditional desire of physicists to simplify the explanation of what mirrors do.

    (B) This explanation does not depend on the false premise that images in mirrors have three-dimensional properties.

    (C) This explanation fails to take into account the point of view and orientation of someone who is observing reflections in the mirror.

    (D) This explanation assumes that people who see something in a mirror do not understand the reality of what they see.

    (E) This explanation is unsuccessful because it involves claims about how people rotate their field of sight rather than claims about what people can imagine.

27. The author mentions the fact that we rarely focus our eyes on mirrors (lines 39–40) primarily in order to

    (A) contrast our capacity to perceive objects with our capacity to imagine objects

    (B) emphasize that it is impossible to perceive reflected objects without using mental constructs of the objects

    (C) clarify the idea that mirrors simulate three-dimensional reality

    (D) illustrate the fact that we typically deal directly with mental constructs rather than with perceptions

    (E) emphasize the degree to which the psychological activity of the observer modifies the shape of the object being perceived

STOP
IF YOU FINISH BEFORE TIME IS CALLED, YOU MAY CHECK YOUR WORK ON THIS SECTION ONLY. DO NOT WORK ON ANY OTHER SECTION IN THE TEST.

LSAT WRITING SAMPLE TOPIC

An organization whose members are professors in a certain discipline holds an important annual conference centered around a full schedule of academic presentations. Most job interviews for positions in the discipline are also conducted at this conference. The organization is deciding whether to continue holding the conference on its usual meeting dates or to hold it two weeks later. Using the facts below, write an essay in which you argue for one option over the other based on the following two criteria:

- The organization wants to encourage its members to attend the conference.
- The organization wants to encourage attendees to go to conference presentations.

The usual meeting dates fall at a time when none of the members' universities hold classes, just after a major family-oriented holiday. In order to spend more time with their families, many potential conference attendees do not attend. The organization recently began offering lodging subsidies and childcare to make attending with family more attractive. Some conference attendees now spend time with their families that they could spend attending presentations. Many members attend the conference to conduct interviews, which take up most of their time.

Air travel to the conference is very expensive during the usual meeting dates. Hotel accommodations cost less than at any other time of year. The later dates fall at a time when a relatively small percentage of members' universities hold classes. These members would be unable to attend or conduct interviews at the conference. No holidays occur within a week of the later dates. The organization could take the money it currently spends on lodging subsidies and childcare and use it to fund additional presentations of interest to more of its members. Air travel is much less expensive during the later dates. Hotel accommodations cost somewhat more.

Directions:

1. Use the Answer Key on the next page to check your answers.

2. Use the Scoring Worksheet below to compute your raw score.

3. Use the Score Conversion Chart to convert your raw score into the 120–180 scale.

Scoring Worksheet

1. Enter the number of questions you answered correctly in each section.

	Number Correct
SECTION I..	_____
SECTION II	_____
SECTION IV	_____
SECTION V	_____

2. Enter the sum here:_____
   This is your Raw Score.

Section Map

SECTION I: PrepTest 71, Section 1
SECTION II: PrepTest 71, Section 2
SECTION III: Experimental (PrepTest 57, Section 3)
SECTION IV: PrepTest 71, Section 3
SECTION V: PrepTest 71, Section 4

Conversion Chart
For Converting Raw Score to the 120–180 LSAT Scaled Score
LSAT Form 3LSN104

Reported Score	Lowest	Highest
180	98	101
179	97	97
178	96	96
177	95	95
176	94	94
175	93	93
174	92	92
173	90	91
172	89	89
171	88	88
170	87	87
169	85	86
168	84	84
167	82	83
166	81	81
165	79	80
164	78	78
163	76	77
162	75	75
161	73	74
160	72	72
159	70	71
158	68	69
157	67	67
156	65	66
155	63	64
154	62	62
153	60	61
152	58	59
151	57	57
150	55	56
149	54	54
148	52	53
147	51	51
146	49	50
145	47	48
144	46	46
143	44	45
142	43	43
141	41	42
140	40	40
139	38	39
138	37	37
137	35	36
136	34	34
135	33	33
134	31	32
133	30	30
132	29	29
131	28	28
130	27	27
129	25	26
128	24	24
127	23	23
126	22	22
125	21	21
124	20	20
123	19	19
122	18	18
121	17	17
120	0	16

*There is no raw score that will produce this scaled score for this form.

SECTION I

1. E	8. D	15. B	22. E
2. D	9. A	16. B	23. C
3. D	10. C	17. B	24. E
4. D	11. E	18. C	25. D
5. E	12. B	19. A	
6. D	13. A	20. C	
7. E	14. C	21. C	

SECTION II

1. E	8. C	15. B	22. E
2. A	9. B	16. D	23. B
3. E	10. C	17. C	
4. D	11. E	18. A	
5. A	12. A	19. C	
6. A	13. A	20. E	
7. B	14. C	21. A	

SECTION III

1. A	8. C	15. C	22. B
2. C	9. D	16. C	23. C
3. A	10. C	17. D	24. C
4. B	11. A	18. B	25. E
5. A	12. E	19. D	
6. A	13. D	20. E	
7. C	14. D	21. B	

SECTION IV

1. C	8. C	15. A	22. B
2. D	9. D	16. B	23. E
3. B	10. A	17. C	24. A
4. E	11. A	18. D	25. A
5. C	12. A	19. D	26. E
6. D	13. E	20. B	
7. A	14. B	21. A	

SECTION V

1. A	8. B	15. E	22. B
2. E	9. C	16. A	23. E
3. D	10. D	17. A	24. D
4. B	11. A	18. C	25. C
5. E	12. A	19. D	26. B
6. D	13. D	20. A	27. C
7. B	14. D	21. B	

TEST ANALYSIS

Section	Overall Performance Score: _____ Percentile: _____		
	Number attempted	Number of guesses	Number correct
Games			
Reading Comprehension			
Arguments 1			
Arguments 2			
TOTAL			

Games			
	Attempted? What order?	Diagram and Elements	Notes
Game 1			
Game 2			
Game 3			
Game 4			

Reading Comprehension

	Attempted? What order?	Passage Notes	Question Notes
Passage 1			
Passage 2			
Passage 3			
Passage 4			

Arguments

Page	Question Number	Question Task	Notes

Arguments			
Page	Question Number	Question Task	Notes

The Official LSAT
PrepTest™ 72
Test code 9728
Form 5LSN113

SECTION I

Time—35 minutes

27 Questions

Directions: The questions in this section are based on the reasoning contained in brief statements or passages. For some questions, more than one of the choices could conceivably answer the question. However, you are to choose the best answer; that is, the response that most accurately and completely answers the question. You should not make assumptions that are by commonsense standards implausible, superfluous, or incompatible with the passage. After you have chosen the best answer, blacken the corresponding space on your answer sheet.

1. Automated flight technology can guide an aircraft very reliably, from navigation to landing. Yet this technology, even when functioning correctly, is not a perfect safeguard against human error.

   Which one of the following, if true, most helps to explain the situation described above?

   (A) Automated flight technology does not always function correctly.
   (B) Smaller aircraft do not always have their automated flight technology updated regularly.
   (C) If a plane's automated flight technology malfunctions, crew members have to operate the plane manually.
   (D) Some airplane crashes are due neither to human error nor to malfunction of automated flight technology.
   (E) Automated flight technology invariably executes exactly the commands that humans give it.

2. To keep one's hands warm during the winter, one never needs gloves or mittens. One can always keep one's hands warm simply by putting on an extra layer of clothing, such as a thermal undershirt or a sweater. After all, keeping one's vital organs warm can keep one's hands warm as well.

   Which one of the following, if true, most weakens the argument?

   (A) Maintaining the temperature of your hands is far less important, physiologically, than maintaining the temperature of your torso.
   (B) Several layers of light garments will keep one's vital organs warmer than will one or two heavy garments.
   (C) Wearing an extra layer of clothing will not keep one's hands warm at temperatures low enough to cause frostbite.
   (D) Keeping one's hands warm by putting on an extra layer of clothing is less effective than turning up the heat.
   (E) The physical effort required to put on an extra layer of clothing does not stimulate circulation enough to warm your hands.

3. The reason music with a simple recurring rhythm exerts a strong primordial appeal is that it reminds us of the womb environment. After all, the first sound heard within the womb is the comforting sound of the mother's regular heartbeat. So in taking away from us the warmth and security of the womb, birth also takes away a primal and constant source of comfort. Thus it is extremely natural that in seeking sensations of warmth and security throughout life, people would be strongly drawn toward simple recurring rhythmic sounds.

   Which one of the following most accurately expresses the main conclusion drawn in the reasoning above?

   (A) The explanation of the strong primordial appeal of music with a simple recurring rhythm is that it reminds us of the womb environment.
   (B) The comforting sound of the mother's regular heartbeat is the first sound that is heard inside the womb.
   (C) Birth deprives us of a primal and constant source of comfort when it takes away the warmth and security of the womb.
   (D) People seek sensations of warmth and security throughout life because birth takes away the warmth and security of the womb.
   (E) The comforting sound of the mother's regular heartbeat is a simple recurring rhythmic sound.

GO ON TO THE NEXT PAGE.

4. Linguist: Most people can tell whether a sequence of words in their own dialect is grammatical. Yet few people who can do so are able to specify the relevant grammatical rules.

Which one of the following best illustrates the principle underlying the linguist's statements?

(A) Some people are able to write cogent and accurate narrative descriptions of events. But these people are not necessarily also capable of composing emotionally moving and satisfying poems.
(B) Engineers who apply the principles of physics to design buildings and bridges must know a great deal more than do the physicists who discover these principles.
(C) Some people are able to tell whether any given piece of music is a waltz. But the majority of these people cannot state the defining characteristics of a waltz.
(D) Those travelers who most enjoy their journeys are not always those most capable of vividly describing the details of those journeys to others.
(E) Quite a few people know the rules of chess, but only a small number of them can play chess very well.

5. Company president: For the management consultant position, we shall interview only those applicants who have worked for management consulting firms generally recognized as in the top 1 percent of firms worldwide. When we finally select somebody, then, we can be sure to have selected one of the best management consultants available.

The company president's reasoning is most vulnerable to criticism on the grounds that it

(A) takes for granted that only the best management consultants have worked for the top management consulting firms
(B) generalizes from too small a sample of management consulting firms worldwide
(C) takes for granted that if something is true of each member of a collection, then it is also true of the collection as a whole
(D) presumes, without providing warrant, that persons who have worked for the top companies will accept a job offer
(E) presumes, without providing justification, that highly competent management consultants are highly competent at every task

6. Beginners typically decide each chess move by considering the consequences. Expert players, in contrast, primarily use pattern-recognition techniques. That is, such a player recognizes having been in a similar position before and makes a decision based on information recalled about the consequences of moves chosen on that prior occasion.

Which one of the following is most strongly supported by the information above?

(A) Beginning chess players are better at thinking through the consequences of chess moves than experts are.
(B) A beginning chess player should use pattern-recognition techniques when deciding what move to make.
(C) One's chess skills will improve only if one learns to use pattern-recognition techniques.
(D) In playing chess, an expert player relies crucially on his or her memory.
(E) Any chess player who played other games that require pattern-recognition skills would thereby improve his or her chess skills.

7. Farmer: Because water content is what makes popcorn pop, the kernels must dry at just the right speed to trap the correct amount of water. The best way to achieve this effect is to have the sun dry the corn while the corn is still in the field, but I always dry the ears on a screen in a warm, dry room.

Which one of the following, if true, most helps to resolve the apparent discrepancy between the farmer's theory and practice?

(A) The region in which the farmer grows popcorn experiences a long, cloudy season that begins shortly before the popcorn in fields would begin to dry.
(B) Leaving popcorn to dry on its stalks in the field is the least expensive method of drying it.
(C) Drying popcorn on its stalks in the field is only one of several methods that allow the kernels' water content to reach acceptable levels.
(D) When popcorn does not dry sufficiently, it will still pop, but it will take several minutes to do so, even under optimal popping conditions.
(E) If popcorn is allowed to dry too much, it will not pop.

GO ON TO THE NEXT PAGE.

8. Factory manager: One reason the automobile parts this factory produces are expensive is that our manufacturing equipment is outdated and inefficient. Our products would be more competitively priced if we were to refurbish the factory completely with new, more efficient equipment. Therefore, since to survive in today's market we have to make our products more competitively priced, we must completely refurbish the factory in order to survive.

The reasoning in the factory manager's argument is flawed because this argument

(A) fails to recognize that the price of a particular commodity can change over time
(B) shifts without justification from treating something as one way of achieving a goal to treating it as the only way of achieving that goal
(C) argues that one thing is the cause of another when the evidence given indicates that the second thing may in fact be the cause of the first
(D) recommends a solution to a problem without first considering any possible causes of that problem
(E) fails to make a definite recommendation and instead merely suggests that some possible course of action might be effective

9. Two months ago a major shipment of pythons arrived from Africa, resulting in a great number of inexpensive pythons in pet stores. Anyone interested in buying a python, however, should beware: many pythons hatched in Africa are afflicted with a deadly liver disease. Although a few pythons recently hatched in North America have this disease, a much greater proportion of African-hatched pythons have it. The disease is difficult to detect in its early stages, and all pythons die within six months of contracting the disease.

Which one of the following statements can be properly inferred from the statements above?

(A) Some pythons hatched in North America may appear fine but will die within six months as a result of the liver disease.
(B) Pythons that hatch in Africa are more susceptible to the liver disease than are pythons that hatch in North America.
(C) Any python that has not died by the age of six months does not have the liver disease.
(D) The pythons are inexpensively priced because many of them suffer from the liver disease.
(E) Pythons hatched in neither Africa nor North America are not afflicted with the liver disease.

10. Nutritionists believe that a person's daily requirement for vitamins can readily be met by eating five servings of fruits and vegetables daily. However, most people eat far less than this. Thus, most people need to take vitamin pills.

Which one of the following statements, if true, most seriously weakens the argument?

(A) Even five servings of fruits and vegetables a day is insufficient unless the intake is varied to ensure that different vitamins are consumed.
(B) Certain commonly available fruits and vegetables contain considerably more nutrients than others.
(C) Nutritionists sometimes disagree on how much of a fruit or vegetable constitutes a complete serving.
(D) Many commonly consumed foods that are neither fruits nor vegetables are fortified by manufacturers with the vitamins found in fruits and vegetables.
(E) Fruits and vegetables are also important sources of fiber, in forms not found in vitamin pills.

11. Researcher: This fall I returned to a research site to recover the armadillos I had tagged there the previous spring. Since a large majority of the armadillos I recaptured were found within a few hundred yards of the location of their tagging last spring, I concluded that armadillos do not move rapidly into new territories.

Which one of the following is an assumption required by the researcher's argument?

(A) Of the armadillos living in the area of the tagging site last spring, few were able to avoid being tagged by the researcher.
(B) Most of the armadillos tagged the previous spring were not recaptured during the subsequent fall.
(C) Predators did not kill any of the armadillos that had been tagged the previous spring.
(D) The tags identifying the armadillos cannot be removed by the armadillos, either by accident or deliberately.
(E) A large majority of the recaptured armadillos did not move to a new territory in the intervening summer and then move back to the old territory by the fall.

GO ON TO THE NEXT PAGE.

12. Sahira: To make a living from their art, artists of great potential would have to produce work that would gain widespread popular acclaim, instead of their best work. That is why governments are justified in subsidizing artists.

Rahima: Your argument for subsidizing art depends on claiming that to gain widespread popular acclaim, artists must produce something other than their best work; but this need not be true.

In her argument, Rahima

(A) disputes an implicit assumption of Sahira's
(B) presents independent support for Sahira's argument
(C) accepts Sahira's conclusion, but for reasons different from those given by Sahira
(D) uses Sahira's premises to reach a conclusion different from that reached by Sahira
(E) argues that a standard that she claims Sahira uses is self-contradictory

13. Adult frogs are vulnerable to dehydration because of their highly permeable skins. Unlike large adult frogs, small adult frogs have such a low ratio of body weight to skin surface area that they cannot survive in arid climates. The animals' moisture requirements constitute the most important factor determining where frogs can live in the Yucatán peninsula, which has an arid climate in the north and a wet climate in the south.

The information above most strongly supports which one of the following conclusions about frogs in the Yucatán peninsula?

(A) Large adult frogs cannot coexist with small adult frogs in the wet areas.
(B) Frogs living in wet areas weigh more on average than frogs in the arid areas.
(C) Large adult frogs can live in more of the area than small adult frogs can.
(D) Fewer small adult frogs live in the south than do large adult frogs.
(E) Small adult frogs in the south have less permeable skins than small adult frogs in the north.

14. Editorial: A recent survey shows that 77 percent of people feel that crime is increasing and that 87 percent feel the judicial system should be handing out tougher sentences. Therefore, the government must firmly address the rising crime rate.

The reasoning in the editorial's argument is most vulnerable to criticism on the grounds that the argument

(A) appeals to survey results that are inconsistent because they suggest that more people are concerned about the sentencing of criminals than are concerned about crime itself
(B) presumes, without providing justification, that there is a correlation between criminal offenders being treated leniently and a high crime rate
(C) fails to consider whether other surveys showing different results have been conducted over the years
(D) fails to distinguish between the crime rate's actually rising and people's believing that the crime rate is rising
(E) presumes, without providing justification, that tougher sentences are the most effective means of alleviating the crime problem

15. Proofs relying crucially on computers provide less certainty than do proofs not requiring computers. Human cognition alone cannot verify computer-dependent proofs; such proofs can never provide the degree of certainty that attends our judgments concerning, for instance, simple arithmetical facts, which can be verified by human calculation. Of course, in these cases one often uses electronic calculators, but here the computer is a convenience rather than a supplement to human cognition.

The statements above, if true, most strongly support which one of the following?

(A) Only if a proof's result is arrived at without the help of a computer can one judge with any degree of certainty that the proof is correct.
(B) We can never be completely sure that proofs relying crucially on computers do not contain errors that humans do not detect.
(C) Whenever a computer replaces human calculation in a proof, the degree of certainty provided by the proof is reduced.
(D) If one can corroborate something by human calculation, one can be completely certain of it.
(E) It is impossible to supplement the cognitive abilities of humans by means of artificial devices such as computers.

GO ON TO THE NEXT PAGE.

16. Madden: Industrialists address problems by simplifying them, but in farming that strategy usually leads to oversimplification. For example, industrialists see water retention and drainage as different and opposite functions—that good topsoil both drains and retains water is a fact alien to industrial logic. To facilitate water retention, they use a terrace or a dam; to facilitate drainage, they use drain tile, a ditch, or a subsoiler. More farming problems are created than solved when agriculture is the domain of the industrialist, not of the farmer.

The situation as Madden describes it best illustrates which one of the following propositions?

(A) The handling of water drainage and retention is the most important part of good farming.
(B) The problems of farming should be viewed in all their complexity.
(C) Farmers are better than anyone else at solving farming problems.
(D) Industrial solutions for problems in farming should never be sought.
(E) The approach to problem solving typical of industrialists is fundamentally flawed.

17. Critic: Works of modern literature cannot be tragedies as those of ancient playwrights and storytellers were unless their protagonists are seen as possessing nobility, which endures through the calamities that befall one. In an age that no longer takes seriously the belief that human endeavors are governed by fate, it is therefore impossible for a contemporary work of literature to be a tragedy.

Which one of the following is an assumption required by the critic's argument?

(A) Whether or not a work of literature is a tragedy should not depend on characteristics of its audience.
(B) The belief that human endeavors are governed by fate is false.
(C) Most plays that were once classified as tragedies were misclassified.
(D) Those whose endeavors are not regarded as governed by fate will not be seen as possessing nobility.
(E) If an ignoble character in a work of literature endures through a series of misfortunes, that work of literature is not a tragedy.

18. Despite the efforts of a small minority of graduate students at one university to unionize, the majority of graduate students there remain unaware of the attempt. Most of those who are aware believe that a union would not represent their interests or that, if it did, it would not effectively pursue them. Thus, the graduate students at the university should not unionize, since the majority of them obviously disapprove of the attempt.

The reasoning in the argument is most vulnerable to criticism on the grounds that the argument

(A) tries to establish a conclusion simply on the premise that the conclusion agrees with a long-standing practice
(B) fails to exclude alternative explanations for why some graduate students disapprove of unionizing
(C) presumes that simply because a majority of a population is unaware of something, it must not be a good idea
(D) ignores the possibility that although a union might not effectively pursue graduate student interests, there are other reasons for unionizing
(E) blurs the distinction between active disapproval and mere lack of approval

19. Anyone who believes in democracy has a high regard for the wisdom of the masses. Griley, however, is an elitist who believes that any artwork that is popular is unlikely to be good. Thus, Griley does not believe in democracy.

The conclusion follows logically if which one of the following is assumed?

(A) Anyone who believes that an artwork is unlikely to be good if it is popular is an elitist.
(B) Anyone who believes that if an artwork is popular it is unlikely to be good does not have a high regard for the wisdom of the masses.
(C) If Griley is not an elitist, then he has a high regard for the wisdom of the masses.
(D) Anyone who does not have a high regard for the wisdom of the masses is an elitist who believes that if an artwork is popular it is unlikely to be good.
(E) Unless Griley believes in democracy, Griley does not have a high regard for the wisdom of the masses.

GO ON TO THE NEXT PAGE.

20. A recent study confirmed that salt intake tends to increase blood pressure and found that, as a result, people with high blood pressure who significantly cut their salt intake during the study had lower blood pressure by the end of the study. However, it was also found that some people who had very high salt intake both before and throughout the study maintained very low blood pressure.

Which one of the following, if true, contributes the most to an explanation of the results of the study?

(A) Study participants with high blood pressure who cut their salt intake only slightly during the study did not have significantly lower blood pressure by the end of the study.

(B) Salt intake is only one of several dietary factors associated with high blood pressure.

(C) For most people who have high blood pressure, reducing salt intake is not the most effective dietary change they can make to reduce their blood pressure.

(D) At the beginning of the study, some people who had very low salt intake also had very high blood pressure.

(E) Persons suffering from abnormally low blood pressure have heightened salt cravings, which ensure that their blood pressure does not drop too low.

21. The odds of winning any major lottery jackpot are extremely slight. However, the very few people who do win major jackpots receive a great deal of attention from the media. Thus, since most people come to have at least some awareness of events that receive extensive media coverage, it is likely that many people greatly overestimate the odds of their winning a major jackpot.

Which one of the following is an assumption on which the argument depends?

(A) Most people who overestimate the likelihood of winning a major jackpot do so at least in part because media coverage of other people who have won major jackpots downplays the odds against winning such a jackpot.

(B) Very few people other than those who win major jackpots receive a great deal of attention from the media.

(C) If it were not for media attention, most people who purchase lottery tickets would not overestimate their chances of winning a jackpot.

(D) Becoming aware of individuals who have won a major jackpot leads at least some people to incorrectly estimate their own chances of winning such a jackpot.

(E) At least some people who are heavily influenced by the media do not believe that the odds of their winning a major jackpot are significant.

GO ON TO THE NEXT PAGE.

22. A book tour will be successful if it is well publicized and the author is an established writer. Julia is an established writer, and her book tour was successful. So her book tour must have been well publicized.

Which one of the following exhibits a pattern of flawed reasoning most closely parallel to the pattern of flawed reasoning exhibited by the argument above?

(A) This recipe will turn out only if one follows it exactly and uses high-quality ingredients. Arthur followed the recipe exactly and it turned out. Thus, Arthur must have used high-quality ingredients.

(B) If a computer has the fastest microprocessor and the most memory available, it will meet Aletha's needs this year. This computer met Aletha's needs last year. So it must have had the fastest microprocessor and the most memory available last year.

(C) If cacti are kept in the shade and watered more than twice weekly, they will die. This cactus was kept in the shade, and it is now dead. Therefore, it must have been watered more than twice weekly.

(D) A house will suffer from dry rot and poor drainage only if it is built near a high water table. This house suffers from dry rot and has poor drainage. Thus, it must have been built near a high water table.

(E) If one wears a suit that has double vents and narrow lapels, one will be fashionably dressed. The suit that Joseph wore to dinner last night had double vents and narrow lapels, so Joseph must have been fashionably dressed.

23. Eight large craters run in a long straight line across a geographical region. Although some of the craters contain rocks that have undergone high-pressure shocks characteristic of meteorites slamming into Earth, these shocks could also have been caused by extreme volcanic events. Because of the linearity of the craters, it is very unlikely that some of them were caused by volcanoes and others were caused by meteorites. Thus, since the craters are all different ages, they were probably caused by volcanic events rather than meteorites.

Which one of the following statements, if true, would most strengthen the argument?

(A) A similar but shorter line of craters that are all the same age is known to have been caused by volcanic activity.

(B) No known natural cause would likely account for eight meteorite craters of different ages forming a straight line.

(C) There is no independent evidence of either meteorites or volcanic activity in the region where the craters are located.

(D) There is no independent evidence of a volcanic event strong enough to have created the high-pressure shocks that are characteristic of meteorites slamming into Earth.

(E) No known single meteor shower has created exactly eight impact craters that form a straight line.

GO ON TO THE NEXT PAGE.

24. The genuine creative genius is someone who is dissatisfied with merely habitual assent to widely held beliefs; thus these rare innovators tend to anger the majority. Those who are dissatisfied with merely habitual assent to widely held beliefs tend to seek out controversy, and controversy seekers enjoy demonstrating the falsehood of popular viewpoints.

The conclusion of the argument follows logically if which one of the following is assumed?

(A) People become angry when they are dissatisfied with merely habitual assent to widely held beliefs.

(B) People who enjoy demonstrating the falsehood of popular viewpoints anger the majority.

(C) People tend to get angry with individuals who hold beliefs not held by a majority of people.

(D) People who anger the majority enjoy demonstrating the falsehood of popular viewpoints.

(E) People who anger the majority are dissatisfied with merely habitual assent to widely held beliefs.

25. Claude: When I'm having lunch with job candidates, I watch to see if they salt their food without first tasting it. If they do, I count that against them, because they're making decisions based on inadequate information.

Larissa: That's silly. It's perfectly reasonable for me to wear a sweater whenever I go into a supermarket, because I already know supermarkets are always too cool inside to suit me. And I never open a credit card offer that comes in the mail, because I already know that no matter how low its interest rate may be, it will never be worthwhile for me.

The two analogies that Larissa offers can most reasonably be interpreted as invoking which one of the following principles to criticize Claude's policy?

(A) In matters involving personal preference, performing an action without first ascertaining whether it is appropriate in the specific circumstances should not be taken as good evidence of faulty decision making, because the action may be based on a reasoned policy relating to knowledge of a general fact about the circumstances.

(B) In professional decision-making contexts, those who have the responsibility of judging other people's suitability for a job should not use observations of job-related behavior as a basis for inferring general conclusions about those people's character.

(C) General conclusions regarding a job candidate's suitability for a position should not be based exclusively on observations of the candidate's behavior in situations that are neither directly job related nor likely to be indicative of a pattern of behavior that the candidate engages in.

(D) Individuals whose behavior in specific circumstances does not conform to generally expected norms should not automatically be considered unconcerned with meeting social expectations, because such individuals may be acting in accordance with reasoned policies that they believe should be generally adopted by people in similar circumstances.

(E) Evidence that a particular individual uses bad decision-making strategies in matters of personal taste should not be considered sufficient to warrant a negative assessment of his or her suitability for a job, because any good decision maker can have occasional lapses of rationality with regard to such matters.

STOP
IF YOU FINISH BEFORE TIME IS CALLED, YOU MAY CHECK YOUR WORK ON THIS SECTION ONLY. DO NOT WORK ON ANY OTHER SECTION IN THE TEST.

SECTION II

Time—35 minutes

23 Questions

Directions: Each set of questions in this section is based on a single passage or a pair of passages. The questions are to be answered on the basis of what is <u>stated</u> or <u>implied</u> in the passage or pair of passages. For some of the questions, more than one of the choices could conceivably answer the question. However, you are to choose the <u>best</u> answer; that is, the response that most accurately and completely answers the question, and blacken the corresponding space on your answer sheet.

In the last half-century, firefighters in North America have developed a powerful system for fighting wildfires using modern technology. But at the same time, foresters and ecologists are increasingly
(5) aware that too much firefighting can be worse than none at all. Over the millennia, many forest ecosystems have evolved in such a way that they are dependent on periodic fires for renewal and for limiting damage when fires do occur. Ancient ponderosa forests, for
(10) example, were stable in part because low-intensity fires maintained open forests with low levels of fuel for future fires. These fires burned lightly around the bases of mature trees, leaving these trees alive and clearing the understory of brush and young trees.
(15) Scientists can easily count the regular recurrence of fires in these forests over the centuries by examining the scars left on trunks; the typical interval between fires could be as short as 5 years and rarely extended beyond 25 years.
(20)   If fires are kept out of forests, however, deadwood and other fuels build up; then, when fire is sparked by lightning or some other cause, what results is a fire so large that it leaves total devastation. Such fires often kill off wildlife that might escape low-intensity fires,
(25) and they also reach the crowns of centuries-old trees, destroying them and ultimately enabling rains to erode the unprotected topsoil. Because of the relative success of fire-suppression efforts, many forests, including ponderosa forests, have now been free of fire for
(30) 50 years or longer, leaving them vulnerable to these devastating crown fires. It is therefore increasingly necessary for land managers in North America to strive to manage rather than eliminate fires; land management policies should recognize the essential
(35) role that fire plays in many ecosystems.
        Fire behavior depends on the complex interaction of three factors—topography, weather, and fuel—and since topography is fixed and weather is unpredictable, fuel is the only element that land managers can
(40) control. Land managers should therefore focus their efforts on fuel. A new kind of wildfire management that is designed to simulate the natural role of fire through a combination of selective harvesting and prescribed fires is the most promising method for
(45) controlling fuel. Selective timber harvesting focuses on smaller trees—markets for this smaller material do exist—leaving the larger, fire-tolerant trees on the land and thinning the forest, thereby re-creating the conditions that allow for low-intensity burns.
(50) Prescribed fire management includes both the

intentional lighting of controlled burns and the policy of allowing fires set by lightning to burn when the weather is damp enough to reduce the risk of extensive damage. Once fuels are reduced by these fires, (55)
(55) maintenance burns at 15- to 20-year intervals will be needed. When wildfires inevitably occur, they will be more easily controlled and do much less damage.

1.   The primary purpose of the passage is to

(A)   claim that ideological dogma may be impeding the enactment of a fundamental and necessary policy change
(B)   compare the actual effects that have resulted from two different policies designed to have the same effect
(C)   contend that a recently implemented policy requires a substantial increase in funding
(D)   recommend a fundamental policy change in light of evidence that current policy has created undesirable conditions
(E)   argue that two seemingly contradictory goals of a policy are actually compatible in a fundamental way

2.   By "maintenance burns" (line 55) the author most clearly refers to

(A)   the low-intensity fires that regularly occurred in ancient forests
(B)   fires that reduce the population density of mature trees
(C)   the types of fires that are likely to occur in North American forest ecosystems today
(D)   a type of fire that used to occur at intervals greater than 50 years
(E)   naturally or intentionally set fires that are allowed to burn to eliminate fuel

GO ON TO THE NEXT PAGE.

3. Which one of the following sentences would most logically complete the last paragraph of the passage?

(A) However, if homes were not built in such close proximity to forests, the damage to developed property would be limited substantially.

(B) Unfortunately, until foresters recognize the dangers posed by excess fuel in forests, these proposals are likely to meet with resistance in the forestry community.

(C) But even with these policies, which require some years to achieve their intended effects, large, devastating fires will remain a threat in the near term.

(D) Yet, because smaller trees will likely yield less profit for timber companies, the ecological benefits of the new plans must be weighed carefully against their economic impact.

(E) But given the large financial resources needed to operate a prescribed fire management system, the chances of such policies being implemented are quite small.

4. The author cites the factors of topography, weather, and fuel in the last paragraph primarily as part of

(A) the support provided for the contention that land managers must focus on fuel to reduce the risk of crown fires

(B) an argument that, given the interaction among these factors, land managers' efforts to control wildfires will always be somewhat ineffective

(C) an attempt to provide a clearer understanding of why forest fires have become unnaturally devastating

(D) an argument that specific fuel types and forest densities are dependent on topographic and weather conditions

(E) the suggestion that fires started by lightning will continue to be a factor in wildfire suppression efforts

5. The passage provides the most support for inferring that which one of the following is true of ancient ponderosa forests?

(A) Ponderosas that thrived in these forests probably differed genetically from modern ponderosas in subtle, though significant, ways.

(B) The population density of trees in these forests was generally lower than it is in many ponderosa forests today.

(C) Weather patterns in these forests were substantially different from weather patterns in ponderosa forests today.

(D) The diversity of plant species was greater in these forests than it is in ponderosa forests today.

(E) In addition to clearing out excess fuel, periodic low-intensity fires helped to control wildlife populations in these forests.

6. It can be inferred from the passage that the author would be most likely to regard a policy in which all forest fires that were started by lightning were allowed to burn until they died out naturally as

(A) a viable means of restoring forests currently vulnerable to catastrophic fires to a cycle of periodic low-intensity fires

(B) an essential component of a new wildfire management plan that would also involve the regulation of timber harvests

(C) beneficial to forests that have centuries-old trees, though harmful to younger forests

(D) currently too extreme and likely to cause the destruction land managers are seeking to avoid

(E) politically infeasible given the public perception of the consequences of such fires

GO ON TO THE NEXT PAGE.

The government of Mali passed a law against excavating and exporting the wonderful terra-cotta sculptures from the old city of Djenne-jeno, but it could not enforce it. And it certainly could not afford
(5) to fund thousands of archaeological excavations. The result was that many fine Djenne-jeno terra-cotta sculptures were illicitly excavated in the 1980s and sold to foreign collectors who rightly admired them. Because these sites were looted, much of what we
(10) would most like to know about this culture—much that we could have learned had the sites been preserved by careful archaeology—may now never be known.

It has been natural to condemn such pillaging. And, through a number of declarations from UNESCO and
(15) other international bodies, a protective doctrine has evolved concerning the ownership of many forms of cultural property (the "UNESCO doctrine"). Essentially the doctrine provides that cultural artifacts should be regarded as the property of the culture. For
(20) an individual belonging to that culture, such works are, using UNESCO's terminology, part of an "artistic and cultural patrimony." Further, a number of countries have strengthened the UNESCO doctrine by declaring all antiquities that originate within their borders to be
(25) state property that cannot be freely exported.

Accordingly, it seems reasonable that the government of Mali, within whose borders the Djenne-jeno antiquities are buried, be the one to regulate excavating Djenne-jeno and to decide where
(30) the statues should go. Regrettably, and this is a painful irony, regulations prohibiting export and requiring repatriation can discourage recording and preserving information about cultural antiquities, one of the key reasons for the UNESCO regulations. For example, if
(35) someone in London sells a figure from Djenne-jeno with documentation that it came out of the ground there after the regulations were implemented, then the authorities committed to the restitution of objects taken illegally out of Mali have the very evidence
(40) they need to seize the figure.

Suppose that from the beginning, Mali had been helped by UNESCO to exercise its trusteeship of the Djenne-jeno terra-cotta sculptures by licensing excavations and educating people to recognize that
(45) such artifacts have greater value when they are removed carefully from the earth with accurate records of location. Suppose Mali had required that objects be recorded and registered before leaving the excavation site, and had imposed a tax on exported objects to
(50) fund acquisitions of important pieces for the national museum. The excavations encouraged by such a system may have been less well conducted and less informative than proper, professionally administered excavations by accredited archaeologists. Some people
(55) would still have avoided the rules. But would this not have been better than what actually happened?

7. Which one of the following most accurately expresses the main point of the passage?

(A) Declarations from UNESCO and other international bodies concerning the ownership of cultural artifacts gave rise to a doctrine based on the notion of artistic and cultural patrimony.
(B) Preserving cultural knowledge at sites like Djenne-jeno requires solutions that are more flexible than simply passing laws prohibiting the excavation and export of antiquities.
(C) Rather than acceding to the dictates of international bodies, countries like Mali must find their own unique solutions to problems concerning the preservation of cultural heritage.
(D) The government of Mali should have exercised its trusteeship of the Djenne-jeno terra-cotta sculptures by licensing only accredited archaeologists for the excavations.
(E) The idea that a culture's artistic and cultural patrimony is the property of the state does more harm than good in countries like Mali.

8. The passage indicates that some countries have made use of the UNESCO doctrine in which one of the following ways?

(A) requiring the origins of all antiquities sold to collectors to be fully documented
(B) restricting the export of antiquities and declaring all antiquities originating within the country's borders to be state property
(C) adopting plans to teach people to recognize that antiquities have greater value when they are removed carefully from the earth with accurate records of location
(D) encouraging trade in a particular ancient culture's artifacts among countries each of which contains within its boundaries a portion of that ancient culture's territory
(E) committing substantial resources to the restoration of antiquities taken illegally out of countries like Mali

9. The author asks the reader to suppose that Mali had imposed a tax on exported objects (lines 49–51) primarily in order to

(A) draw attention to the role of museums in preserving cultural patrimonies
(B) praise one of the Malian government's past policies concerning cultural antiquities
(C) present one part of a more pragmatic approach to regulating the trade in cultural antiquities
(D) suggest a means of giving people who excavate cultural antiquities incentive to keep careful records
(E) highlight a flaw in the UNESCO doctrine

GO ON TO THE NEXT PAGE.

10. The author of the passage would be most likely to agree with which one of the following statements about UNESCO?

(A) It can play an important role in stemming abuses that arise from the international trade in cultural artifacts.

(B) Its stance on cultural artifacts emerged for the most part in response to Mali's loss of terra-cotta sculptures from Djenne-jeno.

(C) It is more effective with initiatives that involve individual states than initiatives that involve several states.

(D) It pays too little attention to the concerns of countries like Mali.

(E) Its effectiveness in limiting the loss of cultural knowledge has been hampered by inadequate funding.

11. The author of the passage would be most likely to agree with which one of the following statements about regulations governing the trade in cultural antiquities in countries like Mali?

(A) Such regulations must be approved by archaeologists before being enacted.

(B) Such regulations must have as their goal maximizing the number of cultural antiquities that ultimately remain in these countries.

(C) Such regulations can be beneficial even if not all people strictly comply with them.

(D) Such regulations must be accompanied by very strict punishments for violators.

(E) Such regulations are most effective when they are very simple and easily understood.

12. The author of the passage would be most likely to agree with which one of the following statements about cultural antiquities?

(A) They must be owned and protected by a country's national museum.

(B) They must remain within the boundaries of the country in which they were found.

(C) They are too valuable to be owned exclusively by the state.

(D) They should be excavated by professional archaeologists when possible.

(E) They belong to whoever finds them and registers them with the state.

13. Which one of the following is an element of the author's attitude toward foreign collectors of terra-cotta sculptures from Djenne-jeno?

(A) appreciation of their efforts to preserve cultural artifacts

(B) approval of their aesthetic judgment

(C) dismay at their failure to take action against illegal exportation of cultural artifacts

(D) frustration with their lack of concern for the people of Mali

(E) sympathy with their motives

GO ON TO THE NEXT PAGE.

The following passage is based on an article published in 1987.

Medical practitioners are ethically required to prescribe the best available treatments. In ordinary patient-physician interactions, this obligation is unproblematic, but when physicians are clinical
(5) researchers in comparative studies of medical treatments, special issues arise. Comparative clinical trials involve withholding one or more of the treatments from at least one group of patients. Traditionally, most physicians and ethicists have agreed that in testing a
(10) new treatment on a patient population for which there exists a currently accepted treatment, the participating physicians should have no opinion as to which treatment is clinically superior—a state of mind usually termed "equipoise."
(15) Unfortunately, the conception of equipoise that is typically employed—which I will term "theoretical equipoise"—may be too strict. Theoretical equipoise exists only when the overall evidence for each of two treatment regimens is judged by each clinical researcher
(20) to be exactly balanced—an ideal hardly attainable in practice. Clinical researchers commonly have some preference for one of the treatments being tested, an intuitive preference perhaps, or one based on their interpretation and balancing of various sources of
(25) evidence. Even if researchers judged the evidence to be balanced at the start of a comparative clinical trial, such a balance would be extremely fragile, liable to be "tipped" by small accretions of evidence as the study progresses. Consequently, if the standard of theoretical
(30) equipoise is adhered to, few comparative clinical trials could commence and even fewer could proceed to completion.

These difficulties associated with theoretical equipoise suggest that a different notion of equipoise
(35) should be developed, one that I will label "clinical equipoise." Clinical equipoise would impose rigorous ethical standards on comparative clinical trials without unreasonably constricting them. One reason for conducting comparative clinical trials is to resolve
(40) a current or imminent conflict in the expert clinical community over what treatment is to be preferred for patients with a given illness. It could be that the standard treatment is A but new evidence suggests that B will be superior. Medical experts may be divided as
(45) to which treatment is better, with each side recognizing that opposing experts can differ honestly in their interpretation of the evidence.

The very absence of consensus within the expert clinical community is what makes clinical equipoise
(50) possible. One or more of a comparative clinical trial's researchers may have a decided treatment preference based on their assessments of the evidence. But that is no ethical bar to participation in the trial. The clinical researchers must simply each recognize that their less-
(55) favored treatment is preferred by a sizable constituency within the medical profession as a whole.

14. The author's primary purpose in the passage is to

(A) explain the difference between two conceptions of an ethical standard together with how these conceptions would affect comparative clinical trials
(B) argue for a more reasonable, less restrictive interpretation of an ethical requirement than the one traditionally given by ethicists and physicians
(C) demonstrate that a change in the standards governing comparative clinical trials will endanger the ability of researchers to derive valuable information from such trials
(D) demonstrate the need for clinical researchers to more closely examine the conceptions embodied in the ethical standards to which these researchers adhere
(E) argue for a change in the scientific methods used for gathering evidence in comparative clinical trials

15. The primary purpose of the second paragraph of the passage is to

(A) provide a view that contrasts with arguments in favor of clinical equipoise
(B) explore the factors underlying physicians' preferences regarding competing treatments
(C) undermine the moral principle that underlies the theory of theoretical equipoise
(D) state the main difficulty with adhering to the standards of theoretical equipoise
(E) illustrate the conflicts inherent in the general notion of equipoise

16. According to the passage, which one of the following is true?

(A) Comparative clinical trials that meet the standard of theoretical equipoise generally present no ethical problems.
(B) Clinical researchers are often forced to suspend comparative clinical trials prematurely because initial data from the trials strongly favors one treatment over another.
(C) A clinical trial comparing treatments is not rendered unethical merely because one of the participating physicians has come to favor one of the treatments over the other.
(D) A comparative clinical trial that meets the standard of clinical equipoise would therefore also meet the standard of theoretical equipoise.
(E) Medical researchers generally try to conduct comparative clinical trials in accordance with the standard of clinical equipoise.

GO ON TO THE NEXT PAGE.

17. Suppose two medical treatments are being compared in a clinical trial for their effectiveness in treating a condition. Based on the passage, which one of the following scenarios would be significantly more likely to jeopardize theoretical equipoise than clinical equipoise?

(A) The initial results of the trial so strikingly favored one treatment that they were published and widely disseminated before the study was even half over; as a result, most physicians who specialize in treating the condition came to favor the more effective treatment before the trial had ended.

(B) Preliminary results in the trial suggest that the two treatments are equally effective in treating the condition; but these results are not reported while the trial is underway and thus few in the expert clinical community are aware of them.

(C) Several of the physicians participating in the trial think that one treatment is more effective at treating the condition than the other; in this they agree with the consensus view within the expert clinical community.

(D) Initial results from the trial convince several of the participating physicians that one treatment more effectively treats the condition than the other does; this does not affect their recognition of the lack of consensus among experts in treating the disease.

(E) There is consensus among physicians participating in the trial that both treatments are equally effective at treating the condition; however, there is no consensus within the expert medical community as to the relative effectiveness of the treatments.

18. Which one of the following most accurately expresses the main point of the passage?

(A) The ethical requirement that physicians prescribe the best available treatment to their patients is jeopardized by an overly strict conception of equipoise.

(B) Medical research conducted through comparative clinical trials is able to achieve more if the ethical requirements it is bound by are not overly restrictive.

(C) It is sometimes ethically acceptable for a physician to participate in a clinical trial in which the physician has a decided treatment preference in favor of one of the treatments being tested.

(D) Clinical equipoise should be adopted because it is less likely to unreasonably constrict the conducting of comparative clinical trials than is theoretical equipoise.

(E) Even though comparative clinical trials often fail to meet the standard of theoretical equipoise, they should not, for that reason, be considered unethical.

19. As used in line 41 of the passage, the term "community" most nearly refers to a group of people

(A) who focus on a common set of problems using a shared body of knowledge

(B) who live and work in the same geographical area as one another

(C) who share opinions that differ significantly from those of other groups

(D) whose association with one another is based on their similar ethical values

(E) whose similar research methods are employed in unrelated disciplines

20. According to the passage, which one of the following is true?

(A) Most clinical trials that are conducted meet the appropriate ethical standards.

(B) Clinical trials would be conducted more often if there were a more reasonable ethical standard in place.

(C) Theoretical equipoise imposes an ethical standard on clinical trials that is rarely if ever met.

(D) Most physicians and ethicists believe that the currently accepted ethical requirements for comparative clinical trials are adequate.

(E) Most comparative clinical trials are undertaken to help resolve a conflict of opinion in the expert clinical community concerning the best available treatment.

21. The author's argument in the third and fourth paragraphs would be most weakened if which one of the following were true?

(A) In most comparative clinical trials, the main purpose is to prove definitively that a treatment considered best by a consensus of relevant experts is in fact superior to the alternative being tested.

(B) Physicians participating in comparative clinical trials rarely ask to leave the trials because early data favors one of the treatments being tested over another.

(C) The number of comparative clinical trials that are conducted annually is increasing rapidly, but the level of ethical oversight of these trials is decreasing.

(D) Medical ethicists are more inclined than are clinical researchers to favor an ethical requirement based on theoretical equipoise over one based on clinical equipoise.

(E) In clinical trials comparing two treatments, it rarely occurs that researchers who begin the trial with no preference for either of the treatments later develop a strong preference on the basis of data obtained early in the study.

GO ON TO THE NEXT PAGE.

Passage A

In 1994, Estonia became the first country to introduce a "flat tax" on personal and corporate income. Income is taxed at a single uniform rate of 26 percent: no schedule of rates, no deductions. So far eight
(5) countries have followed Estonia's example. An old idea that for decades elicited the response, "Fine in theory, just not practical in the real world," seems to be working as well in practice as it does on the blackboard.

Practical types who said that flat taxes cannot
(10) work offer a further instant objection, once they are shown such taxes working, namely, that they are unfair. Enlightened countries, it is argued, have "progressive" tax systems, requiring high-income earners to forfeit a bigger share of their incomes in tax than low-income
(15) earners have to pay. A flat tax seems to rule this out in principle.

Not so. A flat tax on personal incomes combines a threshold (that is, an exempt amount) with a single rate of tax on all income above it. The extent to which
(20) such a system is progressive can be varied within wide limits using just these two variables. Under the systems operating in most developed countries, the incentives for high-income earners to avoid tax (legally or otherwise) are enormous; and the opportunities to do
(25) so, which arise from the very complexity of the codes, are commensurately large. So it is unsurprising that high-income earners usually pay about as much tax under new flat-tax regimes as they would have paid under the previous codes.

Passage B

(30)   A lot of people don't understand graduated, as opposed to "flat," taxes. They think that if you make more money you pay a higher rate on your entire earnings, which seems unfair. Actually, graduated progressive taxes treat all taxpayers equally.
(35) Every taxpayer pays the same rate on equivalent layers of income. People in higher brackets don't pay the higher rate on their entire income, only on the portion of income over a specified amount. People, not dollars, are treated equally.
(40)   All people are created equal, but not all dollars are created equal. Earnings of the working poor go almost entirely for survival expenses such as food, shelter, and clothing. At that level, every dollar is critical; even a small difference causes tremendous
(45) changes in quality of life. Middle-income earners are still very conscious of expenses, but have much greater flexibility in absorbing small fluctuations in income.

Even some of the flat tax proposals recognize this, and want to exempt a primary layer from the tax
(50) system. So, since they recognize that survival dollars are different from discretionary dollars, why go suddenly from one extreme (paying no taxes) to the other (paying the top rate)? Since flat tax proposals are supposed to bring in the same total amount of tax
(55) revenue, if the working poor are going to pay less and the high-income earners are going to pay less, it is naturally going to fall on the middle class to make up the difference.

22. Both passages are concerned with answering which one of the following questions?

(A) Can a flat tax be implemented?
(B) Do graduated progressive taxes treat all taxpayers equally?
(C) Can a flat tax be fair to all taxpayers?
(D) What are some objections to progressive taxes?
(E) Do flat tax regimes reduce illegal tax avoidance?

23. Both passages seek to advance their arguments by means of which one of the following?

(A) accusing opponents of shifting their ground
(B) citing specific historical developments as evidence
(C) arguing on the basis of an analogy
(D) employing rhetorical questions
(E) correcting alleged misunderstandings

24. Which one of the following, if true of countries that have gone from a graduated progressive tax system to a flat tax, would most support the position of passage B over that of passage A?

(A) Revenues from taxation have remained the same as before.
(B) The tax codes in these countries have been greatly simplified.
(C) Most high-income taxpayers believe that they remain overtaxed.
(D) Middle-income taxpayers tend to pay higher taxes than before.
(E) Some legislators favor a return to a graduated progressive system.

25. Which one of the following is a conclusion for which passage A argues but that passage B does not address?

(A) that exempting a threshold amount enables a flat tax to avoid unfairness
(B) that flat tax proposals are not practical in the real world
(C) that higher taxes on high-income earners inhibit investment and economic growth
(D) that a flat tax decreases opportunities and incentives for high-income earners to avoid tax
(E) that a progressive tax is unfair to taxpayers who end up paying more

GO ON TO THE NEXT PAGE.

26. The authors of the two passages would be most likely to disagree over whether

(A) a flat tax system can be progressive
(B) high-income earners would pay less under a flat tax system than under a graduated progressive system
(C) flat tax systems are fine in theory but cannot be put into practice
(D) graduated progressive systems make higher income taxpayers pay a higher rate on their entire earnings
(E) all of an individual's income should be subject to taxation

27. Which one of the following, if true, would be the most reasonable response for the author of passage B to make to the final argument of passage A?

(A) Even under a flat-tax regime, it will be possible for some with high incomes to avoid taxes by underreporting their incomes.
(B) Existing tax codes allow tax avoidance by those with high incomes mainly because they contain loopholes and special deductions, not because they are graduated.
(C) It is unfair to those with high incomes to single them out as tax avoiders, since people at all income levels have been known to try to avoid taxes, sometimes illegally.
(D) Most taxpayers prefer a system that affords them opportunities for avoiding taxes over one that does not afford such opportunities.
(E) The goal of reducing tax avoidance would be advanced by eliminating income taxes altogether in favor of taxes on consumption of goods and services.

S T O P
IF YOU FINISH BEFORE TIME IS CALLED, YOU MAY CHECK YOUR WORK ON THIS SECTION ONLY. DO NOT WORK ON ANY OTHER SECTION IN THE TEST.

SECTION III

Time—35 minutes

26 Questions

Directions: The questions in this section are based on the reasoning contained in brief statements or passages. For some questions, more than one of the choices could conceivably answer the question. However, you are to choose the best answer; that is, the response that most accurately and completely answers the question. You should not make assumptions that are by commonsense standards implausible, superfluous, or incompatible with the passage. After you have chosen the best answer, blacken the corresponding space on your answer sheet.

1. Treat training consists of rewarding dogs with edible treats whenever they respond appropriately to commands. Most dogs will quickly learn what they need to do to receive a treat, so this appears to be an effective training method. However, most dogs who have been treat-trained will not obey commands unless they are shown a treat. Since you cannot always have treats on hand, you should instead use praise and verbal correction to train your dog.

Which one of the following principles, if valid, most helps to justify the reasoning above?

(A) The more quickly a dog learns to respond to a stimulus, the more likely it is that the owner will continue to use that stimulus.

(B) The more often a dog is given a stimulus, the more likely it is that the dog will obey its owner's command even when the owner does not provide that stimulus.

(C) A dog should be trained by the method that results in a high obedience rate in at least some circumstances.

(D) A dog should be trained to respond to a stimulus that its owner can supply in all situations.

(E) A dog should not be trained by a method that has not proven to be effective for any other dogs.

2. Archaeologist: For 2,000 years the ancient Sumerians depended on irrigation to sustain the agriculture that fed their civilization. But eventually irrigation built up in the soil toxic levels of the salts and other impurities left behind when water evaporates. When its soil became unable to support agriculture, Sumerian civilization collapsed. A similar fate is thus likely to befall modern civilizations that continue to rely heavily on irrigation for agriculture.

Which one of the following, if true, most weakens the archaeologist's argument?

(A) Most modern civilizations could not feed themselves through agriculture without relying heavily on irrigation.

(B) Factors unrelated to the use of irrigation would probably have caused Sumerian civilization to collapse sooner or later.

(C) Many modern farmers use irrigation techniques that avoid the buildup of salts and other toxic impurities in the soil.

(D) Many modern civilizations do not rely to any significant extent on irrigation for agriculture.

(E) The soil of ancient Sumeria already contained some toxic salts and other impurities before the Sumerians started using irrigation for agriculture.

3. Researcher: Dinosaur fossils come in various forms, including mineralized bones and tracks in dried mud flats. However, mineralized dinosaur bones and dinosaur tracks in dried mud flats are rarely found together. This isn't surprising, because creatures that scavenged dinosaur carcasses most likely frequented mud flats to find food.

Which one of the following, if true, would most strengthen the researcher's argument?

(A) Dinosaur tracks are also found in locations other than mud flats.

(B) Scavengers commonly drag a carcass away from the site where it was found.

(C) Researchers have found more fossil dinosaur tracks than fossil dinosaur bones.

(D) Dinosaur fossils other than mineralized bone or tracks in dried mud flats are quite common.

(E) It takes longer for bone to mineralize than it takes for tracks to dry in mud flats.

GO ON TO THE NEXT PAGE.

4. Electric stovetop burners would cause fewer fires if their highest temperature were limited to 350°C (662°F), which provides more than enough heat for efficient and effective cooking. The lowest temperature at which cooking oil and most common fibers ignite is 387°C, and electric burners on high go well above 700°C.

Which one of the following most accurately expresses the conclusion drawn in the argument?

(A) Electric stovetop burners would cause fewer fires if their highest temperature were limited to 350°C.
(B) A maximum temperature of 350°C provides more than enough heat for efficient and effective cooking.
(C) The lowest ignition temperature for cooking oil and most common fibers is 387°C.
(D) Electric burners on high go well above 700°C.
(E) Electric stovetop burners cause fires because they go well above 700°C when set on high.

5. Jenkins maintains that the movie *Firepower* was not intended to provoke antisocial behavior, arguing that, on the contrary, it is in the interest of *Firepower*'s director to prevent such behavior. Yet Jenkins's conclusion must be rejected, because the movie has clearly produced antisocial behavior among many of those who have seen it.

The reasoning in the argument is flawed in that it

(A) rejects an argument on the grounds that it was offered by a person who was biased
(B) concludes from a mere correlation between certain phenomena that those phenomena are causally related
(C) infers that something is true of a whole solely on the grounds that it is true of a part of the whole
(D) overlooks the possibility that people can act in a way that is contrary to their expressed interest
(E) concludes from the mere fact that an action had a certain effect that the effect was intended by the person who performed the action

6. The word "loophole" is a loaded, partisan word, one that implies wrongdoing and scandal. When "loophole" creeps into news stories, they start to read like editorials. So news reporters should not use the term "loophole" in their stories unless they provide evidence of wrongdoing.

Which one of the following principles, if valid, most helps to justify the reasoning in the argument?

(A) Making use of a loophole never constitutes wrongdoing or scandal.
(B) Editorials should meet the same journalistic standards as news stories.
(C) News stories need to give evidence to back up any suggestions of misconduct.
(D) Editorial writers should be free to use loaded, partisan words.
(E) News reporters should not report on wrongdoing and scandal that is not a matter of public interest.

7. Expert: Some people claim that, since food production has thus far increased faster than population has, there is no need to be concerned about widespread food shortages. These people fail to recognize that the planet's resources allow for food to be produced at only a few times the current amount, beyond which no increase in production will be possible. Thus, widespread food shortages are inevitable.

Which one of the following, if true, most strengthens the expert's reasoning?

(A) The world's food resources, though limited, are renewable.
(B) Food resources from the world's oceans will eventually be fully utilized.
(C) The world's population has recently remained fairly stable because of falling birth rates.
(D) Periodic regional food shortages have occurred at least briefly throughout history.
(E) Population will continue to grow at least briefly when food production has reached its maximum level.

GO ON TO THE NEXT PAGE.

8. In the earliest video games, the player typically controlled the movements of a simple icon on the screen. But in newer video games, players often control the movements of detailed human figures—a feature possible because of the greater technical sophistication of these games. It is hard for players to identify with these figures, since the players can see that the figures represent other people. Thus, in this respect the technical sophistication of the newer video games often makes them less compelling to players.

The conclusion of the argument can be properly drawn if which one of the following is assumed?

(A) There are no newer, more technically sophisticated video games in which the player controls the movements of a simple icon on the screen.

(B) Most early video games in which the player controlled a simple icon on the screen were in other respects less compelling to players than newer video games.

(C) The technical sophistication necessary for creating detailed human figures in video games cannot in itself make those video games fully compelling even to players who identify with those figures.

(D) When players cannot easily identify with the figure or icon whose movements they control in a video game, they usually find that game less compelling than it otherwise would be.

(E) If some aspect of a video game's technical sophistication makes it less compelling to players, then that video game contains a human figure with whom it is difficult for players to identify.

9. There are many agricultural regions in North America where the growing season is long enough to allow pumpkin production well into autumn with no risk of frost. Nonetheless, pumpkin production in North America is concentrated in regions with long, cold winters, where the growing season is delayed and pumpkin crops are exposed to risk of damage or destruction by early autumn frosts.

Which one of the following, if true, most helps to resolve the apparent discrepancy in the information above?

(A) Pumpkins are usually grown to reach maturity in autumn.

(B) Pumpkins depend on bees for pollination, and bees are active only in warm weather.

(C) More pumpkins are sold to consumers in regions of North America with long growing seasons than to those in regions with short growing seasons.

(D) Prolonged cold temperatures kill soil-borne fungus and other sources of disease that would kill or seriously damage pumpkins.

(E) Most of the pumpkin seed used by growers in North America is produced in areas where the growing season is long, and plants used for seed production are protected in greenhouses.

10. Council chair: The traditional code of parliamentary procedure contains a large number of obscure, unnecessary rules, which cause us to quibble interminably over procedural details and so to appear unworthy of public confidence. Admittedly, the code is entrenched and widely accepted. But success in our endeavors depends on the public's having confidence in our effectiveness. Therefore, it is imperative that we adopt the alternate code, which has been in successful use elsewhere for several years.

Which one of the following, if true, most seriously undermines the chair's conclusion?

(A) The council's use of the problematic rules in the traditional code is intermittent.

(B) Those who have adopted the alternate code sometimes attempt to use it to obscure their opponents' understanding of procedures.

(C) Revision of the traditional code is underway that will eliminate the problematic rules.

(D) It is not always reasonable to adopt a different code in order to maintain the public's confidence.

(E) The alternate code contains few provisions that have thus far been criticized as obscure or unnecessary.

GO ON TO THE NEXT PAGE.

11. Businesses frequently use customer surveys in an attempt to improve sales and increase profits. However, a recent study of the effectiveness of these surveys found that among a group of businesses that sold similar products, profits declined in most of the businesses that used surveys during the course of the study but not in most of the businesses that did not use any surveys during the course of the study.

Which one of the following, if true, most helps to explain why the profits of businesses that did not use customer surveys did not decline while the profits of those that used surveys did decline?

(A) When one business increases its profits, its competitors often report a decline in profits.
(B) Some businesses routinely use customer surveys.
(C) Most businesses of the kind included in the study generally administer customer surveys only as a response to complaints by customers.
(D) Customers who complete surveys do not always respond accurately to all the questions on the survey.
(E) Some of the businesses included in the study did not analyze the results of the customer surveys they conducted.

12. Humans' emotional tendencies are essentially unchanged from those of the earliest members of our species. Accordingly, although technology makes possible a wider range of individual and societal choices than in centuries past, humans are generally unable to choose more wisely.

The argument depends on assuming which one of the following?

(A) Humans have undergone no significant changes since the origin of the species.
(B) Humans who make wise choices are generally in control of their emotions.
(C) Human history cannot make humans any wiser unless humans are emotionally disposed to heed the lessons of history.
(D) Regardless of the range of choices available to humans, they choose on the basis of their emotions alone.
(E) Humans would now be able to make wiser choices than in centuries past only if an essential change had taken place in humans' emotional dispositions.

13. Some ornithologists believe that many species of songbirds are threatened by deforestation. Yet they also claim that, despite recent reforestation, matters continue to worsen, since it is fragmentation of forest rather than reduction of forest size that endangers songbird species. The introduction of open spaces and corridors in forests reduces the distance of songbird nests from unforested areas and thus reduces the songbirds' natural shield from predators.

The claim that there has recently been reforestation plays which one of the following roles in the ornithologists' argument?

(A) It is used as evidence that various species of songbirds will continue to be threatened with extinction.
(B) It is presented as a claim that is rejected by ornithologists who present declining songbird populations as evidence of deforestation.
(C) It is presented as a phenomenon that is compatible with the ornithologists' claim that the threat to songbirds continues to worsen.
(D) It is used as evidence that songbirds' predators will continue to have a habitat and so will continue to pose a threat to songbirds.
(E) It is presented as evidence for the claim that songbirds' predators are threatened by extinction unless they have open spaces and corridors that give them access to their prey.

14. Researchers recently studied the relationship between diet and mood, using a diverse sample of 1,000 adults. It was found that those who ate the most chocolate were the most likely to feel depressed. Therefore, by reducing excessive chocolate consumption, adults can almost certainly improve their mood.

The argument is most vulnerable to criticism on which one of the following grounds?

(A) It improperly infers from the fact that a substance causally contributes to a condition that a reduction in the consumption of the substance is likely to eliminate that condition.
(B) It draws a conclusion about the population as a whole on the basis of a sample that is unlikely to be representative of that population.
(C) It draws a conclusion about a causal relationship between two phenomena from evidence that merely suggests that there is a correlation between those phenomena.
(D) It confuses a condition that is necessary for establishing the truth of the conclusion with a condition that is sufficient for establishing the truth of the conclusion.
(E) Its conclusion is worded too vaguely to evaluate the degree to which the premises support the truth of the conclusion.

GO ON TO THE NEXT PAGE.

15. Among the many temptations of the digital age, manipulation of photographs has proved particularly troublesome for science. Recently, a journal of cellular biology began using a software tool to examine the digital images submitted along with articles for publication. It discovered that dozens of authors had submitted digital images that had been manipulated in ways that violated the journal's guidelines. Clearly, scientific fraud is a widespread problem among the authors submitting to that journal.

Which one of the following is an assumption required by the argument?

(A) The scientists who submitted manipulated images were aware that the journal used software to examine digital images for evidence of manipulation.
(B) The journal requires that all articles submitted for publication include digital images.
(C) Scientific fraud is possible in the field of cellular biology only if the research is documented with digital images.
(D) Many of the scientists who submitted articles with manipulated images did so in order to misrepresent the information conveyed by those images.
(E) Scientific fraud is a widespread problem only among scientists who submit articles to journals of cellular biology.

16. There are already more great artworks in the world than any human being could appreciate in a lifetime, works capable of satisfying virtually any taste imaginable. Thus, contemporary artists, all of whom believe that their works enable many people to feel more aesthetically fulfilled than they otherwise could, are mistaken.

The argument is most vulnerable to criticism on the grounds that it

(A) overlooks the possibility that not all contemporary artists believe that their works enable many people to feel more aesthetically fulfilled than they otherwise could
(B) presumes, without providing justification, that most human beings are inclined to take the time to appreciate many great artworks
(C) presumes, without providing justification, that the value of an artwork depends on the degree to which human beings appreciate it
(D) overlooks the possibility that the work of at least one contemporary artist is appreciated by many people whose access to the great majority of other artworks is severely restricted
(E) presumes, without providing justification, that the number and variety of great artworks already in the world affects the amount of aesthetic fulfillment derivable from any contemporary artwork

17. The government health service has said that it definitely will not pay for patients to take the influenza medicine Antinfia until the drug's manufacturer, PharmCo, provides detailed information about Antinfia's cost-effectiveness. PharmCo has responded that obtaining such information would require massive clinical trials. These trials cannot be performed until the drug is in widespread circulation, something that will happen only if the government health service pays for Antinfia.

If the statements of both the government health service and PharmCo are true, which one of the following is most likely to also be true?

(A) The government health service never pays for any medicine unless that medicine has been shown to be cost-effective.
(B) Antinfia will never be in widespread circulation.
(C) If the government health service does not pay for Antinfia, then many patients will pay for Antinfia themselves.
(D) The government health service should pay for patients to take Antinfia.
(E) Antinfia is not cost-effective.

18. Journalist: Scientists took blood samples from two large, diverse groups of volunteers. All the volunteers in one group reported that they enjoyed eating vegetables, whereas all those in the other group disliked vegetables. When the blood samples from the group that disliked vegetables were analyzed, it was discovered that all the volunteers in that group had a gene in common, the XRV2G gene. This strongly suggests that a dislike of vegetables is, at least in some cases, genetically determined.

The journalist's argument is most vulnerable to criticism on which one of the following grounds?

(A) It presumes that all human traits are genetically determined.
(B) It overlooks the possibility that the volunteers in one or both of the two groups may not have been representative of the human population as a whole in one or more respects.
(C) It overlooks the possibility that even when one phenomenon always produces another phenomenon, the latter phenomenon may often be present when the former is absent.
(D) It overlooks the possibility that even if a dislike of vegetables is genetically determined, it may be strongly influenced by genes other than the XRV2G gene.
(E) It takes for granted that the volunteers in the group that enjoyed eating vegetables did not also all have the XRV2G gene in common.

GO ON TO THE NEXT PAGE.

19. Ana: On libertarian principles, I oppose the proposed smoking ban. It is not the government's business to prevent people from doing things that harm only themselves.

    Pankaj: But keep in mind that the ban would apply only to smoking in public places. People could still smoke all they want in private.

    The dialogue provides the most support for the claim that Ana and Pankaj disagree over whether

    (A) it is the government's business to prevent people from harming themselves
    (B) government should be restrained by libertarian principles
    (C) the proposed smoking ban is intended to prevent harm only to smokers themselves
    (D) the proposed ban would prohibit smoking in public places
    (E) there are cases in which government should attempt to regulate private behavior

20. Agricultural scientist: Wild apples are considerably smaller than cultivated apples found in supermarkets. In one particular region, archaeologists have looked for remains of cultivated apples dating from 5,000 years ago, around the time people first started cultivating fruit. But the only remains of apples that archaeologists have found from this period are from fruits the same size as the wild apples native to the region. So apples were probably not cultivated in this region 5,000 years ago.

    The agricultural scientist's argument is most vulnerable to criticism on the grounds that the argument

    (A) fails to consider that even if a plant was not cultivated in a given region at a specific time, it may have been cultivated in nearby regions at that time
    (B) fails to consider that plants that have been cultivated for only a short time may tend to resemble their wild counterparts much more closely than plants that have been cultivated for a long time
    (C) takes for granted that all apples are either the size of wild apples or the size of the cultivated apples now found in supermarkets
    (D) employs a premise that is incompatible with the conclusion it is supposed to justify
    (E) uses a claim that presupposes the truth of its main conclusion as part of the justification for that conclusion

21. Genuine happiness consists not in pleasurable feelings but instead in one's sense of approval of one's character and projects. Thus the happy life, in fact, tends to be the good life, where the good life is understood not—as it usually is these days—as a life of material well-being but rather as a morally virtuous life.

    Which one of the following is an assumption required by the argument?

    (A) A morally virtuous life requires the rejection of material well-being.
    (B) People who approve of their own character and projects tend to lead morally virtuous lives.
    (C) Approval of one's own character and projects tends not to result in pleasurable feelings.
    (D) Attaining happiness is the real goal of people who strive for material well-being.
    (E) Material well-being does not increase one's sense of approval of one's character and projects.

GO ON TO THE NEXT PAGE.

22. The return of organic wastes to the soil is a good solution to waste disposal problems only if the wastes are nontoxic and not too much energy is expended in transporting them. In small-scale organic farming, the wastes are nontoxic and not too much energy is expended in transporting them. Hence, returning organic wastes to the soil is a good way for small-scale organic farms to solve their waste disposal problems.

Which one of the following exhibits flawed reasoning most similar to the flawed reasoning exhibited by the argument above?

(A) Plants thrive if they get an abundance of moisture, light, and nutrients. In greenhouses, plants get an optimal combination of all three, which is why commercially produced plants are so healthy when you first buy them.

(B) When every country has equal access to markets, which will be the case 20 years from now, globalization of markets will provide a way for each country to optimize its use of resources. So, globalization of markets will show the desired results 20 years from now.

(C) To be viable, a business idea must be clear, cost-effective, practical, and responsive to a market demand. Your idea for a website information service has all these properties, so it is viable.

(D) Those competitors—and only those—who meet all of the following criteria are eligible for the award: they must be under 19 years of age, be in secondary school, and have played the sport for at least the two years immediately preceding the competition. You meet all the criteria, so you are eligible.

(E) A meal is nutritious only if it includes both carbohydrates and protein. Almost 80 percent of the calories in what I ate for lunch were from fat, so what I ate for lunch was not nutritious.

23. Scientist: Some colonies of bacteria produce antibiotic molecules called phenazines, which they use to fend off other bacteria. We hypothesize that phenazines also serve as molecular pipelines that give interior bacteria access to essential nutrients in the environment surrounding the colony.

Which one of the following, if true, provides the most support for the scientist's hypothesis?

(A) Bacteria colonies that do not produce phenazines form wrinkled surfaces, thus increasing the number of bacteria that are in direct contact with the surrounding environment.

(B) The rate at which a bacteria colony produces phenazines is determined by the number of foreign bacteria in the environment immediately surrounding the colony.

(C) When bacteria colonies that do not produce phenazines are buried in nutrient-rich soil, they grow as quickly as colonies that do produce phenazines.

(D) Bacteria colonies that produce phenazines are better able to fend off other bacteria than are bacteria colonies that do not produce phenazines.

(E) Within bacteria colonies that produce phenazines, interior bacteria are more likely to die than are bacteria along the edges.

24. Library preservationist: Due to the continual physical deterioration of the medieval manuscripts in our library's collection, we have decided to restore most of our medieval manuscripts that are of widely acknowledged cultural significance, though this means that some medieval manuscripts whose authenticity is suspect will be restored. However, only manuscripts whose safety can be ensured during the restoration process will be restored, and manuscripts that are not frequently consulted by researchers will not be restored.

If all of the library preservationist's statements are true, which one of the following must be true of the medieval manuscripts in the library's collection?

(A) Some of the medieval manuscripts whose authenticity is suspect are frequently consulted by researchers.

(B) All of the medieval manuscripts widely acknowledged to be of cultural significance are manuscripts whose safety can be ensured during the restoration process.

(C) All of the medieval manuscripts whose safety can be ensured during the restoration process are frequently consulted by researchers.

(D) The medieval manuscripts most susceptible to deterioration are those most frequently consulted by researchers.

(E) None of the medieval manuscripts that are rarely consulted by researchers is widely acknowledged to be of cultural significance.

GO ON TO THE NEXT PAGE.

25. Direct-mail advertising usually consists of advertisements for products to be purchased from the home, so the perception that it is bad for the environment is misguided. Because of direct-mail advertising, millions of people buy products by phone or online—products whose purchase would otherwise require the use of a car, thus adding pollutants to the air.

Which one of the following, if true, would most strengthen the argument?

(A) Although the primary intent of most direct-mail advertisers is to convince people to buy products from their homes, direct mail can also lead to increased sales in stores by customers who prefer to see a product prior to purchasing it.

(B) Most of the products purchased in response to direct-mail advertisements would be purchased even without the direct-mail advertisements.

(C) A person who receives and reads a direct-mail advertisement is more likely to purchase the product advertised than is a person who reads an advertisement for a product in a magazine that they subscribe to.

(D) Usually, a company that sends out direct-mail advertisements has good reason to think that the person to whom the advertisement is sent would be more interested in the product than would the average person.

(E) Products purchased as the result of direct-mail advertising comprise an increasingly large portion of the consumer products purchased each year.

26. The older a country is, the more likely it is to be ruled by a monarch. Thus, since most countries are not ruled by monarchs, if a country is particularly new it is probably not ruled by a monarch.

The pattern of reasoning in the argument above is most similar to that in which one of the following arguments?

(A) Most novels are not made into movies. However, the more popular a novel is, the more likely it is to be made into a movie. Thus, if a movie is quite unpopular, it was probably not based on a novel.

(B) Most novels are not made into movies. However, the more popular a movie is, the more likely it is that the movie was based on a novel. Thus, if a novel is particularly popular, it will probably be made into a movie.

(C) Most novels are not made into movies. Moreover, if a novel is particularly unpopular, it will probably not be made into a movie. Thus, the more popular a novel is, the more likely it is to be made into a movie.

(D) Most novels are not made into movies. However, the more popular a novel is, the more likely it is to be made into a movie. Thus, if a novel is quite unpopular, it will probably not be made into a movie.

(E) Most novels are not made into movies. Moreover, the more complex a novel's plot, the less likely the novel is to be made into a movie. Thus, if a novel has a particularly simple plot, it will probably be made into a movie.

STOP
IF YOU FINISH BEFORE TIME IS CALLED, YOU MAY CHECK YOUR WORK ON THIS SECTION ONLY. DO NOT WORK ON ANY OTHER SECTION IN THE TEST.

SECTION IV

Time—35 minutes

25 Questions

<u>Directions</u>: The questions in this section are based on the reasoning contained in brief statements or passages. For some questions, more than one of the choices could conceivably answer the question. However, you are to choose the <u>best</u> answer; that is, the response that most accurately and completely answers the question. You should not make assumptions that are by commonsense standards implausible, superfluous, or incompatible with the passage. After you have chosen the best answer, blacken the corresponding space on your answer sheet.

1. Dentist: I recommend brushing one's teeth after every meal to remove sugars that facilitate the growth of certain bacteria; these bacteria produce acid that dissolves minerals in tooth enamel, resulting in cavities. And when brushing is not practical, I recommend chewing gum—even gum that contains sugar—to prevent the formation of cavities.

   Which one of the following, if true, would most help to reconcile the dentist's apparently paradoxical recommendations?

   (A) A piece of chewing gum that contains sugar contains far less sugar than does the average meal.
   (B) Tooth decay can be stopped and reversed if it is caught before a cavity develops.
   (C) Chewing gum stimulates the production of saliva, which reduces acidity in the mouth and helps remineralize tooth enamel.
   (D) Sugars can be on teeth for as long as 24 hours before the teeth-damaging bacteria whose growth they facilitate begin to proliferate.
   (E) Chewing gum exercises and relaxes the jaw muscles and so contributes to the overall health of the oral tract.

2. When the ancient fossils of a primitive land mammal were unearthed in New Zealand, they provided the first concrete evidence that the island country had once had indigenous land mammals. Until that discovery, New Zealand had no known native land mammals. The discovery thus falsifies the theory that New Zealand's rich and varied native bird population owes its existence to the lack of competition from mammals.

   Which one of the following, if true, most seriously weakens the argument?

   (A) The unearthed land mammal is only one of several ancient land mammals that were indigenous to New Zealand.
   (B) The recently discovered land mammal became extinct long before the native bird population was established.
   (C) The site at which the primitive land mammal was unearthed also contains the fossils of primitive reptile and insect species.
   (D) Countries with rich and varied native land mammal populations do not have rich and varied native bird populations.
   (E) Some other island countries that are believed to have no native land mammals in fact had indigenous land mammals at one time.

GO ON TO THE NEXT PAGE.

3. Restaurant owner: The newspaper reporter who panned my restaurant acknowledges having no special expertise about food and its preparation. His previous job was as a political reporter. He is a good writer, but he is not a true restaurant critic. A newspaper would never call someone a drama critic who had no special training in theater.

Which one of the following most accurately expresses the conclusion drawn in the restaurant owner's argument?

(A) The newspaper reporter who panned the restaurant acknowledges having no special expertise about food and its preparation.
(B) The previous job of the newspaper reporter who panned the restaurant was as a political reporter.
(C) The newspaper reporter who panned the restaurant is a good writer.
(D) The newspaper reporter who panned the restaurant is not a true restaurant critic.
(E) A newspaper would never call someone a drama critic who had no special training in theater.

4. It has been hypothesized that our solar system was formed from a cloud of gas and dust produced by a supernova—an especially powerful explosion of a star. Supernovas produce the isotope iron-60, so if this hypothesis were correct, then iron-60 would have been present in the early history of the solar system. But researchers have found no iron-60 in meteorites that formed early in the solar system's history, thereby disproving the hypothesis.

Which one of the following is an assumption required by the argument?

(A) If a meteorite is formed early in the solar system's history, it contains chemical elements that are unlikely to be found in gas and dust produced by a supernova.
(B) Other solar systems are not formed from clouds of gas and dust produced by supernovas.
(C) Supernovas do not produce significant quantities of any form of iron other than iron-60.
(D) Researchers have found iron-60 in meteorites that were formed relatively late in the solar system's history.
(E) If there had been iron-60 present in the early history of the solar system, it would be found in meteorites formed early in the solar system's history.

5. Safety expert: Tuna is often treated with carbon monoxide so that it will not turn brown as it ages. Treating tuna with carbon monoxide does not make it harmful in any way. Nonetheless, there is a danger that such treatment will result in more people getting sick from eating tuna.

Which one of the following, if true, most helps to resolve the apparent discrepancy in the safety expert's statements?

(A) Workers in fish processing plants can be sickened by exposure to carbon monoxide if the appropriate safety procedures are not followed at those plants.
(B) Over the last several years, tuna consumption has increased in most parts of the world.
(C) Tuna that is treated with carbon monoxide provides no visible indication when it has spoiled to the point that it can cause food poisoning.
(D) Treating tuna with carbon monoxide is the only way to keep it from turning brown as it ages.
(E) Most consumers strongly prefer tuna that is not brown because they believe that brown tuna is not fresh.

6. Astrophysicist: Gamma ray bursts (GRBs)—explosions of powerful radiation from deep space—have traditionally been classified as either "short" or "long," terms that reflect the explosion's relative duration. However, an unusual GRB has been sighted. Its duration was long, but in every other respect it had the properties of a short GRB. Clearly, the descriptive labels "short" and "long" have now outlived their usefulness.

The conclusion of the astrophysicist's argument is most strongly supported if which one of the following is assumed?

(A) No other GRBs with unusual properties have been sighted.
(B) The classification of GRBs can sometimes be made on the basis of duration alone.
(C) Properties other than duration are more important than duration in the proper classification of the unusual GRB.
(D) GRBs cannot be classified according to the different types of cosmic events that create them.
(E) Descriptive labels are easily replaced with nondescriptive labels such as "type I" and "type II."

GO ON TO THE NEXT PAGE.

7. In one study, hospital patients' immune systems grew stronger when the patients viewed comic videos. This indicates that laughter can aid recovery from illness. But much greater gains in immune system strength occurred in the patients whose tendency to laugh was greater to begin with. So hospital patients with a greater tendency to laugh are helped more in their recovery from illness even when they laugh a little than other patients are helped when they laugh a greater amount.

The argument is most vulnerable to criticism on the grounds that it

(A) overlooks the possibility that the patients whose tendency to laugh was greater to begin with laughed more at the comic videos than did the other patients

(B) fails to address adequately the possibility that the patients whose tendency to laugh was greatest to begin with already had stronger immune systems than the other patients

(C) presumes, without providing justification, that hospital patients have immune systems representative of those of the entire population

(D) takes for granted that the gains in immune system strength did not themselves influence the patients' tendency to laugh

(E) presumes, without providing justification, that the patients whose tendency to laugh was greatest to begin with recovered from their illnesses more rapidly than the other patients

8. A study of guppy fish shows that a male guppy will alter its courting patterns in response to feedback from a female guppy. Males with more orange on one side than the other were free to vary which side they showed to a female. Females were drawn to those males with more orange showing, and males tended to show the females their more orange side when courting.

Which one of the following, if true, provides the most support for the argument?

(A) When a model of a female guppy was substituted for the female guppy, male guppies still courted, but were not more likely to show their side with more orange.

(B) In many other species females show a preference for symmetry of coloring rather than quantity of coloring.

(C) No studies have been done on whether male guppies with more orange coloring father more offspring than those with less orange coloring.

(D) Female guppies have little if any orange coloring on their sides.

(E) The male and female guppies were kept in separate tanks so they could see each other but not otherwise directly interact.

9. Politician: Some proponents of unilateral nuclear arms reduction argue that it would encourage other countries to reduce their own nuclear arsenals, eventually leading to an international agreement on nuclear arms reduction. Our acting on the basis of this argument would be dangerous, because the argument ignores the countries presently on the verge of civil wars. These countries, many of which have nuclear capability, cannot be relied upon to conform to any international military policy.

Which one of the following most accurately expresses the conclusion of the politician's argument?

(A) Countries that are on the verge of civil wars are unlikely to agree to reduce either their nuclear arms or their conventional weapons.

(B) Unilateral nuclear arms reduction by the politician's country would encourage all countries to reduce their nuclear arsenals.

(C) Many countries cannot be relied upon to disclose the extent of their nuclear capability.

(D) It is unlikely that an international agreement on nuclear disarmament will ever be achieved.

(E) It is risky for the politician's country to unilaterally reduce nuclear arms in hopes of achieving an international agreement on arms reduction.

GO ON TO THE NEXT PAGE.

10. Advertisement: Auto accidents are the most common cause of whiplash injury, a kind of injury that is caused by a sudden sharp motion of the neck. However, many other types of accidents can produce a sudden sharp motion of the neck and thereby result in whiplash injury. A sudden sharp motion of the neck can be caused by a fall, a bump on the head, or even by being shoved from behind. That is why you should insist on receiving Lakeside Injury Clinic's complete course of treatment for whiplash after any accident that involves a fall or a bump on the head.

Which one of the following, if true, provides the strongest basis for criticizing the reasoning in the advertisement?

(A) Being shoved from behind rarely causes whiplash.
(B) Auto accidents often involve falling or being bumped on the head.
(C) Nonautomobile accidents other than those involving falls or bumps on the head also occasionally cause whiplash injuries.
(D) It is very uncommon for falling or being bumped on the head to result in a sudden sharp motion of the neck.
(E) The appropriate treatment for whiplash caused by a fall or a bump on the head is no different from that for whiplash caused by an auto accident.

11. A group of citizens opposes developing a nearby abandoned railroad grade into a hiking trail. Its members argue that trail users will likely litter the area with food wrappers and other debris. But this objection is groundless. Most trail users will be dedicated hikers who have great concern for the environment. Consequently, development of the trail should proceed.

The argument above is flawed in that it

(A) bases its conclusion mainly on a claim that an opposing argument is weak
(B) illicitly infers that because each member of a set has a certain property that set itself has the property
(C) illicitly assumes as one of its premises the contention it purports to show
(D) illicitly infers that an attribute of a few users of the proposed trail will characterize a majority of users of the trail
(E) attacks the citizens in the group rather than their objection to developing the trail

12. For years, university administrators, corporations, and government agencies have been predicting an imminent and catastrophic shortage of scientists and engineers. But since there is little noticeable upward pressure on the salaries of scientists and engineers, and unemployment is as high in these fields as any other, these doomsayers are turning out to be wrong.

Which one of the following would, if true, most strengthen the argument above?

(A) The proportion of all research in science and engineering being carried out by corporations is larger than it was five years ago.
(B) Most students choose fields of study that offer some prospect of financial success.
(C) The number of students in university programs in science and engineering has increased significantly in the last five years.
(D) Certain specializations in science and engineering have an oversupply of labor and others have shortages.
(E) The knowledge and skills acquired during university programs in science and engineering need to be kept current through periodic retraining and professional experience.

13. Rhonda: As long as the cost is not too great, you should use your time, energy, or money to help others. People who are active participants in charitable causes have richer lives than miserly hermits, however prosperous the hermits may be.

Brad: You should ignore the problems of complete strangers and focus your generosity on your immediate relatives and close friends, since these are the people who will remember your sacrifices and return the kindness when you yourself need help.

Which one of the following principles, if valid, would most help to justify both Rhonda's and Brad's arguments?

(A) One should always do what will produce the most benefit for the most people.
(B) One should treat others as one expects to be treated by them.
(C) One should act in ways that will benefit oneself.
(D) One should make sacrifices for others only if they will eventually return the favor.
(E) One should always act in a manner that one can reflect on with pride.

GO ON TO THE NEXT PAGE.

14. Columnist: Wildlife activists have proposed that the practice of stringing cable TV lines from the same poles that carry electric power lines should be banned because cable TV lines, while electrically neutral themselves, make it easier for animals to climb near electric power lines, risking electrocution. This particular argument for banning the practice fails, however, since some animals are electrocuted by power lines even where cable TV lines are all underground.

Which one of the following most accurately describes a flaw in the columnist's reasoning?

(A) It takes a sufficient condition for an argument's being inadequate to be a necessary condition for its being inadequate.

(B) It rejects an argument for a proposal merely on the grounds that the proposal would not completely eliminate the problem it is intended to address.

(C) It fails to consider the additional advantageous effects that a proposal to address a problem might have.

(D) It rejects an argument by criticizing the argument's proponents rather than by criticizing its substance.

(E) It rejects a proposal to address a problem merely on the grounds that other proposals to address the problem would also be effective.

15. The ancient reptile *Thrinaxodon*, an ancestor of mammals, had skull features suggesting that it had sensory whiskers. If *Thrinaxodon* had whiskers, it clearly also had hair on other parts of its body, which would have served as insulation that regulated body temperature. Therefore, *Thrinaxodon* was probably warm-blooded, for such insulation would be of little use to a cold-blooded animal.

Which one of the following most accurately describes the role played in the argument by the statement that if *Thrinaxodon* had whiskers, it clearly also had hair on other parts of its body, which would have served as insulation that regulated body temperature?

(A) It is a premise offered in support of the conclusion that insulation regulating body temperature would be of little use to a cold-blooded animal.

(B) It is a premise offered in support of the main conclusion drawn in the argument.

(C) It is a conclusion for which the claim that *Thrinaxodon* had skull features suggesting that it had sensory whiskers is offered as support.

(D) It is a statement of a hypothesis that the argument attempts to show is false.

(E) It is offered as an explanation of the phenomenon described by the argument's main conclusion, but it is not itself used to provide support for that conclusion.

16. Economist: Currently, many countries rely primarily on taxing income to fund government expenditures. But taxing income does nothing to promote savings and investment. Taxing consumption, on the other hand, would encourage savings. The most important challenge facing these countries is improving their economies, and the only way to accomplish this is to increase their savings rates. Hence, _____.

Which one of the following most logically completes the economist's argument?

(A) most governments should stop taxing savings and investment

(B) the economies of countries will rapidly improve if their governments adopt tax policies that encourage savings and investment

(C) in most countries taxes on consumption alone could raise adequate revenues to fund government expenditures

(D) the tax laws of many countries should be revised to focus on taxing consumption rather than income

(E) it is detrimental to the economic improvement of any country to continue to tax income

17. Meade: People who are injured as a result of their risky behaviors not only cause harm to themselves but, because we all have important ties to other people, inevitably impose emotional and financial costs on others. To protect the interests of others, therefore, governments are justified in outlawing behavior that puts one's own health at risk.

Which one of the following principles, if valid, most undermines the reasoning in Meade's argument?

(A) Endangering the social ties that one has to other people is itself a harm to oneself.

(B) People who have important ties to others have a personal obligation not to put their own health at risk.

(C) Governments are not justified in limiting an individual's behavior unless that behavior imposes emotional or financial costs on others.

(D) Preventing harm to others is not by itself a sufficient justification for laws that limit personal freedom.

(E) People's obligation to avoid harming others outweighs their obligation to avoid harming themselves.

GO ON TO THE NEXT PAGE.

18. Sanderson intentionally did not tell his cousin about overhearing someone say that the factory would close, knowing that if he withheld this information, his cousin would assume it would remain open. Clearly this was morally wrong. After all, lying is morally wrong. And making a statement with the intention of misleading someone is lying. True, it was Sanderson's failing to state something that misled his cousin. Yet there is no moral difference between stating and failing to state if they are done with the same intention.

Which one of the following is an assumption required by the argument?

(A) Sanderson believed that his cousin would not want to be informed about the factory closing.

(B) No one ever told Sanderson's cousin about the factory closing.

(C) Sanderson believed that the factory would in fact be closing.

(D) Sanderson would have lied to his cousin if his cousin had asked him whether the factory would be closing.

(E) Sanderson had something to gain by his cousin's continuing to believe that the factory would remain open.

19. After a judge has made the first ruling on a particular point of law, judges must follow that precedent if the original ruling is not contrary to the basic moral values of society. In the absence of precedent, when judges' own legal views do not contradict any widespread public opinion—and only then—they may abide by their own legal views in deciding a case.

Of the rulings described below, which one conforms most closely to the principles stated above?

(A) Judge Swoboda is confronted with a legal issue never before decided. Realizing that his own view on the issue contradicts what most people believe, he nonetheless issues a ruling that accords with his own legal views.

(B) Judge Valenzuela decides, in the absence of any precedent, whether children as young as twelve can be legally tried as adults. There is overwhelming public support for trying children twelve and older as adults, a practice that violates Judge Valenzuela's personal moral views. So Judge Valenzuela rules, in keeping with his own legal beliefs, against trying twelve-year-olds as adults.

(C) Judge Levinsky sets a legal precedent when she rules that the "starfish exception" applies to children. In deciding a later case concerning the starfish exception, Judge Wilson adheres to his own legal views rather than Judge Levinsky's ruling, even though he does not believe that Judge Levinsky's ruling opposes the basic moral values of society.

(D) Judge Watanabe must decide a case that depends on an issue for which no legal precedent exists. There is no widespread public opinion on the issue, so Judge Watanabe rules against the defendant because that conforms to her own legal view about the issue.

(E) Judge Balila rules against the defendant because doing so conforms to her own views about the legal issues involved. However, this ruling is contrary to relevant precedents, all of which conform to the basic moral values of society.

GO ON TO THE NEXT PAGE.

20. Neuroscientists subjected volunteers with amusia—difficulty telling different melodies apart and remembering simple tunes—to shifts in pitch comparable to those that occur when someone plays one piano key and then another. The volunteers were unable to discern a difference between the tones. But the volunteers were able to track timed sequences of musical tones and perceive slight changes in timing.

The statements above, if true, most strongly support which one of the following hypotheses?

(A) People who are unable to discern pitch compensate by developing a heightened perception of timing.
(B) Amusia results more from an inability to discern pitch than from an inability to discern timing.
(C) People who are unable to tell pitches apart in isolation are able to do so in the context of a melody by relying upon timing.
(D) The ability to tell melodies apart depends on the discernment of pitch alone and not at all on the perception of timing.
(E) Whereas perception of timing can apparently be learned, discernment of pitch is most likely innate.

21. Literary critic: There is little of social significance in contemporary novels, for readers cannot enter the internal world of the novelist's mind unless they experience that world from the moral perspective of the novel's characters. But in contemporary novels, the transgressions committed by some characters against others are sensationalistic spectacles whose only purpose is to make readers wonder what will happen next, rather than events whose purpose is to be seen as the injustices they are.

Which one of the following principles, if valid, would most help to justify the literary critic's argument?

(A) An artist who wants to engage the moral sensibilities of his or her audience should not assume that forms of artistic expression that previously served this purpose continue to do so.
(B) A novelist who wants to make a reader empathize with a victim of injustice should avoid sensationalistic spectacles whose only purpose is to make readers wonder what will happen next.
(C) A work of art is socially important only if it engages the moral sensibilities of its audience.
(D) If a novel allows a reader to understand injustice from the point of view of its victims, it will be socially significant.
(E) Novels have social significance only to the extent that they allow readers to enter the internal world of the novelist's mind.

22. A recent study revealed that people who follow precisely all the standard recommendations for avoidance of infection by pathogenic microorganisms in meat-based foods are more likely to contract diseases caused by these pathogens than are those who deviate considerably from the standard recommendations. Hence, the standard recommendations for avoidance of infection by these pathogens must be counterproductive.

The argument is most vulnerable to criticism on the grounds that it fails to take into account which one of the following possibilities?

(A) Pathogenic microorganisms can reproduce in foods that are not meat-based.
(B) Many people do follow precisely all the standard recommendations for avoidance of infection by pathogenic microorganisms in meat-based foods.
(C) Not all diseases caused by microorganisms have readily recognizable symptoms.
(D) Preventing infection by pathogenic microorganisms is simply a matter of following the appropriate set of recommendations.
(E) Those most concerned with avoiding pathogenic infections from meat-based foods are those most susceptible to them.

GO ON TO THE NEXT PAGE.

23. No nonfiction book published by Carriage Books has ever earned a profit. Since Carriage Books earned a profit on every book it published last year, it clearly did not publish a nonfiction book last year.

    The pattern of reasoning in the argument above is most similar to that in which one of the following arguments?

    (A) No actor represented by the talent agent Mira Roberts has ever won an important role in a major movie. Since every actor represented by Ms. Roberts had at least one important acting role last year, it is clear that none of those actors worked in a movie last year.

    (B) No hotel owned by the Bidmore Group specializes in serving business travelers. Since the Cray Springs Hotel is owned by the Bidmore Group, it clearly does not specialize in serving business travelers.

    (C) Pranwich Corporation has never given a bonus to an employee in its marketing division. Since Pranwich gave bonuses to every one of its systems analysts last year, it is clear that the company employed no systems analysts in its marketing division at that time.

    (D) James Benson has never done business with the city of Waldville. Since Waldville only maintains business files on individuals that it does business with, it clearly does not have a business file on James Benson.

    (E) Conway Flooring has never installed hardwood flooring for any customer in Woodridge. Since Conway Flooring has had a lot of customers in Woodridge, the company clearly does not install hardwood flooring.

24. All unemployed artists are sympathetic to social justice. And no employed artists are interested in the prospect of great personal fame.

    If the claims made above are true, then which one of the following must be true?

    (A) If there are artists interested in the prospect of great personal fame, they are sympathetic to social justice.

    (B) All artists uninterested in the prospect of great personal fame are sympathetic to social justice.

    (C) Every unemployed artist is interested in the prospect of great personal fame.

    (D) If an artist is sympathetic to social justice, that artist is unemployed.

    (E) All artists are either sympathetic to social justice or are interested in the prospect of great personal fame.

25. The police department has two suspects for the burglary that occurred last night, Schaeffer and Forster. Schaeffer has an ironclad alibi, so Forster must be the burglar.

    Which one of the following arguments exhibits a flawed pattern of reasoning that is most similar to that exhibited by the argument above?

    (A) It has been known for some time that the Wrightsburg Zoo might build a new primate house and that it might refurbish its polar bear exhibit. There is now good reason to believe the zoo will build a new primate house. Therefore, the zoo will not refurbish its polar bear exhibit.

    (B) If Watson, a robbery suspect, had been picked out of a police lineup by the victim, then charging Watson with robbery would have been reasonable. But the victim did not pick Watson out of the lineup. So Watson should not be charged.

    (C) If Iano Industries does not borrow money so that it can upgrade its factories, it will be unable to compete. While it is undesirable for Iano to take on more debt, being unable to compete would be even worse. So Iano should borrow the money needed to upgrade its factories.

    (D) Baxim Corporation announced last year that it was considering moving its headquarters to Evansville and that it was also considering moving to Rivertown. But Baxim has now decided not to move to Evansville. Thus, we can be sure that Baxim will move to Rivertown.

    (E) The only viable candidates in the mayoral race are Slater and Gonzales. Political analysts believe that Slater has little chance of winning. Therefore, it is likely that Gonzales will win the election.

STOP

IF YOU FINISH BEFORE TIME IS CALLED, YOU MAY CHECK YOUR WORK ON THIS SECTION ONLY. DO NOT WORK ON ANY OTHER SECTION IN THE TEST.

SECTION V

Time—35 minutes

23 Questions

Directions: Each group of questions in this section is based on a set of conditions. In answering some of the questions, it may be useful to draw a rough diagram. Choose the response that most accurately and completely answers each question and blacken the corresponding space on your answer sheet.

Questions 1–6

A radio station airs hourly news updates every morning. Each update consists of exactly five reports—two of general interest: international and national; and three of local interest: sports, traffic, and weather. Each update must be structured as follows:

There are exactly two segments, the first segment containing three reports and the second segment containing two.

Within each segment, reports are ordered by length, from longest to shortest.

Each segment contains at least one report of local interest.

The national report is always the longest of the five reports.

The sports report is always the shortest of the five reports.

The international report is always longer than the weather report.

1. Which one of the following could be an accurate matching of reports to their segments, with the reports listed in order from earliest to latest?

(A) first segment: international, national, sports second segment: traffic, weather

(B) first segment: national, international, sports second segment: weather, traffic

(C) first segment: national, international, weather second segment: sports, traffic

(D) first segment: national, weather, international second segment: traffic, sports

(E) first segment: traffic, weather, sports second segment: national, international

GO ON TO THE NEXT PAGE.

2. If the traffic report is the last report in the first segment, then which one of the following must be true?

    (A) The national report is the first report in the first segment.
    (B) The international report is the second report in the first segment.
    (C) The weather report is the second report in the first segment.
    (D) The national report is the first report in the second segment.
    (E) The sports report is the last report in the second segment.

3. If the national report is the first report in the second segment, then exactly how many of the reports are there any one of which could be the first report in the first segment?

    (A) one
    (B) two
    (C) three
    (D) four
    (E) five

4. Which one of the following CANNOT be true?

    (A) The international report is the first report in the first segment.
    (B) The national report is the first report in the first segment.
    (C) The national report is the first report in the second segment.
    (D) The weather report is the first report in the first segment.
    (E) The weather report is the last report in the second segment.

5. The order of the reports is fully determined if which one of the following is true?

    (A) The international report is the last report in the first segment.
    (B) The national report is the first report in the first segment.
    (C) The national report is the first report in the second segment.
    (D) The sports report is the last report in the second segment.
    (E) The weather report is the last report in the first segment.

6. If the traffic report is the first report in the first segment, then which one of the following could be true?

    (A) The international report is the first report in the second segment.
    (B) The national report is the second report in the first segment.
    (C) The weather report is the second report in the first segment.
    (D) The weather report is the first report in the second segment.
    (E) The weather report is the last report in the second segment.

GO ON TO THE NEXT PAGE.

<u>Questions 7–12</u>

On a single day, a realtor will show a client five houses, exactly one house in each of five neighborhoods—Quarry, Riverton, Shelburne, Townsend, and Valencia. Each house will be shown to the client exactly once. The order in which the houses are shown is subject to the following constraints:

The house in Riverton must be shown either first or second.

The house in Townsend must be shown either first or fifth.

The third house shown must be the house in Quarry or the house in Valencia.

The house in Quarry cannot be shown either immediately before or immediately after the house in Shelburne.

7. If the house in Quarry is shown fourth, which one of the following must be true?

(A) The house in Riverton is shown first.
(B) The house in Riverton is shown second.
(C) The house in Shelburne is shown second.
(D) The house in Townsend is shown first.
(E) The house in Valencia is shown third.

GO ON TO THE NEXT PAGE.

8. The order in which the houses are shown is fully determined if which one of the following is true?

    (A) The house in Quarry is shown third.
    (B) The house in Riverton is shown first.
    (C) The house in Shelburne is shown second.
    (D) The house in Townsend is shown fifth.
    (E) The house in Valencia is shown fourth.

9. If the house in Shelburne is shown earlier than the house in Quarry, which one of the following must be true?

    (A) The house in Quarry is shown fourth.
    (B) The house in Riverton is shown second.
    (C) The house in Shelburne is shown first.
    (D) The house in Townsend is shown fifth.
    (E) The house in Valencia is shown third.

10. Which one of the following could be true?

    (A) The house in Quarry is shown first.
    (B) The house in Quarry is shown fifth.
    (C) The house in Valencia is shown first.
    (D) The house in Valencia is shown second.
    (E) The house in Valencia is shown fifth.

11. If the house in Valencia is shown third, which one of the following must be true?

    (A) The house in Quarry is shown fourth.
    (B) The house in Riverton is shown second.
    (C) The house in Shelburne is shown first.
    (D) The house in Shelburne is shown fourth.
    (E) The house in Townsend is shown fifth.

12. Which one of the following, if substituted for the constraint that the house in Riverton must be shown either first or second, would have the same effect on the order in which the houses are shown?

    (A) The house in Riverton cannot be shown fourth.
    (B) The house in Riverton must be shown earlier than the house in Valencia.
    (C) The house in Valencia must be shown either third or fourth.
    (D) The house in Quarry must be shown either immediately before or immediately after the house in Riverton.
    (E) If the house in Townsend is not shown fifth, then it must be shown immediately before the house in Riverton.

GO ON TO THE NEXT PAGE.

Questions 13–18

Five artifacts—V, W, X, Y, and Z—recovered from a sunken ship are each known to have originated in Iceland, Norway, or Sweden. These artifacts, together with the surviving fragments of a cargo list, have enabled historians to determine the following:

> W and Y originated in the same country.
> X originated in Norway or Sweden.
> More of the artifacts originated in Iceland than in Norway.
> If V originated in Iceland, then Z originated in Sweden.

13. Which one of the following could be an accurate matching of the artifacts to their origins?

(A) Iceland: V, W
    Norway: X
    Sweden: Y, Z

(B) Iceland: W, Y
    Norway: none
    Sweden: V, X, Z

(C) Iceland: W, Y
    Norway: V, Z
    Sweden: X

(D) Iceland: V, W, Y
    Norway: Z
    Sweden: X

(E) Iceland: W, X, Y
    Norway: Z
    Sweden: V

GO ON TO THE NEXT PAGE.

14. If Y and Z originated in Iceland, then what is the minimum number of artifacts that originated in Sweden?

    (A) zero
    (B) one
    (C) two
    (D) three
    (E) four

15. Which one of the following CANNOT be true?

    (A) V and X both originated in Norway.
    (B) V and Y both originated in Iceland.
    (C) W and Z both originated in Iceland.
    (D) W and Z both originated in Sweden.
    (E) W and Y both originated in Norway.

16. If W and X originated in Sweden, then which one of the following must be true?

    (A) None of the artifacts originated in Norway.
    (B) None of the artifacts originated in Iceland.
    (C) V originated in Sweden.
    (D) Z originated in Iceland.
    (E) Z originated in Sweden.

17. Exactly how many of the artifacts are there any one of which could have originated in Norway?

    (A) one
    (B) two
    (C) three
    (D) four
    (E) five

18. Which one of the following CANNOT be true?

    (A) Only V originated in Sweden.
    (B) Only V and Z originated in Sweden.
    (C) Only W and Y originated in Sweden.
    (D) Only X and Z originated in Sweden.
    (E) Only V, W, X, and Y originated in Sweden.

GO ON TO THE NEXT PAGE.

<u>Questions 19–23</u>

The employees of the Summit Company—J, K, L, and M—work a four-day workweek from Monday through Thursday. Every Monday, work begins on four raw workpieces, each of which is worked on for four consecutive days. On any given day, an employee works on exactly one workpiece. At the beginning of each workday after Monday, each workpiece is transferred from the employee who worked on it the previous day to another one of the employees, who will work on it that day. Workpieces cannot be transferred in any of the following ways:

    From J to M
    From K to J
    From L to J

19.   Which one of the following describes four transfers of workpieces that could all occur together at the beginning of a particular workday?

(A)   From J to K; from K to L; from L to M; from M to J

(B)   From J to K; from K to M; from L to K; from M to J

(C)   From J to L; from K to M; from L to J; from M to K

(D)   From J to L; from K to J; from L to M; from M to K

(E)   From J to M; from K to L; from L to K; from M to J

GO ON TO THE NEXT PAGE.

20. Which one of the following transfers must occur at the beginning of any workday that is not a Monday?

    (A) From J to K
    (B) From J to L
    (C) From K to L
    (D) From L to M
    (E) From M to J

21. If one workpiece is worked on by only two of the four employees in the course of an entire workweek, those two employees must be

    (A) J and K
    (B) J and L
    (C) K and L
    (D) K and M
    (E) L and M

22. If L works on the same workpiece both on Tuesday and on Thursday, which one of the following must be true about that workpiece?

    (A) J works on it on Monday.
    (B) K works on it on Monday.
    (C) M works on it on Monday.
    (D) J works on it on Wednesday.
    (E) K works on it on Wednesday.

23. Which one of the following could be true about Tuesday?

    (A) Transfers from J to K and from K to M occur.
    (B) Transfers from J to L and from L to M occur.
    (C) Transfers from J to M and from M to J occur.
    (D) Transfers from K to L and from L to K occur.
    (E) Transfers from K to L and from L to M occur.

STOP
IF YOU FINISH BEFORE TIME IS CALLED, YOU MAY CHECK YOUR WORK ON THIS SECTION ONLY. DO NOT WORK ON ANY OTHER SECTION IN THE TEST.

LSAT WRITING SAMPLE TOPIC

A successful and politically active lawyer is deciding between two career moves: either to accept an appointment as a judge in the regional courts, or to run, with support from a major party, for a seat in the national legislature. Using the facts below, write an essay in which you argue for one choice over the other based on the following two criteria:

• The lawyer wants to have a significant impact on public policy and the future of the country.

• The lawyer wants to maintain a close-knit and prosperous family.

The judicial appointment is a permanent position. Regional judges are rarely removed from office. The regional courts decide at most one or two cases of wide significance in a year. A few regional judges advance to positions in the national courts where most significant cases are decided. Regional judges train law clerks, many of whom go on to important positions in public life. Judges work regular hours and are not required to travel. Judges have personal contact with important figures in government and business. Judges rarely have success in seeking other political office.

The legislative seat is in a highly competitive district and the holder faces frequent elections. New legislators seldom have much effect on legislation or government policy. Successful long-time legislators can greatly affect government policies and programs. The legislature is in session 36 weeks of the year. Legislators spend many hours campaigning and fundraising. They travel frequently between the national capital and their district. The national capital is a short flight from the lawyer's legislative district. Legislators are widely known in their districts and some eventually gain national recognition. A close and supportive family is a strong asset in politics.

Directions:

1. Use the Answer Key on the next page to check your answers.

2. Use the Scoring Worksheet below to compute your raw score.

3. Use the Score Conversion Chart to convert your raw score into the 120–180 scale.

Scoring Worksheet

1. Enter the number of questions you answered correctly in each section.

	Number Correct
SECTION II	_____
SECTION III	_____
SECTION IV	_____
SECTION V	_____

2. Enter the sum here: _____
   This is your Raw Score.

Section Map

SECTION I: Experimental (PrepTest 58, Section 4)
SECTION II: PrepTest 72, Section 1
SECTION III: PrepTest 72, Section 2
SECTION IV: PrepTest 72, Section 3
SECTION V: PrepTest 72, Section 4

Conversion Chart
For Converting Raw Score to the 120–180 LSAT Scaled Score
LSAT Form 5LSN113

Reported Score	Lowest	Highest
180	99	101
179	98	98
178	97	97
177	96	96
176	95	95
175	94	94
174	93	93
173	92	92
172	90	91
171	89	89
170	88	88
169	87	87
168	85	86
167	84	84
166	82	83
165	81	81
164	79	80
163	77	78
162	76	76
161	74	75
160	72	73
159	71	71
158	69	70
157	67	68
156	65	66
155	64	64
154	62	63
153	60	61
152	58	59
151	56	57
150	55	55
149	53	54
148	51	52
147	49	50
146	48	48
145	46	47
144	44	45
143	43	43
142	41	42
141	39	40
140	38	38
139	36	37
138	35	35
137	33	34
136	32	32
135	30	31
134	29	29
133	28	28
132	26	27
131	25	25
130	24	24
129	23	23
128	22	22
127	21	21
126	20	20
125	19	19
124	18	18
123	17	17
122	16	16
121	15	15
120	0	14

*There is no raw score that will produce this scaled score for this form.

SECTION I

1.	E	8.	B	15.	B	22.	C
2.	C	9.	A	16.	B	23.	B
3.	A	10.	D	17.	D	24.	B
4.	C	11.	E	18.	E	25.	A
5.	A	12.	A	19.	B		
6.	D	13.	C	20.	E		
7.	A	14.	D	21.	D		

SECTION II

1.	D	8.	B	15.	D	22.	C
2.	E	9.	C	16.	C	23.	E
3.	C	10.	A	17.	D	24.	D
4.	A	11.	C	18.	D	25.	D
5.	B	12.	D	19.	A	26.	B
6.	D	13.	B	20.	C	27.	B
7.	B	14.	B	21.	A		

SECTION III

1.	D	8.	D	15.	D	22.	C
2.	C	9.	D	16.	D	23.	A
3.	B	10.	C	17.	B	24.	A
4.	A	11.	C	18.	E	25.	B
5.	E	12.	E	19.	C	26.	D
6.	C	13.	C	20.	B		
7.	E	14.	C	21.	B		

SECTION IV

1.	C	8.	A	15.	B	22.	E
2.	D	9.	E	16.	D	23.	C
3.	B	10.	D	17.	D	24.	A
4.	E	11.	A	18.	C	25.	D
5.	C	12.	C	19.	D		
6.	C	13.	C	20.	B		
7.	A	14.	B	21.	E		

SECTION V

1.	B	8.	C	15.	E	22.	E
2.	E	9.	D	16.	A	23.	E
3.	B	10.	A	17.	C		
4.	D	11.	E	18.	C		
5.	A	12.	B	19.	A		
6.	E	13.	B	20.	E		
7.	E	14.	A	21.	C		

TEST ANALYSIS

Section	Overall Performance Score: _____ Percentile: _____		
	Number attempted	Number of guesses	Number correct
Games			
Reading Comprehension			
Arguments 1			
Arguments 2			
TOTAL			

Games			
	Attempted? What order?	Diagram and Elements	Notes
Game 1			
Game 2			
Game 3			
Game 4			

Reading Comprehension

	Attempted? What order?	Passage Notes	Question Notes
Passage 1			
Passage 2			
Passage 3			
Passage 4			

Arguments

Page	Question Number	Question Task	Notes

Arguments			
Page	Question Number	Question Task	Notes

The Official LSAT
PrepTest™ 73
Test code 9738
Form 4LSN110

SECTION I

Time—35 minutes

27 Questions

<u>Directions</u>: Each set of questions in this section is based on a single passage or a pair of passages. The questions are to be answered on the basis of what is <u>stated</u> or <u>implied</u> in the passage or pair of passages. For some of the questions, more than one of the choices could conceivably answer the question. However, you are to choose the <u>best</u> answer; that is, the response that most accurately and completely answers the question, and blacken the corresponding space on your answer sheet.

Charles Darwin objected to all attempts to reduce his theory of evolution to its doctrine of natural selection. "Natural selection has been the main but not the exclusive means of modification," he declared.
(5)   Nonetheless, a group of self-proclaimed strict constructionist Darwinians has recently risen to prominence by reducing Darwin's theory in just this way. These theorists use the mechanism of natural selection to explain all biological phenomena; they
(10) assert that natural selection is responsible for every aspect of every species' form and behavior, and for the success or failure of species in general.

Natural selection is generally held to result in adaptation, the shaping of an organism's form and
(15) behavior in response to environmental conditions to achieve enhanced reproductive success. If the strict constructionists are right, the persistence of every attribute and the survival of every species are due to such adaptation. But in fact, nature provides numerous
(20) examples of attributes that are not adaptations for reproductive success and of species whose success or failure had little to do with their adaptations.

For example, while it is true that some random mutations of genetic material produce attributes that
(25) enhance reproductive success and are thus favored by natural selection, and others produce harmful attributes that are weeded out, we now know from population genetics that most mutations fall into neither category. Research has revealed that neutral, nonadaptive
(30) changes account to a large extent for the evolution of DNA. Most substitutions of one unit of DNA for another within a population have no effect on reproductive success. These alterations often change the attributes of species, but their persistence from
(35) one generation to the next is not explainable by natural selection.

Additionally, the study of mass extinctions in paleontology has undermined the strict constructionist claim that natural selection can account for every
(40) species' success or failure. The extinction of the dinosaurs some 65 million years ago was probably caused by the impact of an extraterrestrial body. Smaller animal species are generally better able to survive the catastrophic changes in climate that we
(45) would expect to follow from such an impact, and mammals in the Cretaceous period were quite small because they could not compete on the large scale of the dominant dinosaurs. But while this scenario explains why dinosaurs died off and mammals fared
(50) relatively well, it does not conform to the strict

constructionist view of the adaptive reasons for the success of species. For that view assumes that adaptations are a response to conditions that are already in place at the time the adaptations occur,
(55) and mammals could not have adapted in advance to conditions caused by the impact. In a sense, their success was the result of dumb luck.

1.   Which one of the following most accurately expresses the main point of the passage?

   (A)   Evidence from two areas of science undermines the strict constructionist claim that natural selection is the only driving force behind evolution.
   (B)   According to strict constructionist Darwinians, new evidence suggests that natural selection is responsible for the failure of most extinct species.
   (C)   New evidence demonstrates that natural selection can produce nonadaptive as well as adaptive changes.
   (D)   Strict constructionist followers of Darwin maintain that natural selection is responsible for all evolutionary change.
   (E)   Evidence from the study of population genetics helps to disprove the claim that natural selection results in the survival of the fittest species.

2.   According to the author, mammals were able to survive catastrophic environmental changes that occurred roughly 65 million years ago because they

   (A)   had adapted previously to similar changes
   (B)   were relatively small
   (C)   were highly intelligent
   (D)   lived in a wide range of environments
   (E)   were able to reproduce quickly

GO ON TO THE NEXT PAGE.

3. The author asserts which one of the following regarding mutations of genetic material?

(A) The majority of such mutations are not passed on to subsequent generations.
(B) The majority of such mutations occur during periods when mass extinctions take place.
(C) The majority of such mutations change species' behavior rather than their appearance.
(D) The majority of such mutations have no effect on reproductive success.
(E) The majority of such mutations occur in larger rather than smaller species.

4. The author would be most likely to agree with which one of the following statements?

(A) Natural selection is responsible for almost none of the characteristics of existing species.
(B) The fact that a species flourishes in a certain environment is not proof of its adaptation to that environment.
(C) Only evolutionary changes that provide some advantage to a species are transmitted to subsequent generations.
(D) Large animal species are generally unable to survive in harsh environmental conditions.
(E) Natural selection is useful for explaining the form but not the behavior of most species.

5. The author's stance toward the arguments of the strict constructionist Darwinians can most accurately be described as one of

(A) emphatic disagreement
(B) mild disapproval
(C) open-minded neutrality
(D) conditional agreement
(E) unreserved endorsement

6. Which one of the following most accurately and completely describes the function of the second paragraph of the passage?

(A) It outlines the objections to traditional evolutionary theory raised by the strict constructionists mentioned in the first paragraph.
(B) It lists recent evidence suggesting that the strict constructionist claims described in the first paragraph are incorrect.
(C) It describes the strict constructionists' view of evolutionary theory in order to explain why the evidence described in subsequent paragraphs has recently gotten so much attention.
(D) It enumerates the arguments for the strict constructionist position that are rebutted in the paragraphs that follow.
(E) It explains the ramifications of the strict constructionists' claims and helps clarify the relevance of evidence offered in subsequent paragraphs.

7. The primary purpose of the passage is to

(A) argue in favor of a recently proposed hypothesis
(B) summarize a contemporary debate
(C) demonstrate that a particular view is incorrect
(D) criticize the proponents of a traditional theory
(E) explain why a particular theory is gaining popularity

GO ON TO THE NEXT PAGE.

From a critical discussion of the work of Victorian photographer Julia Margaret Cameron.

What Cameron called her "fancy-subject" pictures—photographs in which two or more costumed sitters enacted, under Cameron's direction, scenes from the Bible, mythology, Shakespeare, or Tennyson—
(5) bear unmistakable traces of the often comical conditions under which they were taken. In many respects they have more connection to the family album pictures of recalcitrant relatives who have been herded together for the obligatory group picture than they do to the
(10) masterpieces of Western painting. In Raphael and Giotto there are no infant Christs whose faces are blurred because they moved, or who are looking at the viewer with frank hatred. These traces, of course, are what give the photographs their life and charm. If
(15) Cameron had succeeded in her project of making seamless works of illustrative art, her work would be among the curiosities of Victorian photography—like Oscar Gustave Rejlander's extravagantly awful *The Two Ways of Life*—rather than among its most
(20) vital images.

It is precisely the camera's realism—its stubborn obsession with the surface of things—that has given Cameron's theatricality and artificiality its atmosphere of truth. It is the truth of the sitting, rather than the
(25) fiction which all the dressing up was in aid of, that wafts out of these wonderful and strange, not-quite-in-focus photographs. They are what they are: pictures of housemaids and nieces and husbands and village children who are dressed up as Mary Madonnas and
(30) infant Jesuses and John the Baptists and Lancelots and Guineveres and trying desperately hard to sit still. The way each sitter endures his or her ordeal is the collective action of the photograph, its "plot" so to speak. When we look at a narrative painting we can
(35) suspend our disbelief; when we look at a narrative photograph we cannot. We are always aware of the photograph's doubleness—of each figure's imaginary and real personas. Theater can transcend its doubleness, can make us believe (for at least some of the time) that
(40) we are seeing only Lear or Medea. Still photographs of theatrical scenes can never escape being pictures of actors.

What gives Cameron's pictures of actors their special quality—their status as treasures of photography
(45) of an unfathomably peculiar sort—is their singular combination of amateurism and artistry. In *The Passing of Arthur,* for example, the mast and oar of the makeshift boat representing a royal barge are obviously broomsticks and the water is white muslin
(50) drapery. But these details are insignificant. For once, the homely truth of the sitting gives right of place to the romantic fantasy of its director. The picture, a night scene, is magical and mysterious. While Cameron's fancy-subject pictures have been compared
(55) to poor amateur theatricals, *The Passing of Arthur* puts one in mind of good amateur theatricals one has seen, and recalls with shameless delight.

8. Which one of the following most accurately expresses the main point of the passage?

(A) The circumstances under which Cameron's fancy-subject pictures were taken render them unintentionally comical.
(B) The peculiar charm of Cameron's fancy-subject pictures derives from the viewer's simultaneous awareness of the fictional scene portrayed and the circumstances of its portrayal.
(C) The implicit claim of Cameron's fancy-subject pictures to comparison with the masterpieces of Western painting is undermined by the obtrusiveness of the sitters.
(D) The most successful of Cameron's fancy-subject pictures from an aesthetic point of view are those in which the viewer is completely unaware that the sitters are engaged in role playing.
(E) The interest of Cameron's fancy-subject pictures consists in what they tell us about the sitters and not in the imaginary scenes they portray.

9. The author mentions the props employed in *The Passing of Arthur* as

(A) examples of amateurish aspects of the work
(B) evidence of the transformative power of theater
(C) testimonies to Cameron's ingenuity
(D) indications that the work is intended ironically
(E) support for a negative appraisal of the work

10. Which one of the following, if true, would most help to explain the claim about suspension of disbelief in lines 34–36?

(A) Sitting for a painting typically takes much longer than sitting for a photograph.
(B) Paintings, unlike photographs, can depict obviously impossible situations.
(C) All of the sitters for a painting do not have to be present at the same time.
(D) A painter can suppress details about a sitter that are at odds with an imaginary persona.
(E) Paintings typically bear the stylistic imprint of an artist, school, or period.

GO ON TO THE NEXT PAGE.

11. Based on the passage, Cameron is most like which one of the following in relation to her fancy-subject pictures?

(A) a playwright who introduces incongruous elements to preserve an aesthetic distance between characters and audience
(B) a rap artist whose lyrics are designed to subvert the meaning of a song sampled in his recording
(C) a sculptor whose works possess a certain grandeur even though they are clearly constructed out of ordinary objects
(D) an architect whose buildings are designed to be as functional as possible
(E) a film director who employs ordinary people as actors in order to give the appearance of a documentary

12. Based on the passage, the author would agree with each of the following statements EXCEPT:

(A) A less realistic medium can be more conducive to suspension of disbelief than a more realistic medium.
(B) Amateurishness is a positive quality in some works of art.
(C) What might appear to be an incongruity in a narrative photograph can actually enhance its aesthetic value.
(D) We are sometimes aware of both the real and the imaginary persona of an actor in a drama.
(E) A work of art succeeds only to the extent that it realizes the artist's intentions.

13. The passage provides the most support for inferring that in Cameron's era

(A) there was little interest in photographs documenting contemporary life
(B) photography was practiced mainly by wealthy amateurs
(C) publicity stills of actors were coming into vogue
(D) there were no professional artist's models
(E) the time required to take a picture was substantial

14. The discussion of suspension of disbelief in the second paragraph serves which one of the following purposes?

(A) It is the main conclusion of the passage, for which the discussion of Cameron's fancy-subject pictures serves as a case study.
(B) It introduces a contrast the author uses in characterizing the peculiar nature of our response to Cameron's fancy-subject pictures.
(C) It is the key step in an argument supporting the author's negative appraisal of the project of narrative photography.
(D) It is used to explain a criticism of Cameron's fancy-subject pictures that the author shows to be conceptually confused.
(E) It draws a contrast between narrative painting and drama to support the author's conclusion that Cameron's fancy-subject pictures are more like the former.

15. The main purpose of the passage is

(A) to chronicle Cameron's artistic development as a photographer, which culminated in her masterpiece *The Passing of Arthur*
(B) to argue that the tension between Cameron's aims and the results she achieved in some of her works enhances the works' aesthetic value
(C) to show that Cameron's essentially theatrical vision accounts for both the strengths and the weaknesses of her photographic oeuvre
(D) to explain why Cameron's project of acquiring for photography the prestige accorded to painting was doomed to failure
(E) to defend Cameron's masterpiece *The Passing of Arthur* against its detractors by showing that it transcends the homely details of its setting

GO ON TO THE NEXT PAGE.

Some critics of advertising have assumed that the creation of false needs in consumers is the principal mechanism underlying what these critics regard as its manipulative and hegemonic power. Central to this
(5) type of critique are the writings of political theorist Herbert Marcuse, who maintained that modern people succumb to oppression by believing themselves satisfied in spite of their living in an objectively unsatisfying world. This process occurs because in
(10) mass market culture the powerful psychological techniques of advertising create "needs" that are false and whose satisfaction thus contributes, not to the genuine well-being of consumers, but rather to the profit—and thereby the disproportionate power—
(15) of corporations.

Marcuse supposed that we all have certain real needs, both physical and psychological. Advertising appropriates these needs for its own purposes, forging psychological associations between them and
(20) consumer items, e.g., between sex and perfume, thereby creating a false "need" for these items. Since the quest for fulfillment is thus displaced from its true objects to consumer items, the implicit promises of advertisements are never really fulfilled
(25) and the consumer remains at some level unsatisfied.

Unfortunately, the distinction between real and false needs upon which this critique depends is extremely problematic. If Marcusians are right, we cannot, with any assurance, separate our real needs
(30) from the alleged false needs we feel as a result of the manipulation of advertisers. For, in order to do so, it would be necessary to eliminate forces of persuasion that are so prevalent in society that they have come to inform our instinctive judgments about things.

(35) But, in fact, Marcusians make a major mistake in assuming that the majority of consumers who respond to advertising do not do so autonomously. Advertising techniques are unable to induce unwilling behavior in rational, informed adults, and regulations prohibit
(40) misinformation in advertising claims. Moreover, evidence suggests that most adults understand and recognize the techniques used and are not merely passive instruments. If there is a real need for emotional fulfillment, and if we can freely and
(45) authentically choose our means of obtaining it, then free, informed individuals may choose to obtain it through the purchase of commodities or even through the enjoyment occasionally provided by advertisements themselves. It is no doubt true that in many—perhaps
(50) even most—cases the use of an advertised product does not yield the precise sort of emotional dividend that advertisements seem to promise. This does not mean, however, that consumers do not freely and intentionally use the product as a means to another sort
(55) of fulfillment, or even that its genuine fulfillment of needs must be less than the advertisement suggests.

16. Which one of the following most accurately expresses the main point of the passage?

(A) Advertising has greater social value than Marcusians have supposed, because it is both an effective means of informing consumers and often an intrinsically entertaining medium of mass communication.

(B) Even if, as Marcusians have argued, there is a theoretical difference between real and false needs, that difference is obscured in practice by the relationship of consumers to the forces of persuasion in profit-motivated, consumer oriented societies.

(C) Marcusian arguments regarding advertisers' creation of false needs are mistaken, because individuals are able to make autonomous decisions regarding their needs and are even able to use the elements of mass market culture to achieve genuine fulfillment.

(D) Critics of advertising typically focus on the development of false needs in the consumer and do not fully consider the ability of people to make independent choices by distinguishing their own real needs from the apparent needs that advertising induces.

(E) The problematic distinction that Marcusians have drawn between real and false needs provides an inadequate basis for their attacks on advertising, because the distinction overlooks consumers' physical and psychological needs.

17. The author states that Marcuse believed that advertisers

(A) base many of their manipulative strategies on psychological research findings

(B) appeal to people's real needs in order to create false needs

(C) are restricted to a degree by regulations prohibiting misinformation

(D) exaggerate the consumer's need for independent decision-making

(E) deny that the needs they create in people are less real than other needs

GO ON TO THE NEXT PAGE.

18. The main function of the first paragraph is to

(A) summarize the political and economic context from which Marcusian critiques of advertising arise
(B) outline the mechanisms by which false needs originate in mass market culture
(C) evaluate the psychological processes by which the manipulative techniques of mass market advertising influence individuals
(D) describe the prevailing views among contemporary critics of advertising and categorize Marcuse's theories in relation to those views
(E) describe Marcusian views regarding mass market manipulation and indicate their role in certain criticisms of advertising

19. Which one of the following is a claim that the author attributes to Marcuse?

(A) In modern society, advertising helps lead people to think that they are satisfied.
(B) Modern societies differ from earlier societies in that they fail to satisfy basic physical needs.
(C) It is impossible to draw any meaningful distinction between real and false psychological needs in modern society.
(D) Advertising in modern society has sometimes become a tool of oppression working to the benefit of totalitarian political systems.
(E) Advertising exploits basic human needs by deriving from them certain secondary needs which, though they become real needs, subtly work to the detriment of consumers.

20. By the term "forces of persuasion" (line 32), the author most probably refers to

(A) intentionally dishonest claims that some theorists argue are common in advertising
(B) innate, instinctual drives that some theorists say are fundamental to human behavior
(C) emotional pressures that some theorists claim are exerted over individuals by society as a whole
(D) subtle practices of social indoctrination that some theorists say are sponsored by the state
(E) manipulative influences that some theorists say go unrecognized by those affected by them

21. Which one of the following sentences would most logically complete the passage?

(A) Therefore, while in principle there might be grounds for holding that advertising is detrimental to society, the Marcusian critique does not provide such grounds.
(B) Therefore, although Marcusian claims about advertising are rationally justified, the mistake of many recent critics of advertising is in their use of these claims for political gain.
(C) Therefore, any shift in basic assumptions required to correct the abuses of advertising will require a change in the perception of human nature held by corporate leaders.
(D) Therefore, while emphasizing only detrimental social aspects of advertising, Marcusians have failed to consider that such aspects are clearly outweighed by numerous social benefits.
(E) Therefore, the Marcusian critique of advertising is mistaken except in its claim that advertisers exert economic power over those few people who are unable or unwilling to distinguish real from false needs.

GO ON TO THE NEXT PAGE.

Passage A

There are two principles that are fundamental to a theory of justice regarding property. The principle of justice in acquisition specifies the conditions under which someone can legitimately come to own
(5) something that was previously not owned by anyone. The principle of justice in transfer specifies the conditions under which the transfer of property from one person to another is justified.

Given such principles, if the world were wholly
(10) just, the following definition would exhaustively cover the subject of justice regarding property:

1. A person who acquires property in accordance with the principle of justice in acquisition is entitled to that property.

(15) 2. A person who acquires property in accordance with the principle of justice in transfer, from someone else who is entitled to the property, is entitled to the property.

3. No one is entitled to any property except by
(20) (repeated) applications of 1 and 2.

However, not all actual situations are generated in accordance with the principles of justice in acquisition and justice in transfer. Some people steal from others or defraud them, for example. The existence of past
(25) injustice raises the issue of the rectification of injustice. If past injustice has shaped present ownership in various ways, what, if anything, ought to be done to rectify that injustice? A principle of rectification would use historical information about previous
(30) situations and injustices done in them, and information about the actual course of events that flowed from these injustices, to produce a description of the property ownership that should have resulted. Actual ownership of property must then be brought
(35) into conformity with this description.

Passage B

In 1790, the United States Congress passed the Indian Nonintercourse Act, which requires that all transfers of lands from Native Americans to others be approved by the federal government. The law has not
(40) been changed in any relevant respect, and it remains in effect today. Its purpose is clear. It was meant to guarantee security to Native Americans against fraudulent acquisition by others of the Native Americans' land holdings. Several suits have been
(45) initiated by Native American tribes for recovery of lands held by them when the Nonintercourse Act took effect.

One natural (one might almost say obvious) way of reasoning about Native American claims to land in
(50) North America is this: Native Americans were the first human occupants of this land. Before the European invasion of North America, the land belonged to them.

In the course of that invasion and its aftermath, the land was illicitly taken from them. The current owners
(55) lack a well-founded right to the land, which now lies

illicitly in their hands. Ideally, the land should be restored to its rightful owners. This may be impractical; compromises might have to be made. But the original wrong can most easily be righted by returning the land
(60) to them—or by returning it wherever that is feasible.

22. Which one of the following most accurately describes the main purpose for which passage A was written and the main purpose for which passage B was written?

(A) Passage A: to propose a solution to a moral problem
Passage B: to criticize a proposed solution to a moral problem

(B) Passage A: to sketch a general outline of a branch of moral theory
Passage B: to give a particular moral analysis of a real case

(C) Passage A: to spell out the details of two fundamental principles
Passage B: to examine a case that exemplifies a moral ideal

(D) Passage A: to argue for a particular moral ideal
Passage B: to question the assumptions of a moral theory

(E) Passage A: to advocate the use of certain moral principles
Passage B: to provide a counterexample to some widely held moral principles

23. Both passages explicitly mention which one of the following?

(A) transfer of property from one owner to another
(B) a legal basis for recovery of property
(C) entitlement to property in a wholly just world
(D) practicability of rectification of past injustice
(E) injustice committed as part of an invasion

24. Which one of the following is true of the relationship between passage A and the second paragraph of passage B?

(A) The second paragraph of passage B attempts to develop a broader version of the theory presented in passage A.
(B) The second paragraph of passage B purports to state facts that bolster the argument made in passage A.
(C) The argument in the second paragraph of passage B is structurally parallel to the argument in passage A, but the subject matter of the two is different.
(D) Passage A presents a theory that tends to support the argument presented in the second paragraph of passage B.
(E) The second paragraph of passage B attempts to undermine the theory presented in passage A.

GO ON TO THE NEXT PAGE.

25.   Based on what can be inferred from their titles, the relationship between which one of the following pairs of documents is most analogous to the relationship between passage A and passage B?

(A)   "Card Counting for Everyone: A Can't-Lose System for Beating the Dealer"
      "The Evils of Gambling"
(B)   "Mayor McConnell Is Unfit to Serve"
      "Why Mayor McConnell Should be Reelected"
(C)   "Pruning Fruit Trees: A Guide for the Novice"
      "Easy Recipes for Beginning Cooks"
(D)   "Notable Failures of the STORM Weather Forecasting Model"
      "Meteorologists' Best Tool Yet: The STORM Forecasting Model"
(E)   "Fundamentals of Building Construction and Repair"
      "Engineering Report: The Repairs Needed by the Thales Building"

26.   The author of passage A would be most likely to characterize the purpose of the Indian Nonintercourse Act as which one of the following?

(A)   legitimization of actual property holdings during the eighteenth century
(B)   clarification of existing laws regarding transfer of property
(C)   assurance of conformity to the principle of justice in acquisition
(D)   prevention of violations of the principle of justice in transfer
(E)   implementation of a principle of rectification

27.   Which one of the following most accurately describes the difference in approach taken by passage A as compared to passage B?

(A)   Passage A espouses a general view without providing details, while passage B sketches an argument that it does not necessarily endorse.
(B)   Passage A argues for the superiority of one view over competing views, while passage B considers only a single view.
(C)   Passage A invokes commonly held principles to support a policy recommendation, while passage B relies on the views of established authorities to support its claims.
(D)   Passage A briefly states a view and then provides an argument for it, while passage B provides a detailed statement of a view but no argument.
(E)   Passage A provides an argument in support of a view, while passage B attempts to undermine a view.

STOP
IF YOU FINISH BEFORE TIME IS CALLED, YOU MAY CHECK YOUR WORK ON THIS SECTION ONLY. DO NOT WORK ON ANY OTHER SECTION IN THE TEST.

SECTION II

Time—35 minutes

25 Questions

Directions: The questions in this section are based on the reasoning contained in brief statements or passages. For some questions, more than one of the choices could conceivably answer the question. However, you are to choose the <u>best</u> answer; that is, the response that most accurately and completely answers the question. You should not make assumptions that are by commonsense standards implausible, superfluous, or incompatible with the passage. After you have chosen the best answer, blacken the corresponding space on your answer sheet.

1. When politicians resort to personal attacks, many editorialists criticize these attacks but most voters pay them scant attention. Everyone knows such attacks will end after election day, and politicians can be excused for mudslinging. Political commentators, however, cannot be. Political commentators should be engaged in sustained and serious debate about ideas and policies. In such a context, personal attacks on opponents serve not to beat those opponents but to cut off the debate.

   Which one of the following most accurately states the main point of the argument?

   (A) Personal attacks on opponents serve a useful purpose for politicians.
   (B) Political commentators should not resort to personal attacks on their opponents.
   (C) Editorialists are right to criticize politicians who resort to personal attacks on their opponents.
   (D) The purpose of serious debate about ideas and policies is to counteract the effect of personal attacks by politicians.
   (E) Voters should be concerned about the personal attacks politicians make on each other.

2. Throughout the Popoya Islands community pressure is exerted on people who win the national lottery to share their good fortune with their neighbors. When people living in rural areas win the lottery they invariably throw elaborate neighborhood feasts, often wiping out all of their lottery winnings. However, in the cities, lottery winners frequently use their winnings for their own personal investment rather than sharing their good fortune with their neighbors.

   Which one of the following, if true, contributes most to an explanation of the difference between the behavior of lottery winners in rural areas and those in cities?

   (A) Twice as many Popoyans live in rural areas as live in the city.
   (B) Popoyan city dwellers tend to buy several lottery tickets at a time, but they buy tickets less frequently than do rural dwellers.
   (C) Lottery winners in rural areas are notified of winning by public posting of lists of winners, but notification in the city is by private mail.
   (D) Families in rural areas in the Popoyas may contain twelve or fourteen people, but city families average six or seven.
   (E) Twice as many lottery tickets are sold in rural areas as are sold in the city.

GO ON TO THE NEXT PAGE.

3. A new medication for migraine seems effective, but there is concern that the medication might exacerbate heart disease. If patients with heart disease take the medication under careful medical supervision, however, harmful side effects can definitely be averted. The concern about those side effects is thus unfounded.

    The argument depends on which one of the following assumptions?

    (A) The new medication actually is effective when taken by patients with heart disease.
    (B) No migraine sufferers with heart disease will take the new medication except under careful medical supervision.
    (C) Most migraine sufferers who have taken the new medication in trials also had heart disease.
    (D) The new medication has various other side effects, but none as serious as that of exacerbating heart disease.
    (E) The new medication will displace all migraine medications currently being used.

4. The highest-ranking detectives in the city's police department are also the most adept at solving crimes. Yet in each of the past ten years, the average success rate for the city's highest-ranking detectives in solving criminal cases has been no higher than the average success rate for its lowest-ranking detectives.

    Which one of the following, if true, most helps to resolve the apparent paradox?

    (A) The detectives who have the highest success rate in solving criminal cases are those who have worked as detectives the longest.
    (B) It generally takes at least ten years for a detective to rise from the lowest to the highest ranks of the city's detective force.
    (C) Those detectives in the police department who are the most adept at solving criminal cases are also those most likely to remain in the police department.
    (D) The police department generally gives the criminal cases that it expects to be the easiest to solve to its lowest-ranking detectives.
    (E) None of the lowest-ranking detectives in the police department had experience in solving criminal cases prior to joining the police department.

5. Irrigation runoff from neighboring farms may well have increased the concentration of phosphorus in the local swamp above previous levels, but the claim that the increase in phosphorus is harming the swamp's native aquatic wildlife is false; the phosphorus concentration in the swamp is actually less than that found in certain kinds of bottled water that some people drink every day.

    The argument is vulnerable to criticism on the ground that it

    (A) makes exaggerations in formulating the claim against which it argues
    (B) bases its conclusion on two contradictory claims
    (C) relies on evidence the relevance of which has not been established
    (D) concedes the very point that it argues against
    (E) makes a generalization that is unwarranted because the sources of the data on which it is based have not been specified

6. Copyright laws protect the rights of writers to profits earned from their writings, whereas patent laws protect inventors' rights to profits earned from their inventions. In Jawade, when computer-software writers demanded that their rights to profit be protected, the courts determined that information written for a machine does not fit into either the copyright or the patent category. Clearly, therefore, the profit rights of computer-software writers remain unprotected in Jawade.

    Which one of the following is an assumption on which the argument depends?

    (A) Computer-software writers are not an influential enough group in Jawade for the government to consider modifying existing copyright laws in order to protect this group's profit rights.
    (B) No laws exist, other than copyright laws and patent laws, that would protect the profit rights of computer-software writers in Jawade.
    (C) Most of the computer software used in Jawade is imported from other countries.
    (D) Computer software is more similar to writings covered by copyright laws than it is to inventions covered by patent laws.
    (E) Copyright laws and patent laws in Jawade have not been modified since their original adoption.

GO ON TO THE NEXT PAGE.

7. Brownlea's post office must be replaced with a larger one. The present one cannot be expanded. Land near the present location in the center of town is more expensive than land on the outskirts of town. Since the cost of acquiring a site is a significant part of the total construction cost, the post office clearly could be built more cheaply on the outskirts of town.

Which one of the following, if true, most seriously undermines the argument's stated conclusion?

(A) The new post office will have to be built in accordance with a demanding new citywide building code.
(B) If the new post office is built on the outskirts of town, it will require a parking lot, but if sited near the present post office it will not.
(C) If the new post office is built on the outskirts of town, current city bus routes will have to be expanded to provide access.
(D) If the new post office is built on the outskirts of town, residents will make decreased use of post office boxes, with the result that mail carriers will have to deliver more mail to homes.
(E) If the new post office is built near the center of town, disruptions to city traffic would have to be minimized by taking such steps as doing some construction work in stages at night and on weekends.

8. In the past, the railroads in Ostronia were run as regional monopolies and operated with little regard for what customers wanted. In recent years, with improvements to the Ostronian national highway network, the railroad companies have faced heavy competition from long-distance trucking companies. But because of government subsidies that have permitted Ostronain railroad companies to operate even while incurring substantial losses, the companies continue to disregard customers' needs and desires.

If the statements above are true, which one of the following must also be true on the basis of them?

(A) If the government of Ostronia ceases to subsidize railroad companies, few of those companies will continue to operate.
(B) Few companies in Ostronia that have received subsidies from the government have taken the needs and desires of their customers into account.
(C) Without government subsidies, railroad companies in Ostronia would have to increase the prices they charge their customers.
(D) The transportation system in Ostronia is no more efficient today than in was in the past.
(E) In recent years, some companies in Ostronia that have had little regard for the desires of their customers have nonetheless survived.

9. Although Damon had ample time earlier in the month to complete the paper he is scheduled to present at a professional conference tomorrow morning, he repeatedly put off doing it. Damon could still get the paper ready in time, but only if he works on it all evening without interruption. However, his seven-year-old daughter's tap-dance recital takes place this evening, and Damon had promised both to attend and to take his daughter and her friends out for ice cream afterward. Thus, because of his procrastination, Damon will be forced to choose between his professional and his family responsibilities.

The argument proceeds by

(A) providing evidence that one event will occur in order to establish that an alternative event cannot occur
(B) showing that two situations are similar in order to justify the claim that someone with certain responsibilities in the first situation has similar responsibilities in the second situation
(C) invoking sympathy for someone who finds himself in a dilemma in order to excuse that person's failure to meet all of his responsibilities
(D) making clear the extent to which someone's actions resulted in harm to others in order to support the claim that those actions were irresponsible
(E) demonstrating that two situations cannot both occur by showing that something necessary for one of those situations is incompatible with something necessary for the other situation

10. The increase in the price of jet fuel is due to a sharp decrease over the past year in the supply of jet fuel available relative to demand. Nonetheless, the amount of jet fuel available for sale is larger today than it was last year.

If the statements above are true, which one of the following conclusions can be properly drawn on the basis of them?

(A) The demand for jet fuel has increased over the past year.
(B) The fuel efficiency of jet engines has increased over the past year.
(C) The number of jet airline flights has decreased over the past year.
(D) The cost of refining petroleum for jet fuel has increased over the past year.
(E) The supply of petroleum available for jet fuel has decreased over the past year.

GO ON TO THE NEXT PAGE.

Questions 11–12

Alan: Government subsidies have been proposed in Cariana to encourage farmers in Rochelle, the country's principal agricultural region, to implement certain new farming techniques. Unless these techniques are implemented, erosion of productive topsoil cannot be controlled. Unfortunately, farmers cannot afford to shoulder the entire cost of the new techniques, which are more expensive than those currently used. Therefore, without subsidies, agricultural output in Rochelle will inevitably decline.

Betty: But erosion in Rochelle is caused by recurring floods, which will end next year once Cariana completes the hydroelectric dam it is building across the region's major river. Therefore, Rochelle's total agricultural output will stabilize at its present level even without subsidies.

11. Which one of the following is an assumption on which Betty's argument depends?

(A) Building a dam across Rochelle's major river will not reduce any recurrent flooding that occurs in regions of Cariana other than Rochelle.

(B) The new farming techniques that must be implemented to control soil erosion in Rochelle are not well suited to other regions of Cariana.

(C) The current yearly output, if any, from Rochelle's land that will be permanently under water once the dam is completed will at least be matched by additional yearly output from Rochelle's remaining land.

(D) The cost to the government of Cariana to operate the hydroelectric dam will not be greater than the projected cost of subsidizing the farmers of Rochelle in the implementation of the new farming techniques.

(E) The government of Cariana has sufficient financial resources both to subsidize its farmers' implementation of new farming techniques and to operate a hydroelectric dam.

12. Betty uses which one of the following argumentative techniques in countering Alan's argument?

(A) showing the one premise in Alan's argument is inconsistent with another premise in his argument

(B) making additional claims that, if correct, undermine a premise in Alan's argument

(C) demonstrating that Alan's conclusion is true but not for the reasons Alan gives to support it

(D) presenting evidence indicating that the policy Alan argues in favor of would have damaging consequences that outweigh its positive consequences

(E) pointing out that Alan's argument mistakenly identifies something as the cause of a trend when it is really an effect of that trend

13. Astronomers have long thought that the irregularity in the orbit of the planet Neptune was adequately explained by the gravitational pull exerted on Neptune by the planet Pluto. The most recent observations of Pluto, however, indicate that this planet is much too small to exert the amount of gravitational pull on Neptune that astronomers once thought it did.

If the statements above are true, they provide the most support for which one of the following?

(A) Neptune is somewhat larger than scientists once believed it to be.

(B) The orbit on Neptune is considerably more irregular than scientists once thought it was.

(C) There exists another, as yet undiscovered planet with an orbit beyond that of Pluto.

(D) The gravitational pull of Pluto is not the sole cause of Neptune's irregular orbit.

(E) Further observations of Pluto will eventually show it to be even smaller than it is now thought to be.

GO ON TO THE NEXT PAGE.

Questions 14–15

In most corporations the salaries of executives are set by a group from the corporation's board of directors. Since the board's primary mission is to safeguard the economic health of the corporation rather than to make its executives rich, this way of setting executives' salaries is expected to prevent excessively large salaries. But, clearly, this expectation is based on poor reasoning. After all, most members of a corporation's board are themselves executives of some corporation and can expect to benefit from setting generous benchmarks for executives' salaries.

14. The point made by the author is that the most common way of setting executives' salaries might not keep those salaries in bounds because

(A)   most corporate executives, thanks to their generous salaries, are not financially dependent on money earned as board members

(B)   most corporate executive might be less generous in setting their own salaries than the board members actually setting them are

(C)   many board members might let their self-interest as executives interfere with properly discharging their role, as board members, in setting executives' salaries

(D)   many board members who set executives' salaries unreasonably high do so because they happen to be on the board of a corporation of which they expect later to become executives

(E)   many board members are remunerated generously and wish to protect this source of income by pleasing the executives to whom they owe their appointments on the board.

15. Which one of the following practices is vulnerable to a line of criticism most parallel to that used in the argument in the passage?

(A)   in medical malpractice suits, giving physicians not directly involved in a suit a major role in determining the damages due to successful plaintiffs

(B)   in a legislature, allowing the legislators to increase their own salaries only if at least two-thirds of them vote in favor of an increase

(C)   on a factory floor, giving workers an incentive to work both fast and accurately by paying them by the piece but counting only pieces of acceptable quality

(D)   in a sports competition decided by judges' scores, selecting the judges from among people retired from that sport after successful careers

(E)   in a business organization, distributing a group bonus among the members of a task force on the basis of a confidential evaluation, by each member, of the contribution made by each of the others

16. Consumer advocate: One advertisement that is deceptive, and thus morally wrong, states that "gram for gram, the refined sugar used in our chocolate pies is no more fattening than the sugars found in fruits and vegetables." This is like trying to persuade someone that chocolate pies are not fattening by saying that, calorie for calorie, they are no more fattening than celery. True, but it would take a whole shopping cart full of celery to equal a chocolate pie's worth of calories.

Advertiser: This advertisement cannot be called deceptive. It is, after all, true.

Which one of the following principles, if established, would do most to support the consumer advocate's position against the advertiser's response?

(A)   It is morally wrong to seek to persuade by use of deceptive statements.

(B)   A true statement should be regarded as deceptive only if the person making the statement believes it to be false, and thus intends the people reading or hearing it to acquire a false belief.

(C)   To make statements that impart only a small proportion of the information in one's possession should not necessarily be regarded as deceptive.

(D)   It is morally wrong to make a true statement in a manner that will deceive hearers or readers of the statement into believing that it is false.

(E)   A true statement should be regarded as deceptive if it is made with the expectation that people hearing or reading the statement will draw a false conclusion from it.

GO ON TO THE NEXT PAGE.

17. Members of the Amazonian Akabe people commonly take an early-morning drink of a tea made from the leaves of a forest plant. Although they greatly enjoy this drink, at dawn they drink it only in small amounts. Anthropologists hypothesize that since this tea is extraordinarily high in caffeine, the explanation for the Akabe's not drinking more of it at dawn is that high caffeine intake would destroy the surefootedness that their daily tasks require.

Which one of the following, if true, most seriously calls the anthropologists' explanation into question?

(A) The drink is full of nutrients otherwise absent from the Akabe diet.
(B) The Akabe also drink the tea in the evening, after their day's work is done.
(C) The leaves used for the tea contain a soluble narcotic.
(D) Akabe children are introduced to the tea in only a very weak form.
(E) When celebrating, the Akabe drink the tea in large quantities.

18. All of the cargo ships of the Blue Star Line are over 100 meters long, and all of its passenger ships are under 100 meters long. Most of the ships of the Blue Star Line were built before 1980. All of the passenger and cargo ships of the Gold Star line were built after 1980, and all are under 100 meters long. The dockside facilities of Port Tropica, which is open only to ships of these two lines, can accommodate only those ships that are less than 100 meters long. The S.S. Coral is a cargo ship that is currently docked at Port Tropica.

If the statements above are true, which one of the following must be true on the basis of them?

(A) The S.S. Coral was built after 1980.
(B) The S.S. Coral belongs to the Blue Star Line.
(C) Port Tropica is served only by cargo ships.
(D) Port Tropica is not served by ships of the Blue Star Line.
(E) All of the ships of the Blue Star Line are older than any of the ships of the Gold Star Line.

19. Spectroscopic analysis has revealed the existence of frozen nitrogen, methane, and carbon monoxide on the surface of Pluto. Such ices have a tendency to vaporize, producing an atmosphere. Since the proportion of any gas in such an atmosphere depends directly on how readily the corresponding ice vaporizes, astronomers have concluded that the components of Pluto's atmosphere are nitrogen, carbon monoxide, and methane, in order of decreasing abundance.

The astronomers' argument relies on which one of the following assumptions?

(A) There is no more frozen nitrogen on the surface of Pluto than there is either frozen carbon monoxide or methane.
(B) Until space probes reach Pluto, direct analysis of the atmosphere is impossible.
(C) There is no frozen substance on the surface of Pluto that vaporizes more readily than methane but less readily than carbon monoxide.
(D) Nitrogen is found in the atmosphere of a planet only if nitrogen ice is found on the surface of that planet.
(E) A mixture of nitrogen, carbon monoxide, and methane is characteristic of the substances from which the Solar System formed.

GO ON TO THE NEXT PAGE.

20. Ann will either take a leave of absence from Technocomp and return in a year or else she will quit her job there; but she would not do either one unless she were offered a one-year teaching fellowship at a prestigious university. Technocomp will allow her to take a leave of absence if it does not find out that she has been offered the fellowship, but not otherwise. Therefore, Ann will quit her job at Technocomp only if Technocomp finds out she has been offered the fellowship.

Which one of the following, if assumed, allows the conclusion above to be properly drawn?

(A) Technocomp will find out about Ann being offered the fellowship only if someone informs on her.

(B) The reason Ann wants the fellowship is so she can quit her job at Technocomp.

(C) Technocomp does not allow any of its employees to take a leave of absence in order to work for one of its competitors.

(D) Ann will take a leave of absence if Technocomp allows her to take a leave of absence.

(E) Ann would be offered the fellowship only if she quit her job at Technocomp.

21. If a mechanical aerator is installed in a fish pool, the water in the pool can be properly aerated. So, since John's fish pool does not have a mechanical aerator, it must be that his pool is not properly aerated. Without properly aerated water, fish cannot thrive. Therefore, any fish in John's fish pool will not thrive.

Which one of the following arguments contains an error of reasoning that is also contained in the argument above?

(A) If alum is added to pickle brine, brine can replace the water in the pickles. Therefore, since Paula does not add alum to her pickle brine, the water in the pickles cannot be replaced by brine. Unless their water is replaced with brine, pickles will not stay crisp. Thus, Paula's pickles will not stay crisp.

(B) If pectin is added to jam, the jam will gel. Without a setting agent such as pectin, jam will not gel. So in order to make his jam gel, Harry should add a setting agent such as pectin to the jam.

(C) If stored potatoes are not exposed to ethylene, the potatoes will not sprout. Beets do not release ethylene. Therefore, if Sara stores her potatoes together with beets, the potatoes will not sprout.

(D) If a carrot patch is covered with mulch in the fall, the carrots can be left in the ground until spring. Without a mulch cover, carrots stored in the ground can suffer frost damage. Thus, since Kevin covers his carrot patch with mulch in the fall, the carrots can safely be left in the ground.

(E) If tomatoes are not stored in a dark place, their seeds sometimes sprout. Sprouted seeds can make tomatoes inedible. Therefore, since Maria does not store her tomatoes in a dark place, some of Maria's tomatoes could be inedible.

GO ON TO THE NEXT PAGE.

Questions 22–23

Antinuclear activist: The closing of the nuclear power plant is a victory for the antinuclear cause. It also represents a belated acknowledgment by the power industry that they cannot operate such plants safely.

Nuclear power plant manager: It represents no such thing. The availability of cheap power from nonnuclear sources, together with the cost of mandated safety inspections and safety repairs, made continued operation uneconomic. Thus it was not safety considerations but economic considerations that dictated the plant's closing.

22. The reasoning in the manager's argument is flawed because the argument

(A) fails to acknowledge that the power industry might now believe nuclear power plants to be unsafe even though this plant was not closed for safety reasons
(B) overlooks the possibility that the sources from which cheap power is available might themselves be subject to safety concerns
(C) mistakes the issue of what the closure of the plant represents to the public for the issue of what the managers' reasons for the closure were
(D) takes as one of its premises a view about the power industry's attitude toward nuclear safety that contradicts the activist's view
(E) counts as purely economic considerations some expenses that arise as a result of the need to take safety precautions

23. Which one of the following, if true, most strongly supports the activist's claim of victory?

(A) The plant had reached the age at which its operating license expired.
(B) The mandate for inspections and repairs mentioned by the manager was recently enacted as a result of pressure from antinuclear groups.
(C) The plant would not have closed if cheap power from nonnuclear sources had not been available.
(D) Per unit of electricity produced, the plant had the highest operating costs of any nuclear power plant.
(E) The plant that closed had been able to provide backup power to an electrical network when parts of the network became overloaded.

Questions 24–25

Statistician: Changes in the Sun's luminosity correlate exceedingly well with average land temperatures on Earth. Clearly and contrary to accepted opinion among meteorologists, the Sun's luminosity essentially controls land temperatures on Earth.

Meteorologist: I disagree. Any professional meteorologist will tell you that in a system as complicated as that giving rise to the climate, no significant aspect can be controlled by a single variable.

24. The rejection by the meteorologist of the statistician's conclusion employs which one of the following techniques of argumentation?

(A) supporting a conclusion about a specific case by invoking a relevant generalization
(B) producing a single counterexample that establishes that a generalization is false as stated
(C) reanalyzing a correlation as reflecting the multiple effects of a single cause
(D) rejecting a conclusion because it is a proposition that cannot be experimentally tested
(E) pointing out that potentially unfavorable evidence has been systematically neglected

25. The reasoning in the meteorologist's counterargument is questionable because that argument

(A) rejects a partial explanation, not because it is incorrect, but only because it is not complete
(B) fails to distinguish phenomena that exist independently of a particular system from phenomena that exist only as part of the system
(C) calls into question the existence of a correlation when the only real issue is that of how to interpret the correlation
(D) dismisses a hypothesis on the grounds that it fails to deal with any matters of the scientific significance
(E) appeals to the authoritativeness of an opinion without evaluating the merit of a putative counterexample

STOP

IF YOU FINISH BEFORE TIME IS CALLED, YOU MAY CHECK YOUR WORK ON THIS SECTION ONLY. DO NOT WORK ON ANY OTHER SECTION IN THE TEST.

SECTION III

Time—35 minutes

25 Questions

Directions: The questions in this section are based on the reasoning contained in brief statements or passages. For some questions, more than one of the choices could conceivably answer the question. However, you are to choose the best answer; that is, the response that most accurately and completely answers the question. You should not make assumptions that are by commonsense standards implausible, superfluous, or incompatible with the passage. After you have chosen the best answer, blacken the corresponding space on your answer sheet.

1. Editorial: The city has chosen a contractor to upgrade the heating systems in public buildings. Only 40 percent of the technicians employed by this contractor are certified by the Heating Technicians Association. So the city selected a contractor 60 percent of whose technicians are unqualified, which is an outrage.

    Which one of the following is an assumption required by the argument in the editorial?

    (A) Certified technicians receive higher pay than uncertified technicians.
    (B) There are no contractors with fewer than 40 percent of their technicians certified.
    (C) Technicians who lack certification are not qualified technicians.
    (D) Qualified technicians installed the heating systems to be upgraded.
    (E) The contractor hired by the city has personal ties to city officials.

2. Jeneta: Increasingly, I've noticed that when a salesperson thanks a customer for making a purchase, the customer also says "Thank you" instead of saying "You're welcome." I've even started doing that myself. But when a friend thanks a friend for a favor, the response is always "You're welcome."

    Which one of the following, if true, most helps to explain the discrepancy that Jeneta observes in people's responses?

    (A) Customers regard themselves as doing salespeople a favor by buying from them as opposed to someone else.
    (B) Salespeople are often instructed by their employers to thank customers, whereas customers are free to say what they want.
    (C) Salespeople do not regard customers who buy from them as doing them a favor.
    (D) The way that people respond to being thanked is generally determined by habit rather than by conscious decision.
    (E) In a commercial transaction, as opposed to a favor, the customer feels that the benefits are mutual.

3. Some video game makers have sold the movie rights for popular games. However, this move is rarely good from a business perspective. After all, StarQuanta sold the movie rights to its popular game Nostroma, but the poorly made film adaptation of the game was hated by critics and the public alike. Subsequent versions of the *Nostroma* video game, although better than the original, sold poorly.

    The reasoning in the argument is most vulnerable to criticism in that the argument

    (A) draws a general conclusion on the basis of just one individual case
    (B) infers that a product will be disliked by the public merely from the claim that the product was disliked by critics
    (C) restates as a conclusion a claim earlier presented as evidence for that conclusion
    (D) takes for granted that products with similar content that are in different media will be of roughly equal popularity
    (E) treats a requirement for a product to be popular as something that ensures that a product will be popular

GO ON TO THE NEXT PAGE.

4. Principle: The executive in a given company whose compensation package is determined by advice of an external consultant is likely to be overcompensated if the consultant also has business interests with the company the executive manages.

Which one of the following judgments conforms most closely to the principle stated above?

(A) The president of the Troskco Corporation is definitely overpaid, since he receives in salary and benefits almost 40 times more than the average employee of Troskco receives.

(B) The president of the Troskco Corporation is probably overpaid, since his total annual compensation package was determined five years ago, when the company's profits were at an all-time high.

(C) The president of the Troskco Corporation is probably not overpaid, since his total compensation package was determined by the Troskco board of directors without retaining the services of an external compensation consultant.

(D) The president of Troskco Corporation is probably overpaid, since the Troskco board of directors determined his compensation by following the advice of an external consultant who has many other contracts with Troskco.

(E) The president of Troskco Corporation is definitely not overpaid, since the external consultant the board of directors retained to advise on executive salaries has no other contracts with Troskco.

5. Science writer: Lemaître argued that the universe began with the explosion of a "primeval atom," a singular point of infinite gravity in space and time. If this is correct, our current observations should reveal galaxies accelerating away from one another. This is precisely what we observe. Yet because there is another theory—the oscillating universe theory—that makes exactly this same prediction, Lemaître's theory must be considered inadequate.

Which one of the following most accurately describes a flaw in the science writer's reasoning?

(A) The conclusion is derived partly from assertions attributed to a purported expert whose credibility is not established.

(B) The conclusion is based on a shift in meaning of a key term from one part of the argument to another part.

(C) The science writer takes for granted the existence of a causal connection between observed phenomena.

(D) The science writer fails to see that one theory's correctly predicting observed data cannot itself constitute evidence against an alternative theory that also does this.

(E) The science writer presumes, without providing justification, that there are only two possible explanations for the phenomena in question.

6. Critic: The criticism of the popular film comedy Quirks for not being realistic is misguided. It is certainly true that the characters are too stylized to be real people. That could be problematic, but in this case the resulting film is funny. And that is the important thing for a comedy.

Which one of the following principles, if valid, most helps to justify the reasoning in the critic's argument?

(A) Films should be judged on how well they accurately capture the world.

(B) Films are successful as long as they are popular.

(C) Film comedies should find their humor in their stylistic portrayals.

(D) Films are successful if they succeed within their genre.

(E) Films should try to stay entirely within a single genre.

GO ON TO THE NEXT PAGE.

7. Party X has recently been accused by its opposition, Party Y, of accepting international campaign contributions, which is illegal. Such accusations are, however, ill founded. Three years ago, Party Y itself was involved in a scandal in which it was discovered that its national committee seriously violated campaign laws.

Which one of the following contains flawed reasoning most similar to the flawed reasoning in the argument above?

(A) The plaintiff accuses the defendant of violating campaign laws, but the accusations are ill founded. While the defendant's actions may violate certain laws, they are not immoral, because the laws in question are unjust.

(B) The plaintiff accuses the defendant of violating campaign laws, but these accusations show the plaintiff to be hypocritical, because the plaintiff has engaged in similar conduct.

(C) The plaintiff accuses the defendant of violating campaign laws, and, in the past, courts have declared such violations illegal. Nevertheless, because the plaintiff recently engaged in actions that were similar to those of the defendant, the plaintiff's accusations are ill founded.

(D) The plaintiff accuses the defendant of violating campaign laws, but these accusations are ill founded. They are clearly an attempt to stir up controversy, because they were made just two weeks before the election.

(E) The plaintiff accuses the defendant of voting only for campaign laws that would favor the defendant's party. This accusation is ill founded, however, because it attacks the defendant's motivations instead of addressing the arguments the defendant has put forth justifying these votes.

8. Biologist: Marine animals known as box jellyfish have eyes with well-formed lenses capable of producing sharp images that reveal fine detail. But the box jellyfish's retinas are too far forward to receive a clear image, so these jellyfish can receive only a blurry image that reveals prominent features of objects but not fine detail. This example shows that eyes are adapted only to an animal's needs rather than to some abstract sense of how a good eye would be designed.

The argument requires assuming which one of the following?

(A) Box jellyfish are the only kind of jellyfish with retinas that do not focus clearly.

(B) Box jellyfish have a need to detect prominent features of objects but not fine details.

(C) Box jellyfish would benefit from having retinas that allowed their eyes to focus more sharply.

(D) Box jellyfish developed from jellyfish whose retinas received clear images.

(E) Box jellyfish use vision as their main means of detecting prey.

9. Columnist: Research shows significant reductions in the number of people smoking, and especially in the number of first-time smokers in those countries that have imposed stringent restrictions on tobacco advertising. This provides substantial grounds for disputing tobacco companies' claims that advertising has no significant causal impact on the tendency to smoke.

Which one of the following, if true, most undermines the columnist's reasoning?

(A) People who smoke are unlikely to quit merely because they are no longer exposed to tobacco advertising.

(B) Broadcast media tend to have stricter restrictions on tobacco advertising than do print media.

(C) Restrictions on tobacco advertising are imposed only in countries where a negative attitude toward tobacco use is already widespread and increasing.

(D) Most people who begin smoking during adolescence continue to smoke throughout their lives.

(E) People who are largely unaffected by tobacco advertising tend to be unaffected by other kinds of advertising as well.

GO ON TO THE NEXT PAGE.

10. Actor: Bertolt Brecht's plays are not genuinely successful dramas. The roles in Brecht's plays express such incongruous motives and beliefs that audiences, as well as the actors playing the roles, invariably find it difficult, at best, to discern any of the characters' personalities. But, for a play to succeed as a drama, audiences must care what happens to at least some of its characters.

The conclusion of the actor's argument can be properly drawn if which one of the following is assumed?

(A) An audience that cannot readily discern a character's personality will not take any interest in that character.
(B) A character's personality is determined primarily by the motives and beliefs of that character.
(C) The extent to which a play succeeds as a drama is directly proportional to the extent to which the play's audiences care about its characters.
(D) If the personalities of a play's characters are not readily discernible by the actors playing the roles, then those personalities are not readily discernible by the play's audience.
(E) All plays that, unlike Brecht's plays, have characters with whom audiences empathize succeed as dramas.

11. Municipal legislator: The mayor proposes that the city accept a lighting company's gift of several hightech streetlights. Surely there would be no problem in accepting these despite some people's fear that the company wants to influence the city's decision regarding park lighting contracts. The only ulterior motive I can find is the company's desire to have its products seen by mayors who will visit the city for an upcoming convention. In any case, favoritism in city contracts is prevented by our competitive bidding procedure.

Which one of the following most accurately expresses the main conclusion of the municipal legislator's argument?

(A) Some people's fear that the company wants to influence the city's decision regarding park lighting contracts is unfounded.
(B) The mayor's proposal to accept the gift of streetlights should not be considered problematic.
(C) It is not appropriate that any company should have the unique opportunity to display its products to mayors attending the upcoming convention.
(D) The city's competitive-bidding procedure prevents favoritism in the dispensing of city contracts.
(E) The lighting company's desire to display its products to visiting mayors is the real motivation behind the suggested gift of streetlights.

12. The chairperson should not have released the Election Commission's report to the public, for the chairperson did not consult any other members of the commission about releasing the report before having it released.

The argument's conclusion can be properly inferred if which one of the following is assumed?

(A) It would have been permissible for the chairperson to release the commission's report to the public only if most other members of the commission had first given their consent.
(B) All of the members of the commission had signed the report prior to its release.
(C) The chairperson would not have been justified in releasing the commission's report if any members of the commission had serious reservations about the report's content.
(D) The chairperson would have been justified in releasing the report only if each of the commission's members would have agreed to its being released had they been consulted.
(E) Some members of the commission would have preferred that the report not be released to the public.

13. Reformer: A survey of police departments keeps track of the national crime rate, which is the annual number of crimes per 100,000 people. The survey shows no significant reduction in the crime rate in the past 20 years, but the percentage of the population in prison has increased substantially, and public expenditure on prisons has grown at an alarming rate. This demonstrates that putting more people in prison cannot help to reduce crime.

A flaw in the reformer's argument is that it

(A) infers without justification that because the national crime rate has increased, the number of crimes reported by each police department has increased
(B) ignores the possibility that the crime rate would have significantly increased if it had not been for the greater rate of imprisonment
(C) overlooks the possibility that the population has increased significantly over the past 20 years
(D) presumes, without providing warrant, that alternative measures for reducing crime would be more effective than imprisonment
(E) takes for granted that the number of prisoners must be proportional to the number of crimes committed

GO ON TO THE NEXT PAGE.

14. Inez: Space-exploration programs pay for themselves many times over, since such programs result in technological advances with everyday, practical applications. Space exploration is more than the search for knowledge for its own sake; investment in space exploration is such a productive investment in developing widely useful technology that we can't afford not to invest in space exploration.

Winona: It is absurd to try to justify funding for space exploration merely by pointing out that such programs will lead to technological advances. If technology with practical applications is all that is desired, then it should be funded directly.

Winona responds to Inez by

(A) showing that there is no evidence that the outcome Inez anticipates will in fact be realized

(B) suggesting that Inez has overlooked evidence that directly argues against the programs Inez supports

(C) demonstrating that the pieces of evidence that Inez cites contradict each other

(D) providing evidence that the beneficial effects that Inez desires can be achieved only at great expense

(E) claiming that a goal that Inez mentions could be pursued without the programs Inez endorses

15. Marketing consultant: Last year I predicted that LRG's latest advertising campaign would be unpopular with customers and ineffective in promoting new products. But LRG ignored my predictions and took the advice of a competing consultant. This season's sales figures show that sales are down and LRG's new products are selling especially poorly. Thus, the advertising campaign was ill conceived.

The marketing consultant's reasoning is most vulnerable to criticism on the grounds that

(A) it takes for granted that LRG's sales would not have been lower still in the absence of the competitor's advertising campaign

(B) it fails to consider that economic factors unrelated to the advertising campaign may have caused LRG's low sales figures

(C) it takes for granted that in LRG's industry, new products should outsell established products

(D) it takes for granted that the higher sales of established products are due to effective advertising

(E) it confuses a condition necessary for increasing product sales with a condition that will ensure increased sales

16. The top prize in architecture, the Pritzker Prize, is awarded for individual achievement, like Nobel Prizes for science. But architects are judged by their buildings, and buildings are the result of teamwork. As achievements, buildings are not like scientific discoveries, but like movies, which compete for awards for best picture. Thus, it would be better if the top prize in architecture were awarded to the best building rather than the best architect.

The argument proceeds by

(A) reaching a conclusion about the way something should be done in one field on the basis of comparisons with corresponding practices in other fields

(B) making a distinction between two different types of objects in order to conclude that one has more inherent value than the other

(C) pointing to similarities between two practices as a basis for concluding that criticisms of one practice can rightly be applied to the other

(D) arguing that because two different fields are disanalogous, the characteristics of one field are not relevant to justifying a conclusion about the other

(E) contending that an action is inappropriate by presenting an argument that a corresponding action in an analogous case is inappropriate

17. If Suarez is not the most qualified of the candidates for sheriff, then Anderson is. Thus, if the most qualified candidate is elected and Suarez is not elected, then Anderson will be.

The reasoning in which one of the following is most similar to the reasoning in the argument above?

(A) If the excavation contract does not go to the lowest bidder, then it will go to Caldwell. So if Qiu gets the contract and Caldwell does not, then the contract will have been awarded to the lowest bidder.

(B) If the lowest bidder on the sanitation contract is not Dillon, then it is Ramsey. So if the contract goes to the lowest bidder and it does not go to Dillon, then it will go to Ramsey.

(C) If Kapshaw is not awarded the landscaping contract, then Johnson will be. So if the contract goes to the lowest bidder and it does not go to Johnson, then it will go to Kapshaw.

(D) If Holihan did not submit the lowest bid on the maintenance contract, then neither did Easton. So if the contract goes to the lowest bidder and it does not go to Easton, then it will not go to Holihan either.

(E) If Perez is not the lowest bidder on the catering contract, then Sullivan is. So if Sullivan does not get the contract and Perez does not get it either, then it will not be awarded to the lowest bidder.

GO ON TO THE NEXT PAGE.

18. Critic: An art historian argues that because fifteenth-century European paintings were generally more planimetric (that is, two-dimensional with no attempt at suggesting depth) than were sixteenth-century paintings, fifteenth-century painters had a greater mastery of painting than did sixteenth century painters. However, this conclusion is wrong. Fifteenth-century European painters did not have a greater mastery of painting, for the degree to which a painting is planimetric is irrelevant to the painter's mastery.

The argument is flawed in that it

(A) rejects a position merely because the proponent of the position has other objectionable views
(B) illicitly relies on two different meanings of the term "mastery"
(C) takes a necessary condition for an argument's being inadequate to be a sufficient condition for an argument's being inadequate
(D) bases its conclusion on two claims that contradict each other
(E) rejects a position on the grounds that an inadequate argument has been made for it

19. A carved flint object depicting a stylized human head with an open mouth was found in a Stone Age tomb in Ireland. Some archaeologists believe that the object was a weapon—the head of a warrior's mace—but it is too small for that purpose. Because of its size and the fact that an open mouth symbolizes speaking, the object was probably the head of a speaking staff, a communal object passed around a small assembly to indicate who has the right to speak.

Which one of the following, if true, would most weaken the argument?

(A) The tomb in which the object was found did not contain any other objects that might have been weapons.
(B) Communal objects were normally passed from one generation to the next in Stone Age Ireland.
(C) The object was carved with an artistry that was rare in Stone Age Ireland.
(D) The tomb in which the object was found was that of a politically prominent person.
(E) A speaking staff with a stone head is thought to symbolize a warrior's mace.

20. The advent of chemical fertilizers led the farmers in a certain region to abandon the practice of periodically growing a "green-manure" crop, such as alfalfa, in a field to rejuvenate its soil. As a result, the soil structure in a typical farm field in the region is poor. So to significantly improve the soil structure, farmers will need to abandon the use of chemical fertilizers.

The argument relies on the assumption that

(A) most, if not all, farmers in the region who abandon the use of chemical fertilizers will periodically grow alfalfa
(B) applying chemical fertilizers to green-manure crops, such as alfalfa, has no positive effect on their growth
(C) the most important factor influencing the soil quality of a farm field is soil structure
(D) chemical fertilizers themselves have a destructive effect on the soil structure of farm fields
(E) many, if not all, farmers in the region will not grow green-manure crops unless they abandon the use of chemical fertilizers

GO ON TO THE NEXT PAGE.

21. Most of the students who took Spanish 101 at the university last semester attended every class session. However, each student who received a grade lower than B minus missed at least one class session.

Which one of the following statements about the students who took Spanish 101 at the university last semester can be properly inferred from the information above?

(A) At least some of the students who received a grade of A minus or higher attended every class session.

(B) Most, if not all, of the students who missed at least one class session received a grade lower than B minus.

(C) Most of the students received a grade higher than B minus.

(D) At least one student who received a grade of B minus or higher missed one or more class sessions.

(E) More than half of the students received a grade of B minus or higher.

22. Because the native salmon in Lake Clearwater had nearly disappeared, sockeye salmon were introduced in 1940. After being introduced, this genetically uniform group of sockeyes split into two distinct populations that do not interbreed, one inhabiting deep areas of the lake and the other inhabiting shallow areas. Since the two populations now differ genetically, some researchers hypothesize that each has adapted genetically to its distinct habitat.

Which of the following, if true, most strongly supports the researchers' hypothesis?

(A) Neither of the two populations of sockeyes has interbred with the native salmon.

(B) When the native salmon in Lake Clearwater were numerous, they comprised two distinct populations that did not interbreed.

(C) Most types of salmon that inhabit lakes spend part of the time in shallow water and part in deeper water.

(D) One of the populations of sockeyes is virtually identical genetically to the sockeyes originally introduced in 1940.

(E) The total number of sockeye salmon in the lake is not as large as the number of native salmon had been many years ago.

23. A developing country can substantially increase its economic growth if its businesspeople are willing to invest in modern industries that have not yet been pursued there. But being the first to invest in an industry is very risky. Moreover, businesspeople have little incentive to take this risk since if the business succeeds, many other people will invest in the same industry, and the competition will cut into their profits.

The statements above, if true, most strongly support which one of the following claims?

(A) Once a developing country has at least one business in a modern industry, further investment in that industry will not contribute to the country's economic growth.

(B) In developing countries, there is greater competition within modern industries than within traditional industries.

(C) A developing country can increase its prospects for economic growth by providing added incentive for investment in modern industries that have not yet been pursued there.

(D) A developing country will not experience economic growth unless its businesspeople invest in modern industries.

(E) Investments in a modern industry in a developing country carry little risk as long as the country has at least one other business in that industry.

GO ON TO THE NEXT PAGE.

24. A survey of a city's concertgoers found that almost all of them were dissatisfied with the local concert hall. A large majority of them expressed a strong preference for wider seats and better acoustics. And, even though the survey respondents were told that the existing concert hall cannot feasibly be modified to provide these features, most of them opposed the idea of tearing down the existing structure and replacing it with a concert hall with wider seats and better acoustics.

Which one of the following, if true, most helps to explain the apparent conflict in the concertgoers' views, as revealed by the survey?

(A) Before any of the survey questions were asked, the respondents were informed that the survey was sponsored by a group that advocates replacing the existing concert hall.

(B) Most of the people who live in the vicinity of the existing concert hall do not want it to be torn down.

(C) The city's construction industry will receive more economic benefit from the construction of a new concert hall than from renovations to the existing concert hall.

(D) A well-publicized plan is being considered by the city government that would convert the existing concert hall into a public auditorium and build a new concert hall nearby.

(E) Many popular singers and musicians who currently do not hold concerts in the city would begin to hold concerts there if a new concert hall were built.

25. Student: Before completing my research paper, I want to find the book from which I copied a passage to quote in the paper. Without the book, I will be unable to write an accurate citation, and without an accurate citation, I will be unable to include the quotation. Hence, since the completed paper will be much better with the quotation than without, _____.

Which one of the following most logically completes the student's argument?

(A) I will have to include an inaccurate citation

(B) I will be unable to complete my research paper

(C) if I do not find the book, my research paper will suffer

(D) if I do not find the book, I will include the quotation without an accurate citation

(E) if I do not find the book, I will be unable to complete my research paper

STOP
IF YOU FINISH BEFORE TIME IS CALLED, YOU MAY CHECK YOUR WORK ON THIS SECTION ONLY. DO NOT WORK ON ANY OTHER SECTION IN THE TEST.

SECTION IV

Time—35 minutes

23 Questions

<u>Directions</u>: Each group of questions in this section is based on a set of conditions. In answering some of the questions, it may be useful to draw a rough diagram. Choose the response that most accurately and completely answers each question and blacken the corresponding space on your answer sheet.

Questions 1–7

A record producer is planning the contents of a CD consisting of a sequence of exactly five instrumental pieces—*Reciprocity, Salammbo, Trapezoid, Vancouver,* and *Wisteria.* To create and sustain certain moods, the sequence of pieces will satisfy the following constraints:

> *Salammbo* must be earlier than *Vancouver.*
> *Trapezoid* must either be earlier than both *Reciprocity* and *Salammbo* or later than both *Reciprocity* and *Salammbo.*
> *Wisteria* must either be earlier than both *Reciprocity* and *Trapezoid* or later than both *Reciprocity* and *Trapezoid.*

1. The five pieces could appear in which one of the following sequences on the CD, in order from first to last?

    (A) *Reciprocity, Trapezoid, Wisteria, Salammbo, Vancouver*

    (B) *Salammbo, Reciprocity, Trapezoid, Vancouver, Wisteria*

    (C) *Trapezoid, Wisteria, Salammbo, Vancouver, Reciprocity*

    (D) *Vancouver, Wisteria, Salammbo, Reciprocity, Trapezoid*

    (E) *Wisteria, Salammbo, Vancouver, Trapezoid, Reciprocity*

GO ON TO THE NEXT PAGE.

2. If *Salammbo* is the fourth piece on the CD, then which one of the following must be true?

   (A) *Reciprocity* is earlier on the CD than *Wisteria*.
   (B) *Salammbo* is earlier on the CD than *Trapezoid*.
   (C) *Trapezoid* is earlier on the CD than *Reciprocity*.
   (D) *Vancouver* is earlier on the CD than *Wisteria*.
   (E) *Wisteria* is earlier on the CD than *Trapezoid*.

3. If *Reciprocity* is the first piece on the CD, then which one of the following could be true?

   (A) *Trapezoid* is the second piece on the CD.
   (B) *Vancouver* is the third piece on the CD.
   (C) *Wisteria* is the third piece on the CD.
   (D) *Salammbo* is the fourth piece on the CD.
   (E) *Trapezoid* is the last piece on the CD.

4. If *Trapezoid* is the second piece on the CD, then which one of the following could be true?

   (A) *Salammbo* is the first piece on the CD.
   (B) *Reciprocity* is the first piece on the CD.
   (C) *Vancouver* is the third piece on the CD.
   (D) *Wisteria* is the fourth piece on the CD.
   (E) *Reciprocity* is the last piece on the CD.

5. The first and second pieces on the CD, listed in order, could be

   (A) *Reciprocity* and *Vancouver*
   (B) *Reciprocity* and *Wisteria*
   (C) *Salammbo* and *Trapezoid*
   (D) *Trapezoid* and *Wisteria*
   (E) *Wisteria* and *Salammbo*

6. If *Vancouver* is the second piece on the CD, then which one of the following could be true?

   (A) *Wisteria* is the first piece on the CD.
   (B) *Salammbo* is the third piece on the CD.
   (C) *Trapezoid* is the third piece on the CD.
   (D) *Reciprocity* is the fourth piece on the CD.
   (E) *Reciprocity* is the last piece on the CD.

7. If *Wisteria* is the first piece on the CD, then which one of the following CANNOT be true?

   (A) *Trapezoid* is the third piece on the CD.
   (B) *Vancouver* is the third piece on the CD.
   (C) *Salammbo* is the fourth piece on the CD.
   (D) *Vancouver* is the fourth piece on the CD.
   (E) *Trapezoid* is the last piece on the CD.

GO ON TO THE NEXT PAGE.

Questions 8–13

At a business symposium there will be exactly five speakers: Long, Molina, Xiao, Yoshida, and Zimmerman. Each speaker will give exactly one speech, in either the Gold Room or the Rose Room. In each room, there will be exactly one speech at 1 P.M. and one speech at 2 P.M. In one of the rooms, yet to be determined, there will also be a speech at 3 P.M. The schedule of speeches is constrained by the following:

    Molina's speech must be earlier than Long's, and in the same room.

    Neither Xiao's speech nor Yoshida's speech can be earlier than Zimmerman's.

    If Long's speech is in the Gold Room, then Xiao's and Zimmerman's speeches must both be in the Rose Room.

8. Which one of the following could be the speeches given in each room, listed in the order in which they occur?

(A)   Gold Room: Molina's, Long's
       Rose Room: Zimmerman's, Xiao's, Yoshida's

(B)   Gold Room: Molina's, Yoshida's, Long's
       Rose Room: Xiao's, Zimmerman's

(C)   Gold Room: Xiao's, Molina's, Long's
       Rose Room: Zimmerman's, Yoshida's

(D)   Gold Room: Yoshida's, Long's, Molina's
       Rose Room: Zimmerman's, Xiao's

(E)   Gold Room: Zimmerman's, Molina's
       Rose Room: Xiao's, Yoshida's, Long's

GO ON TO THE NEXT PAGE.

9. Which one of the following pairs of speeches CANNOT be given at the same time?

    (A) Long's and Yoshida's
    (B) Long's and Zimmerman's
    (C) Molina's and Xiao's
    (D) Xiao's and Yoshida's
    (E) Yoshida's and Zimmerman's

10. If Xiao's speech is at 3 P.M., which one of the following CANNOT be true?

    (A) Long's speech is in the same room as Yoshida's.
    (B) Molina's speech is in the same room as Xiao's.
    (C) Xiao's speech is in the same room as Yoshida's.
    (D) Xiao's speech is in the same room as Zimmerman's.
    (E) Yoshida's speech is in the same room as Zimmerman's.

11. Which one of the following could be a complete and accurate list of the speeches given in the Gold Room, in the order in which they occur?

    (A) Long's, Molina's
    (B) Molina's, Yoshida's
    (C) Molina's, Yoshida's, Long's
    (D) Yoshida's, Zimmerman's, Xiao's
    (E) Zimmerman's, Molina's, Long's

12. If Yoshida's speech is at 1 P.M., which one of the following could be true?

    (A) Long's speech is at 1 P.M. in the Gold Room.
    (B) Long's speech is at 2 P.M. in the Rose Room.
    (C) Molina's speech is at 2 P.M. in the Gold Room.
    (D) Xiao's speech is at 3 P.M. in the Gold Room.
    (E) Xiao's speech is at 1 P.M. in the Rose Room.

13. Which one of the following, if substituted for the constraint that neither Xiao's speech nor Yoshida's speech can be earlier than Zimmerman's, would have the same effect in determining the schedule of speeches with regard to rooms and times?

    (A) Long's speech must be at 3 P.M.
    (B) Molina's speech cannot be earlier than Zimmerman's.
    (C) Either Xiao's speech or Yoshida's speech must be after Zimmerman's.
    (D) Either Xiao's speech or Yoshida's speech or both must be at 2 P.M.
    (E) Zimmerman's speech must be at 1 P.M.

GO ON TO THE NEXT PAGE.

Questions 14–18

During the seventeenth century, three families—the Trents, the Williamses, and the Yandells—owned the five buildings that constituted the center of their village—the forge, the granary, the inn, the mill, and the stable. Each family owned at least one of the buildings and each building was owned by exactly one of the families. The historical evidence establishes the following about the ownership of the buildings:

> The Williamses owned more of the buildings than the Yandells owned.
> Neither the inn nor the mill belonged to the owner of the forge.
> Either the Trents owned the stable or the Yandells owned the inn, or both.

14. Which one of the following could be an accurate matching of each family to the building or buildings it owned?

(A) Trents: the granary, the stable
     Williamses: the inn, the mill
     Yandells: the forge

(B) Trents: the granary, the mill
     Williamses: the inn, the stable
     Yandells: the forge

(C) Trents: the forge, the mill
     Williamses: the granary, the stable
     Yandells: the inn

(D) Trents: the forge, the granary
     Williamses: the mill
     Yandells: the inn, the stable

(E) Trents: the stable
     Williamses: the inn, the mill
     Yandells: the forge, the granary

GO ON TO THE NEXT PAGE.

15. Which one of the following is a pair of buildings that CANNOT both have been owned by the Trents?

   (A) the forge, the granary
   (B) the granary, the mill
   (C) the granary, the stable
   (D) the inn, the mill
   (E) the inn, the stable

16. If the Yandells owned the mill, which one of the following must be true?

   (A) The Trents owned the forge.
   (B) The Trents owned the inn.
   (C) The Williamses owned the forge.
   (D) The Williamses owned the granary.
   (E) The Williamses owned the inn.

17. If one of the families owned both the granary and the inn, which one of the following could be true?

   (A) The Trents owned the granary.
   (B) The Trents owned the mill.
   (C) The Williamses owned the forge.
   (D) The Williamses owned the stable.
   (E) The Yandells owned the inn.

18. If the Trents owned exactly one of the buildings, which one of the following is a complete and accurate list of the buildings any one of which could be the building that the Trents owned?

   (A) the forge
   (B) the forge, the mill
   (C) the inn, the stable
   (D) the forge, the granary, the mill
   (E) the forge, the mill, the stable

GO ON TO THE NEXT PAGE.

<u>Questions 19–23</u>

A florist is filling a customer's order for three bouquets—bouquet 1, bouquet 2, and bouquet 3. Each of the bouquets is to be composed of one or more of five kinds of flowers—lilies, peonies, roses, snapdragons, and tulips—subject to the following conditions:

Bouquets 1 and 3 cannot have any kind of flower in common.

Bouquets 2 and 3 must have exactly two kinds of flowers in common.

Bouquet 3 must have snapdragons.

If a bouquet has lilies, that bouquet must also have roses but cannot have snapdragons.

If a bouquet has tulips, that bouquet must also have peonies.

19. Which one of the following could be a complete and accurate list of the kinds of flowers in each of the bouquets?

(A) bouquet 1: lilies, roses
bouquet 2: peonies, roses, tulips
bouquet 3: peonies, snapdragons, tulips

(B) bouquet 1: peonies, roses
bouquet 2: peonies, snapdragons
bouquet 3: peonies, snapdragons, tulips

(C) bouquet 1: peonies, tulips
bouquet 2: roses, snapdragons, tulips
bouquet 3: roses, snapdragons

(D) bouquet 1: roses
bouquet 2: peonies, snapdragons
bouquet 3: lilies, peonies, snapdragons

(E) bouquet 1: snapdragons
bouquet 2: lilies, roses
bouquet 3: lilies, roses

GO ON TO THE NEXT PAGE.

20. If lilies are in bouquet 1, which one of the following must be true?

    (A) Lilies are in bouquet 2.
    (B) Peonies are in bouquet 3.
    (C) Roses are in bouquet 2.
    (D) Tulips are in bouquet 2.
    (E) Tulips are in bouquet 3.

21. If tulips are in bouquet 1, which one of the following could be a complete and accurate list of the kinds of flowers in bouquet 2?

    (A) peonies, tulips
    (B) peonies, snapdragons
    (C) peonies, snapdragons, tulips
    (D) peonies, roses, tulips
    (E) peonies, roses, snapdragons, tulips

22. Which one of the following CANNOT be a complete and accurate list of the kinds of flowers in bouquet 2?

    (A) lilies, roses
    (B) peonies, tulips
    (C) peonies, roses, snapdragons
    (D) peonies, roses, tulips
    (E) peonies, roses, snapdragons, tulips

23. Which one of the following CANNOT be true?

    (A) Lilies and roses are the only kinds of flowers in bouquet 1.
    (B) Peonies and tulips are the only kinds of flowers in bouquet 1.
    (C) Lilies, peonies, and roses are the only kinds of flowers in bouquet 2.
    (D) Peonies, roses, and snapdragons are the only kinds of flowers in bouquet 2.
    (E) Peonies, snapdragons, and tulips are the only kinds of flowers in bouquet 3.

STOP
IF YOU FINISH BEFORE TIME IS CALLED, YOU MAY CHECK YOUR WORK ON THIS SECTION ONLY. DO NOT WORK ON ANY OTHER SECTION IN THE TEST.

SECTION V

Time—35 minutes

26 Questions

Directions: The questions in this section are based on the reasoning contained in brief statements or passages. For some questions, more than one of the choices could conceivably answer the question. However, you are to choose the best answer; that is, the response that most accurately and completely answers the question. You should not make assumptions that are by commonsense standards implausible, superfluous, or incompatible with the passage. After you have chosen the best answer, blacken the corresponding space on your answer sheet.

1. In an experiment, ten people were asked to taste samples of coffee and rank them. Five of the people were given chocolate with the coffee, and this group subsequently reported that all the coffee samples tasted pretty much the same as one another. Five others tasted coffee only, and they were able to detect differences. Clearly, then, chocolate interferes with one's ability to taste coffee.

   Which one of the following, if true, most undermines the conclusion drawn above?

   (A) The ten people were randomly assigned to either the group that tasted only coffee or the group that was also given chocolate, although some people had asked to be in the group that received chocolate.

   (B) Similar results were achieved when the experiment was repeated with a different, larger group of people.

   (C) Chocolate is normally consumed as a solid, whereas coffee is normally consumed as a liquid.

   (D) The five people who were originally given chocolate were asked a week later to taste coffee samples without chocolate, and they still detected no differences between the coffee samples.

   (E) Some subjects who tasted just coffee reported only subtle differences between the coffee samples, while others thought the differences were considerable.

2. Residents of a coastal community are resisting the efforts of one family to build a large house on the family's land. Although the house would not violate any town codes, the land in question is depicted in a painting by a famous and beloved landscape painter who recently died. Residents argue that the house would alter the pristine landscape and hence damage the community's artistic and historic heritage.

   Which one of the following principles, if valid, most helps to justify the reasoning of the residents opposed to building the house?

   (A) Every possible effort should be made to preserve historic buildings that are well known and well loved.

   (B) Communities that seek to preserve undeveloped areas of landscape or historic neighborhoods should purchase those properties for the public trust.

   (C) Artists who choose to represent actual landscapes in their paintings have the right to demand that the owners of the land represented do not significantly alter the landscape.

   (D) The right to build on one's own property is constrained by the artistic and historical interests of the community at large.

   (E) In historic communities, the building and zoning regulations should prohibit construction that obstructs access to historic sites.

GO ON TO THE NEXT PAGE.

3. Moore: Sunscreen lotions, which are designed to block skin-cancer-causing ultraviolet radiation, do not do so effectively. Many scientific studies have shown that people who have consistently used these lotions develop, on average, as many skin cancers as those who have rarely, if ever, used them.

    The reasoning in Moore's argument is most vulnerable to criticism on the grounds that the argument

    (A) takes for granted that there are no other possible health benefits of using sunscreen lotions other than blocking skin-cancer-causing ultraviolet radiation

    (B) fails to distinguish between the relative number of cases of skin cancer and the severity of those cases in measuring effectiveness at skin cancer prevention

    (C) fails to consider the effectiveness of sunscreen lotions that are not specifically designed to block skin-cancer-causing ultraviolet radiation

    (D) relies on evidence regarding the probability of people in different groups developing cancer that, in principle, would be impossible to challenge

    (E) overlooks the possibility that people who consistently use sunscreen lotions spend more time in the sun, on average, than people who do not

4. Psychologist: Some have argued that Freudian psychotherapy is the most effective kind because it is so difficult and time consuming. But surely this does not follow. Similar reasoning—e.g., concluding that a car-repair chain has the most effective technique for repairing cars because the cars it services receive so much work and spend so much time in the shop—would never be accepted.

    The reasoning technique employed by the psychologist is that of attempting to undermine an argument by

    (A) introducing a principle that contradicts the one on which the argument is based

    (B) questioning the truth of its premises

    (C) presenting an analogous argument whose conclusion is thought to be obviously false

    (D) claiming that the argument is based on a false analogy

    (E) suggesting that a supposed cause of a phenomenon is actually an effect of that phenomenon

5. While biodiversity is indispensable to the survival of life on Earth, biodiversity does not require the survival of every currently existing species. For there to be life on Earth, various ecological niches must be filled; many niches, however, can be filled by more than one species.

    Which one of the following statements most accurately expresses the conclusion drawn in the argument?

    (A) Biodiversity does not require that all existing species continue to exist.

    (B) There are various ecological niches that must be filled if there is to be life on Earth.

    (C) The survival of life on Earth depends upon biodiversity.

    (D) There are many ecological niches that can be filled by more than one species.

    (E) The species most indispensable for biodiversity fill more than one ecological niche.

6. Clinician: Patients with immune system disorders are usually treated with a class of drugs that, unfortunately, increase the patient's risk of developing osteoporosis, a bone-loss disease. So these patients take another drug that helps to preserve existing bone. Since a drug that enhances the growth of new bone cells has now become available, these patients should take this new drug in addition to the drug that helps to preserve existing bone.

    Which one of the following would be most useful to know in order to evaluate the clinician's argument?

    (A) How large is the class of drugs that increase the risk of developing osteoporosis?

    (B) Why are immune system disorders treated with drugs that increase the risk of developing osteoporosis?

    (C) Is the new drug more expensive than the drug that helps to preserve existing bone?

    (D) How long has the drug that helps to preserve existing bone been in use?

    (E) To what extent does the new drug retain its efficacy when used in combination with the other drugs?

GO ON TO THE NEXT PAGE.

7. Critic: The perennial image of the "city on a hill" associates elevated locations with elevated purposes. The city's concert hall—its newest civic building— is located on a spectacular hilltop site. But because it is far from the center of the city, it cannot fulfill the purpose of a civic building. An example of a successful civic building is the art museum, which is situated in a densely populated downtown area. It encourages social cohesion and makes the city more alive.

The critic's reasoning most closely conforms to which one of the following principles?

(A) A civic building that is located in a downtown area should, if possible, be located on an elevated site.
(B) A city needs to have civic buildings if it is to have social cohesion.
(C) A civic building with an elevated purpose should be located on a spectacular site.
(D) The downtown area of a city should be designed in a way that complements the area's civic buildings.
(E) The purpose of a civic building is to encourage social cohesion and to make a city more alive.

8. Fluoride enters a region's groundwater when rain dissolves fluoride-bearing minerals in the soil. In a recent study, researchers found that when rainfall, concentrations of fluoride-bearing minerals, and other relevant variables are held constant, fluoride concentrations in groundwater are significantly higher in areas where the groundwater also contains a high concentration of sodium.

Which one of the following can most reasonably be concluded on the basis of the researchers' findings?

(A) Fluoride-bearing minerals are not the primary source of fluoride found in groundwater.
(B) Rainfall does not affect fluoride concentrations in groundwater.
(C) Sodium-bearing minerals dissolve at a faster rate than fluoride-bearing minerals.
(D) Sodium in groundwater increases the rate at which fluoride-bearing minerals dissolve.
(E) Soil that contains high concentrations of sodium-bearing minerals also contains high concentrations of fluoride-bearing minerals.

9. Fraenger's assertion that the artist Hieronymus Bosch belonged to the Brethren of the Free Spirit, a nonmainstream religious group, is unlikely to be correct. Fraenger's hypothesis explains much of Bosch's unusual subject matter. However, there is evidence that Bosch was a member of a mainstream church, and no evidence that he was a member of the Brethren.

The statement that there is no evidence that Bosch was a member of the Brethren figures in the argument in which one of the following ways?

(A) It is a premise that, when combined with the other premises, guarantees the falsity of Fraenger's assertion.
(B) It is used to support the claim that Bosch was a member of a mainstream church.
(C) It is used to dispute Fraenger's hypothesis by questioning Fraenger's credibility.
(D) It is intended to cast doubt on Fraenger's hypothesis by questioning the sufficiency of Fraenger's evidence.
(E) It is intended to help show that Bosch's choice of subject matter remains unexplained.

10. Vacuum cleaner salesperson: To prove that this Super XL vacuum cleaner is better than your old vacuum cleaner, I ran your old vacuum once over this dirty carpet. Then I ran the Super XL over the same area. All that dirt that the Super XL picked up is dirt your old vacuum left behind, proving the Super XL is the better vacuum.

The vacuum cleaner salesperson's argument is most vulnerable to the criticism that it

(A) ignores the possibility that dirt remained in the carpet even after the Super XL had been used in the test
(B) takes for granted that the Super XL will still perform better than the old vacuum cleaner when it is the same age as the old vacuum cleaner
(C) takes for granted that because the Super XL outperforms one vacuum cleaner it is the best vacuum cleaner available
(D) ignores the possibility that the amount of dirt removed in the test by the old vacuum cleaner is greater than the amount of dirt removed by the Super XL
(E) ignores the possibility that if the Super XL had been used first it would have left behind just as much dirt as did the old vacuum cleaner

GO ON TO THE NEXT PAGE.

11. Manager: This company's supply chain will develop significant weaknesses unless we make changes to our vendor contracts now. Some will argue that this problem is so far in the future that there is no need to address it today. But that is an irresponsible approach. Just imagine if a financial planner offered the same counsel to a 30-year-old client: "Don't worry, Jane, retirement is 35 years away; you don't need to save anything now." That planner would be guilty of gross malpractice.

Which one of the following most accurately expresses the overall conclusion drawn in the manager's argument?

(A) Some people argue that the supply-chain problem is so far in the future that there is no need to address it now.

(B) It would be irresponsible to postpone changes to the vendor contracts just because the supply chain will not develop weaknesses for a long time.

(C) If no changes are made to the vendor contracts, the supply chain will eventually develop significant weaknesses.

(D) In planning to meet its future obligations, a company should follow the same practices that are appropriate for an individual who is planning for retirement.

(E) Financial planners should advise their clients to save money for retirement only if retirement is many years away.

12. Worldwide, more books were sold last year than in any previous year. In particular, there were more cookbooks sold. For the first time ever, most of the cookbooks sold were not intended for beginners. Indeed, more cookbooks than ever were purchased by professional cooks. However, one of the few books available on every continent is a cookbook written for beginners, entitled *Problem-Free Cooking.*

Which one of the following is most strongly supported by the information above?

(A) Last year there were more cookbooks sold that were not intended for beginners than in any previous year.

(B) The best-selling cookbook last year was a cookbook that was intended for beginners.

(C) Sales of cookbooks intended for beginners were lower last year than in previous years.

(D) Most of the cookbooks purchased last year that were not intended for beginners were purchased by professional cooks.

(E) *Problem-Free Cooking* sold more copies last year than did any cookbook written for professional cooks.

13. In early 2003, scientists detected methane in the atmosphere of Mars. Methane is a fragile compound that falls apart when hit by the ultraviolet radiation in sunlight. So any methane in the Martian atmosphere must have been released into the atmosphere relatively recently.

The argument relies on the assumption that

(A) Mars had no methane in its atmosphere prior to 2003

(B) all methane in the Martian atmosphere is eventually exposed to sunlight

(C) methane cannot be detected until it has started to fall apart

(D) the methane that the scientists detected had been exposed to ultraviolet radiation

(E) methane in Earth's atmosphere does not fall apart as a result of exposure to ultraviolet radiation

14. Environmentalist: Pollution from gasoline burned by cars contributes to serious environmental problems. But the cost of these problems is not reflected in gasoline prices, and hence usually does not affect consumers' decisions about how much to drive. Heavier taxes on gasoline, however, would reflect this cost, and as a result consumers would pollute less.

The environmentalist's statements, if true, most strongly support which one of the following?

(A) The cost of pollution from driving should not be reflected in the price of gasoline unless the amount of pollution produced would be reduced as a result.

(B) Heavier taxes on gasoline would increase consumers' awareness of the kinds of environmental problems to which pollution from driving contributes.

(C) Consumers would purchase less gasoline, on average, if the cost of the environmental problems to which pollution from driving contributes were fully reflected in the price of gasoline.

(D) The only cost considered by most consumers when they are deciding how much to drive is the cost of gasoline.

(E) Pollution from gasoline burned by cars will be reduced only if consumers give more consideration to the cost of that pollution when deciding how much to drive.

GO ON TO THE NEXT PAGE.

15. Hine's emerald dragonflies are an endangered species that live in wetlands. The larvae of these dragonflies can survive only in the water, where they are subject to predation by several species including red devil crayfish. Surprisingly, the dragonfly populations are more likely to remain healthy in areas where red devil crayfish are present than in areas without red devil crayfish.

Which one of the following, if true, most helps to explain the surprising fact?

(A) Red devil crayfish dig chambers that remain filled with water even when the surrounding wetlands dry up.
(B) Red devil crayfish present no threat to adult Hine's emerald dragonflies.
(C) The varied diet of the red devil crayfish does not include any animal species that prey on dragonfly larvae.
(D) Red devil crayfish are found in many more locations than Hine's emerald dragonflies are.
(E) Populations of red devil crayfish in a wetland do not drop significantly if the local population of Hine's emerald dragonflies dies out.

16. Stress is a common cause of high blood pressure. By calming their minds and thereby reducing stress, some people can lower their blood pressure. And most people can calm their minds, in turn, by engaging in exercise.

Which one of the following is most strongly supported by the information above?

(A) For at least some people, having lower blood pressure has at least some tendency to cause their stress levels to be reduced.
(B) Most people with high blood pressure can lower their blood pressure by reducing their stress levels.
(C) Most people who do not exercise regularly have higher stress levels as a result.
(D) Engaging in exercise can directly lower one's blood pressure.
(E) For at least some people, engaging in exercise can cause their stress levels to be reduced.

17. A positive correlation has been found between the amount of soot in the atmosphere of cities and the frequency of a certain ailment among those cities' populations. However, the soot itself probably does not cause this ailment, since in cities where there are large amounts of soot in the air, there are usually also high concentrations of many other air pollutants.

Which one of the following statements, if true, most weakens the argument?

(A) In cities where there are high concentrations of many air pollutants but little if any soot in the air, the frequency of the ailment is just as high, on average, as it is in cities where there are large amounts of soot in the air.
(B) If the ailment rarely occurs except in cities in which there are large amounts of soot in the air, then the soot is probably the cause of the ailment.
(C) In each of the cities where there are large amounts of soot in the air but little other air pollution, the frequency of the ailment is at least as high as it is anywhere else.
(D) If high concentrations of many different pollutants in a city's air are correlated with a high frequency of the ailment among that city's population, then it is possible that two or more of those pollutants each causally contributes to the ailment.
(E) In cities in which there are high concentrations of many air pollutants, there are generally also high concentrations of other forms of pollution that are very likely to contribute causally to the ailment.

GO ON TO THE NEXT PAGE.

18. So far this summer there has been no rain in the valley. But usually a few inches of rain fall there each summer. Since only one week of summer is left, it will probably rain in the valley within the next week.

The flawed pattern of reasoning in the argument above is most similar to that in which one of the following arguments?

(A) Aisha has finished proofreading all but the last two pages of an issue of the journal *Periodos* and has encountered no errors. However, there are sometimes a few errors in an issue of the journal *Periodos*. So there may be errors in the pages that Aisha has not yet checked.

(B) There are generally few errors in an issue of the journal *Periodos*. Aisha has finished proofreading all but the last two pages of an issue of this journal but has encountered no errors. Hence, there are probably no errors in the pages that Aisha has not yet checked in this issue of the journal.

(C) On average, there are a few errors in an issue of the journal *Periodos*. Aisha has finished proofreading all but the last two pages of an issue of this journal but has encountered no errors. So there are probably errors in the pages she has not yet checked in this issue of the journal.

(D) Aisha has proofread several issues of the journal *Periodos* and has encountered no errors. But there are seldom any errors in an issue of this journal. So there will probably be no errors in the next issue of the journal Periodos that she proofreads.

(E) There usually are errors in each issue of the journal *Periodos*. Since Aisha has finished proofreading the latest issue of this journal and has detected no errors, Aisha has probably made a mistake in her proofreading.

19. Young people believe efforts to reduce pollution, poverty, and war are doomed to failure. This pessimism is probably harmful to humanity's future, because people lose motivation to work for goals they think are unrealizable. We must do what we can to prevent this loss of motivation and therefore must enable our children to believe that better futures are possible.

Which one of the following is an assumption on which the argument depends?

(A) Motivating people to work to solve humanity's problems will enable them to believe that the future can be better and will cause them to be less pessimistic.

(B) Enabling people to believe that better futures are possible will help prevent the loss of motivation that results from pessimistic beliefs about the future.

(C) Optimism about the future is better than pessimism, even if that optimism is based on an illusory vision of what is likely to occur.

(D) If future generations believe that the future can be better, then pollution, poverty, and war will be eliminated.

(E) The current prevalence of such problems as pollution and poverty stems from previous generations' inability to believe that futures can be better.

20. In a recent study of stroke patients, those who exhibited continuing deterioration of the nerve cells in the brain after the stroke also exhibited the highest levels of the protein glutamate in their blood. Glutamate, which functions within nerve cells as a neurotransmitter, can kill surrounding nerve cells if it leaks from damaged or oxygen-starved nerve cells. Thus glutamate leaking from damaged or oxygen-starved nerve cells is a cause of long-term brain damage resulting from strokes.

Which one of the following, if true, most strengthens the argument?

(A) Any neurotransmitter that leaks from a damaged or oxygen-starved nerve cell will damage surrounding nerve cells.

(B) Stroke patients exhibit a wide variety of abnormal chemical levels in their blood.

(C) Glutamate is the only neurotransmitter that leaks from oxygen-starved or physically damaged nerve cells.

(D) Leakage from damaged or oxygen-starved nerve cells is the only possible source of glutamate in the blood.

(E) Nerve cells can suffer enough damage to leak glutamate without being destroyed themselves.

GO ON TO THE NEXT PAGE.

21. The only songs Amanda has ever written are blues songs and punk rock songs. Most punk rock songs involve no more than three chords. So if the next song Amanda writes is not a blues song, it probably will not involve more than three chords.

The reasoning in which one of the following arguments is most similar to that in the argument above?

(A) The only pets the Gupta family has ever owned are fish and parrots. Most parrots are very noisy. So if the next pet the Gupta family owns is a parrot, it will probably be very noisy.
(B) Most parrots are very noisy. The Gupta family has never owned any pets other than fish and parrots. So if the Gupta family has ever owned a noisy pet, it was probably a parrot.
(C) All the pets the Gupta family has ever owned have been fish and parrots. Most parrots are very noisy. So any pet the Gupta family ever owns that is not a fish will probably be very noisy.
(D) Every pet the Gupta family has ever owned has been a fish or a parrot. Most parrots are very noisy. So if the next pet the Gupta family owns is not a parrot, it will probably not be very noisy.
(E) The Gupta family has never owned any pets other than fish and parrots. Most parrots are very noisy. So the next pet the Gupta family owns will probably be very noisy if it is not a fish.

22. Advertising tends to have a greater influence on consumer preferences regarding brands of yogurt than it does on consumer preferences regarding brands of milk. Yet, since the LargeCo supermarket chain began advertising its store-brand products, sales of its store-brand milk increased more than sales of its store-brand yogurt.

Which one of the following, if true, most helps to resolve the apparent discrepancy described above?

(A) There has recently been increased demand at LargeCo stores for the chain's own brand of yogurt as well as for other brands of yogurt.
(B) The typical shopper going to LargeCo for the purpose of buying milk does not go with the intention of also buying yogurt.
(C) Shoppers at LargeCo tend to purchase the chain's own brand of dairy products more frequently than other brands of dairy products.
(D) Supermarkets throughout the entire nation have experienced a sharp decrease in sales of yogurt recently.
(E) Consumers tend to purchase store brands of yogurt, but purchase whichever brand of milk is least expensive.

23. Problem: If Shayna congratulates Daniel on his award, she will misrepresent her true feelings. However, if Shayna does not congratulate Daniel, she will hurt his feelings.

Principle: One should never be insincere about one's feelings, except possibly where one believes that the person with whom one is speaking would prefer kindness to honesty.

The principle, if valid, most helps to justify the reasoning in which one of the following arguments concerning the problem?

(A) If Shayna congratulates Daniel, she will avoid hurting his feelings, so she should congratulate him.
(B) Daniel might prefer for Shayna to congratulate him—even if insincerely—rather than for her to express her true feelings, and so Shayna would be doing nothing wrong in insincerely congratulating Daniel.
(C) Shayna believes that kindness should be preferred to dishonesty when speaking to others, so she should not tell Daniel her true feelings.
(D) Daniel's feelings would be hurt if he knew that congratulations from Shayna were insincere, so Shayna should not congratulate him.
(E) Shayna has no opinion about whether Daniel would prefer kindness to honesty, so she should not congratulate him.

24. Clearly, a democracy cannot thrive without effective news media. After all, a democracy cannot thrive without an electorate that is knowledgeable about important political issues, and an electorate can be knowledgeable in this way only if it has access to unbiased information about the government.

The argument's conclusion is properly inferred if which one of the following is assumed?

(A) All societies that have effective news media are thriving democracies.
(B) If an electorate has access to unbiased information about the government, then that electorate will be knowledgeable about important political issues.
(C) A democracy will thrive if its electorate is knowledgeable about important political issues.
(D) A democracy cannot thrive if the electorate is exposed to biased information about the government.
(E) Without effective news media, an electorate will not have access to unbiased information about the government.

GO ON TO THE NEXT PAGE.

25. Roberta is irritable only when she is tired, and loses things only when she is tired. Since she has been yawning all day, and has just lost her keys, she is almost certainly irritable.

The reasoning above is flawed in that it

(A) infers from a correlation between tiredness and yawning that tiredness causes yawning
(B) assumes the conclusion that it sets out to prove
(C) generalizes on the basis of a single instance
(D) takes a necessary condition for Roberta's losing things to be a sufficient condition
(E) takes a necessary condition for Roberta's being irritable to be a sufficient condition

26. Farmer: Crops genetically engineered to produce toxins that enable them to resist insect pests do not need to be sprayed with insecticides. Since excessive spraying of insecticides has harmed wildlife populations near croplands, using such genetically engineered crops more widely is likely to help wildlife populations to recover.

Which one of the following is an assumption the farmer's argument requires?

(A) Use of the crops that have been genetically engineered to resist insect pests in place of crops that have been sprayed with insecticides will cause less harm to wildlife populations.
(B) Wildlife populations that have been harmed by the excessive spraying of insecticides on croplands are likely to recover if the amount of insecticides sprayed on those croplands is reduced even slightly.
(C) Crops that have been genetically engineered to resist insect pests are never sprayed with insecticides that harm wildlife populations.
(D) Use of crops that have been genetically engineered to resist insect pests is no more costly to farmers than the use of insecticides on crops that are not genetically engineered.
(E) If a wider use of certain crops that have been genetically engineered to resist insect pests is likely to help at least some wildlife populations to recover, it is likely to have that effect only because its use will prevent excessive and ineffective spraying of insecticides on croplands.

STOP
IF YOU FINISH BEFORE TIME IS CALLED, YOU MAY CHECK YOUR WORK ON THIS SECTION ONLY. DO NOT WORK ON ANY OTHER SECTION IN THE TEST.

LSAT WRITING SAMPLE TOPIC

Directions: The scenario presented below describes two choices, either one of which can be supported on the basis of the information given. Your essay should consider both choices and argue for one over the other, based on the two specified criteria and the facts provided. There is no "right" or "wrong" choice: a reasonable argument can be made for either.

A medium-sized company is located in a technology park in a sparsely populated area outside a major city. It has had difficulty retaining employees because of the long and expensive commute between the city and work that nearly all of its employees face. Consequently, the company will implement a commuting assistance plan. It must decide between operating a free bus for employees and subsidizing employees' costs of using public transportation. Using the facts below, write an essay in which you argue for one plan over the other based on the following two criteria:

- The company wants to minimize its employees' commuting expenses and frustrations.
- The company wants reliability and flexibility in its employees' work schedules.

Under the first plan, the company would lease a bus and hire a driver. The bus would make several daily circuits between the company's location and a single downtown stop, accessible by public transportation and close to a large, inexpensive parking garage. The only riders on the bus would be the company's employees. The bus has reclining seats and free Wi-Fi. The average total commute time for an employee would be 75 minutes each way. A breakdown of the bus would be disruptive to the company's operations.

Under the second plan, the company would partially reimburse employees' cost of using public transportation to commute to work. The average savings for an employee would be about 80 percent. Most of the employees live within walking distance to a bus stop. Most employees would have to make one or two transfers. Buses are scheduled to arrive every half hour at a bus shelter in the technology park. Buses are sometimes late. None of them have Wi-Fi. The average total commute time for an employee would be 60 minutes each way.

Directions:

1. Use the Answer Key on the next page to check your answers.

2. Use the Scoring Worksheet below to compute your raw score.

3. Use the Score Conversion Chart to convert your raw score into the 120–180 scale.

Scoring Worksheet

1. Enter the number of questions you answered correctly in each section.

	Number Correct
SECTION I..	_____
SECTION III	_____
SECTION IV	_____
SECTION V	_____

2. Enter the sum here:_____
   This is your Raw Score.

Section Map

SECTION I: PrepTest 73, Section 1
SECTION II: Experimental (PrepTest 21, Section 2)
SECTION III: PrepTest 73, Section 2
SECTION IV: PrepTest 73, Section 3
SECTION V: PrepTest 73, Section 4

Conversion Chart
For Converting Raw Score to the 120–180 LSAT Scaled Score
LSAT Form 4LSN110

Reported Score	Lowest	Highest
180	98	101
179	97	97
178	*	*
177	96	96
176	95	95
175	94	94
174	93	93
173	92	92
172	91	91
171	90	90
170	89	89
169	87	88
168	86	86
167	85	85
166	83	84
165	82	82
164	80	81
163	79	79
162	77	78
161	75	76
160	74	74
159	72	73
158	70	71
157	69	69
156	67	68
155	65	66
154	63	64
153	61	62
152	60	60
151	58	59
150	56	57
149	54	55
148	53	53
147	51	52
146	49	50
145	47	48
144	46	46
143	44	45
142	43	43
141	41	42
140	39	40
139	38	38
138	37	37
137	35	36
136	34	34
135	32	33
134	31	31
133	30	30
132	29	29
131	27	28
130	26	26
129	25	25
128	24	24
127	23	23
126	22	22
125	21	21
124	20	20
123	19	19
122	18	18
121	17	17
120	0	16

*There is no raw score that will produce this scaled score for this form.

SECTION I

1.	A	8.	B	15.	B	22.	B
2.	B	9.	A	16.	C	23.	A
3.	D	10.	D	17.	B	24.	D
4.	B	11.	C	18.	E	25.	E
5.	A	12.	E	19.	A	26.	D
6.	E	13.	E	20.	E	27.	A
7.	C	14.	B	21.	A		

SECTION II

1.	B	8.	E	15.	A	22.	E
2.	C	9.	E	16.	E	23.	B
3.	B	10.	A	17.	C	24.	A
4.	D	11.	C	18.	A	25.	E
5.	C	12.	B	19.	C		
6.	B	13.	D	20.	D		
7.	B	14.	C	21.	A		

SECTION III

1.	C	8.	B	15.	B	22.	A
2.	E	9.	C	16.	A	23.	C
3.	A	10.	A	17.	B	24.	D
4.	D	11.	B	18.	E	25.	C
5.	D	12.	A	19.	B		
6.	D	13.	B	20.	E		
7.	C	14.	E	21.	E		

SECTION IV

1.	B	8.	A	15.	D	22.	A
2.	C	9.	B	16.	D	23.	C
3.	B	10.	A	17.	B		
4.	E	11.	C	18.	E		
5.	E	12.	C	19.	A		
6.	D	13.	E	20.	B		
7.	A	14.	A	21.	E		

SECTION V

1.	D	8.	D	15.	A	22.	D
2.	D	9.	D	16.	E	23.	E
3.	E	10.	E	17.	C	24.	E
4.	C	11.	B	18.	C	25.	E
5.	A	12.	A	19.	B	26.	A
6.	E	13.	B	20.	D		
7.	E	14.	C	21.	E		

TEST ANALYSIS

Section	Overall Performance	Score: _____	Percentile: _____
	Number attempted	Number of guesses	Number correct
Games			
Reading Comprehension			
Arguments 1			
Arguments 2			
TOTAL			

Games			
	Attempted? What order?	Diagram and Elements	Notes
Game 1			
Game 2			
Game 3			
Game 4			

Reading Comprehension

	Attempted? What order?	Passage Notes	Question Notes
Passage 1			
Passage 2			
Passage 3			
Passage 4			

Arguments

Page	Question Number	Question Task	Notes

Arguments

Page	Question Number	Question Task	Notes

The Official LSAT PrepTest™ 74
Test code 9748
Form 4LSN111

SECTION I

Time—35 minutes

25 Questions

<u>Directions</u>: The questions in this section are based on the reasoning contained in brief statements or passages. For some questions, more than one of the choices could conceivably answer the question. However, you are to choose the <u>best</u> answer; that is, the response that most accurately and completely answers the question. You should not make assumptions that are by commonsense standards implausible, superfluous, or incompatible with the passage. After you have chosen the best answer, blacken the corresponding space on your answer sheet.

1. Children should be discouraged from reading Jones's books. Reading them is like eating candy, which provides intense, short-term sensory stimulation but leaves one poorly nourished and dulls one's taste for better fare. In other words, the problem with letting children read Jones's books is that _____.

Which one of the following most logically completes the argument above?

(A) it will lead them to develop a taste for candy and sweets
(B) too many children may become frustrated by their difficulty and stop reading altogether
(C) their doing so interferes with the development of appreciation for more challenging literature
(D) their message may undermine the positive teaching done by parents
(E) children may become so enthralled with books that they will want to spend all their time reading

2. Archaeologist: How did the Parthenon's stonemasons manage to carve columns that all bulged outward in the center in precisely the same way? One hypothesis is suggested by the discovery of a scale drawing of a column etched into the stone of a Greek temple at Didyma. The drawing is a profile view of a column surrounded by a grid, which makes it possible to determine the correct width at every height of the column. The stonemasons who carved the Parthenon's columns may have relied on a drawing like the one at Didyma.

Which one of the following, if true, adds the most support for the archaeologist's hypothesis?

(A) Modern attempts to recreate columns like those at the Parthenon have only been partially successful.
(B) The construction of the temple at Didyma was begun over a century after the Parthenon was constructed.
(C) Scale drawings were commonly used in many types of construction in ancient Greece.
(D) The surviving columns at Didyma are almost twice as tall as the columns at the Parthenon.
(E) The Parthenon's stonemasons had considerable experience carving columns before they started work on the Parthenon.

3. Editorial: The government should not fund any part of its health services with lottery revenue. These health services are essential to our community, but lottery revenue could decline at some time in the future, leaving the government scrambling to make up a budget shortfall.

The argument in the editorial most closely conforms to which one of the following principles?

(A) Governments should spend more of their revenue on essential services than on nonessential services.
(B) Essential government services must be funded from reliable sources of revenue.
(C) No government service should be entirely dependent on lottery revenue for its funding.
(D) Governments should consider all health services to be essential to the community.
(E) At least some lottery revenue must be set aside in case of budget shortfalls in the future.

GO ON TO THE NEXT PAGE.

4. Scientist: Rattlesnakes prey on young California ground squirrels. Protective adult squirrels harass a threatening rattlesnake by puffing up their tails and wagging them. New results show that the squirrel's tail also heats up when harassing a rattlesnake. Since rattlesnakes have an infrared sensing organ that detects body heat, the heating up of the squirrel's tail probably plays a role in repelling rattlesnakes.

Which one of the following, if true, most helps to support the scientist's hypothesis?

(A) Rattlesnakes do not have the ability to increase the temperature of their tails.
(B) Squirrels puff up their tails and wag them when they attempt to attract the attention of other squirrels.
(C) Rattlesnakes react much more defensively when confronted with a squirrel whose tail is heated up than when confronted with one whose tail is not.
(D) The rattlesnake is not the only predator of the California ground squirrel that causes it to engage in harassing behavior as a defensive mechanism.
(E) Mammals such as the California ground squirrel have no organ for sensing infrared energy.

5. Critic: Fillmore, an influential television executive, argues that watching television regularly is not detrimental to very young children. Fillmore bases this on the claim, which I grant, that children can learn much that is beneficial from television. But we should reject Fillmore's argument, because clearly it is to Fillmore's benefit to convince parents that television is not harmful to their children.

Which one of the following most accurately describes a flaw in the critic's reasoning?

(A) It takes a necessary condition for something's being harmful to be a sufficient condition for being harmful.
(B) It concludes that something is true merely on the grounds that there is no evidence to the contrary.
(C) It rejects an argument solely on the grounds that the argument could serve the interests of the person making that argument.
(D) It is based on an appeal to the views of someone with questionable authority on the subject matter.
(E) It bases its conclusion on claims that are inconsistent with one another.

6. While grapefruit juice is a healthy drink, it has been discovered that a chemical in the juice affects how certain medicines are absorbed, with the result that normal medicinal doses act like higher doses. Getting the wrong dose is dangerous. Since it is always desirable to take the lowest effective dose, the best medical approach would be to take lower doses of these medicines along with prescribed amounts of grapefruit juice.

Which one of the following, if true, most seriously weakens the argument?

(A) The amount of the chemical in grapefruit juice is highly unpredictable from glass to glass.
(B) Grapefruit juice is less expensive than most of the medicines with which it interacts.
(C) When scientists removed the chemical from grapefruit juice, the juice no longer affected how certain medicines were absorbed.
(D) The chemical in grapefruit juice works by inhibiting an enzyme in the body that affects how certain medicines are metabolized.
(E) Long before the chemical in grapefruit juice was identified, doctors were advising patients who took certain medicines to avoid grapefruit juice.

7. A landlord needed to replace the air-conditioning unit in a small rental home. The salesperson at the appliance store showed the landlord two air-conditioning units with identical prices. She told the landlord that the Sno-Queen was the most powerful unit for the price, but advised him to purchase the less powerful FreezAll unit, saying that the FreezAll was powerful enough for his needs.

The salesperson's advice to the landlord most closely conforms to which one of the following principles?

(A) When the prices of two different brands of a particular home appliance are identical, either of the products can satisfy the needs of the consumer.
(B) When a consumer is choosing between two different brands of a particular home appliance, the consumer should select the less powerful product only if it is also less expensive.
(C) A salesperson should always recommend that a customer buy the product that represents the best value.
(D) When advising customers about a purchase of a home appliance, a salesperson should direct the customer toward the product that yields the highest commission for the salesperson.
(E) When a consumer is choosing a home appliance, that consumer should choose the least powerful product that meets his or her needs.

GO ON TO THE NEXT PAGE.

8. Editorial: Our political discussions tend to focus largely on the flaws of our nation's leaders, but we need to remind ourselves that these leaders were chosen democratically. The real question that needs answering is how our nation's institutions and procedures enable such people to attain positions of power. Thus, to focus our attention on the flaws of our leaders is to indulge in a pointless distraction.

Which one of the following is an assumption that the argument requires?

(A) Examining an individual leader's personal flaws does not reveal anything about how the nation's institutions and procedures influence the selection of leaders.
(B) Political discussions that focus on the flaws of the nation's leaders will become even more common if the nation's institutions and procedures are not examined.
(C) The workings of the nation's current institutions and procedures ensure that only flawed individuals will attain positions of power.
(D) As yet, no one in the nation has made the effort to critically examine the details of the nation's institutions and procedures.
(E) Concentrating on the flaws of the nation's leaders creates greater dissatisfaction with those leaders.

9. Many calcium supplements contain lead, a potentially dangerous substance even in small amounts. The body can safely store in bones trace amounts of lead from food, but high levels of lead in the blood are a major public health concern, associated with anemia and nerve damage. Despite this, many doctors contend that for some people calcium supplements containing lead are preferable to no calcium supplements at all.

Which one of the following, if true, would most help to resolve the apparent discrepancy in the information above?

(A) Some fruits and vegetables contain trace amounts of lead derived from the soil in which they are grown.
(B) It is difficult to ensure that one has completely eliminated trace amounts of lead from one's diet.
(C) Lead is only one of the common public health concerns that are associated with anemia and nerve damage.
(D) A high-calcium diet decreases the amount of lead that the body is able to tolerate safely.
(E) When calcium intake is insufficient, the body draws calcium from bones, releasing stored lead into the bloodstream.

10. Principle: People should buy an expensive antique only if they can be confident of its authenticity and they find the piece desirable for its intrinsic qualities and not just for its value as an investment.

Application: Matilde should not buy the expensive antique vase offered for sale on the Internet.

Which one of the following, if true, most helps to justify the above application of the principle?

(A) While this style of vase is not currently sought after by other collectors, Matilde has acquired quite a few similar pieces and has developed significant expertise in identifying counterfeits.
(B) Although the seller is willing to take back the vase if Matilde cannot independently authenticate it, Matilde is not sure that the vase will appreciate much in value in the future.
(C) The seller of the vase has offered documentation of its age and origin, and Matilde is highly attracted to its shape and color; moreover, she suspects that it will be highly desirable to other collectors in the future.
(D) The asking price for the vase is significantly less than the amount Matilde thinks it is worth, and the vase is of a style that Matilde particularly likes.
(E) While Matilde likes the color and features of the vase, its particular style has frequently been reproduced for the mass market, and the vase cannot be examined closely or authenticated over the Internet.

GO ON TO THE NEXT PAGE.

11. Critic: In her presentation of important works of art in her art history textbook, Waverly claims to have presented only objective accounts: "I have sought neither to advocate nor to denigrate what I included." In writing about art, a pretense of objectivity never succeeds: clearly, Waverly writes much better about art she likes than about art to which she is indifferent.

The critic's statements, if true, most strongly support which one of the following?

(A) Waverly believes that a historian of art should not prefer certain works of art to other works of art.
(B) Waverly has only included works of art that she has strong opinions about in her textbook.
(C) Waverly wrote her textbook with the intention of advocating the works of art that she likes best.
(D) Waverly has not succeeded in her intended objectivity about works of art discussed in her textbook.
(E) Waverly does not really believe that objectivity is a desirable trait in an art history textbook.

12. Archaeologists are discovering a great deal about the Sals culture. For example, recent excavations have unearthed smelting furnaces and tools of smelted copper and bronze. There were distinct Sals words for copper and for bronze, but none for iron. Thus, the Sals did not smelt iron.

The conclusion drawn above follows logically if which one of the following is assumed?

(A) If a culture had a distinct word for a metal, then it smelted that metal.
(B) If a culture was unfamiliar with a metal, then it did not have a distinct word for that metal.
(C) If a culture smelted copper and bronze, then it had distinct words for copper and bronze.
(D) If a culture did not smelt a metal, then it was unfamiliar with that metal.
(E) If a culture smelted a metal, then it had a distinct word for that metal.

13. Community organizations wanting to enhance support for higher education programs need to convince the public that such programs benefit society as a whole. Taking this approach makes the public more receptive. It is much easier, for example, to get the public to support road building, which is seen as benefiting everyone, than it is to get them to support programs that are seen as benefiting only a relatively small segment of society.

Which one of the following most accurately expresses the overall conclusion drawn in the argument?

(A) Community organizations seeking to encourage higher education programs must persuade the public that these programs benefit society as a whole.
(B) It is easier to get the public to support programs that are seen as benefiting everyone than it is to get them to support programs that are seen as benefiting only a small segment of society.
(C) It is easy to get the public to support road building, because road building is seen as benefiting society as a whole.
(D) Convincing the public that higher education programs will benefit society as a whole makes the public more receptive to those programs.
(E) Higher education is similar to road building in that both are beneficial to society as a whole.

14. Currently, no satellite orbiting Earth is at significant risk of colliding with other satellites or satellite fragments, but the risk of such a collision is likely to increase dramatically in the future. After all, once such a collision occurs, it will probably produce thousands of satellite fragments, each large enough to shatter other satellites. The resulting collisions will produce many more fragments, and so on, causing the space around Earth to become quite heavily cluttered with dangerous debris.

Which one of the following most accurately describes the role played in the argument by the claim that the risk of a satellite orbiting Earth colliding with other satellites or satellite fragments is likely to increase dramatically in the future?

(A) It is an unsupported claim that is used to provide support for the argument's conclusion.
(B) It is an unsupported claim that is used to support another claim that in turn supports the argument's conclusion.
(C) It is a claim for which the argument provides some support, and which in turn is used to support the argument's conclusion.
(D) It is a claim that serves as the argument's conclusion.
(E) It is a claim that provides nonessential background information for the argument's conclusion.

GO ON TO THE NEXT PAGE.

15. Researcher: *Salmonella* bacteria are a major cause of illness in humans who consume poultry. Young chicks that underwent a new treatment exhibited a lower incidence of *Salmonella* infection than did untreated chicks, although one week after the treatment was administered the treated chicks had higher concentrations of a variety of bacteria than did untreated chicks.

Which one of the following, if true, most helps to explain the concentrations of bacteria one week after the treatment?

(A) The new treatment takes several weeks to administer.
(B) Levels of *Salmonella* bacteria in young chicks are generally not high to begin with.
(C) Most chicks develop resistance to many harmful bacteria by the time they reach adulthood.
(D) The untreated chicks experienced a higher incidence of illness from infection by bacteria other than *Salmonella* than did treated chicks.
(E) The bacteria found in the treated chicks were nonvirulent types whose growth is inhibited by *Salmonella* bacteria.

16. Debater: As a pedagogical practice, lecturing embodies hierarchy, since the lecturer is superior to the student in mastery of the subject. But people learn best from peer interaction. Thus, the hierarchy in lecturing is a great weakness.

Respondent: By definition, all teaching and learning are hierarchical, for all teaching and learning must proceed from simple to complex. In teaching mathematics, for example, arithmetic must precede calculus. Thus, the hierarchy in lecturing is a strength.

The respondent's reply to the debater's argument is most vulnerable to criticism on the grounds that the respondent

(A) concedes one of the major assumptions on which the debater's argument depends
(B) takes for granted that teaching methods that are effective in mathematics are also effective in other academic disciplines
(C) fails to consider the possibility that some characteristics of lecturing other than hierarchy are weaknesses
(D) applies a key concept to a different aspect of education than the aspect to which the debater applied it
(E) takes for granted that the conceptual structure of mathematics is sufficiently representative of the conceptual structure of at least some other academic disciplines

17. How the pigment known as Han purple was synthesized by the ancient Chinese of the Qin and Han dynasties has puzzled scientists. The Chinese chemists employed the same chemical ingredients used for Han purple in the production of a common type of white glass during that period. Both were produced in processes that involved subjecting the mixtures to high heat and mixing in lead to decrease the melting temperature. Thus, Han purple was probably discovered by fortuitous accident during glass production.

Which one of the following, if true, would most strengthen the argument?

(A) Chemical analysis shows that most of the known fragments of both Han purple and the white glass were produced within a small geographical radius.
(B) Han purple was used for luxury and ceremonial items, whereas the white glass was used to make certain household items.
(C) The technique used for producing Han purple was known to very few people during the Qin and Han dynasties.
(D) The ingredients used in producing both Han purple and the white glass were easily obtainable during the Qin and Han dynasties.
(E) The white glass is found in more surviving artifacts from the Qin and Han dynasties than Han purple is.

GO ON TO THE NEXT PAGE.

18. Medical researcher: A survey of more than 1 million adults found that there was a greater frequency of illness among people who regularly slept at least 8 hours a night than among people who slept significantly less. This shows that mild sleep deprivation is not unhealthy and, in fact, probably bolsters the body's defenses against illness.

The reasoning in the medical researcher's argument is most vulnerable to criticism on the grounds that the argument

(A) fails to address the possibility that an observed correlation between two phenomena is due to another factor that causally contributes to both phenomena

(B) fails to consider that even if a given factor causally contributes to the occurrence of a given phenomenon, it may not be the only factor affecting the occurrence of that phenomenon

(C) concludes, from the claim that a certain phenomenon occurs and the claim that a certain condition is sufficient for that phenomenon to occur, that the condition also exists

(D) takes for granted that there will be an observable correlation between two phenomena if either of those phenomena causally contributes to the other

(E) fails to consider that even if a specific negative consequence is not associated with a given phenomenon, that phenomenon may have other negative consequences

19. If temperatures had dropped below freezing when I was gone last week, the impatiens in my garden would have died. If the impatiens had died, they obviously could not continue to bloom. However, since the impatiens in my garden are still in bloom today, temperatures did not drop below freezing last week.

The pattern of reasoning in which one of the following arguments most closely parallels that in the argument above?

(A) If a species is highly adaptable, it will thrive when introduced into a new environment. If a species thrives in its new environment, it will have an adverse effect on species already existing in that environment. But, since this species has not had an adverse effect on any species already existing in its new environment, it is not highly adaptable.

(B) If a species thrives in a new environment, that species is adaptable. Species that adapt to new environments adversely affect some species already existing in those environments. So, if a species does not adversely affect any species already existing in its new environment, it has not adapted to it.

(C) If a species is introduced into a new environment, it adversely affects some species already existing in that environment, but only if it adapts well to it. Therefore, if a species does not adapt well to a new environment, it will not adversely affect any species already existing in it.

(D) If the introduction of a new species would adversely affect some species already existing in an environment, that species should not be introduced into it. Therefore, since the introduction of species into new environments will result in some species in those environments being adversely affected, species should probably not be introduced into new environments.

(E) If a new species would damage an environment, that species should not be introduced into it. If a new species is introduced, the risk can be reduced by controlling its population. Therefore, because the introduction of species into new environments is likely to happen, their populations should be controlled.

GO ON TO THE NEXT PAGE.

20. If the city builds the proposed convention center, several national professional organizations will hold conventions there. And if several large conventions are held in the city, the total number of visitors will of course increase. Tax revenues will certainly increase if the number of visitors increases. Thus, building the convention center will increase the city's tax revenues.

The conclusion of the argument follows logically if which one of the following is assumed?

(A) If the number of visitors to the city does not increase, then the city's tax revenues will not increase.
(B) If the number of visitors to the city increases, then the amount of money spent by visitors will increase.
(C) The city's tax revenues will not increase unless the convention center is built.
(D) People who are now regular visitors to the city will continue to visit the city if the new convention center is built.
(E) If several national professional organizations hold their conventions in the convention center, those conventions will be large.

21. In a study, pairs of trained dogs were placed side by side and given a command such as "sit." After both obeyed the command, one dog was given a treat while its partner was given no reward at all. Over time, the dogs who went unrewarded began to disobey the command. This shows that dogs have an aversion to being treated unfairly.

Which one of the following would be most useful to know in order to evaluate the argument?

(A) Were dogs who were accustomed to receiving regular rewards prior to the study more inclined to obey the command?
(B) Is there a decline in obedience if rewards are withheld from both dogs in the pair?
(C) Were dogs who received treats in one trial ever used as dogs that did not receive treats in other trials?
(D) Were there any cases in which the dog who was given a reward became more inclined to obey the command?
(E) How many repetitions were required before the unrewarded dogs began to disobey the command?

22. A study of 20,000 20- to 64-year-olds found that people's satisfaction with their incomes is not strongly correlated with the amount they make. People tend to live in neighborhoods of people from their same economic class, and the study shows that people's satisfaction with their incomes depends largely on how favorably their incomes compare with those of their neighbors.

The statements above, if true, most strongly support which one of the following hypotheses?

(A) People with high incomes are consistently more satisfied with their incomes than are people in the middle class.
(B) Older people are generally more satisfied with their incomes than are younger people.
(C) Satisfaction with income is strongly correlated with neighborhood.
(D) In general, people's income levels have little effect on their level of satisfaction with life as a whole.
(E) An increase in everyone's incomes is not likely to greatly increase people's levels of satisfaction with their own incomes.

23. Geologist: The dominant view that petroleum formed from the fossilized remains of plants and animals deep in the earth's crust has been challenged by scientists who hold that it formed, not from living material, but from deep carbon deposits dating from the formation of the earth. But their theory is refuted by the presence in petroleum of biomarkers, molecules indicating the past or present existence of a living organism.

Which one of the following, if true, most weakens the geologist's argument?

(A) Fossils have been discovered that are devoid of biomarkers.
(B) Living organisms only emerged long after the earth's formation.
(C) It would take many millions of years for organisms to become petroleum.
(D) Certain strains of bacteria thrive deep inside the earth's crust.
(E) Some carbon deposits were formed from the fossilized remains of plants.

GO ON TO THE NEXT PAGE.

24. Any driver involved in an accident leading to personal injury or property damage exceeding $500 is legally required to report the accident to the department of motor vehicles, unless the driver is incapable of doing so. Ted is not required to report the accident in which he was involved as a driver.

Which one of the following can be properly inferred from the statements above?

(A) If Ted is incapable of reporting the accident, then the accident did not lead to property damage exceeding $500.

(B) If Ted's car was damaged in excess of $500 in the accident, then he is incapable of reporting the accident to the department of motor vehicles.

(C) Someone other than Ted is legally required to report the accident to the department of motor vehicles.

(D) If Ted is incapable of reporting the accident to the department of motor vehicles, then he was injured in the accident.

(E) Either no one was injured in the accident or the accident did not lead to property damage exceeding $500.

25. Student: If a person has an immunity to infection by a microorganism, then that microorganism does not cause them to develop harmful symptoms. Since many people are exposed to staphylococcus without developing any harmful symptoms, it follows that they have an immunity to infection by this microorganism.

The student's argument is most similar in its flawed pattern of reasoning to which one of the following?

(A) Everything morally right is just, but some actions that best serve the interests of everyone are not just. Thus, some morally right actions do not serve the interests of everyone.

(B) Advertisers try to persuade people that certain claims are true. Since writers of fiction are not advertisers, they probably never try to persuade people that certain claims are true.

(C) Isabel said that she would take the medication. Obviously, though, she did not do so, because medication either cures disease or alleviates its symptoms, and Isabel is still quite ill.

(D) When business owners are subjected to excessive taxation, they become less willing to expand their businesses. The recent decline in business expansions thus shows that their taxes are too high.

(E) Studies show that doctors tend to wash their hands less often than any other health care professionals. This shows that the procedure cannot be of much value in preventing disease.

STOP
IF YOU FINISH BEFORE TIME IS CALLED, YOU MAY CHECK YOUR WORK ON THIS SECTION ONLY. DO NOT WORK ON ANY OTHER SECTION IN THE TEST.

SECTION II

Time—35 minutes

25 Questions

Directions: Each group of questions in this section is based on a set of conditions. In answering some of the questions, it may be useful to draw a rough diagram. Choose the response that most accurately and completely answers each question and blacken the corresponding space on your answer sheet.

Questions 1–5

A concert is given by a six-member band—guitarist, keyboard player, percussionist, saxophonist, trumpeter, violinist. During the concert, each member performs exactly one solo. The following restrictions apply:

    The guitarist does not perform the fourth solo.

    The percussionist performs a solo at some time before the keyboard player does.

    The keyboard player performs a solo at some time after the violinist does and at some time before the guitarist does.

    The saxophonist performs a solo at some time after either the percussionist does or the trumpeter does, but not both.

1. Which one of the following is an acceptable ordering of solos from first to last?

    (A) violinist, percussionist, saxophonist, guitarist, trumpeter, keyboard player

    (B) percussionist, violinist, keyboard player, trumpeter, saxophonist, guitarist

    (C) violinist, trumpeter, saxophonist, percussionist, keyboard player, guitarist

    (D) keyboard player, trumpeter, violinist, saxophonist, guitarist, percussionist

    (E) guitarist, violinist, keyboard player, percussionist, saxophonist, trumpeter

GO ON TO THE NEXT PAGE.

2. If the percussionist performs a solo at some time before the saxophonist does, then which one of the following must be true?

(A) The percussionist performs the first solo.
(B) The percussionist performs the second solo.
(C) The violinist performs a solo at some time before the saxophonist does.
(D) The percussionist performs a solo at some time before the trumpeter does.
(E) The saxophonist performs a solo at some time before the keyboard player does.

3. Each of the following must be false EXCEPT:

(A) The keyboard player performs the first solo.
(B) The guitarist performs the second solo.
(C) The guitarist performs a solo at some time before the saxophonist does.
(D) The guitarist performs a solo at some time before the percussionist does.
(E) The keyboard player performs a solo at some time before the saxophonist does.

4. Which one of the following CANNOT perform the third solo?

(A) guitarist
(B) keyboard player
(C) saxophonist
(D) trumpeter
(E) violinist

5. If the violinist performs the fourth solo, then each of the following must be true EXCEPT:

(A) The percussionist performs a solo at some time before the violinist does.
(B) The trumpeter performs a solo at some time before the violinist does.
(C) The trumpeter performs a solo at some time before the guitarist does.
(D) The saxophonist performs a solo at some time before the violinist does.
(E) The trumpeter performs a solo at some time before the saxophonist does.

GO ON TO THE NEXT PAGE.

Questions 6–10

Four art historians—Farley, Garcia, Holden, and Jiang—will give a series of four public lectures, each lecture on a different topic—lithographs, oil paintings, sculptures, and watercolors. The lectures will be given one at a time, with each art historian giving a lecture on a different one of the topics. The schedule of the lectures is subject to the following constraints:

    The oil paintings lecture and the watercolors lecture must both be earlier than the lithographs lecture.

    Farley's lecture must be earlier than the oil paintings lecture.

    Holden's lecture must be earlier than both Garcia's lecture and Jiang's lecture.

6. Which one of the following is an acceptable ordering of the lectures, from first to fourth?

(A) Farley: sculptures; Holden: lithographs; Garcia: oil paintings; Jiang: watercolors

(B) Farley: watercolors; Jiang: oil paintings; Holden: sculptures; Garcia: lithographs

(C) Garcia: sculptures; Farley: watercolors; Holden: oil paintings; Jiang: lithographs

(D) Holden: oil paintings; Jiang: watercolors; Farley: lithographs; Garcia: sculptures

(E) Holden: sculptures; Farley: watercolors; Jiang: oil paintings; Garcia: lithographs

GO ON TO THE NEXT PAGE.

7. Which one of the following must be true?

(A) Farley's lecture is earlier than the sculptures lecture.
(B) Holden's lecture is earlier than the lithographs lecture.
(C) The sculptures lecture is earlier than Garcia's lecture.
(D) The sculptures lecture is earlier than Jiang's lecture.
(E) The watercolors lecture is earlier than Garcia's lecture.

8. If the watercolors lecture is third, which one of the following could be true?

(A) Farley gives the watercolors lecture.
(B) Garcia gives the oil paintings lecture.
(C) Garcia gives the sculptures lecture.
(D) Holden gives the sculptures lecture.
(E) Jiang gives the lithographs lecture.

9. Which one of the following CANNOT be true?

(A) Farley gives the lithographs lecture.
(B) Garcia gives the sculptures lecture.
(C) Garcia gives the watercolors lecture.
(D) Holden gives the oil paintings lecture.
(E) Jiang gives the watercolors lecture.

10. If Garcia gives the sculptures lecture, which one of the following could be true?

(A) The lithographs lecture is third.
(B) The oil paintings lecture is third.
(C) The sculptures lecture is first.
(D) The sculptures lecture is second.
(E) The watercolors lecture is second.

GO ON TO THE NEXT PAGE.

<u>Questions 11–16</u>

Three rugs will be woven out of colored thread. Six colors of thread are available—forest, olive, peach, turquoise, white, and yellow—exactly five of which will be used to weave the rugs. Each color that is used will be used in only one of the rugs. The rugs are either solid—woven in a single color—or multicolored. The rugs must be woven according to the following rules:

In any rug in which white is used, two other colors are also used.

In any rug in which olive is used, peach is also used.

Forest and turquoise are not used together in a rug.

Peach and turquoise are not used together in a rug.

Peach and yellow are not used together in a rug.

11. Which one of the following could be the colors of the three rugs?

(A) forest only;
turquoise only;
olive, peach, and white

(B) forest only;
turquoise only;
olive, peach, and yellow

(C) peach only;
turquoise only;
forest, olive, and white

(D) yellow only;
forest and turquoise;
olive and peach

(E) yellow only;
olive and peach;
turquoise and white

GO ON TO THE NEXT PAGE.

12. Which one of the following must be true?

(A) There are no multicolored rugs in which forest is used.
(B) There are no multicolored rugs in which turquoise is used.
(C) Peach is used in one of the rugs.
(D) Turquoise is used in one of the rugs.
(E) Yellow is used in one of the rugs.

13. If one of the rugs is solid peach, which one of the following must be true?

(A) One of the rugs is solid forest.
(B) One of the rugs is solid turquoise.
(C) One of the rugs is solid yellow.
(D) Forest and white are used together in a rug.
(E) White and yellow are used together in a rug.

14. If there are exactly two solid rugs, then the colors of those two rugs CANNOT be

(A) forest and peach
(B) forest and yellow
(C) peach and turquoise
(D) peach and yellow
(E) turquoise and yellow

15. If forest and peach are used together in a rug, which one of the following could be true?

(A) There is exactly one solid rug.
(B) White is not used in any of the rugs.
(C) Yellow is not used in any of the rugs.
(D) Turquoise and white are used together in a rug.
(E) Turquoise and yellow are used together in a rug.

16. If one of the rugs is solid yellow, then any of the following could be true EXCEPT:

(A) There is exactly one solid color rug.
(B) One of the rugs is solid forest.
(C) Turquoise is not used in any of the rugs.
(D) Forest and olive are used together in a rug.
(E) Peach and white are used together in a rug.

GO ON TO THE NEXT PAGE.

Questions 17–23

The manager of a photography business must assign at least two photographers to each of two graduation ceremonies—one at Silva University and the other at Thorne University. Exactly six photographers are available—Frost, Gonzalez, Heideck, Knutson, Lai, and Mays—but not all have to be assigned. No photographer can be assigned to both ceremonies. The following constraints apply:

    Frost must be assigned together with Heideck to one of the graduation ceremonies.

    If Lai and Mays are both assigned, it must be to different ceremonies.

    If Gonzalez is assigned to the Silva University ceremony, then Lai must be assigned to the Thorne University ceremony.

    If Knutson is not assigned to the Thorne University ceremony, then both Heideck and Mays must be assigned to it.

17. Which one of the following is an acceptable assignment of photographers to the two graduation ceremonies?

(A) Silva University: Gonzalez, Lai
    Thorne University: Frost, Heideck, Mays
(B) Silva University: Gonzalez, Mays
    Thorne University: Knutson, Lai
(C) Silva University: Frost, Gonzalez, Heideck
    Thorne University: Knutson, Lai, Mays
(D) Silva University: Frost, Heideck, Mays
    Thorne University: Gonzalez, Lai
(E) Silva University: Frost, Heideck, Mays
    Thorne University: Gonzalez, Knutson, Lai

GO ON TO THE NEXT PAGE.

18. If Heideck is assigned to the same graduation ceremony as Lai, then which one of the following must be true?

(A) Frost is assigned to the Thorne University ceremony.
(B) Gonzalez is assigned to the Silva University ceremony.
(C) Gonzalez is assigned to neither graduation ceremony.
(D) Knutson is assigned to the Thorne University ceremony.
(E) Lai is assigned to the Thorne University ceremony.

19. Which one of the following could be the complete assignment of photographers to the Silva University ceremony?

(A) Frost, Gonzalez, Heideck, Knutson
(B) Frost, Gonzalez, Heideck
(C) Gonzalez, Knutson
(D) Heideck, Lai
(E) Knutson, Mays

20. Which one of the following is a complete and accurate list of all of the photographers who must be assigned?

(A) Frost, Heideck
(B) Frost, Heideck, Knutson
(C) Frost, Heideck, Knutson, Lai
(D) Frost, Gonzalez, Heideck
(E) Frost, Gonzalez, Heideck, Mays

21. If exactly four of the photographers are assigned to the graduation ceremonies, then which one of the following must be assigned to the Silva University ceremony?

(A) Frost
(B) Gonzalez
(C) Knutson
(D) Lai
(E) Mays

22. Which one of the following CANNOT be the complete assignment of photographers to the Thorne University ceremony?

(A) Frost, Gonzalez, Heideck, Mays
(B) Frost, Heideck, Knutson, Mays
(C) Gonzalez, Knutson, Lai
(D) Gonzalez, Knutson, Mays
(E) Knutson, Mays

23. Which one of the following, if substituted for the constraint that if Knutson is not assigned to the Thorne University ceremony, then both Heideck and Mays must be assigned to it, would have the same effect in determining the assignment of photographers to the graduation ceremonies?

(A) If Knutson is assigned to the Silva University ceremony, then Heideck and Mays cannot both be assigned to that ceremony.
(B) If Knutson is assigned to the Silva University ceremony, then Lai must also be assigned to that ceremony.
(C) Unless Knutson is assigned to the Thorne University ceremony, both Frost and Mays must be assigned to that ceremony.
(D) Unless Knutson is assigned to the Thorne University ceremony, Heideck cannot be assigned to the same ceremony as Lai.
(E) Unless either Heideck or Mays is assigned to the Thorne University ceremony, Knutson must be assigned to that ceremony.

S T O P
IF YOU FINISH BEFORE TIME IS CALLED, YOU MAY CHECK YOUR WORK ON THIS SECTION ONLY. DO NOT WORK ON ANY OTHER SECTION IN THE TEST.

SECTION III

Time—35 minutes

25 Questions

<u>Directions</u>: The questions in this section are based on the reasoning contained in brief statements or passages. For some questions, more than one of the choices could conceivably answer the question. However, you are to choose the <u>best</u> answer; that is, the response that most accurately and completely answers the question. You should not make assumptions that are by commonsense standards implausible, superfluous, or incompatible with the passage. After you have chosen the best answer, blacken the corresponding space on your answer sheet.

1. A research study revealed that, in most cases, once existing highways near urban areas are widened and extended in an attempt to reduce traffic congestion and resulting delays for motorists, these problems actually increase rather than decrease.

    Which one of the following, if true, most helps to explain the discrepancy between the intended results of the highway improvements and the results revealed in the study?

    (A) Widened and extended roads tend to attract many more motorists than used them before their improvement.

    (B) Typically, road widening or extension projects are undertaken only after the population near the road in question has increased and then leveled off, leaving a higher average population level.

    (C) As a general rule, the greater the number of lanes on a given length of highway, the lower the rate of accidents per 100,000 vehicles traveling on it.

    (D) Rural, as compared to urban, traffic usually includes a larger proportion of trucks and vehicles used by farmers.

    (E) Urban traffic generally moves at a slower pace and involves more congestion and delays than rural and suburban traffic.

2. A study found that consumers reaching supermarket checkout lines within 40 minutes after the airing of an advertisement for a given product over the store's audio system were significantly more likely to purchase the product advertised than were consumers who checked out prior to the airing. Apparently, these advertisements are effective.

    Which one of the following, if true, most strengthens the argument?

    (A) During the study, for most of the advertisements more people went through the checkout lines after they were aired than before they were aired.

    (B) A large proportion of the consumers who bought a product shortly after the airing of an advertisement for it reported that they had not gone to the store intending to buy that product.

    (C) Many of the consumers reported that they typically bought at least one of the advertised products every time they shopped at the store.

    (D) Many of the consumers who bought an advertised product and who reached the checkout line within 40 minutes of the advertisement's airing reported that they could not remember hearing the advertisement.

    (E) Many of the consumers who bought an advertised product reported that they buy that product only occasionally.

GO ON TO THE NEXT PAGE.

3. Unless the building permit is obtained by February 1 of this year or some of the other activities necessary for construction of the new library can be completed in less time than originally planned, the new library will not be completed on schedule. It is now clear that the building permit cannot be obtained by February 1, so the new library will not be completed on schedule.

The conclusion drawn follows logically from the premises if which one of the following is assumed?

(A) All of the other activities necessary for construction of the library will take at least as much time as originally planned.
(B) The officials in charge of construction of the new library have admitted that it probably will not be completed on schedule.
(C) The application for a building permit was submitted on January 2 of this year, and processing building permits always takes at least two months.
(D) The application for a building permit was rejected the first time it was submitted, and it had to be resubmitted with a revised building plan.
(E) It is not possible to convince authorities to allow construction of the library to begin before the building permit is obtained.

4. In a study of patients who enrolled at a sleep clinic because of insomnia, those who inhaled the scent of peppermint before going to bed were more likely to have difficulty falling asleep than were patients who inhaled the scent of bitter orange. Since it is known that inhaling bitter orange does not help people fall asleep more easily, this study shows that inhaling the scent of peppermint makes insomnia worse.

Which one of the following, if true, most seriously weakens the argument above?

(A) Several studies have shown that inhaling the scent of peppermint tends to have a relaxing effect on people who do not suffer from insomnia.
(B) The patients who inhaled the scent of bitter orange were, on average, suffering from milder cases of insomnia than were the patients who inhaled the scent of peppermint.
(C) Because the scents of peppermint and bitter orange are each very distinctive, it was not possible to prevent the patients from knowing that they were undergoing some sort of study of the effects of inhaling various scents.
(D) Some of the patients who enrolled in the sleep clinic also had difficulty staying asleep once they fell asleep.
(E) Several studies have revealed that in many cases inhaling certain pleasant scents can dramatically affect the degree to which a patient suffers from insomnia.

5. Dogs learn best when they are trained using both voice commands and hand signals. After all, a recent study shows that dogs who were trained using both voice commands and hand signals were twice as likely to obey as were dogs who were trained using only voice commands.

The claim that dogs learn best when they are trained using both voice commands and hand signals figures in the argument in which one of the following ways?

(A) It is an explicit premise of the argument.
(B) It is an implicit assumption of the argument.
(C) It is a statement of background information offered to help facilitate understanding the issue in the argument.
(D) It is a statement that the argument claims is supported by the study.
(E) It is an intermediate conclusion that is offered as direct support for the argument's main conclusion.

6. Of the many test pilots who have flown the new plane, none has found it difficult to operate. So it is unlikely that the test pilot flying the plane tomorrow will find it difficult to operate.

The reasoning in which one of the following arguments is most similar to the reasoning in the argument above?

(A) All of the many book reviewers who read Rachel Nguyen's new novel thought that it was particularly well written. So it is likely that the average reader will enjoy the book.
(B) Many of the book reviewers who read Wim Jashka's new novel before it was published found it very entertaining. So it is unlikely that most people who buy the book will find it boring.
(C) Neither of the two reviewers who enjoyed Sharlene Lo's new novel hoped that Lo would write a sequel. So it is unlikely that the review of the book in next Sunday's newspaper will express hope that Lo will write a sequel.
(D) Many reviewers have read Kip Landau's new novel, but none of them enjoyed it. So it is unlikely that the reviewer for the local newspaper will enjoy the book when she reads it.
(E) None of the reviewers who have read Gray Ornsby's new novel were offended by it. So it is unlikely that the book will offend anyone in the general public who reads it.

GO ON TO THE NEXT PAGE.

7. Scientist: Any theory that is to be taken seriously must affect our perception of the world. Of course, this is not, in itself, enough for a theory to be taken seriously. To see this, one need only consider astrology.

The point of the scientist's mentioning astrology in the argument is to present

(A) an example of a theory that should not be taken seriously because it does not affect our perception of the world
(B) an example of something that should not be considered a theory
(C) an example of a theory that should not be taken seriously despite its affecting our perception of the world
(D) an example of a theory that affects our perception of the world, and thus should be taken seriously
(E) an example of a theory that should be taken seriously, even though it does not affect our perception of the world

8. Clark: Our local community theater often produces plays by critically acclaimed playwrights. In fact, the production director says that critical acclaim is one of the main factors considered in the selection of plays to perform. So, since my neighbor Michaela's new play will be performed by the theater this season, she must be a critically acclaimed playwright.

The reasoning in Clark's argument is most vulnerable to criticism on the grounds that the argument

(A) takes a condition necessary for a playwright's being critically acclaimed to be a condition sufficient for a playwright's being critically acclaimed
(B) fails to consider that several different effects may be produced by a single cause
(C) treats one main factor considered in the selection of plays to perform as though it were a condition that must be met in order for a play to be selected
(D) uses as evidence a source that there is reason to believe is unreliable
(E) provides no evidence that a playwright's being critically acclaimed is the result rather than the cause of his or her plays being selected for production

9. Legal theorist: Governments should not be allowed to use the personal diaries of an individual who is the subject of a criminal prosecution as evidence against that individual. A diary is a silent conversation with oneself and there is no relevant difference between speaking to oneself, writing one's thoughts down, and keeping one's thoughts to oneself.

Which one of the following principles, if valid, provides the most support for the legal theorist's argument?

(A) Governments should not be allowed to compel corporate officials to surrender interoffice memos to government investigators.
(B) When crime is a serious problem, governments should be given increased power to investigate and prosecute suspected wrongdoers, and some restrictions on admissible evidence should be relaxed.
(C) Governments should not be allowed to use an individual's remarks to prosecute the individual for criminal activity unless the remarks were intended for other people.
(D) Governments should not have the power to confiscate an individual's personal correspondence to use as evidence against the individual in a criminal trial.
(E) Governments should do everything in their power to investigate and prosecute suspected wrongdoers.

10. A ring of gas emitting X-rays flickering 450 times per second has been observed in a stable orbit around a black hole. In light of certain widely accepted physical theories, that rate of flickering can best be explained if the ring of gas has a radius of 49 kilometers. But the gas ring could not maintain an orbit so close to a black hole unless the black hole was spinning.

The statements above, if true, most strongly support which one of the following, assuming that the widely accepted physical theories referred to above are correct?

(A) Black holes that have orbiting rings of gas with radii greater than 49 kilometers are usually stationary.
(B) Only rings of gas that are in stable orbits around black holes emit flickering X-rays.
(C) The black hole that is within the ring of gas observed by the astronomers is spinning.
(D) X-rays emitted by rings of gas orbiting black holes cause those black holes to spin.
(E) A black hole is stationary only if it is orbited by a ring of gas with a radius of more than 49 kilometers.

GO ON TO THE NEXT PAGE.

11. A mass of "black water" containing noxious organic material swept through Laurel Bay last year. Some scientists believe that this event was a naturally occurring but infrequent phenomenon. The black water completely wiped out five species of coral in the bay, including mounds of coral that were more than two centuries old. Therefore, even if this black water phenomenon has struck the bay before, it did not reach last year's intensity at any time in the past two centuries.

Which one of the following is an assumption required by the argument?

(A) Masses of black water such as that observed last summer come into the bay more frequently than just once every two centuries.

(B) Every species of coral in the bay was seriously harmed by the mass of black water that swept in last year.

(C) The mass of black water that swept through the bay last year did not decimate any plant or animal species that makes use of coral.

(D) The mounds of centuries-old coral that were destroyed were not in especially fragile condition just before the black water swept in last year.

(E) Older specimens of coral in the bay were more vulnerable to damage from the influx of black water than were young specimens.

12. Many nurseries sell fruit trees that they label "miniature." Not all nurseries, however, use this term in the same way. While some nurseries label any nectarine trees of the Stark Sweet Melody variety as "miniature," for example, others do not. One thing that is clear is that if a variety of fruit tree is not suitable for growing in a tub or a pot, no tree of that variety can be correctly labeled "miniature."

Which one of the following can be properly inferred from the information above?

(A) Most nurseries mislabel at least some of their fruit trees.

(B) Some of the nurseries have correctly labeled nectarine trees of the Stark Sweet Melody variety only if the variety is unsuitable for growing in a tub or a pot.

(C) Any nectarine tree of the Stark Sweet Melody variety that a nursery labels "miniature" is labeled incorrectly.

(D) Some nectarine trees that are not labeled "miniature" are labeled incorrectly.

(E) Unless the Stark Sweet Melody variety of nectarine tree is suitable for growing in a tub or a pot, some nurseries mislabel this variety of tree.

13. Psychologist: Identical twins are virtually the same genetically. Moreover, according to some studies, identical twins separated at birth and brought up in vastly different environments show a strong tendency to report similar ethical beliefs, dress in the same way, and have similar careers. Thus, many of our inclinations must be genetic in origin, and not subject to environmental influences.

Which one of the following, if true, would most weaken the psychologist's argument?

(A) Many people, including identical twins, undergo radical changes in their lifestyles at some point in their lives.

(B) While some studies of identical twins separated at birth reveal a high percentage of similar personality traits, they also show a few differences.

(C) Scientists are far from being able to link any specific genes to specific inclinations.

(D) Identical twins who grow up together tend to develop different beliefs, tastes, and careers in order to differentiate themselves from each other.

(E) Twins who are not identical tend to develop different beliefs, tastes, and careers.

14. Human beings can live happily only in a society where love and friendship are the primary motives for actions. Yet economic needs can be satisfied in the absence of this condition, as, for example, in a merchant society where only economic utility motivates action. It is obvious then that human beings _____.

Which one of the following most logically completes the argument?

(A) can live happily only when economic utility is not a motivator in their society

(B) cannot achieve happiness unless their economic needs have already been satisfied

(C) cannot satisfy economic needs by means of interactions with family members and close friends

(D) can satisfy their basic economic needs without obtaining happiness

(E) cannot really be said to have satisfied their economic needs unless they are happy

GO ON TO THE NEXT PAGE.

15. Technologically, it is already possible to produce nonpolluting cars that burn hydrogen rather than gasoline. But the national system of fuel stations that would be needed to provide the hydrogen fuel for such cars does not yet exist. However, this infrastructure is likely to appear and grow rapidly. A century ago no fuel-distribution infrastructure existed for gasoline-powered vehicles, yet it quickly developed in response to consumer demand.

Which one of the following most accurately expresses the conclusion drawn in the argument?

(A) It is already technologically possible to produce nonpolluting cars that burn hydrogen rather than gasoline.
(B) The fuel-distribution infrastructure for hydrogen-powered cars still needs to be created.
(C) If a new kind of technology is developed, the infrastructure needed to support that technology is likely to quickly develop in response to consumer demands.
(D) The fuel-distribution infrastructure for hydrogen-powered cars is likely to appear and grow rapidly.
(E) Hydrogen-powered vehicles will be similar to gasoline-powered vehicles with regard to the amount of consumer demand for their fuel-distribution infrastructure.

16. Wildlife management experts should not interfere with the natural habitats of creatures in the wild, because manipulating the environment to make it easier for an endangered species to survive in a habitat invariably makes it harder for nonendangered species to survive in that habitat.

The argument is most vulnerable to criticism on the grounds that it

(A) fails to consider that wildlife management experts probably know best how to facilitate the survival of an endangered species in a habitat
(B) fails to recognize that a nonendangered species can easily become an endangered species
(C) overlooks the possibility that saving an endangered species in a habitat is incompatible with preserving the overall diversity of species in that habitat
(D) presumes, without providing justification, that the survival of each endangered species is equally important to the health of the environment
(E) takes for granted that preserving a currently endangered species in a habitat does not have higher priority than preserving species in that habitat that are not endangered

17. Any food that is not sterilized and sealed can contain disease-causing bacteria. Once sterilized and properly sealed, however, it contains no bacteria. There are many different acceptable food-preservation techniques; each involves either sterilizing and sealing food or else at least slowing the growth of disease-causing bacteria. Some of the techniques may also destroy natural food enzymes that cause food to spoil or discolor quickly.

If the statements above are true, which one of the following must be true?

(A) All food preserved by an acceptable method is free of disease-causing bacteria.
(B) Preservation methods that destroy enzymes that cause food to spoil do not sterilize the food.
(C) Food preserved by a sterilization method is less likely to discolor quickly than food preserved with other methods.
(D) Any nonsterilized food preserved by an acceptable method can contain disease-causing bacteria.
(E) If a food contains no bacteria, then it has been preserved by an acceptable method.

GO ON TO THE NEXT PAGE.

18. Activities that pose risks to life are acceptable if and only if each person who bears the risks either gains some net benefit that cannot be had without such risks, or bears the risks voluntarily.

Which one of the following judgments most closely conforms to the principle above?

(A) A door-to-door salesperson declines to replace his older car with a new model with more safety features; this is acceptable because the decision not to replace the car is voluntary.

(B) A smoker subjects people to secondhand smoke at an outdoor public meeting; the resulting risks are acceptable because the danger from secondhand smoke is minimal outdoors, where smoke dissipates quickly.

(C) A motorcyclist rides without a helmet; the risk of fatal injury to the motorcyclist thus incurred is acceptable because the motorcyclist incurs this risk willingly.

(D) Motor vehicles are allowed to emit certain low levels of pollution; the resulting health risks are acceptable because all users of motor vehicles share the resulting benefit of inexpensive, convenient travel.

(E) A nation requires all citizens to spend two years in national service; since such service involves no risk to life, the policy is acceptable.

19. Ecologist: One theory attributes the ability of sea butterflies to avoid predation to their appearance, while another attributes this ability to various chemical compounds they produce. Recently we added each of the compounds to food pellets, one compound per pellet. Predators ate the pellets no matter which one of the compounds was present. Thus the compounds the sea butterflies produce are not responsible for their ability to avoid predation.

The reasoning in the ecologist's argument is flawed in that the argument

(A) presumes, without providing justification, that the two theories are incompatible with each other

(B) draws a conclusion about a cause on the basis of nothing more than a statistical correlation

(C) treats a condition sufficient for sea butterflies' ability to avoid predators as a condition required for this ability

(D) infers, from the claim that no individual member of a set has a certain effect, that the set as a whole does not have that effect

(E) draws a conclusion that merely restates material present in one or more of its premises

20. Principle: One should criticize the works or actions of another person only if the criticism will not seriously harm the person criticized and one does so in the hope or expectation of benefiting someone other than oneself.

Application: Jarrett should not have criticized Ostertag's essay in front of the class, since the defects in it were so obvious that pointing them out benefited no one.

Which one of the following, if true, justifies the above application of the principle?

(A) Jarrett knew that the defects in the essay were so obvious that pointing them out would benefit no one.

(B) Jarrett's criticism of the essay would have been to Ostertag's benefit only if Ostertag had been unaware of the defects in the essay at the time.

(C) Jarrett knew that the criticism might antagonize Ostertag.

(D) Jarrett hoped to gain prestige by criticizing Ostertag.

(E) Jarrett did not expect the criticism to be to Ostertag's benefit.

21. Safety consultant: Judged by the number of injuries per licensed vehicle, minivans are the safest vehicles on the road. However, in carefully designed crash tests, minivans show no greater ability to protect their occupants than other vehicles of similar size do. Thus, the reason minivans have such a good safety record is probably not that they are inherently safer than other vehicles, but rather that they are driven primarily by low-risk drivers.

Which one of the following, if true, most strengthens the safety consultant's argument?

(A) When choosing what kind of vehicle to drive, low-risk drivers often select a kind that they know to perform particularly well in crash tests.

(B) Judged by the number of accidents per licensed vehicle, minivans are no safer than most other kinds of vehicles are.

(C) Minivans tend to carry more passengers at any given time than do most other vehicles.

(D) In general, the larger a vehicle is, the greater its ability to protect its occupants.

(E) Minivans generally have worse braking and emergency handling capabilities than other vehicles of similar size.

GO ON TO THE NEXT PAGE.

22. Consumer advocate: There is no doubt that the government is responsible for the increased cost of gasoline, because the government's policies have significantly increased consumer demand for fuel, and as a result of increasing demand, the price of gasoline has risen steadily.

Which one of the following is an assumption required by the consumer advocate's argument?

(A) The government can bear responsibility for that which it indirectly causes.

(B) The government is responsible for some unforeseen consequences of its policies.

(C) Consumer demand for gasoline cannot increase without causing gasoline prices to increase.

(D) The government has an obligation to ensure that demand for fuel does not increase excessively.

(E) If the government pursues policies that do not increase the demand for fuel, gasoline prices tend to remain stable.

23. A species in which mutations frequently occur will develop new evolutionary adaptations in each generation. Since species survive dramatic environmental changes only if they develop new evolutionary adaptations in each generation, a species in which mutations frequently occur will survive dramatic environmental changes.

The flawed pattern of reasoning in which one of the following is most closely parallel to that in the argument above?

(A) In a stone wall that is properly built, every stone supports another stone. Since a wall's being sturdy depends upon its being properly built, only walls that are composed entirely of stones supporting other stones are sturdy.

(B) A play that is performed before a different audience every time will never get the same reaction from any two audiences. Since no plays are performed before the same audience every time, no play ever gets the same reaction from any two audiences.

(C) A person who is perfectly honest will tell the truth in every situation. Since in order to be a morally upright person one must tell the truth at all times, a perfectly honest person will also be a morally upright person.

(D) An herb garden is productive only if the soil that it is planted in is well drained. Since soil that is well drained is good soil, an herb garden is not productive unless it is planted in good soil.

(E) A diet that is healthful is well balanced. Since a well-balanced diet includes fruits and vegetables, one will not be healthy unless one eats fruits and vegetables.

GO ON TO THE NEXT PAGE.

24. Music critic: How well an underground rock group's recordings sell is no mark of that group's success as an underground group. After all, if a recording sells well, it may be because some of the music on the recording is too trendy to be authentically underground; accordingly, many underground musicians consider it desirable for a recording not to sell well. But weak sales may simply be the result of the group's incompetence.

Which one of the following principles, if valid, most helps to justify the music critic's argument?

(A) If an underground rock group is successful as an underground group, its recordings will sell neither especially well nor especially poorly.

(B) An underground rock group is unsuccessful as an underground group if it is incompetent or if any of its music is too trendy to be authentically underground, or both.

(C) Whether an underground group's recordings meet criteria that many underground musicians consider desirable is not a mark of that group's success.

(D) An underground rock group is successful as an underground group if the group is competent but its recordings nonetheless do not sell well.

(E) For an underground rock group, competence and the creation of authentically underground music are not in themselves marks of success.

25. Graham: The defeat of the world's chess champion by a computer shows that any type of human intellectual activity governed by fixed principles can be mastered by machines and thus that a truly intelligent machine will inevitably be devised.

Adelaide: But you are overlooking the fact that the computer in the case you cite was simply an extension of the people who programmed it. It was their successful distillation of the principles of chess that enabled them to defeat a chess champion using a computer.

The statements above provide the most support for holding that Graham and Adelaide disagree about whether

(A) chess is the best example of a human intellectual activity that is governed by fixed principles

(B) chess is a typical example of the sorts of intellectual activities in which human beings characteristically engage

(C) a computer's defeat of a human chess player is an accomplishment that should be attributed to the computer

(D) intelligence can be demonstrated by the performance of an activity in accord with fixed principles

(E) tools can be designed to aid in any human activity that is governed by fixed principles

STOP
IF YOU FINISH BEFORE TIME IS CALLED, YOU MAY CHECK YOUR WORK ON THIS SECTION ONLY. DO NOT WORK ON ANY OTHER SECTION IN THE TEST.

SECTION IV

Time—35 minutes

27 Questions

Given the amount of time and effort that curators, collectors, dealers, scholars, and critics spend on formulating judgments of taste in relation to oil paintings, it seems odd that so few are prepared to
(5) apply some of the same skills in exploring works of art that stimulate another sense altogether: that of smell. Why is great perfume not taken more seriously? While art professionals are very serious about many branches of literature, architecture, and music, I have
(10) yet to find a curatorial colleague who regularly beats a path to the fragrance counter in search of, say, *Joy Parfum,* the 1930 masterpiece by Henri Alméras.

And yet, the parallels between what ought to be regarded as sister arts are undeniable. Painters
(15) combine natural and, these days, synthetic pigments with media such as oils and resins, much as the perfumer carefully formulates natural and synthetic chemical compounds. The Old Masters deployed oil paint across the color spectrum, and applied layers on
(20) a determining ground and various kinds of underpainting, slowly building up to the surface, completing their work with thin glazes on top. Thus various types of mashed-up earth and vegetable suspended in linseed or poppy oil are brushed over
(25) a stretch of woven fabric. They begin to dry, and a picture is born. Its appearance changes over time, because the tendency of oil paint is to become gradually more transparent.

So, too, talented "noses" experiment with
(30) complex configurations of olfactory elements and produce in symphonic combination many small sensations, at times discordant, sweet, bitter, melancholy, or happy, as the case may be. These combinations change and develop in sequence or in
(35) unison as the substance and its constituents evaporate at different rates, some quickly, others slowly, thanks to the warmth of our skin. A brilliant perfumer may thus devise an imaginary world no less powerful, or intimate, than that of a great composer or painter,
(40) and in calling on our capacity to discover there some memory of childhood or of a long-forgotten experience, perfumers are in the same business as the artist who creates the illusion of life on canvas.

Perhaps one reason that truly great smells are so
(45) often undervalued is that perfumes are today made and distributed under the not particularly watchful gaze of a few large corporations. The cynical bean counters in Paris and Zurich do not hesitate to tamper with old formulas, insisting on the substitution of cheap
(50) chemical compounds that approximately resemble rarer, better ingredients in an effort to increase profits.

They do not tell their customers when or how they do this; indeed, they presume their customers won't notice the difference. Consequently, fine perfume is
(55) now hopelessly entangled with the international cosmetic dollar, and ill-served by marketing and public relations.

1. Which one of the following most accurately expresses the main point of the passage?

(A) Despite their pursuit of profit, corporations that produce and market perfumes value artistic skill.
(B) A masterpiece perfume evokes reactions that are no less powerful than those evoked by a masterpiece in music or painting.
(C) The corporate nature of the perfume business is the reason that so few truly great perfumes are now produced.
(D) Great perfumes are works of art and deserve respect and attention as such.
(E) Perfume-making and oil painting should be regarded as sister arts, both of which involve the skilled application of complex configurations of ingredients.

2. In which one of the following circumstances would the author of the passage be most likely to believe that a perfume manufacturer is justified in altering the formula of a classic perfume?

(A) The alteration makes the perfume more closely resemble *Joy Parfum.*
(B) The alteration is done to replace an ingredient that is currently very costly.
(C) The alteration replaces a synthetic chemical compound with a natural chemical compound.
(D) The alteration is done to make the perfume popular with a wider variety of customers.
(E) The alteration takes a previously altered perfume closer to its creator's original formula.

GO ON TO THE NEXT PAGE.

3. The word "noses" (line 29) refers to

   (A) perfumers
   (B) perfume collectors
   (C) particular perfumes
   (D) people with expertise in marketing perfumes
   (E) people with expertise in pricing perfumes

4. The passage provides the most support for which one of the following statements about art?

   (A) A work of art can bring about an aesthetic experience through the memories that it evokes.
   (B) In any work of art, one can detect the harmonious combination of many small sensations.
   (C) A work of art will inevitably fail if it is created for the sake of commercial success.
   (D) The best works of art improve with age.
   (E) Some forms of art are superior to others.

5. The author would be most likely to hold which one of the following opinions about *Joy Parfum* by Henri Alméras?

   (A) As time goes on, its artistry is appreciated more and more.
   (B) As a work of art, it is no less important than a great piece of sculpture.
   (C) It was the foremost accomplishment of its time in perfume making.
   (D) It is a fragrance that is appreciated only by people with refined taste.
   (E) Its original formula is similar to many other perfumes of the 1930s.

6. Which one of the following is most analogous to what the author calls the "cynical bean counters" (line 47)?

   (A) an art museum curator who caters to popular tastes in choosing works for an exhibition
   (B) a movie studio executive who imposes cost-saving production restrictions on a film's director
   (C) a director of an art institute who cuts the annual budget because of projections of declining revenues
   (D) a business executive who convinces her company to invest in art merely for the sake of tax benefits
   (E) an art school dean who slashes the budget of one project in order to increase the budget of his pet project

7. The last paragraph most strongly supports which one of the following statements?

   (A) The names of the world's best perfumes are not known to most customers.
   (B) The profitability of a particular perfume is not a good indicator of its quality.
   (C) Companies that sell perfume pay little attention to what their customers want.
   (D) Perfume makers of the past would never tamper with established formulas.
   (E) Companies that sell perfume make most of their profits on perfumes in the least expensive price ranges.

8. Which one of the following most accurately describes the organization of the passage?

   (A) The first paragraph makes an observation, the middle paragraphs elaborate on that observation while considering one possible explanation for it, and the final paragraph delivers an alternative explanation.
   (B) The first paragraph advances a thesis, the middle paragraphs present a case for that thesis, and the final paragraph considers and rejects one particular challenge to that thesis.
   (C) The first paragraph sets out a challenge to received wisdom, the middle paragraphs present a response to that challenge, and the final paragraph presents a concrete example that supports the response.
   (D) The first paragraph poses a question, the middle paragraphs present a case that helps to justify the posing of that question, and the final paragraph presents a possible answer to the question.
   (E) The first paragraph outlines a problem, the middle paragraphs present two consequences of that problem, and the final paragraph attempts to identify the parties that are responsible for the problem.

GO ON TO THE NEXT PAGE.

"Stealing thunder" is a courtroom strategy that consists in a lawyer's revealing negative information about a client before that information is revealed or elicited by an opposing lawyer. While there is no point
(5)　in revealing a weakness that is unknown to one's opponents or that would not be exploited by them, many lawyers believe that if the weakness is likely to be revealed in opposing testimony, it should be volunteered; otherwise, the hostile revelation would
(10)　be more damaging.

Although no empirical research has directly tested the effectiveness of stealing thunder in actual trials, studies involving simulated trial situations have suggested that the technique is, in fact, effective, at
(15)　least within a reasonably broad range of applications. Lawyers' commonly held belief in the value of stealing thunder is not only corroborated by those experimental findings; it is also supported by several psychological explanations of why the technique
(20)　should work. For one thing, volunteering damaging information early may create an image of credibility. Psychological research suggests that people who reveal information that appears to be against their own best interest are likely to be perceived as more credible
(25)　and thus may be more persuasive. Stealing thunder may also provide juries with an impetus for critical assessment by previewing, and thus alerting them to, testimony that the opposition plans to present. In psychological experiments, audiences that were
(30)　previously warned of an upcoming attempt at persuasion became more resistant to the persuasive attempt, forming counterarguments based on the warning. Also, the value placed on a persuasive message is probably much like the value placed on any
(35)　commodity; the scarcer the commodity, the more valuable it is. A persuasive message will thus increase in value and effectiveness to the extent that it is seen as scarce. In the courtroom, a piece of evidence brought by both the prosecution and the defense, as
(40)　when thunder is stolen, may be seen as less scarce—becoming "old news." Thus, unless that evidence is of overriding consequence, it should carry less weight than if it had been included only in hostile testimony.

Finally, stealing thunder may work because the
(45)　lawyer can frame the evidence in his or her own terms and downplay its significance, just as politicians sometimes seek to put their "spin" on potentially damaging information. However, it may therefore be effective only when the negative information can be
(50)　framed positively. Jurors, who often initially have little information about a case, are usually eager to solidify their position regarding the case. They can therefore be expected to use the early positive framing to guide their subsequent analysis of the trial information. But
(55)　this also suggests limitations on the use of the technique: when information is very damaging, stealing thunder may create an early negative impression that forms a cognitive framework for jurors, who then filter subsequent information through this schema.

9. Which one of the following most accurately expresses the main point of the passage?

(A) Although there are limits to the usefulness of stealing thunder, its effectiveness in actual trials has been demonstrated through research conducted by psychologists and legal scholars.

(B) The commonly practiced courtroom strategy of stealing thunder can have unintended consequences if the lawyers using it do not accurately predict jurors' attitudes.

(C) Lawyers' commonly held belief in the value of stealing thunder is supported by several psychological explanations of how that strategy may influence jurors.

(D) The risks involved in stealing thunder can outweigh the probable benefits when the information to be revealed is too readily available or too negative in its impact.

(E) Research designed to confirm the usefulness of stealing thunder has vindicated lawyers' belief in the value of the technique and has identified the general limitations of the strategy's effectiveness.

10. It can be most reasonably inferred from the passage that which one of the following is an example of stealing thunder?

(A) warning jurors that a client on the opposing side has a serious conflict of interest and cannot be trusted

(B) disclosing in opening statements of a defense against copyright infringement that one's client has in the past been guilty of plagiarism

(C) responding to the opposition's revelation that one's client has a minor criminal background by conceding that this is the case

(D) pointing out to jurors during opening statements the mistaken reasoning in the opposition's case

(E) stressing that one's client, while technically guilty, is believable and that mitigating circumstances should be considered

11. Which one of the following does the author mention as a factor that in some instances probably contributes to the success of stealing thunder?

(A) careful timing of the thunder-stealing message to precede the opposition's similar message by only a short time

(B) some lawyers' superior skill in assessing jurors' probable reactions to a message

(C) the willingness of some lawyers' clients to testify in person about their own past mistakes

(D) jurors' desire to arrive at a firm view regarding the case they are hearing

(E) lawyers' careful screening of prospective jurors prior to the beginning of courtroom proceedings

GO ON TO THE NEXT PAGE.

12. The author discusses the "cognitive framework" that jurors create (line 58) primarily to

(A) indicate that at least some information mentioned early in a trial can influence the way jurors evaluate information presented later in the trial

(B) indicate that jurors bring into court with them certain attitudes and biases that at least in part inform their opinions during trials

(C) suggest that damaging evidence that is framed positively early in a trial will have a greater impact than damaging evidence presented later in a trial

(D) theorize that stealing thunder is best done as early as possible in a case, before the opposition has an opportunity to solidify jurors' opinions

(E) speculate that creating credibility in some cases is probably more effective than positively framing very harmful information

13. The author's attitude regarding stealing thunder can most accurately be described as

(A) concerned that the technique may become so common that lawyers will fail to recognize its drawbacks

(B) favorable toward its use by lawyers during the opening statements of a case but skeptical of its value otherwise

(C) concerned that research results supporting it may omit crucial anecdotal evidence indicating pitfalls in its use

(D) approving of its use on the grounds that its success is experimentally supported and can be psychologically explained

(E) skeptical of its suitability for use by lawyers without lengthy experience in courtroom strategies

14. The author's characterization of stealing thunder in the passage is based at least partly on both

(A) informal surveys of lawyers' clients' reactions to stealing thunder and controlled research based on simulated trial situations

(B) statistical surveys of lawyers who steal thunder and observations of lawyers' tactics in trials

(C) records of judges' decisions in court cases and the results of studies involving simulated courtroom situations

(D) informal observations of nontrial uses of techniques analogous to stealing thunder and controlled studies of lawyers' courtroom behavior

(E) research that was not directly concerned with legal proceedings and research in which subjects participated in simulated trial situations

15. By saying that certain studies have suggested that in some applications, "the technique is, in fact, effective" (line 14), the author most likely means that those studies have given evidence that the technique in question

(A) inclines juries to regard the clients of those using the technique more favorably than would be the case if the negative information about them were first divulged by the opposition

(B) is a reliable means, in courtroom settings, of introducing a set of counterarguments that jurors will be able to use in resisting the opposition's subsequent attempts at persuasion

(C) invariably results in cases being decided in favor of the clients of those using the technique rather than in favor of parties opposing those clients, if it is used broadly

(D) appears generally to succeed as a means of forcefully capturing jurors' attention and thus leading them to focus more attentively than they would otherwise on the lawyer's message

(E) more often than not achieves its goal of timing a negative revelation so as to dramatically precede the opposition's revelation of the same information

16. The passage most strongly implies that many lawyers believe which one of the following concerning decisions about whether to steal thunder?

(A) A lawyer should be concerned with how readily the negative information can be positively framed, especially if the information is very negative.

(B) A lawyer should take into account, among other things, whether or not the jurors are already familiar with some of the relevant facts of the case prior to the trial.

(C) The decision should be based on careful deliberations that anticipate both positive and negative reactions of jurors and opposing lawyers.

(D) The decision should depend on how probable it is that the opposition will try to derive an advantage from mentioning the negative information in question.

(E) The decision should be based at least partly on a lawyer's knowledge of relevant psychological research findings and legal statistics.

GO ON TO THE NEXT PAGE.

Passage A

To a neuroscientist, you are your brain; nothing causes your behavior other than the operations of your brain. This viewpoint, together with recent findings in neuroscience, radically changes the way we think
(5) about the law. The official line in the law is that all that matters is whether you are rational, but you can have someone who is totally rational even though their strings are being pulled by something beyond their control. Indeed, people who believe themselves to be
(10) making a free and rational moral choice may really be deluding themselves—a brain scan might show that such a choice correlates with activity in emotional centers in the brain rather than in the region of the brain associated with deliberative problem solving.
(15) This insight suggests that the criminal-justice system should abandon the idea of retribution—the idea that bad people should be punished because of their freely chosen immoral acts—which is now dominant as a justification of punishment. Instead, the law should
(20) focus on deterring future harms. In some cases, this might mean lighter punishments. If it is really true that we do not get any prevention bang from our punishment buck when we punish some person, then it is not worth punishing that person.

Passage B

(25) Neuroscience constantly produces new mechanistic descriptions of how the physical brain causes behavior, adding fuel to the deterministic view that all human action is causally necessitated by events that are independent of the will. It has long been
(30) argued, however, that the concept of free will can coexist with determinism.

In 1954 English philosopher Alfred J. Ayer put forth a theory of "soft determinism." He argued, as the philosopher David Hume had two centuries earlier,
(35) that even in a deterministic world, a person can still act freely. Ayer distinguished between free actions and constrained actions. Free actions are those that are caused by internal sources, by one's own will (unless one is suffering from a disorder). Constrained actions
(40) are those that are caused by external sources, for example, by someone or something forcing you physically or mentally to perform an action, as in hypnosis or in mental disorders such as kleptomania. When someone performs a free action to do A, he or
(45) she could have done B instead, since no external source precluded doing so. When someone performs a constrained action to do A, he or she could have done only A.

Ayer argued that actions are free as long as they
(50) are not constrained. It is not the existence of a cause but the source of the cause that determines whether an action is free. Although Ayer did not explicitly discuss the brain's role, one could make the analogy that those actions—and indeed those wills—that originate from
(55) a disease-free brain are not constrained, and are therefore free, even though they may be determined.

17. Both passages are concerned with answering which one of the following questions?

(A) Should people be punished for actions that are outside of their control?
(B) Does scientific research into the brain have implications regarding freedom of the will?
(C) Can actions that are not free be effectively deterred by the threat of punishment?
(D) Is the view that retribution is a legitimate justification for punishment compatible with the findings of neuroscience?
(E) Can an action be free if someone else physically forced the actor to perform it?

18. Which one of the following concepts plays a role in the argument of passage B but not in that of passage A?

(A) mental disorder
(B) free choice
(C) causality
(D) self-delusion
(E) moral responsibility

19. One purpose of the reference by the author of passage B to David Hume (line 34) is to

(A) characterize Ayer as someone who is not an original thinker
(B) add credence to the theory of soft determinism
(C) suggest that the theory of soft determinism is primarily of historical importance
(D) suggest that the theory of soft determinism has been in existence as long as mechanistic descriptions of the brain have
(E) add intellectual respectability to the view that the brain should not be described mechanistically

GO ON TO THE NEXT PAGE.

20. Passage B differs from passage A in that passage B displays an attitude toward the ideas it discusses that is more

    (A) engaged
    (B) dismissive
    (C) detached
    (D) ironic
    (E) skeptical

21. Which one of the following arguments is most analogous to the argument advanced in passage A?

    (A) Many word processors are packed with nonessential features that only confuse most users and get in the way of important functions. Word processors with fewer features thus enhance productivity.
    (B) Economic models generally presume that actors in an economy are entirely rational. But psychological studies have documented many ways in which people make irrational choices. Thus, economic models, in theory, should not be able to predict human behavior.
    (C) The existing program for teaching mathematics in elementary schools is based on mistaken notions about what sorts of mathematical concepts children can grasp, and it should therefore be replaced.
    (D) Civil disobedience is justified only in those cases in which civil law conflicts with one's sincere moral or religious convictions. Any attempt to justify civil disobedience on something other than moral or religious grounds is therefore illegitimate.
    (E) Being autonomous does not imply having full control over one's behavior. After all, addicted smokers are unable to exercise control over some behaviors but are nevertheless autonomous in the general sense.

GO ON TO THE NEXT PAGE.

This passage is adapted from a review of a 1991 book.

In a recent study, Mario García argues that in the United States between 1930 and 1960 the group of political activists he calls the "Mexican American Generation" was more radical and politically diverse
(5) than earlier historians have recognized. Through analysis of the work of some of the era's most important scholars, García does provide persuasive evidence that in the 1930s and 1940s these activists anticipated many of the reforms proposed by the more
(10) militant Chicanos of the 1960s and 1970s. His study, however, suffers from two flaws.

First, García's analysis of the evidence he provides to demonstrate the Mexican American Generation's political diversity is not entirely
(15) consistent. Indeed, he undermines his primary thesis by emphasizing an underlying consensus among various groups that tends to conceal the full significance of their differences. Groups such as the League of United Latin American Citizens, an
(20) organization that encouraged Mexican Americans to pursue a civil rights strategy of assimilation into the United States political and cultural mainstream, were often diametrically opposed to organizations such as the Congress of Spanish-Speaking People, a coalition
(25) group that advocated bilingual education and equal rights for resident aliens in the United States. García acknowledges these differences but dismisses them as insignificant, given that the goals of groups as disparate as these centered on liberal reform, not
(30) revolution. But one need only note the fierce controversies that occurred during the period over United States immigration policies and the question of assimilation versus cultural maintenance to recognize that Mexican American political history since 1930
(35) has been characterized not by consensus but by intense and lively debate.

Second, García may be exaggerating the degree to which the views of these activists were representative of the ethnic Mexican population residing in the
(40) United States during this period. Noting that by 1930 the proportion of the Mexican American population that had been born in the United States had significantly increased, García argues that between 1930 and 1960 a new generation of Mexican American
(45) leaders appeared, one that was more acculturated and hence more politically active than its predecessor. Influenced by their experience of discrimination and by the inclusive rhetoric of World War II slogans, these leaders, according to García, were determined to
(50) achieve full civil rights for all United States residents of Mexican descent. However, it is not clear how far this outlook extended beyond these activists. Without a better understanding of the political implications of important variables such as patterns of bilingualism and
(55) rates of Mexican immigration and naturalization, and the variations in ethnic consciousness these variables help to create, one cannot assume that an increase in the proportion of Mexican Americans born in the United States necessarily resulted in an increase
(60) in the ethnic Mexican population's political activism.

22. According to the passage, the League of United Latin American Citizens differed from the Congress of Spanish-Speaking People in that the League of United Latin American Citizens

(A) sought the political goals most popular with other United States citizens

(B) fought for equal rights for resident aliens in the United States

(C) favored a more liberal United States immigration policy

(D) encouraged Mexican Americans to speak Spanish rather than English

(E) encouraged Mexican Americans to adopt the culture of the United States

23. It can be inferred from the passage that García would most probably agree with which one of the following statements about the Mexican American political activists of the 1930s and 1940s?

(A) Some of their concerns were similar to those of the Mexican American activists of the 1960s and 1970s.

(B) They were more politically diverse than the Mexican American activists of the 1960s and 1970s.

(C) They were as militant as the Mexican American activists of the 1960s and 1970s.

(D) Most of them advocated bilingual education and equal rights for resident aliens in the United States.

(E) Most of them were more interested in revolution than in liberal reform.

GO ON TO THE NEXT PAGE.

24. The passage suggests that García assumes which one of the following to have been true of Mexican Americans between 1930 and 1960?

(A) Increased ethnic consciousness among Mexican Americans accounted for an increase in political activity among them.

(B) Increased familiarity among Mexican Americans with United States culture accounted for an increase in political activity among them.

(C) The assimilation of many Mexican Americans into United States culture accounted for Mexican Americans' lack of interest in political activity.

(D) Many Mexican Americans were moved to political militancy as a means of achieving full civil rights for all United States residents of Mexican descent.

(E) Many Mexican Americans were moved to political protest by their experience of discrimination and the patronizing rhetoric of World War II slogans.

25. It can be inferred that the author of the passage believes which one of the following about the Mexican American political activists of the 1930s and 1940s?

(A) Their common goal of liberal reform made them less militant than the Mexican American activists of the 1960s and 1970s.

(B) Their common goal of liberal reform did not outweigh their political differences.

(C) Their common goal of liberal reform helped them reach a consensus in spite of their political differences.

(D) They were more or less evenly divided between those favoring assimilation and those favoring cultural maintenance.

(E) They did not succeed in fully achieving their political goals because of their disparate political views.

26. The author of the passage expresses uncertainty with regard to which one of the following?

(A) whether or not one can assume that the increase in the number of Mexican Americans born in the United States led to an increase in Mexican American political activism

(B) whether or not historians preceding García were correct in their assumptions about Mexican Americans who were politically active between 1930 and 1960

(C) whether or not there was general consensus among Mexican American political activists between 1930 and 1960

(D) the extent to which the views of Mexican American activists were shared by the ethnic Mexican population in the United States

(E) the nature of the relationship between the League of United Latin American Citizens and the Congress of Spanish-Speaking People

27. The passage supports which one of the following statements about ethnic consciousness among Mexican Americans?

(A) Ethnic consciousness increases when rates of Mexican immigration and naturalization increase.

(B) Ethnic consciousness increases when the number of Mexican Americans born in the United States increases.

(C) Ethnic consciousness decreases when the number of Mexican Americans assimilating into the culture of the United States increases.

(D) Variations in the influence of Mexican American leaders over the Mexican American population at large account in part for variations in ethnic consciousness.

(E) Variations in rates of Mexican immigration and naturalization account in part for variations in ethnic consciousness.

STOP

IF YOU FINISH BEFORE TIME IS CALLED, YOU MAY CHECK YOUR WORK ON THIS SECTION ONLY. DO NOT WORK ON ANY OTHER SECTION IN THE TEST.

SECTION V

Time—35 minutes

25 Questions

Directions: The questions in this section are based on the reasoning contained in brief statements or passages. For some questions, more than one of the choices could conceivably answer the question. However, you are to choose the best answer; that is, the response that most accurately and completely answers the question. You should not make assumptions that are by commonsense standards implausible, superfluous, or incompatible with the passage. After you have chosen the best answer, blacken the corresponding space on your answer sheet.

1. Ming: Since trans fat is particularly unhealthy, it's fortunate for the consumer that so many cookie manufacturers have completely eliminated it from their products.

   Carol: Why do you say that? Even without trans fat, desserts do not make for healthy eating.

   Carol's response indicates that she interpreted Ming's remarks to mean that

   (A) the more trans fat a cookie contains, the more unhealthy it is
   (B) food that doesn't contain trans fat is healthy food
   (C) if a food is not healthy, then it is unhealthy
   (D) a cookie containing any amount of trans fat is unhealthy
   (E) consumers should purchase cookies only if they do not contain trans fat

2. Historian: During the Industrial Revolution, for the first time in history, the productivity of the economy grew at a faster rate than the population and thus dramatically improved living standards. An economist theorizes that this growth was made possible by the spread of values such as hard work and thrift. But successful explanations need to be based on facts, so no one should accept this explanation until historical evidence demonstrates that a change in values occurred prior to the Industrial Revolution.

   The overall conclusion of the historian's argument is that

   (A) during the Industrial Revolution the productivity of the economy grew at a faster rate than the population
   (B) the fact that the productivity of the economy grew at a faster rate than the population during the Industrial Revolution led to a dramatic improvement in living standards
   (C) no one should accept the economist's explanation until historical evidence demonstrates that a change in values occurred prior to the Industrial Revolution
   (D) the improvement in living standards that occurred during the Industrial Revolution was not due to the spread of a change in values
   (E) values such as hard work and thrift did not become widespread prior to the Industrial Revolution

3. The master plan for the new park calls for the planting of trees of any species native to this area, except for those native trees that grow to be very large, such as the cottonwood. The trees that the community group donated were purchased at Three Rivers Nursery, which sells mostly native trees and shrubs. Thus, the donated trees are probably consistent with the master plan.

   Which one of the following, if true, most strengthens the argument?

   (A) Some tree species that grow to be very large are consistent with the master plan.
   (B) Three Rivers Nursery sells cottonwood trees.
   (C) Many of the native species that Three Rivers Nursery sells are shrubs, not trees.
   (D) Tree species that are not native to this area and that are consistent with the master plan are rare and hard to find.
   (E) Three Rivers Nursery does not sell any tree species that grow to be very large.

GO ON TO THE NEXT PAGE.

4. Paleontologists had long supposed that the dinosaur *Diplodocus* browsed for high-growing vegetation such as treetop leaves by raising its very long neck. But now computer models have shown that the structure of *Diplodocus*'s neck bones would have prevented such movement. The neck could, however, bend downward and even extend below ground level, allowing *Diplodocus* to access underwater vegetation from dry land. Thus, *Diplodocus* must have fed on plants on or near the ground, or underwater.

Which one of the following is an assumption required by the argument?

(A) The same type of neck structure is found in modern ground-feeding animals.

(B) *Diplodocus* was not able to see in front of itself unless its head was angled steeply downward.

(C) It would be impossible for a large animal such as *Diplodocus* to supply blood to an elevated brain.

(D) *Diplodocus* had no other way of accessing high-growing vegetation, such as by rising up on its hind legs.

(E) *Diplodocus* was not able to browse for underwater vegetation by kneeling beside bodies of water or by walking into them.

5. Government official: Although the determination of local residents to rebuild hiking trails recently devastated by a landslide indicates that they are strongly committed to their community, the government should not assist them in rebuilding. The reason is clear: there is a strong likelihood of future landslides in that location that could cause serious injury or worse.

Which one of the following principles, if valid, most helps to justify the reasoning in the government official's argument?

(A) Residents should not be allowed to rebuild trails unless the government assists them in rebuilding.

(B) The determination of residents to rebuild hiking trails devastated by landslides should be what determines government support for the project.

(C) Government agencies should not assist people with projects unless those people are strongly committed to their community.

(D) The government should not assist in projects that are very likely to result in circumstances that could lead to serious injury.

(E) Residents should be discouraged from rebuilding in any area that has had an extensive history of landslides.

6. Scientist: There is a lot of concern that human behavior may be responsible for large-scale climate change. But this should be seen as more of an opportunity than a problem. If human behavior is responsible for climate change, then we can control future climate change to make it less extreme than previous climate shifts.

The scientist's argument requires assuming which one of the following?

(A) The same degree of climate change produces less damage if it is caused by human behavior than if it has a purely natural cause.

(B) Human beings can control the aspects of their behavior that have an impact on climate change.

(C) At least some previous large-scale climate changes have been caused by human behavior.

(D) Large-scale climate change poses a greater danger to human beings than to other species.

(E) It is easier to identify the human behaviors that cause climate change than it is to change those behaviors.

7. In a study of heart patients awaiting treatment for reduced blood flow to the heart, those still waiting to find out whether they would need surgery were less likely to experience pain from the condition than were those who knew what type of treatment they would receive. Assuming that this uncertainty is more stressful than knowing what one's future holds, then it is reasonable to conclude that _____.

Which one of the following most logically completes the argument?

(A) stress sometimes reduces the amount of pain a heart patient experiences

(B) the pain experienced by heart patients is to some extent beneficial

(C) the severity of a heart patient's condition is usually worsened by withholding information from the patient about the treatment that that patient will receive

(D) stress is probably an effect rather than a cause of reduced blood flow to the heart

(E) heart patients suffering from reduced blood flow to the heart who are experiencing pain from the condition are more likely to require surgery than are such patients who are not experiencing pain

GO ON TO THE NEXT PAGE.

8. Given the shape of the hip and foot bones of the Kodiak bear, it has been determined that standing and walking upright is completely natural behavior for these bears. Thus, walking on hind legs is instinctive and not a learned behavior of the Kodiak.

To which one of the following criticisms is the argument most vulnerable?

(A) The argument incorrectly generalizes from the behavior of a few bears in support of its conclusion.

(B) The argument fails to consider the possibility that walking on hind legs is the result of both learning and an innate capacity.

(C) The word "behavior" illicitly changes meaning during the course of the argument.

(D) The argument presumes, without giving justification, that all behavior can be explained in one or both of only two ways.

(E) The argument incorrectly appeals to the authority of science in order to support its conclusion.

9. People are usually interested in, and often even moved by, anecdotes about individuals, whereas they rarely even pay attention to statistical information, much less change their beliefs in response to it. However, although anecdotes are generally misleading in that they are about unrepresentative cases, people tend to have fairly accurate beliefs about society.

Which one of the following, if true, would most help to explain why people tend to have accurate beliefs about society despite the facts described above?

(A) Statistical information tends to obscure the characteristics of individuals.

(B) Most people recognize that anecdotes tend to be about unrepresentative cases.

(C) The more emotionally compelling an anecdote is, the more likely it is to change a person's beliefs.

(D) Statistical information is made more comprehensible when illustrated by anecdotes.

(E) People tend to base their beliefs about other people on their emotional response to those people.

10. In 2005, paleontologist Mary Schweitzer made headlines when she reported finding preserved soft tissue in the bones of a *Tyrannosaurus rex* dinosaur. Analysis of the collagen proteins from the *T. rex* showed them to be similar to the collagen proteins in modern-day chickens. Schweitzer's discovery therefore adds to the mountain of evidence that dinosaurs are closely related to birds.

The answer to which one of the following questions would be most useful to know in order to evaluate the argument?

(A) How rare is it to find preserved soft tissue in the bones of a dinosaur?

(B) Is there any evidence at all against the claim that dinosaurs are closely related to birds?

(C) How likely is it for animals that are not closely related to each other to have similar collagen proteins?

(D) Is it possible that *T. rex* is more closely related to modern-day chickens than to certain other types of dinosaurs?

(E) Before Schweitzer's discovery, did researchers suppose that the collagen proteins in *T. rex* and chickens might be similar?

11. A university professor researching sleep disorders occasionally taught class after spending whole nights working in a laboratory. She found lecturing after such nights difficult: she reported that she felt worn out and humorless, and she had difficulty concentrating and finding the appropriate words. After several weeks of lectures, she asked her students to guess which lectures had been given after nights without sleep. Interestingly, very few students were able to correctly identify them.

Which one of the following statements is most strongly supported by the information above?

(A) The subjective effects of occasional sleep deprivation are more pronounced than are its effects on overt behavior.

(B) No one can assess the overall effects of sleep deprivation on a particular person as well as that sleep-deprived person can.

(C) Sleep deprivation has less effect on professors' job performance than it does on the job performance of others.

(D) Occasional sleep deprivation is not as debilitating as extended sleep deprivation.

(E) University students in a lecture audience tend to be astute observers of human behavior.

GO ON TO THE NEXT PAGE.

12. Prime minister: Our nation's government should give priority to satisfying the needs of our nation's people over satisfying the needs of people of any other nation. This is despite the fact that the people of other nations are equal in worth to the people of our nation, which means that it is objectively no more important to satisfy the needs of our nation's people than to satisfy those of other nations' people.

Which one of the following principles, if valid, most helps to reconcile the apparent conflict among the prime minister's claims?

(A) A nation's government should not attempt to satisfy the needs of a group of people unless the satisfaction of those people's needs is objectively more important than that of any other group's needs.

(B) A nation's government should give priority to satisfying the needs of its own people over satisfying the needs of another nation's people only if its own people are more worthy than the other nation's people.

(C) The priority a nation's government should place on satisfying the needs of a group of people depends mainly on how objectively important it is for the needs of those people to be satisfied.

(D) When the people of two nations are equally worthy, the needs of the people of each of those nations should be satisfied primarily by the people's own governments.

(E) A nation's government should give priority to the satisfaction of the needs of a group of people if, but only if, there is no other way for that group's needs to be satisfied.

13. Mayor: To keep our neighborhoods clean, every street in town will be swept at least once a month. If a neighborhood needs more frequent sweepings, due to excessive dirt from major construction for example, that neighborhood will be qualified for interim sweepings. All requests for interim sweepings from qualified neighborhoods will be satisfied immediately.

If all of the mayor's statements are true, then which one of the following must also be true?

(A) All neighborhoods in which construction is under way are qualified neighborhoods.

(B) All qualified neighborhoods will get their streets swept more than once a month.

(C) No street will be swept more than once a month unless it is located in a qualified neighborhood.

(D) A qualified neighborhood that requests an interim sweeping will have its streets swept more than once a month.

(E) No street in an unqualified neighborhood will be swept more than once a month even if the neighborhood requests it.

14. Journalist: It is unethical for journalists to lie—to say something untrue with the purpose of deceiving the listener—to get a story. However, journalists commonly withhold relevant information in interviews in order to elicit new information. Some argue that this, like lying, is intentional deception and therefore unethical. However, this argument fails to recognize the distinction between failing to prevent a false belief and actively encouraging one. Lying is unethical because it actively encourages a false belief.

The journalist argues by

(A) pointing out a difference between the two cases being compared in order to show that a conclusion based on their similarities should not be drawn

(B) defending what the journalist considers a controversial distinction by offering an example of a clear instance of it

(C) defining a concept and then showing that under this definition the concept applies to all of the cases under discussion

(D) appealing to a counterexample to undermine an ethical principle that supports an argument the journalist is trying to refute

(E) clarifying and defending a moral principle by comparing a case in which it applies to one in which it does not apply

15. Economist: Many of my colleagues are arguing that interest rates should be further lowered in order to stimulate economic growth. However, no such stimulation is needed: the economy is already growing at a sustainable rate. So, currently there is no reason to lower interest rates further.

The reasoning in the economist's argument is questionable in that the argument

(A) relies solely on the testimony of experts

(B) confuses economic growth with what stimulates it

(C) presumes that a need to stimulate economic growth is the only possible reason to lower interest rates now

(D) takes what is merely one way of stimulating economic growth to be the only way of stimulating economic growth

(E) concludes that a further reduction of interest rates would lead to unsustainable economic growth merely from the fact that the economy is already growing at a sustainable rate

GO ON TO THE NEXT PAGE.

16. Most commentators on Baroque painting consider Caravaggio an early practitioner of that style, believing that his realism and novel use of the interplay of light and shadow broke sharply with current styles of Caravaggio's time and significantly influenced seventeenth-century Baroque painting. One must therefore either abandon the opinion of this majority of commentators or reject Mather's definition of Baroque painting, which says that for any painting to be considered Baroque, it must display opulence, heroic sweep, and extravagance.

The conclusion of the argument can be properly drawn if which one of the following is assumed?

(A) Paintings that belong to a single historical period typically share many of the same stylistic features.

(B) A painter who makes use of the interplay of light and shadow need not for that reason be considered a nonrealistic painter.

(C) Realism was not widely used by painters prior to the seventeenth century.

(D) A realistic painting usually does not depict the world as opulent, heroic, or extravagant.

(E) Opulence, heroic sweep, and extravagance are not present in Caravaggio's paintings.

17. Under the legal doctrine of jury nullification, a jury may legitimately acquit a defendant it believes violated a law if the jury believes that law to be unjust. Proponents argue that this practice is legitimate because it helps shield against injustice. But the doctrine relies excessively on jurors' objectivity. When juries are empowered to acquit on grounds of their perceptions of unfairness, they too often make serious mistakes.

The argument uses which one of the following techniques in its attempt to undermine the position that it attributes to the proponents of jury nullification?

(A) attacking the motives of the proponents of the doctrine

(B) identifying an inconsistency within the reasoning used to support the position

(C) attempting to show that a premise put forward in support of the position is false

(D) presenting a purported counterexample to a general claim made by the doctrine's proponents

(E) arguing that the application of the doctrine has undesirable consequences

18. Pharmacist: A large study of people aged 65–81 and suffering from insomnia showed that most of insomnia's symptoms are substantially alleviated by ingesting melatonin, a hormone produced by the pineal gland, which plays a role in the regulation of the body's biological clock. Thus, the recent claims made by manufacturers of melatonin supplements that the pineal gland produces less melatonin as it ages are evidently correct.

The pharmacist's argument is flawed in that it

(A) infers from the effect of an action that the action is intended to produce that effect

(B) relies on the opinions of individuals who are likely to be biased

(C) depends on using two different meanings for the same term to draw its conclusion

(D) confuses an effect of a phenomenon with its cause

(E) relies on a sample that is unrepresentative

GO ON TO THE NEXT PAGE.

19. The recent concert was probably not properly promoted. Wells, who is quite knowledgeable about the concert business, was certain that it would sell out unless it was poorly promoted. But the concert did not sell out.

The pattern of reasoning in which one of the following is most similar to that in the argument above?

(A) Dr. Smith, a well-trained cardiologist, said the patient would probably survive the heart transplant if it were performed by a highly skilled surgeon. Thus, since the patient did not survive the surgery, it probably was not properly performed.

(B) Professor Willis, who is quite knowledgeable about organic chemistry, said that the sample probably did not contain any organic compounds. So, the sample probably is not labeled correctly, for if it were, it would contain organic compounds.

(C) My neighbor, who is an experienced home renovator, said the damage to the wall would not be noticeable if it were properly repaired. Thus, the repair to the wall probably was not properly done, since one can still notice the damage.

(D) The builder said that the school's roof would not require repairs for years, unless it is damaged in a storm. The roof is already leaking. Thus, since there have been no major storms, the builder was probably wrong.

(E) Professor Yanakita, who is an expert on the subject, said that the tests would find lead in the soil if they were properly conducted. So, since the tests did find lead in the soil, they probably were properly conducted.

20. Economist: Global recessions can never be prevented, for they could be prevented only if they were predictable. Yet economists, using the best techniques at their disposal, consistently fail to accurately predict global recessions.

The economist's argument is most vulnerable to the criticism that it

(A) presupposes in a premise the conclusion that it purports to establish

(B) fails to establish that economists claim to be able to accurately predict global recessions

(C) treats the predictability of an event, which is required for the event to be preventable, as a characteristic that assures its prevention

(D) fails to address the possibility that the techniques available to economists for the prediction of global recessions will significantly improve

(E) implicitly bases an inference that something will not occur solely on the information that its occurrence is not predictable

21. Letter to the editor: When your newspaper reported the (admittedly extraordinary) claim by Mr. Hanlon that he saw an alien spaceship, the tone of your article was very skeptical despite the fact that Hanlon has over the years proved to be a trusted member of the community. If Hanlon claimed to have observed a rare natural phenomenon like a large meteor, your article would not have been skeptical. So your newspaper exhibits an unjustified bias.

The argument in the letter conflicts with which one of the following principles?

(A) If a claim is extraordinary, it should not be presented uncritically unless it is backed by evidence of an extraordinarily high standard.

(B) One should be skeptical of claims that are based upon testimonial evidence that is acquired only through an intermediary source.

(C) If a media outlet has trusted a source in the past and the source has a good reputation, the outlet should continue to trust that source.

(D) People who think they observe supernatural phenomena should not publicize that fact unless they can present corroborating evidence.

(E) A newspaper should not publish a report unless it is confirmed by an independent source.

22. Fish with teeth specialized for scraping algae occur in both Flower Lake and Blue Lake. Some biologists argue that because such specialized characteristics are rare, fish species that have them should be expected to be closely related. If they are closely related, then the algae-scraping specialization evolved only once. But genetic tests show that the two algae-scraping species, although possibly related, are not closely related. Thus, the algae-scraping specialization evolved more than once.

The reasoning in the argument is flawed in that it

(A) infers a cause merely from a correlation

(B) infers that just because the evidence for a particular claim has not yet been confirmed, that claim is false

(C) takes a sufficient condition as a necessary one

(D) infers merely because something was likely to occur that it did occur

(E) appeals to the authority of biologists who may not be representative of all biologists with expertise in the relevant area

GO ON TO THE NEXT PAGE.

23. The constitution of Country F requires that whenever the government sells a state-owned entity, it must sell that entity for the highest price it can command on the open market. The constitution also requires that whenever the government sells a state-owned entity, it must ensure that citizens of Country F will have majority ownership of the resulting company for at least one year after the sale.

The government of Country F must violate at least one of the constitutional requirements described above if it is faced with which one of the following situations?

(A) The government will sell StateAir, a state-owned airline. The highest bid received was from a corporation that was owned entirely by citizens of Country F when the bid was received. Shortly after the bid was received, however, noncitizens purchased a minority share in the corporation.

(B) The government has agreed to sell National Silver, a state-owned mine, to a corporation. Although citizens of Country F have majority ownership of the corporation, most of the corporation's operations and sales take place in other countries.

(C) The government will sell PetroNat, a state-owned oil company. World Oil Company has made one of the highest offers for PetroNat, but World Oil's ownership structure is so complex that the government cannot determine whether citizens of Country F have majority ownership.

(D) The government will sell National Telephone, a state-owned utility. The highest bid received was from a company in which citizens of Country F have majority ownership but noncitizens own a minority share. However, the second-highest bid, from a consortium of investors all of whom are citizens of Country F, was almost as high as the highest bid.

(E) The government will sell StateRail, a state-owned railway. The government must place significant restrictions on who can purchase StateRail to ensure that citizens of Country F will gain majority ownership. However, any such restrictions will reduce the price the government receives for StateRail.

24. The makers of Activite, a natural dietary supplement, claim that it promotes energy and mental alertness. To back up their claim, they offer a month's supply of Activite free to new customers. Clearly, Activite must be effective, since otherwise it would not be in the company's interest to make such an offer.

Which one of the following, if true, most weakens the argument?

(A) The nutrients in Activite can all be obtained from a sufficiently varied and well-balanced diet.

(B) There are less expensive dietary supplements on the market that are just as effective as Activite.

(C) A month is not a sufficient length of time for most dietary supplements to be fully effective.

(D) The makers of Activite charge a handling fee that is considerably more than what it costs them to pack and ship their product.

(E) The mere fact that a dietary supplement contains only natural ingredients does not insure that it has no harmful side effects.

GO ON TO THE NEXT PAGE.

25. Of the citizens who disapprove of the prime minister's overall job performance, most disapprove because of the prime minister's support for increasing the income tax. However, Theresa believes that the income tax should be increased. So Theresa probably approves of the prime minister's overall job performance.

Which one of the following arguments exhibits flawed reasoning that is most parallel to that in the argument above?

(A) Of the people who support allowing limited logging in the Grizzly National Forest, most support it because they think it will reduce the risk of fire in the forest. Andy thinks that limited logging will not reduce the risk of fire in the forest, so he probably opposes allowing limited logging there.

(B) Of the people who expect the population in the area to increase over the next ten years, most think that an expected population increase is a good reason to build a new school. Bonita does not expect the population to increase over the next ten years, so she probably does not favor building a new school.

(C) Of the people who believe that the overall economy has improved, most believe it because they believe that their own financial situation has improved. Chung believes that the economy has worsened, so he probably believes that his own financial situation has worsened.

(D) Of the people who oppose funding a study to determine the feasibility of building a light rail line in the Loffoch Valley, most also believe that the Valley Freeway should be built. Donna opposes increasing funding for a study, so she probably supports building the Valley Freeway.

(E) Of the people who believe that there will be a blizzard tomorrow, most believe it because of the weather report on the Channel 9 news. Eduardo believes that there will be a blizzard tomorrow, so he probably saw the weather report on the Channel 9 news.

26. Bird watcher: The decrease in the mourning-dove population in this area is probably a result of the loss of nesting habitat. Many mourning doves had formerly nested in the nearby orchards, but after overhead sprinklers were installed in the orchards last year, the doves ceased building nests there.

Which one of the following, if true, most strengthens the argument?

(A) Mourning doves were recently designated a migratory game species, meaning that they can be legally hunted.

(B) The trees in the nearby orchards were the only type of trees in the area attractive to nesting mourning doves.

(C) Blue jays that had nested in the orchards also ceased doing so after the sprinklers were installed.

(D) Many residents of the area fill their bird feeders with canola or wheat, which are appropriate seeds for attracting mourning doves.

(E) Mourning doves often nest in fruit trees.

STOP
IF YOU FINISH BEFORE TIME IS CALLED, YOU MAY CHECK YOUR WORK ON THIS SECTION ONLY. DO NOT WORK ON ANY OTHER SECTION IN THE TEST.

Acknowledgment is made to the following sources from which material has been adapted for use in this test booklet:

Michael S. Gazzaniga and Megan S. Steven, "Neuroscience and the Law." ©2007 by Scientific American, Inc. http://www.sciammind.com/article.cfm?articleID=00053249-43D1-123A-822283414B7F4945.

Jeffrey Rosen, "The Brain on the Stand." ©2007 by The New York Times Company. http://www.nytimes.com/2007/03/11/magazine/11Neurolaw.t.html?_r=2&oref=slogin&oref=slogin.

Angus Trumble, "Smelly Masterpieces." ©2008 by Times Newspapers Ltd.

Kipling D. Williams, Martin J. Bourgeois, and Robert T. Croyle, "The Effects of Stealing Thunder in Criminal and Civil Trials." ©1993 by Plenum Publishing Corporation.

LSAT WRITING SAMPLE TOPIC

A brother and sister, Hector and Teresa, are deciding whether to spend the upcoming summer recording music and playing in cafes and bars together, or to continue in the summer along their original career paths. Using the facts below, write an essay in which you argue for one option over the other based on the following two criteria:

- They want the risks they take in their lives to reflect the potential rewards.
- They want to be responsible with respect to their educational preparation and the choices they have already made.

Hector and Teresa each have extensive musical training. They are talented enough that if they spend the summer on music, there is a good chance that they will become popular enough to get steady work performing and selling albums. It is unlikely that they will have another occasion to spend so much time together. Spending the summer on music could allow them to develop their sibling relationship, which has not been very close because of their five-year age difference. Spending so much time together could reveal personality clashes.

Teresa is pursuing her PhD in economics. She completed all the coursework and general examinations four years ago. Spending the summer on music might delay finishing her dissertation. This could further jeopardize her job prospects in a field where the opportunities have been diminishing. Hector has been working in a medical laboratory since receiving his undergraduate degree five years ago. To advance in his field, he is scheduled to begin a difficult master's program in biochemistry early in the fall. Hector and Teresa each might have to go into debt as a consequence of spending the summer on music.

Directions:

1. Use the Answer Key on the next page to check your answers.

2. Use the Scoring Worksheet below to compute your raw score.

3. Use the Score Conversion Chart to convert your raw score into the 120–180 scale.

Scoring Worksheet

1. Enter the number of questions you answered correctly in each section.

Number Correct

SECTION I.. _____
SECTION II .... _____
SECTION IV .... _____
SECTION V .... _____

2. Enter the sum here: _____
This is your Raw Score.

Section Map

SECTION I: PrepTest 74, Section 1
SECTION II: PrepTest 74, Section 2
SECTION III: Experimental (PrepTest 60, Section 3)
SECTION IV: PrepTest 74, Section 3
SECTION V: PrepTest 74, Section 4

Conversion Chart
For Converting Raw Score to the 120–180 LSAT Scaled Score
LSAT Form 4LSN111

Reported Score	Lowest	Highest
180	99	101
179	98	98
178	97	97
177	96	96
176	95	95
175	*	*
174	94	94
173	93	93
172	92	92
171	90	91
170	89	89
169	88	88
168	86	87
167	85	85
166	84	84
165	82	83
164	80	81
163	79	79
162	77	78
161	75	76
160	74	74
159	72	73
158	70	71
157	68	69
156	67	67
155	65	66
154	63	64
153	61	62
152	59	60
151	58	58
150	56	57
149	54	55
148	53	53
147	51	52
146	49	50
145	48	48
144	46	47
143	44	45
142	43	43
141	41	42
140	40	40
139	38	39
138	36	37
137	35	35
136	33	34
135	32	32
134	31	31
133	29	30
132	28	28
131	27	27
130	25	26
129	24	24
128	23	23
127	22	22
126	21	21
125	20	20
124	19	19
123	18	18
122	17	17
121	16	16
120	0	15

*There is no raw score that will produce this scaled score for this form.

SECTION I

1.	C	8.	A	15.	E	22.	E
2.	C	9.	E	16.	D	23.	D
3.	B	10.	E	17.	A	24.	B
4.	C	11.	D	18.	A	25.	D
5.	C	12.	E	19.	A		
6.	A	13.	A	20.	E		
7.	E	14.	D	21.	B		

SECTION II

1.	C	8.	E	15.	B	22.	B
2.	D	9.	A	16.	A	23.	C
3.	E	10.	A	17.	E		
4.	A	11.	A	18.	D		
5.	E	12.	C	19.	B		
6.	E	13.	E	20.	B		
7.	B	14.	D	21.	A		

SECTION III

1.	A	8.	C	15.	D	22.	A
2.	B	9.	C	16.	E	23.	C
3.	A	10.	C	17.	D	24.	B
4.	B	11.	D	18.	C	25.	C
5.	D	12.	E	19.	D		
6.	D	13.	D	20.	A		
7.	C	14.	D	21.	E		

SECTION IV

1.	D	8.	D	15.	A	22.	E
2.	E	9.	C	16.	D	23.	A
3.	A	10.	B	17.	B	24.	B
4.	A	11.	D	18.	A	25.	B
5.	B	12.	A	19.	B	26.	D
6.	B	13.	D	20.	C	27.	E
7.	B	14.	E	21.	C		

SECTION V

1.	B	8.	B	15.	C	22.	C
2.	C	9.	B	16.	E	23.	E
3.	E	10.	C	17.	E	24.	D
4.	D	11.	A	18.	E	25.	A
5.	D	12.	D	19.	C	26.	B
6.	B	13.	D	20.	D		
7.	A	14.	A	21.	A		

TEST ANALYSIS

Section	Overall Performance	Score: _____	Percentile: _____
	Number attempted	Number of guesses	Number correct
Games			
Reading Comprehension			
Arguments 1			
Arguments 2			
TOTAL			

Games			
	Attempted? What order?	Diagram and Elements	Notes
Game 1			
Game 2			
Game 3			
Game 4			

Reading Comprehension

	Attempted? What order?	Passage Notes	Question Notes
Passage 1			
Passage 2			
Passage 3			
Passage 4			

Arguments

Page	Question Number	Question Task	Notes

Arguments			
Page	Question Number	Question Task	Notes